DATE DUE

COLLECTION EDITOR: **JENNIFER GRÜNWALD**

ASSISTANT EDITOR: **CAITLIN O'CONNELL**

ASSOCIATE MANAGING EDITOR: **KATERI WOODY**

EDITOR, SPECIAL PROJECTS: **MARK D. BEAZLEY**

VP PRODUCTION & SPECIAL PROJECTS: **JEFF YOUNGQUIST**

SVP PRINT, SALES & MARKETING: **DAVID GABRIEL**

BOOK DESIGNER: **ADAM DEL RE**

EDITOR IN CHIEF: **AXEL ALONSO**

CHIEF CREATIVE OFFICER: **JOE QUESADA**

PRESIDENT: **DAN BUCKLEY**

EXECUTIVE PRODUCER: **ALAN FINE**

THOR CREATED BY **STAN LEE, LARRY LIEBER** & **JACK KIRBY**

MIGHTY THOR VOL. 2: LORDS OF MIDGARD. Contains material originally published in magazine form as MIGHTY THOR #6-12. First printing 2017. ISBN# 978-0-7851-9966-3. Published by M
WORLDWIDE, INC., a subsidiary of MARVEL ENTERTAINMENT, LLC. OFFICE OF PUBLICATION: 135 West 50th Street, New York, NY 10020. Copyright © 2017 MARVEL No similarity between any
names, characters, persons, and/or institutions in this magazine with those of any living or dead person or institution is intended, and any such similarity which may exist is purely coincidental. P
in the U.S.A. DAN BUCKLEY, President, Marvel Entertainment; JOE QUESADA, Chief Creative Officer; TOM BREVOORT, SVP of Publishing; DAVID BOGART, SVP of Business Affairs & Operations, Pub
& Partnership; C.B. CEBULSKI, VP of Brand Management & Development, Asia; DAVID GABRIEL, SVP of Sales & Marketing, Publishing; JEFF YOUNGQUIST, VP of Production & Special Projects; DAN
Executive Director of Publishing Technology; ALEX MORALES, Director of Publishing Operations; SUSAN CRESPI, Production Manager; STAN LEE, Chairman Emeritus. For information regarding adve
in Marvel Comics or on Marvel.com, please contact Vit DeBellis, Integrated Sales Manager, at vdebellis@marvel.com. For Marvel subscription inquiries, please call 888-511-5480. **Manufa**
between 6/2/2017 and 7/4/2017 by LSC COMMUNICATIONS INC., KENDALLVILLE, IN, USA.

10 9 8 7 6 5 4 3 2 1

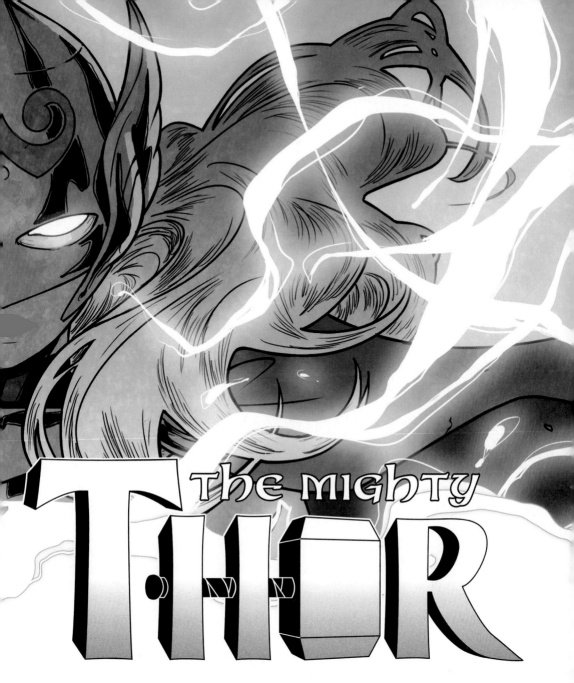

THE MIGHTY THOR

LORDS OF MIDGARD

WRITER	ARTIST	COLOR ARTIST
SON AARON	**RUSSELL DAUTERMAN**	**MATTHEW WILSON**

ART & COLOR, #6-7 VIKING ERA	ART & COLOR, #12 OLD ASGARD
RAFA GARRES	**FRAZER IRVING**

LETTERER	COVER ART
VC's JOE SABINO	**RUSSELL DAUTERMAN & MATTHEW WILSON**

ASSISTANT EDITORS	EDITOR
CHRIS ROBINSON & CHARLES BEACHAM	**WIL MOSS**

WHEN **DR. JANE FOSTER** LIFTS THE MYSTIC HAMMER MJOLNIR, SHE IS
TRANSFORMED INTO **THE GODDESS OF THUNDER, THE MIGHTY THOR!**
HER ENEMIES ARE MANY, AS ASGARD DESCENDS FURTHER INTO CHAOS
AND WAR THREATENS TO SPREAD THROUGHOUT THE TEN REALMS.
YET HER GREATEST BATTLE WILL BE AGAINST A FAR MORE PERSONAL FOE:
THE CANCER THAT IS KILLING HER MORTAL FORM…

DESPITE THOR'S SEEMINGLY DECISIVE DEFEAT OF MALEKITH'S FORCES,
THE KING OF THE DARK ELVES CONVINCED THE ENCHANTRESS
TO CAST A SPELL OF COERCION OVER AELSA, QUEEN OF THE LIGHT ELVES.
UNDER THIS ENCHANTEMENT, AELSA MARRIED MALEKITH,
GIVING THE MONSTER CONTROL OF ALFHEIM. A BEAUTIFUL REALM RICH
WITH RESOURCES, ALFHEIM IS NOW SUBJECT TO THE WILL AND WHIM
OF THE DARK ELF KING AND HIS GREEDY ALLIES…

6

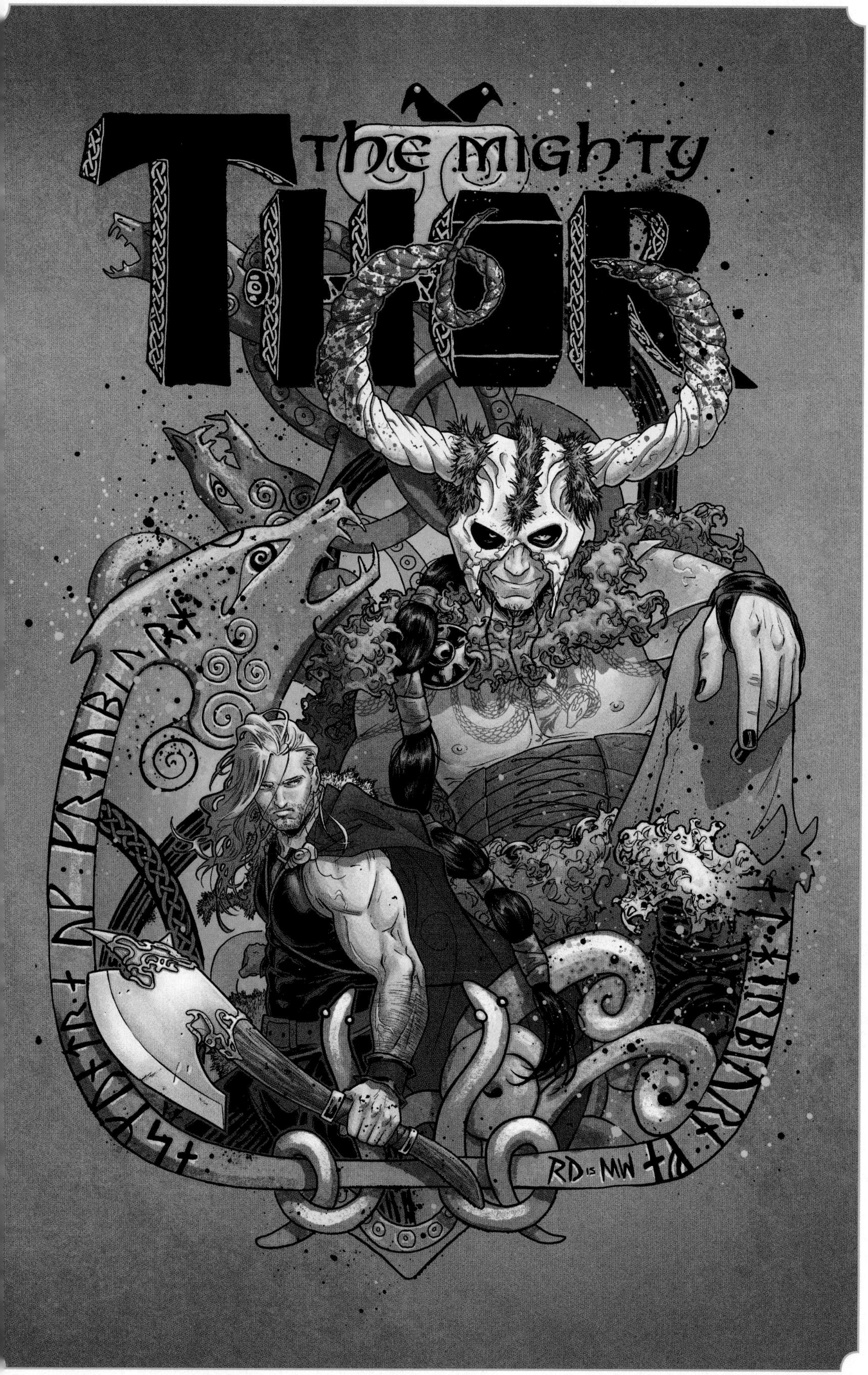
THE MIGHTY
THOR
RD is MW

THE STRONGEST VIKING THERE IS PART I

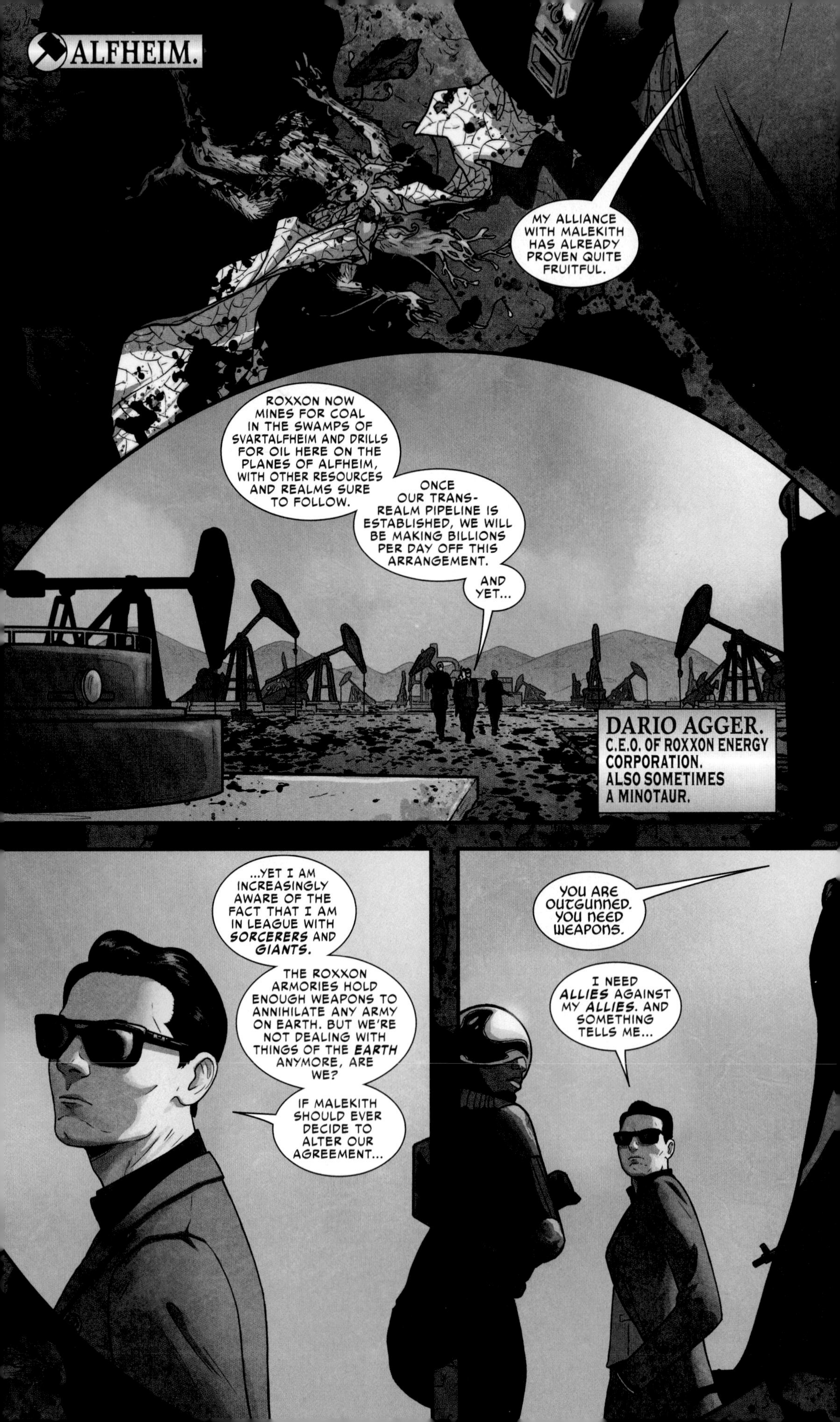
ALFHEIM.
MY ALLIANCE WITH MALEKITH HAS ALREADY PROVEN QUITE FRUITFUL.
ROXXON NOW MINES FOR COAL IN THE SWAMPS OF SVARTALFHEIM AND DRILLS FOR OIL HERE ON THE PLANES OF ALFHEIM, WITH OTHER RESOURCES AND REALMS SURE TO FOLLOW.
ONCE OUR TRANS-REALM PIPELINE IS ESTABLISHED, WE WILL BE MAKING BILLIONS PER DAY OFF THIS ARRANGEMENT.
AND YET...
DARIO AGGER.
C.E.O. OF ROXXON ENERGY CORPORATION.
ALSO SOMETIMES A MINOTAUR.
...YET I AM INCREASINGLY AWARE OF THE FACT THAT I AM IN LEAGUE WITH SORCERERS AND GIANTS.
THE ROXXON ARMORIES HOLD ENOUGH WEAPONS TO ANNIHILATE ANY ARMY ON EARTH. BUT WE'RE NOT DEALING WITH THINGS OF THE EARTH ANYMORE, ARE WE?
IF MALEKITH SHOULD EVER DECIDE TO ALTER OUR AGREEMENT...
YOU ARE OUTGUNNED. YOU NEED WEAPONS.
I NEED ALLIES AGAINST MY ALLIES. AND SOMETHING TELLS ME...

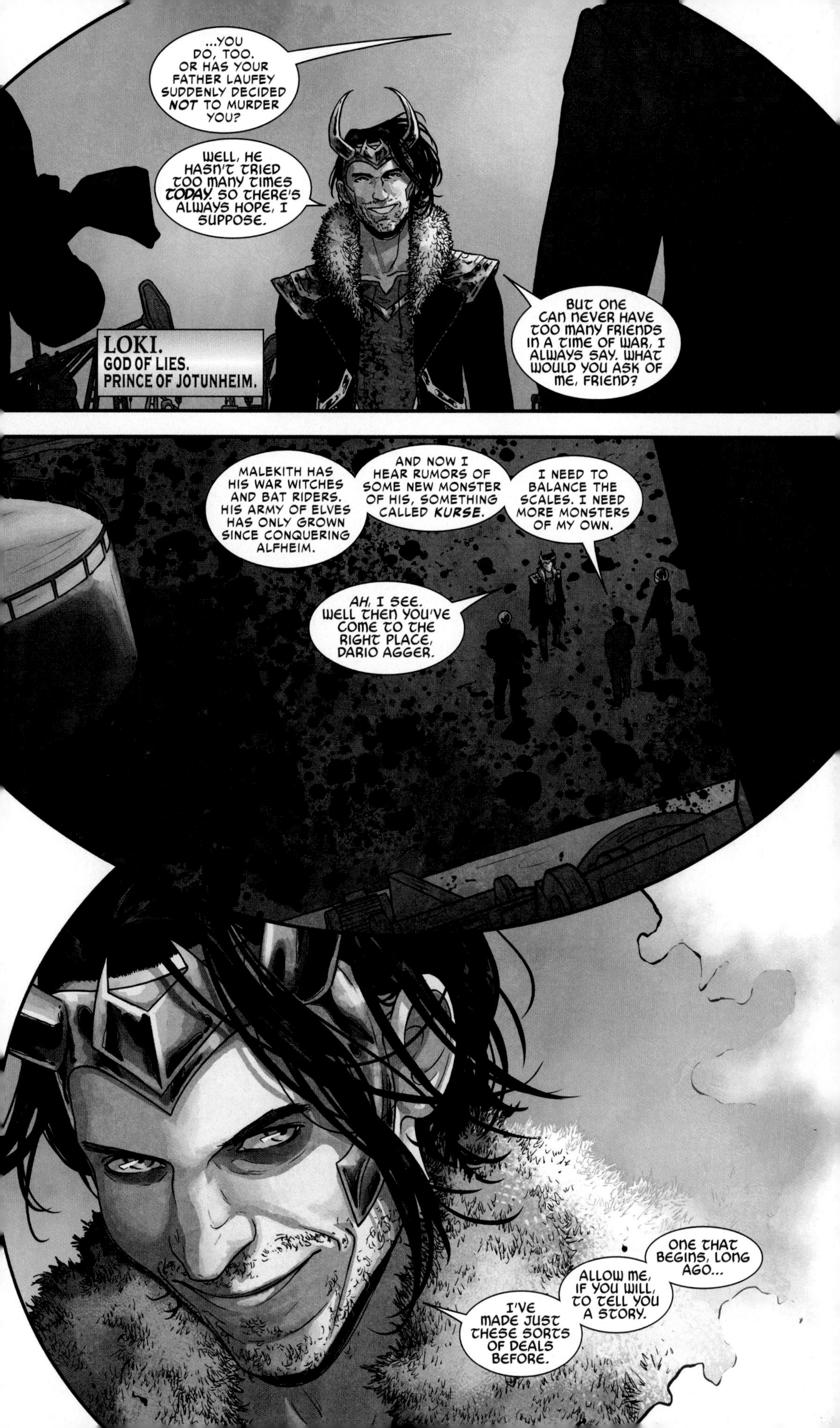
...YOU DO, TOO. OR HAS YOUR FATHER LAUFEY SUDDENLY DECIDED NOT TO MURDER YOU?
WELL, HE HASN'T TRIED TOO MANY TIMES TODAY. SO THERE'S ALWAYS HOPE, I SUPPOSE.
LOKI. GOD OF LIES. PRINCE OF JOTUNHEIM.
BUT ONE CAN NEVER HAVE TOO MANY FRIENDS IN A TIME OF WAR, I ALWAYS SAY. WHAT WOULD YOU ASK OF ME, FRIEND?
MALEKITH HAS HIS WAR WITCHES AND BAT RIDERS. HIS ARMY OF ELVES HAS ONLY GROWN SINCE CONQUERING ALFHEIM.
AND NOW I HEAR RUMORS OF SOME NEW MONSTER OF HIS, SOMETHING CALLED KURSE.
I NEED TO BALANCE THE SCALES. I NEED MORE MONSTERS OF MY OWN.
AH, I SEE. WELL THEN YOU'VE COME TO THE RIGHT PLACE, DARIO AGGER.
I'VE MADE JUST THESE SORTS OF DEALS BEFORE.
ALLOW ME, IF YOU WILL, TO TELL YOU A STORY.
ONE THAT BEGINS, LONG AGO...

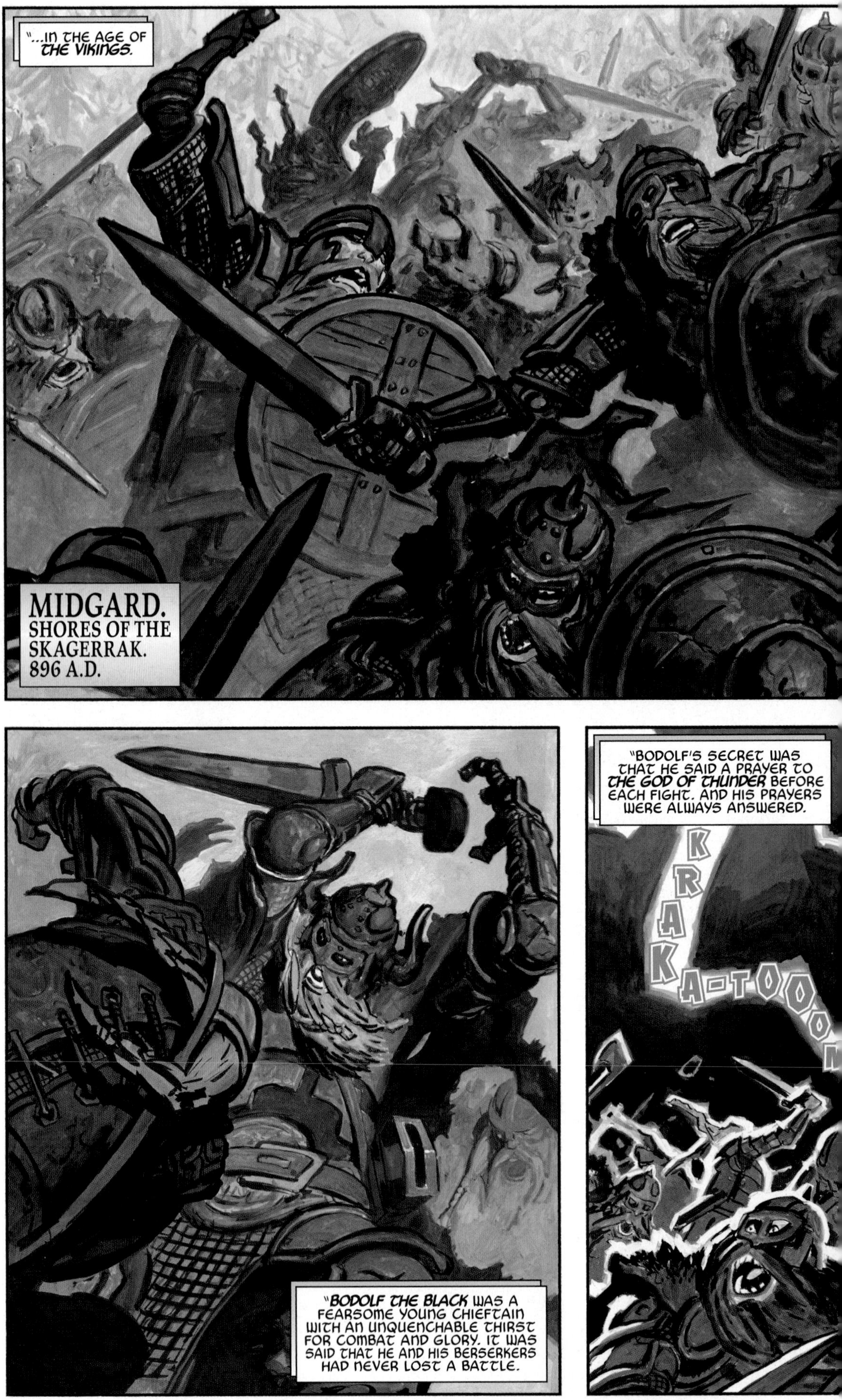
"...IN THE AGE OF THE VIKINGS.
MIDGARD. SHORES OF THE SKAGERRAK. 896 A.D.
"BODOLF THE BLACK WAS A FEARSOME YOUNG CHIEFTAIN WITH AN UNQUENCHABLE THIRST FOR COMBAT AND GLORY. IT WAS SAID THAT HE AND HIS BERSERKERS HAD NEVER LOST A BATTLE.
"BODOLF'S SECRET WAS THAT HE SAID A PRAYER TO THE GOD OF THUNDER BEFORE EACH FIGHT. AND HIS PRAYERS WERE ALWAYS ANSWERED.
KRAKA-TOOOOM

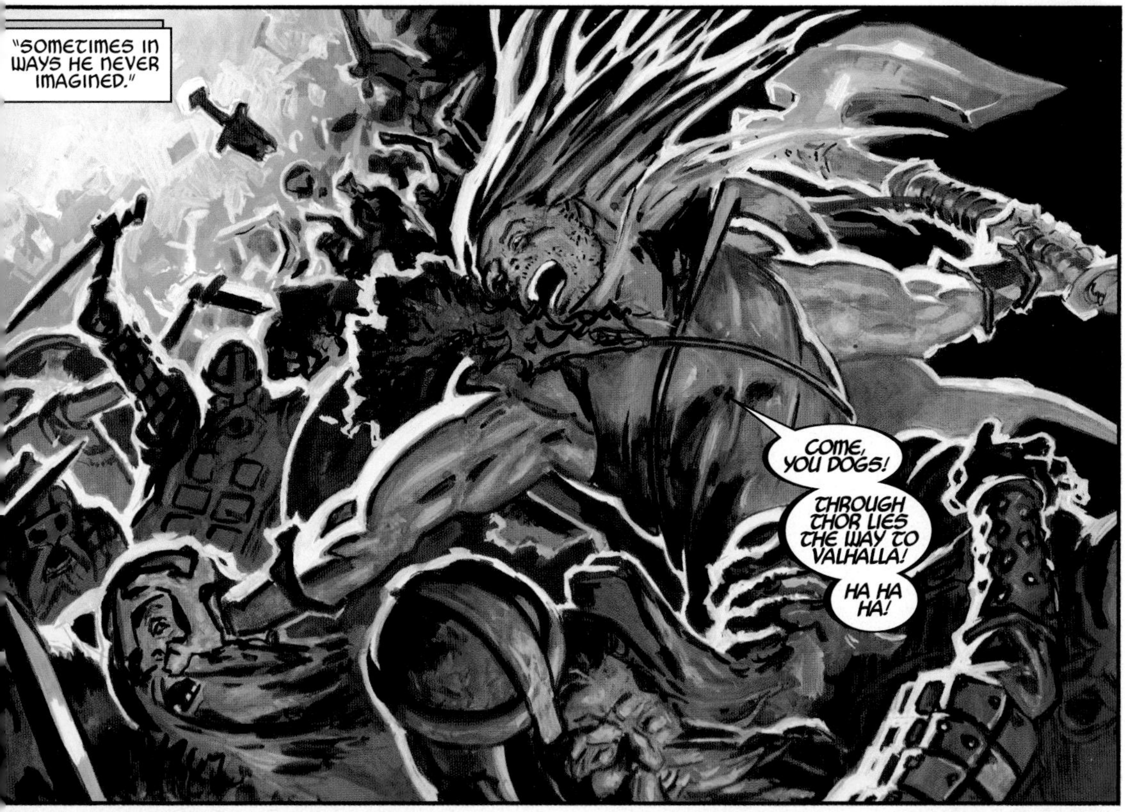
"SOMETIMES IN WAYS HE NEVER IMAGINED."
COME, YOU DOGS!
THROUGH THOR LIES THE WAY TO VALHALLA!
HA HA HA!

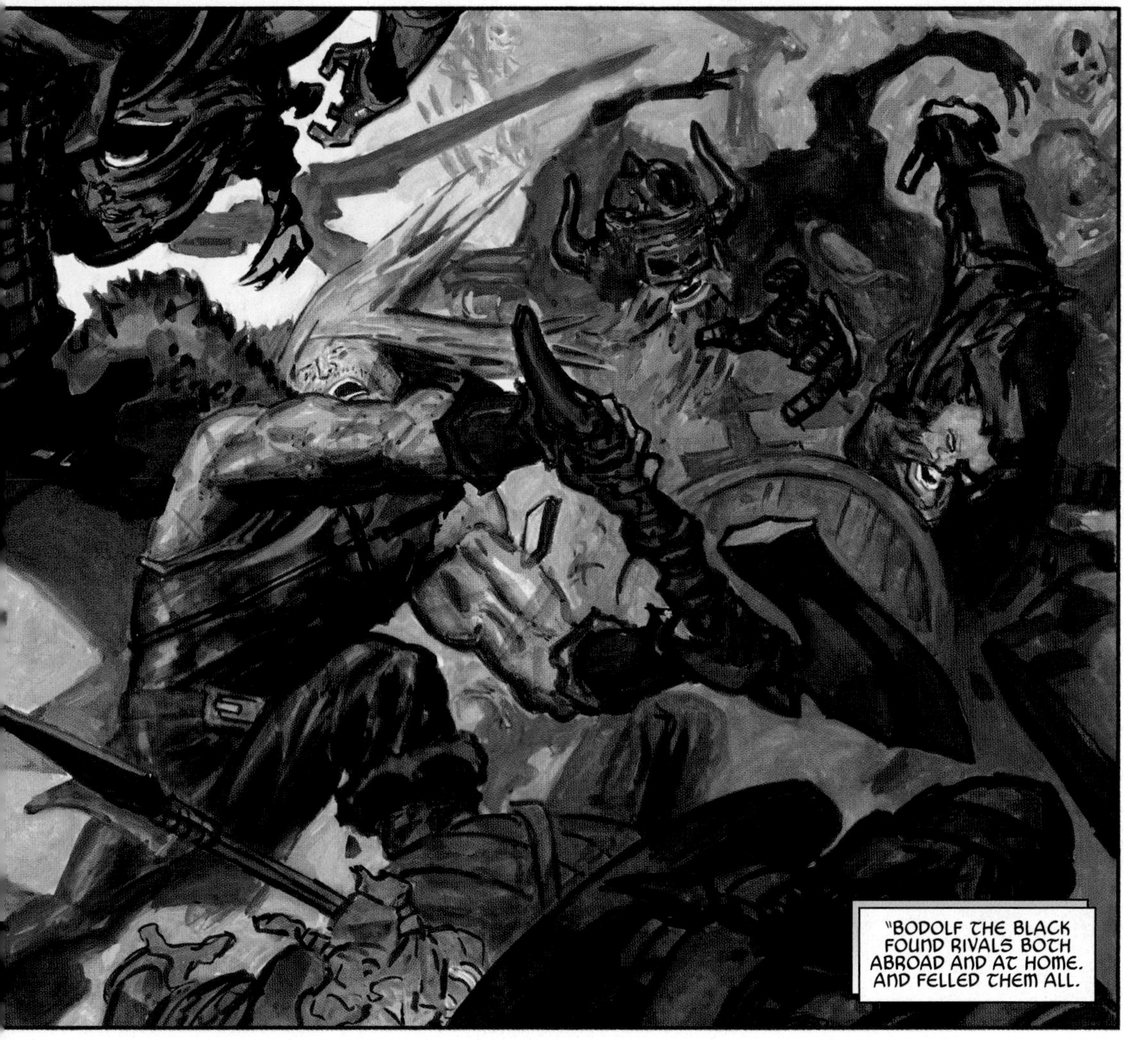
"BODOLF THE BLACK FOUND RIVALS BOTH ABROAD AND AT HOME. AND FELLED THEM ALL.

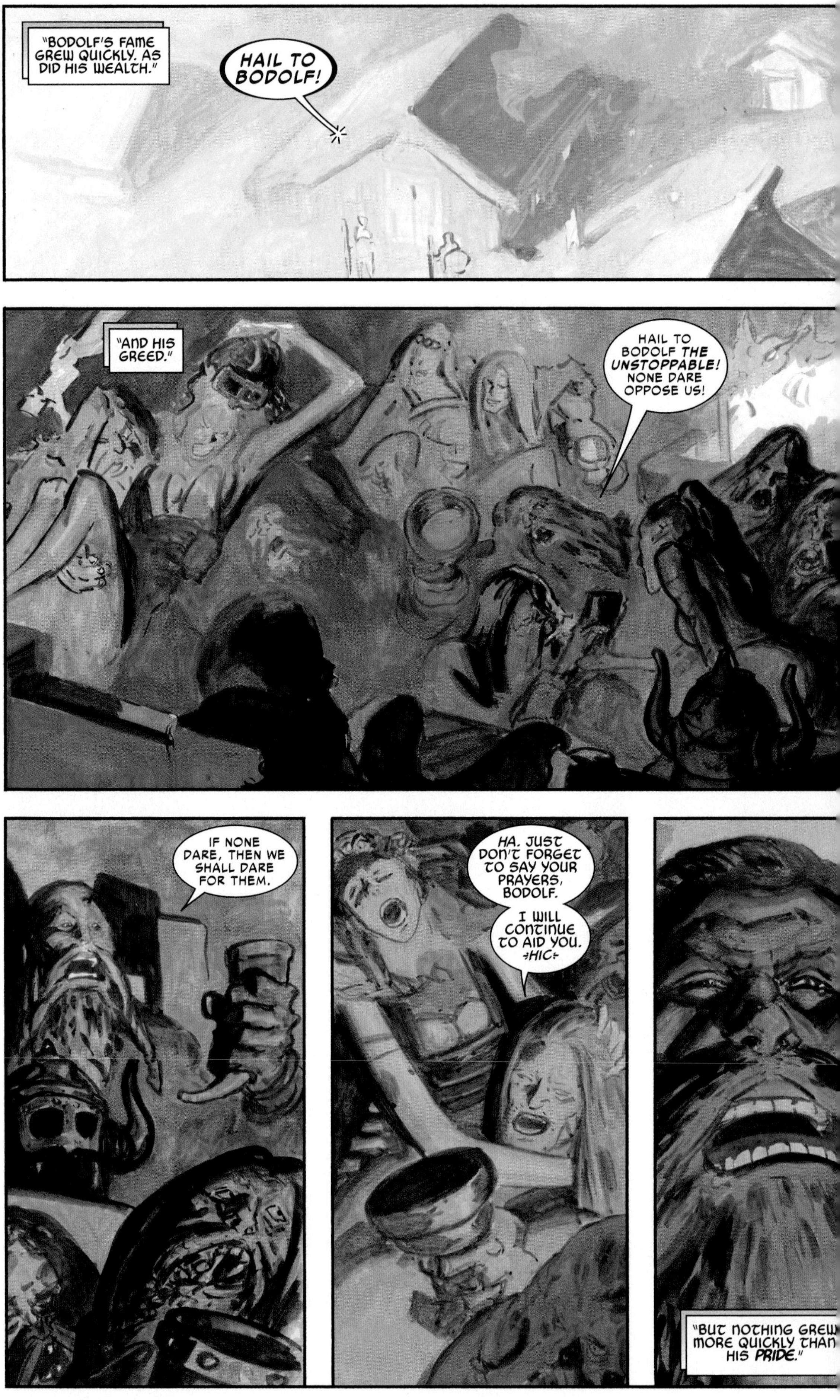

"BODOLF'S FAME GREW QUICKLY. AS DID HIS WEALTH."
HAIL TO BODOLF!
"AND HIS GREED."
HAIL TO BODOLF *THE UNSTOPPABLE!* NONE DARE OPPOSE US!
IF NONE DARE, THEN WE SHALL DARE FOR THEM.
HA. JUST DON'T FORGET TO SAY YOUR PRAYERS, BODOLF.
I WILL CONTINUE TO AID YOU. *HIC*
"BUT NOTHING GREW MORE QUICKLY THAN HIS *PRIDE.*"

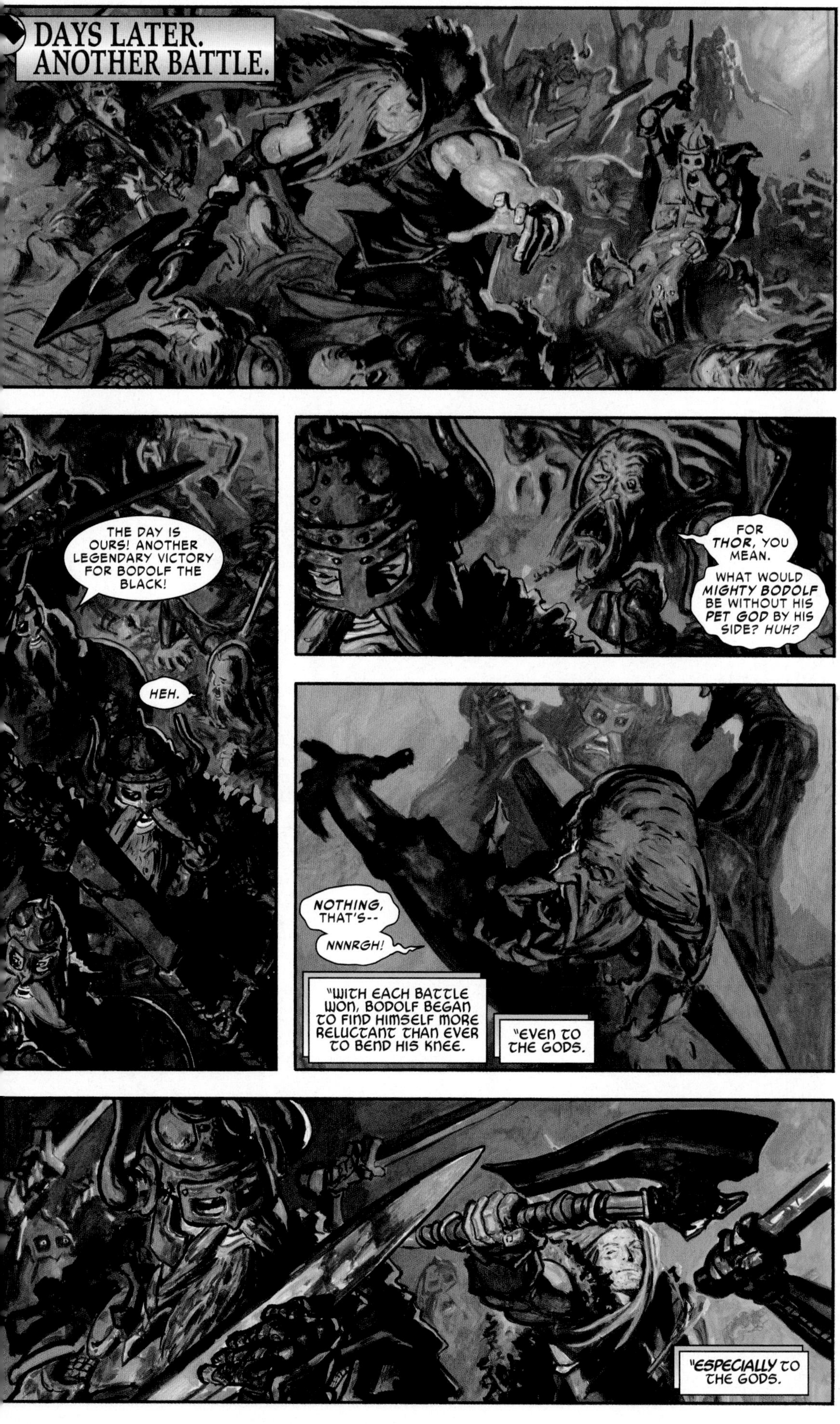
DAYS LATER. ANOTHER BATTLE.
THE DAY IS OURS! ANOTHER LEGENDARY VICTORY FOR BODOLF THE BLACK!
FOR THOR, YOU MEAN.
WHAT WOULD MIGHTY BODOLF BE WITHOUT HIS PET GOD BY HIS SIDE? HUH?
HEH.
NOTHING, THAT'S--
NNNRGH!
"WITH EACH BATTLE WON, BODOLF BEGAN TO FIND HIMSELF MORE RELUCTANT THAN EVER TO BEND HIS KNEE.
"EVEN TO THE GODS.
"ESPECIALLY TO THE GODS.

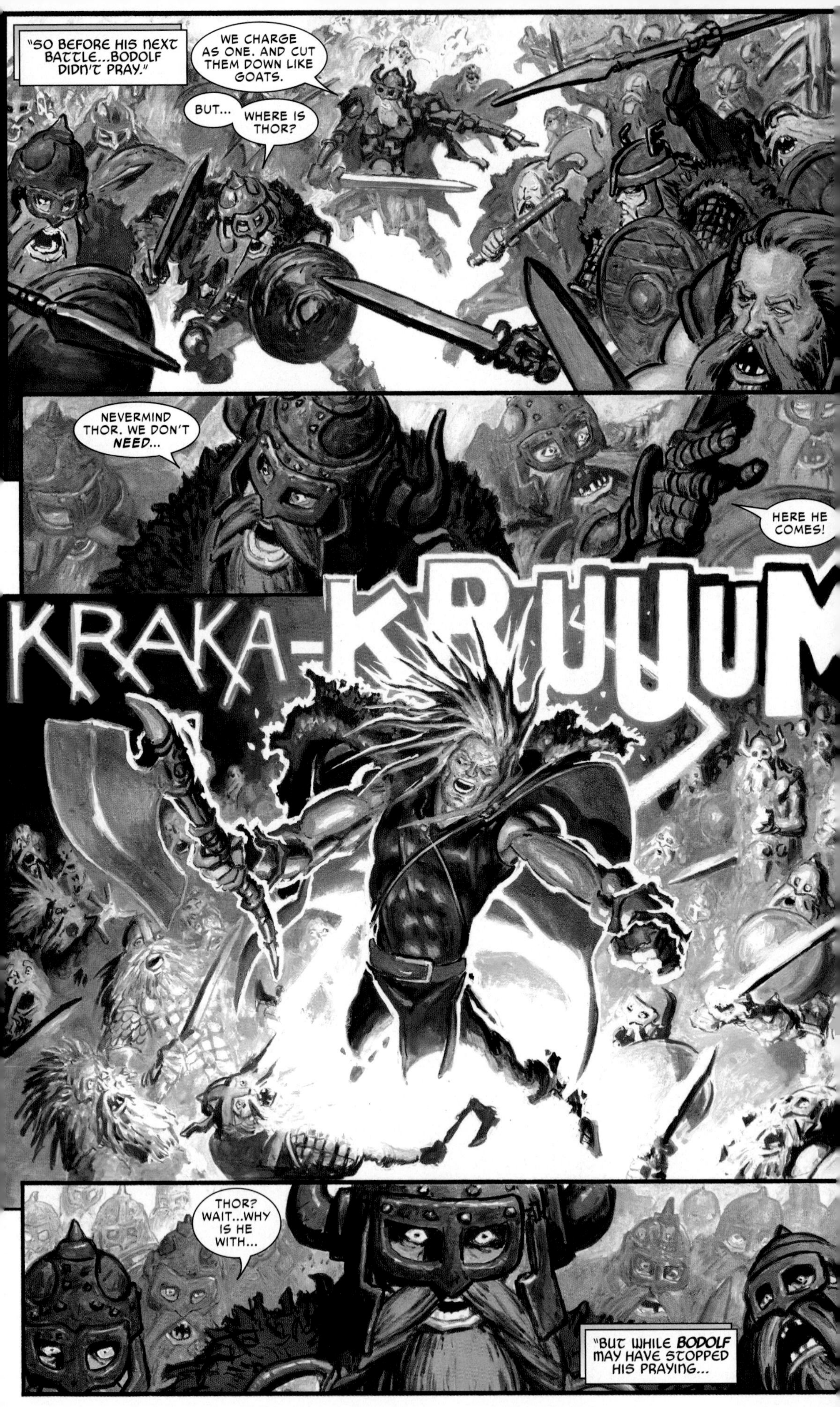
"SO BEFORE HIS NEXT BATTLE...BODOLF DIDN'T PRAY."
WE CHARGE AS ONE. AND CUT THEM DOWN LIKE GOATS.
BUT...
WHERE IS THOR?
NEVERMIND THOR. WE DON'T NEED...
HERE HE COMES!
KRAKA-KRUUUM
THOR? WAIT...WHY IS HE WITH...
"BUT WHILE BODOLF MAY HAVE STOPPED HIS PRAYING...

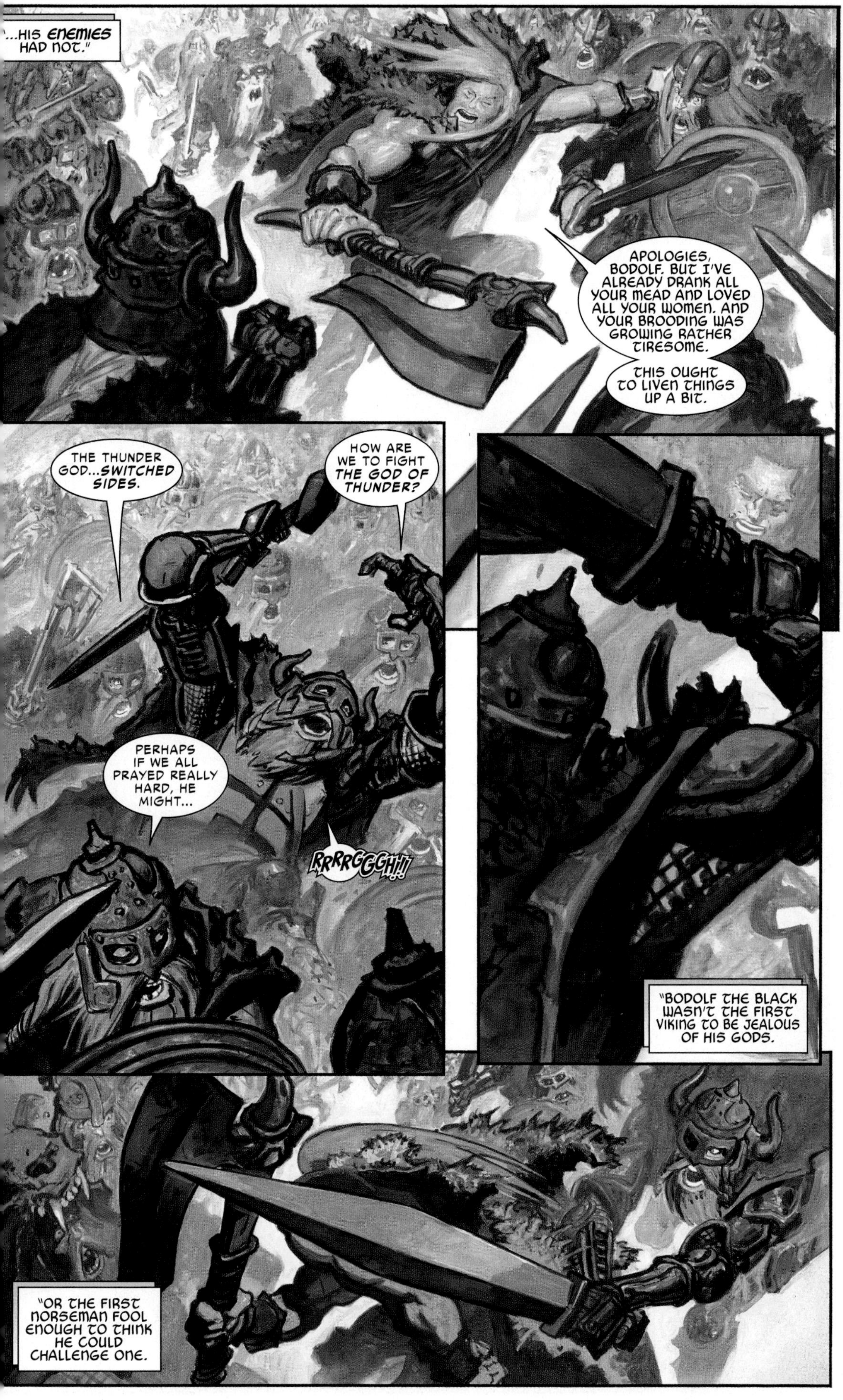
"...HIS ENEMIES HAD NOT."
APOLOGIES, BODOLF. BUT I'VE ALREADY DRANK ALL YOUR MEAD AND LOVED ALL YOUR WOMEN. AND YOUR BROODING WAS GROWING RATHER TIRESOME.
THIS OUGHT TO LIVEN THINGS UP A BIT.
THE THUNDER GOD...SWITCHED SIDES.
HOW ARE WE TO FIGHT THE GOD OF THUNDER?
PERHAPS IF WE ALL PRAYED REALLY HARD, HE MIGHT...
RRRRGGGH!!
"BODOLF THE BLACK WASN'T THE FIRST VIKING TO BE JEALOUS OF HIS GODS.
"OR THE FIRST NORSEMAN FOOL ENOUGH TO THINK HE COULD CHALLENGE ONE.

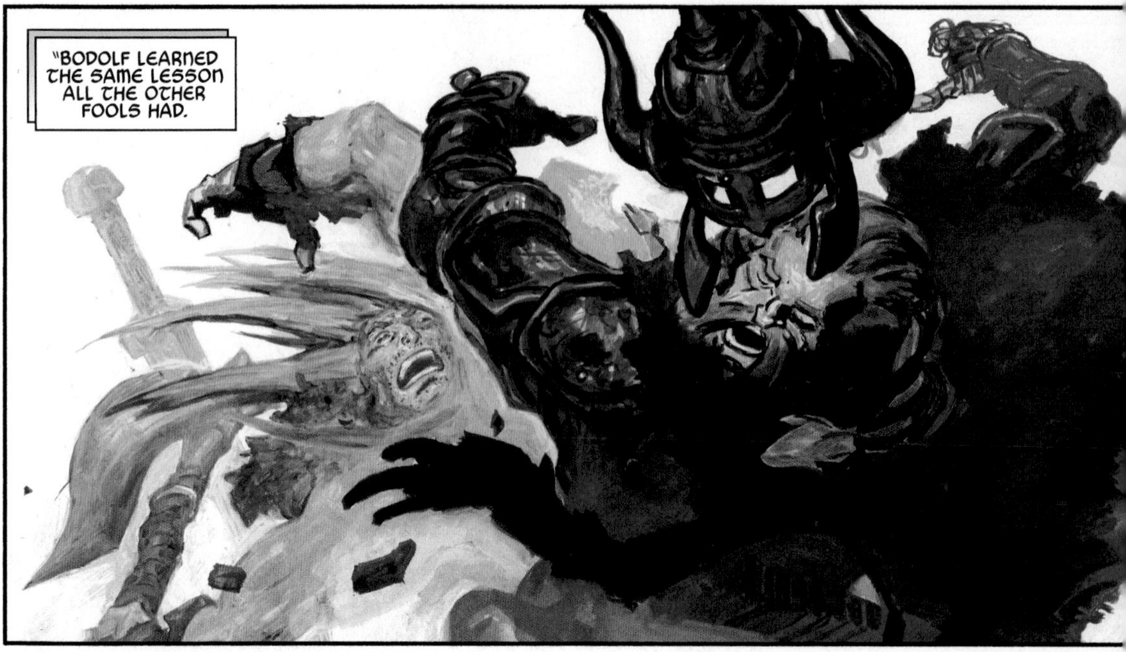
"BODOLF LEARNED THE SAME LESSON ALL THE OTHER FOOLS HAD.

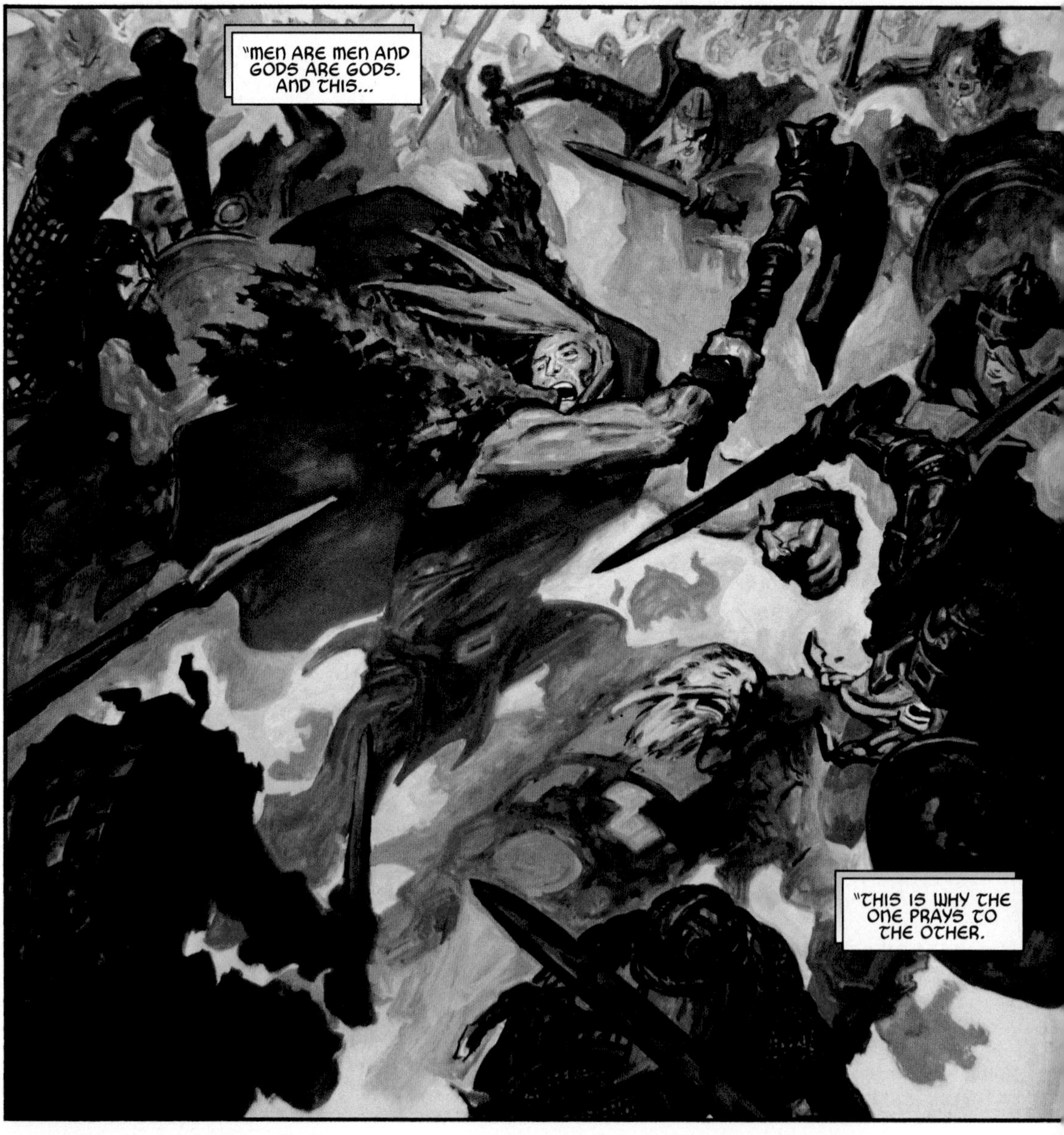
"MEN ARE MEN AND GODS ARE GODS. AND THIS...
"THIS IS WHY THE ONE PRAYS TO THE OTHER.

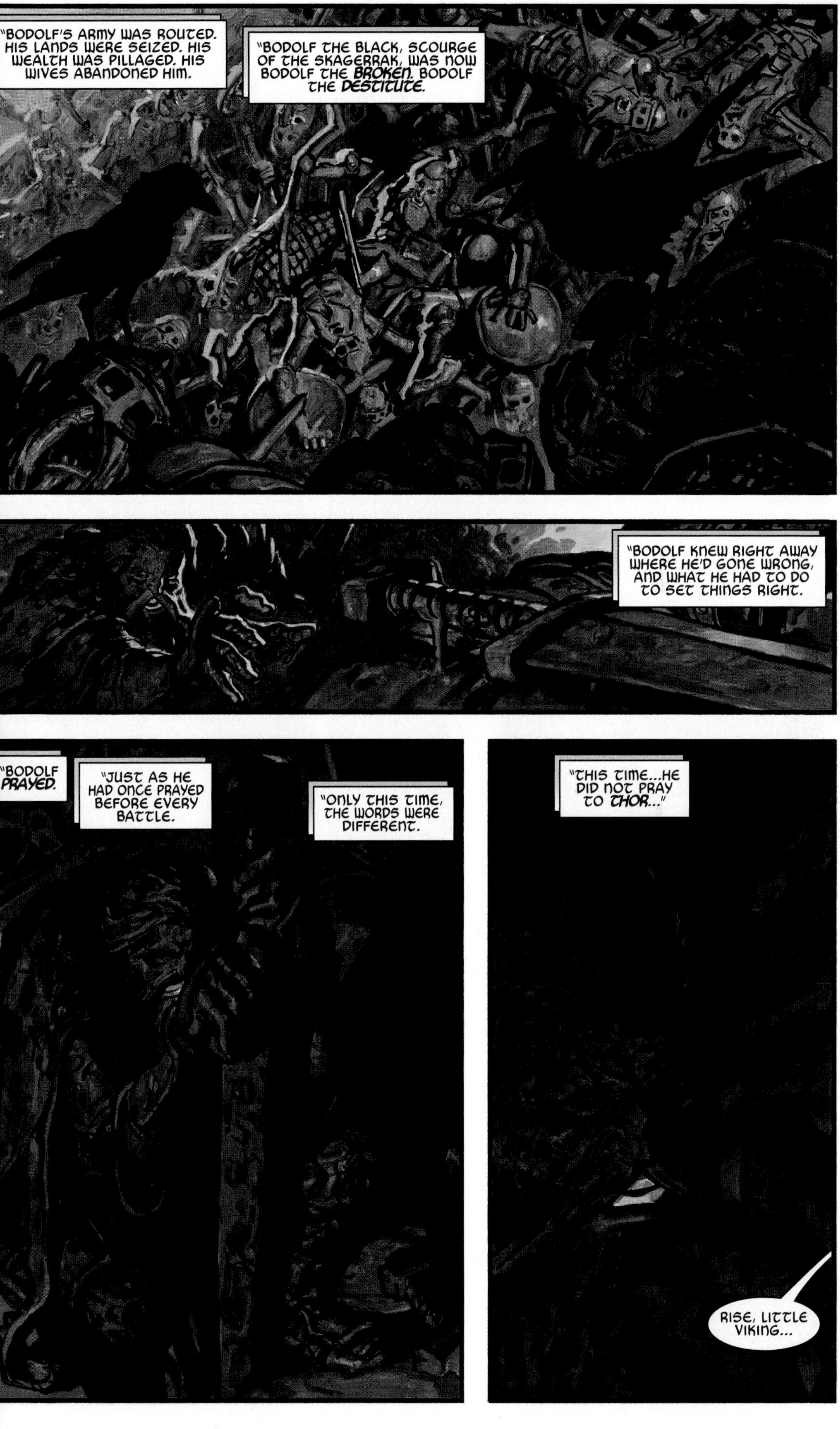
"BODOLF'S ARMY WAS ROUTED. HIS LANDS WERE SEIZED. HIS WEALTH WAS PILLAGED. HIS WIVES ABANDONED HIM.
"BODOLF THE BLACK, SCOURGE OF THE SKAGERRAK, WAS NOW BODOLF THE ***BROKEN***. BODOLF THE ***DESTITUTE***.
"BODOLF KNEW RIGHT AWAY WHERE HE'D GONE WRONG, AND WHAT HE HAD TO DO TO SET THINGS RIGHT.
"BODOLF ***PRAYED***.
"JUST AS HE HAD ONCE PRAYED BEFORE EVERY BATTLE.
"ONLY THIS TIME, THE WORDS WERE DIFFERENT.
"THIS TIME...HE DID NOT PRAY TO ***THOR***..."
RISE, LITTLE VIKING...

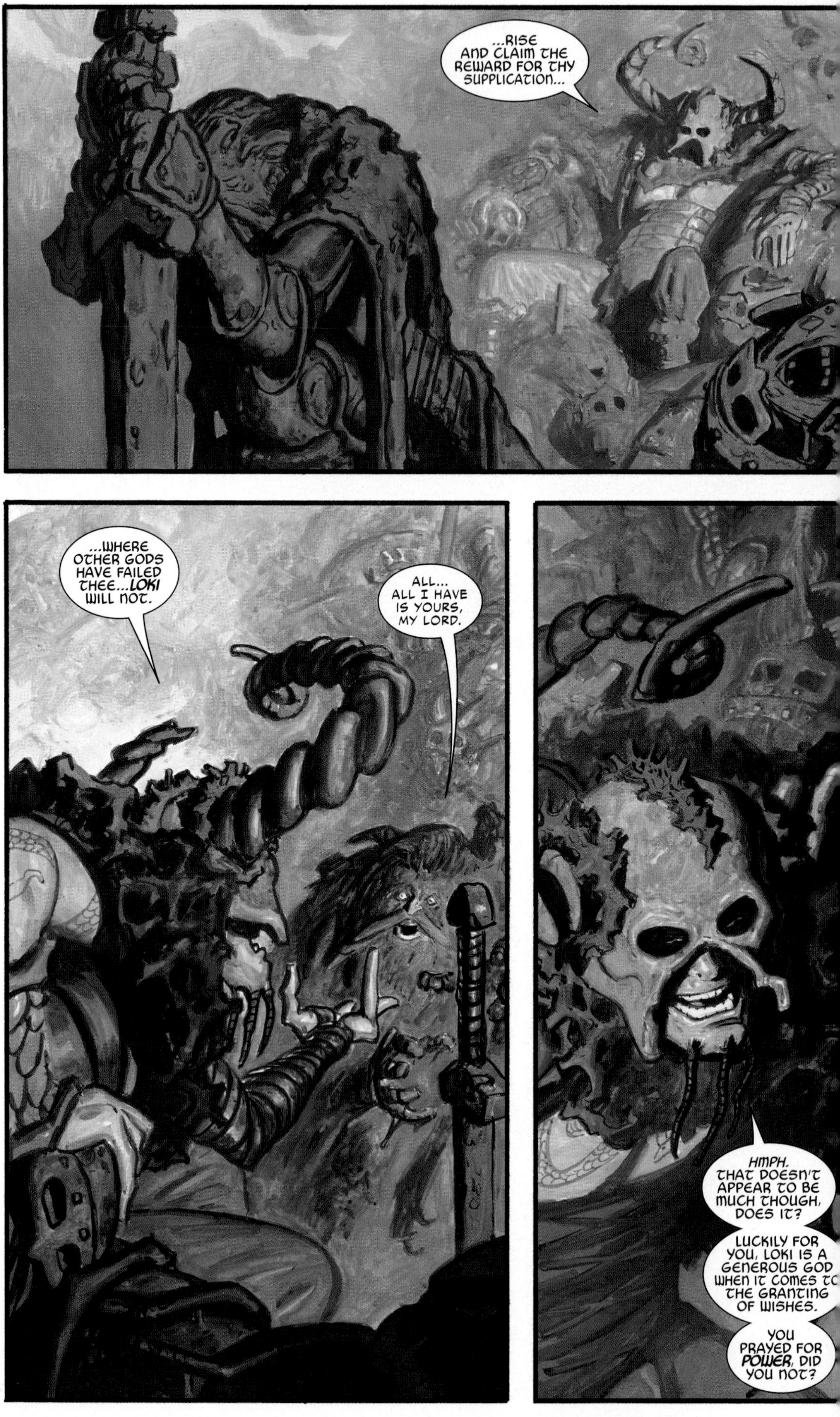
...RISE AND CLAIM THE REWARD FOR THY SUPPLICATION...
...WHERE OTHER GODS HAVE FAILED THEE...LOKI WILL NOT.
ALL... ALL I HAVE IS YOURS, MY LORD.
HMPH. THAT DOESN'T APPEAR TO BE MUCH THOUGH, DOES IT?
LUCKILY FOR YOU, LOKI IS A GENEROUS GOD WHEN IT COMES TO THE GRANTING OF WISHES.
YOU PRAYED FOR POWER, DID YOU NOT?

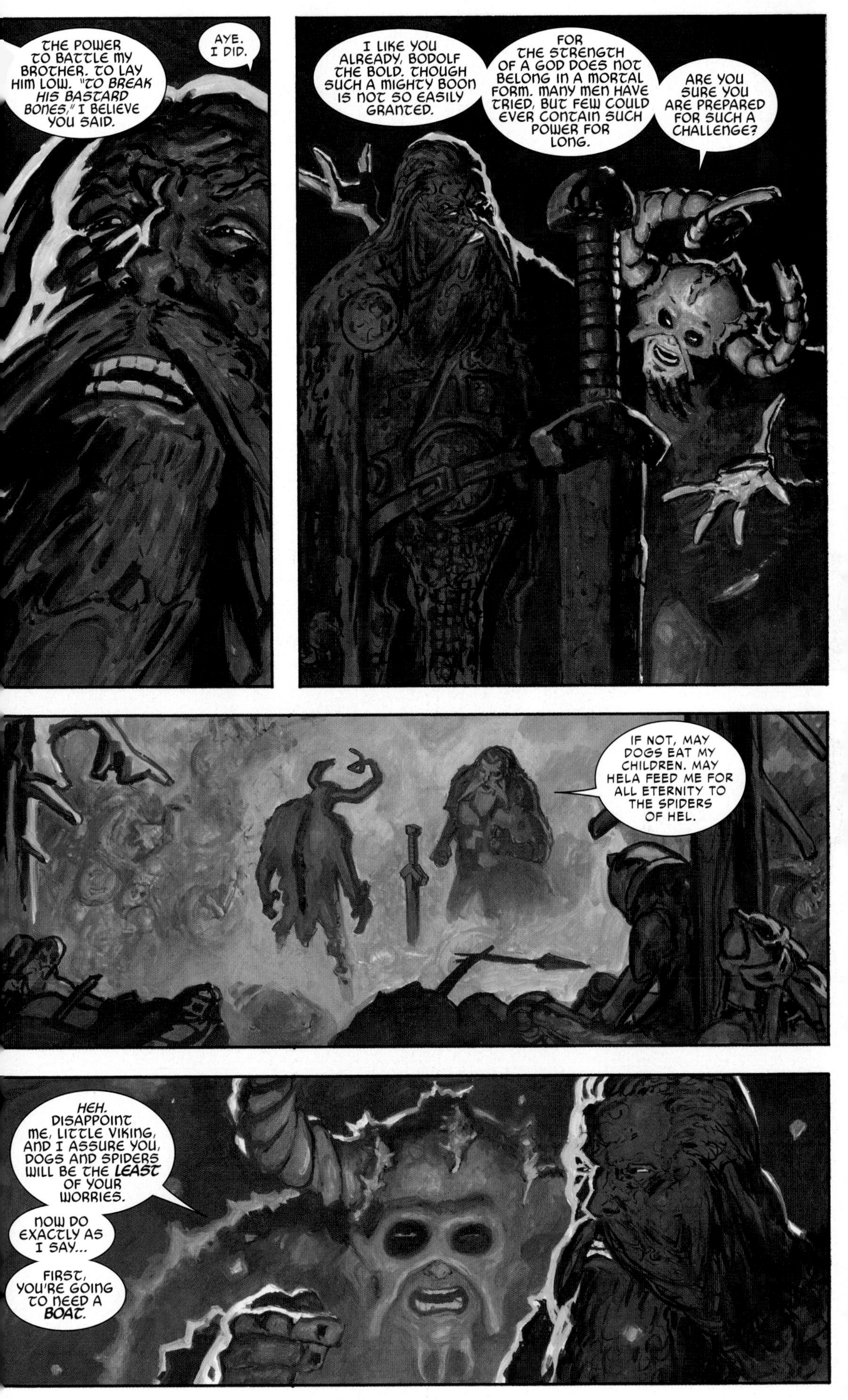
THE POWER TO BATTLE MY BROTHER. TO LAY HIM LOW. "*TO BREAK HIS BASTARD BONES*," I BELIEVE YOU SAID.
AYE. I DID.
I LIKE YOU ALREADY, BODOLF THE BOLD. THOUGH SUCH A MIGHTY BOON IS NOT SO EASILY GRANTED.
FOR THE STRENGTH OF A GOD DOES NOT BELONG IN A MORTAL FORM. MANY MEN HAVE TRIED, BUT FEW COULD EVER CONTAIN SUCH POWER FOR LONG.
ARE YOU SURE YOU ARE PREPARED FOR SUCH A CHALLENGE?
IF NOT, MAY DOGS EAT MY CHILDREN. MAY HELA FEED ME FOR ALL ETERNITY TO THE SPIDERS OF HEL.
HEH. DISAPPOINT ME, LITTLE VIKING, AND I ASSURE YOU, DOGS AND SPIDERS WILL BE THE ***LEAST*** OF YOUR WORRIES.
NOW DO EXACTLY AS I SAY...
FIRST, YOU'RE GOING TO NEED A ***BOAT***.

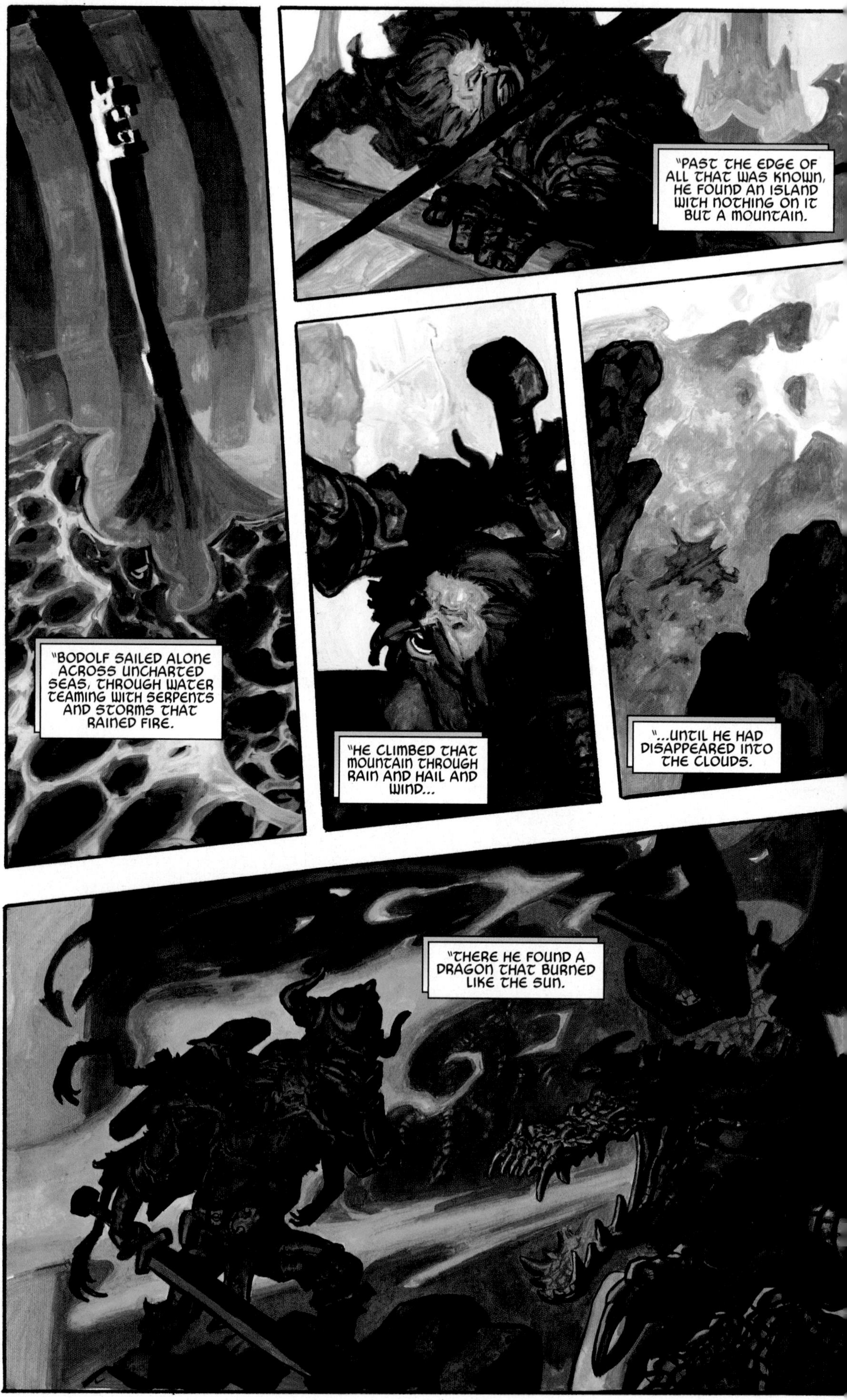

"BODOLF SAILED ALONE ACROSS UNCHARTED SEAS, THROUGH WATER TEAMING WITH SERPENTS AND STORMS THAT RAINED FIRE.
"PAST THE EDGE OF ALL THAT WAS KNOWN, HE FOUND AN ISLAND WITH NOTHING ON IT BUT A MOUNTAIN.
"HE CLIMBED THAT MOUNTAIN THROUGH RAIN AND HAIL AND WIND...
"...UNTIL HE HAD DISAPPEARED INTO THE CLOUDS.
"THERE HE FOUND A DRAGON THAT BURNED LIKE THE SUN.

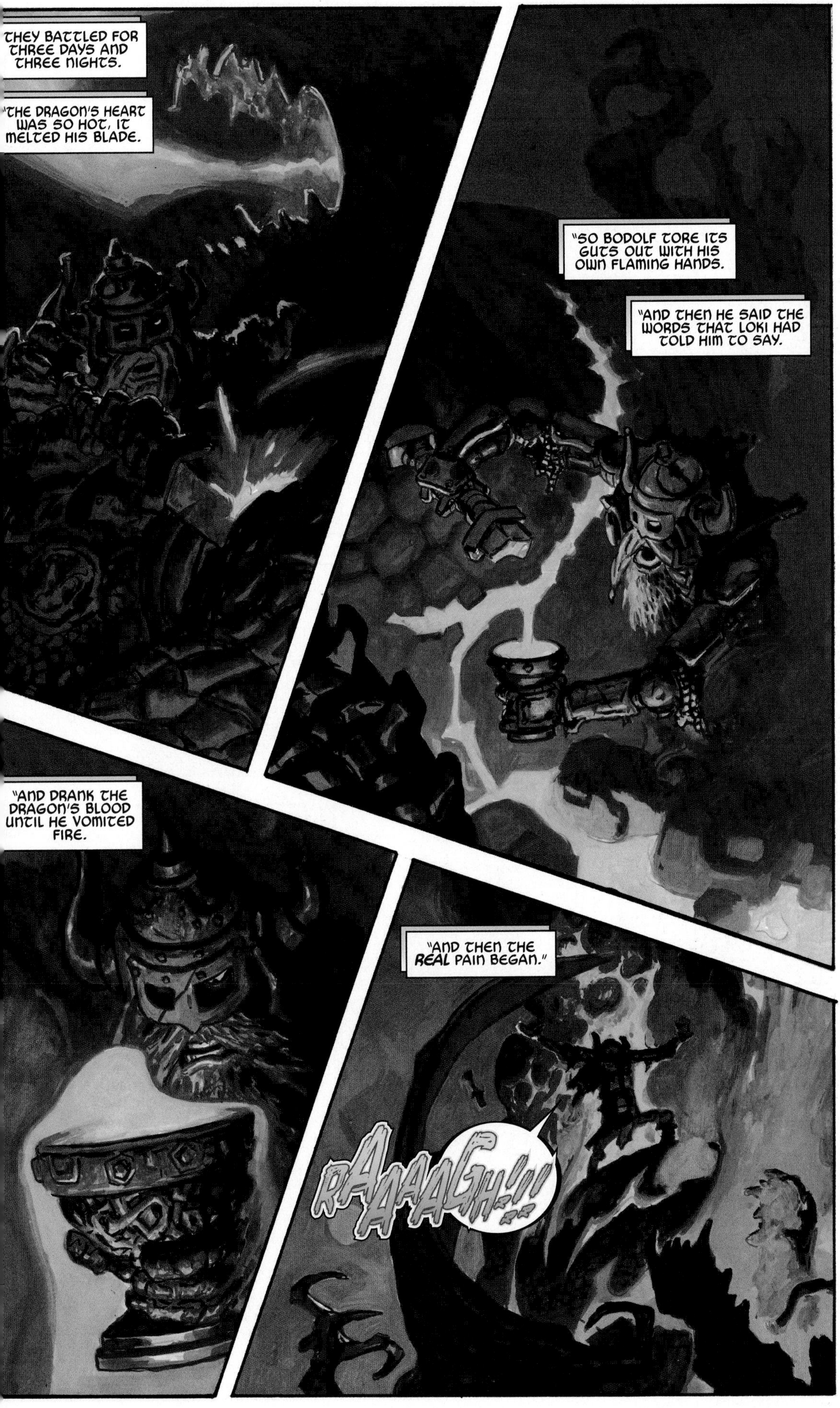
THEY BATTLED FOR THREE DAYS AND THREE NIGHTS.
"THE DRAGON'S HEART WAS SO HOT, IT MELTED HIS BLADE.
"SO BODOLF TORE ITS GUTS OUT WITH HIS OWN FLAMING HANDS.
"AND THEN HE SAID THE WORDS THAT LOKI HAD TOLD HIM TO SAY.
"AND DRANK THE DRAGON'S BLOOD UNTIL HE VOMITED FIRE.
"AND THEN THE REAL PAIN BEGAN."
RAAAAGH!!!

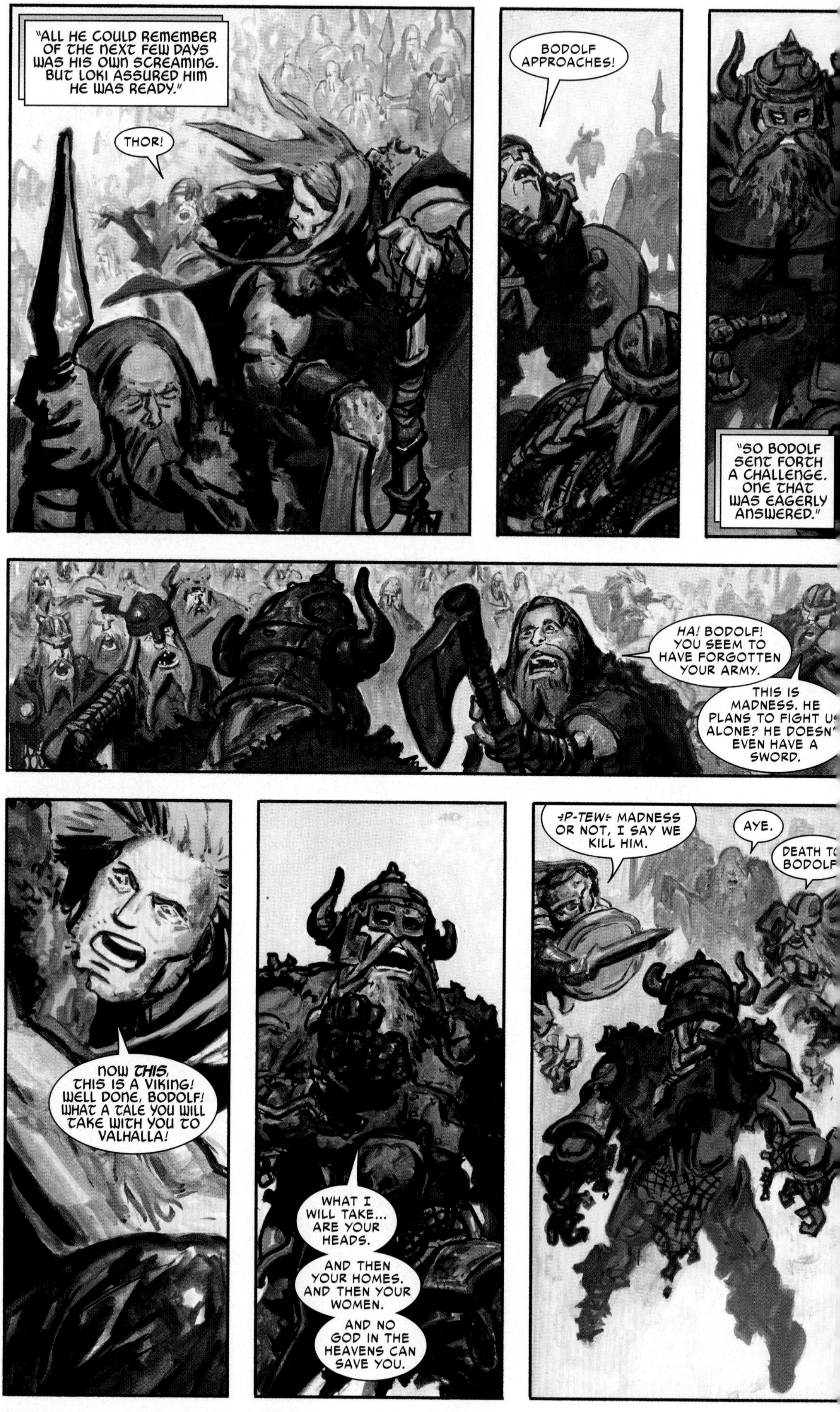
"ALL HE COULD REMEMBER OF THE NEXT FEW DAYS WAS HIS OWN SCREAMING. BUT LOKI ASSURED HIM HE WAS READY."
THOR!
BODOLF APPROACHES!
"SO BODOLF SENT FORTH A CHALLENGE. ONE THAT WAS EAGERLY ANSWERED."
HA! BODOLF! YOU SEEM TO HAVE FORGOTTEN YOUR ARMY.
THIS IS MADNESS. HE PLANS TO FIGHT US ALONE? HE DOESN'T EVEN HAVE A SWORD.
NOW THIS, THIS IS A VIKING! WELL DONE, BODOLF! WHAT A TALE YOU WILL TAKE WITH YOU TO VALHALLA!
WHAT I WILL TAKE... ARE YOUR HEADS.
AND THEN YOUR HOMES. AND THEN YOUR WOMEN.
AND NO GOD IN THE HEAVENS CAN SAVE YOU.
=P-TEW= MADNESS OR NOT, I SAY WE KILL HIM.
AYE.
DEATH TO BODOLF

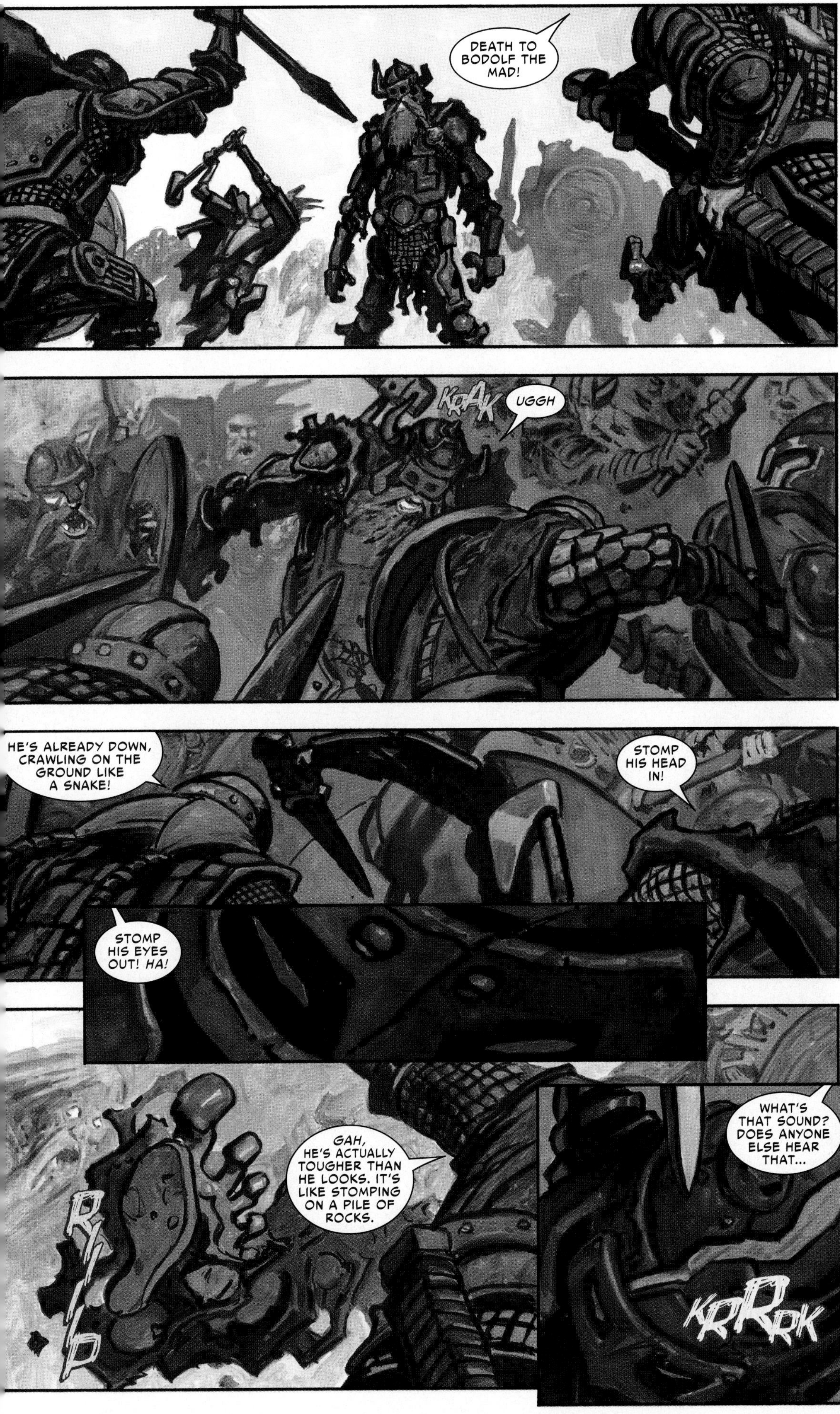
DEATH TO BODOLF THE MAD!
KRAK
UGGH
HE'S ALREADY DOWN, CRAWLING ON THE GROUND LIKE A SNAKE!
STOMP HIS HEAD IN!
STOMP HIS EYES OUT! HA!
GAH, HE'S ACTUALLY TOUGHER THAN HE LOOKS. IT'S LIKE STOMPING ON A PILE OF ROCKS.
WHAT'S THAT SOUND? DOES ANYONE ELSE HEAR THAT...
KRRRK

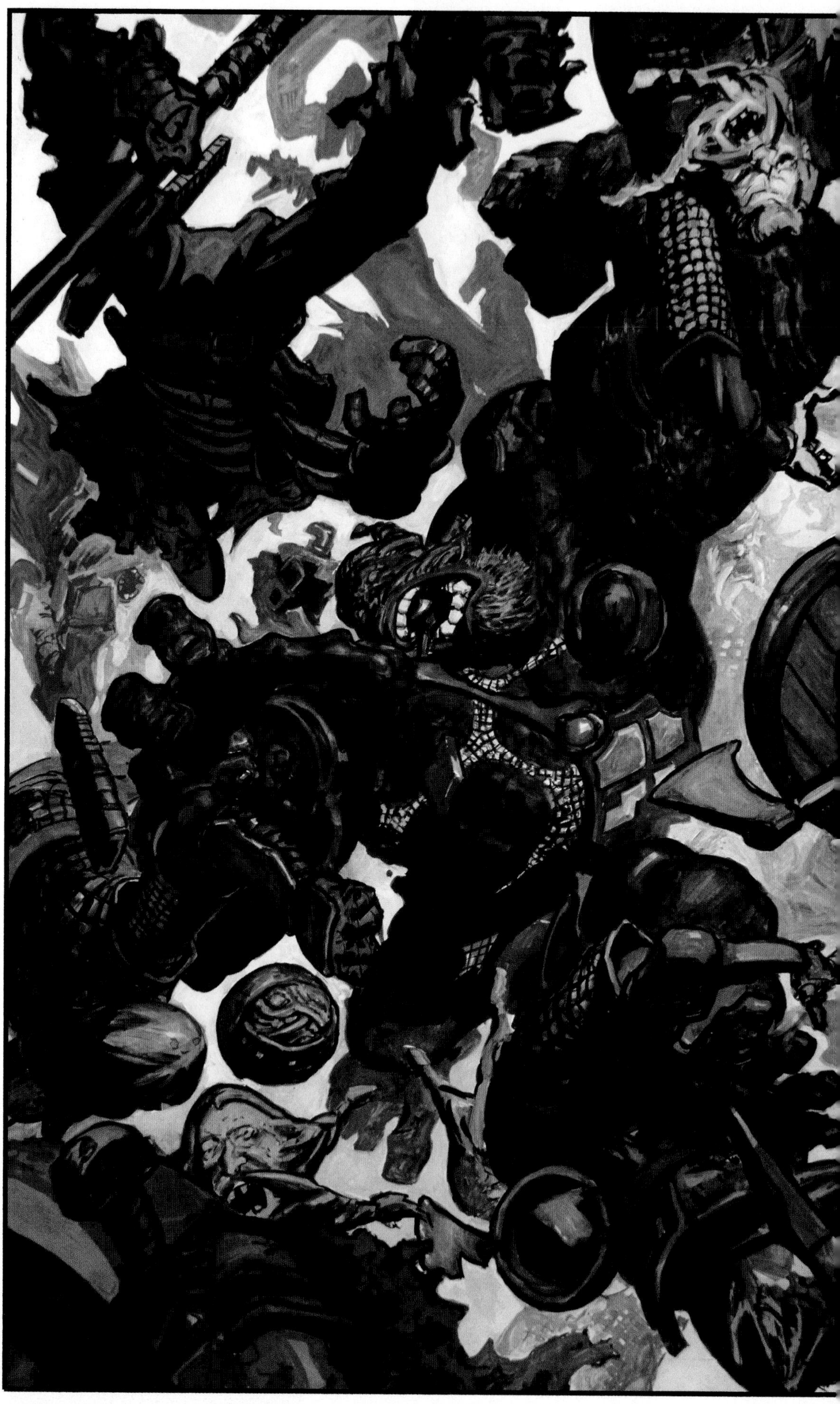

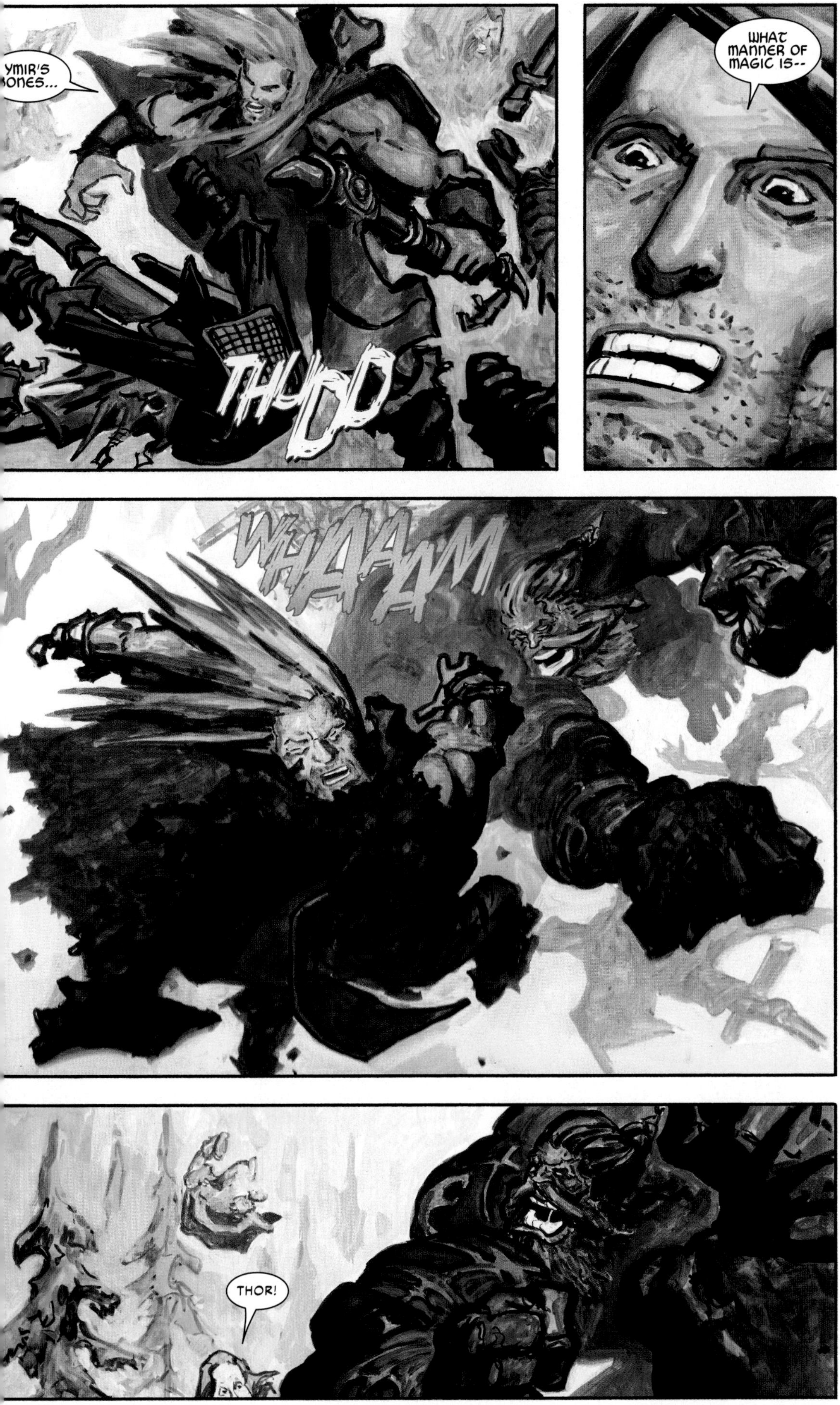
YMIR'S
BONES...
THUDD
WHAT
MANNER OF
MAGIC IS--
WHAAAM
THOR!

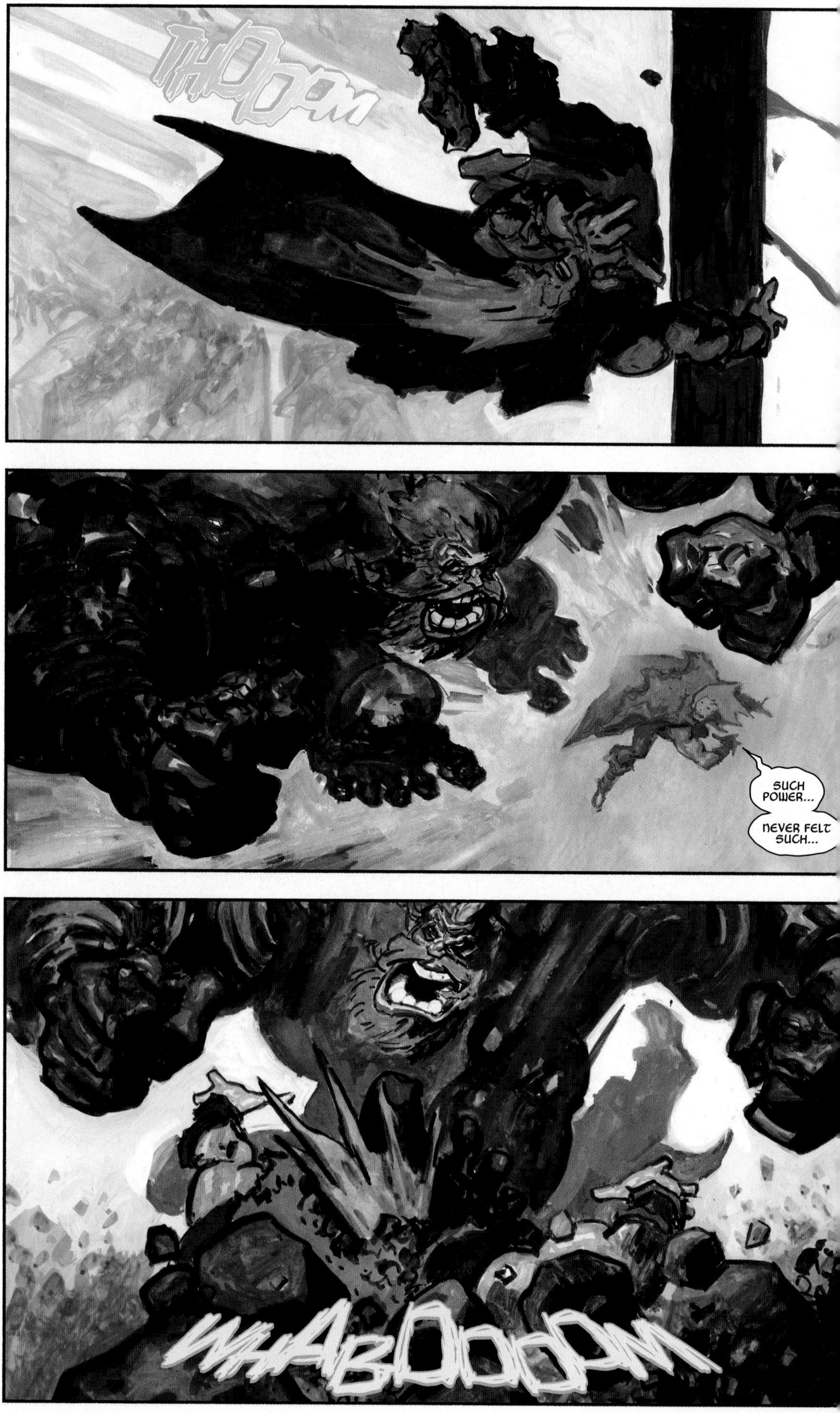
THOOOM
SUCH POWER...
NEVER FELT SUCH...
WHABOOOOM

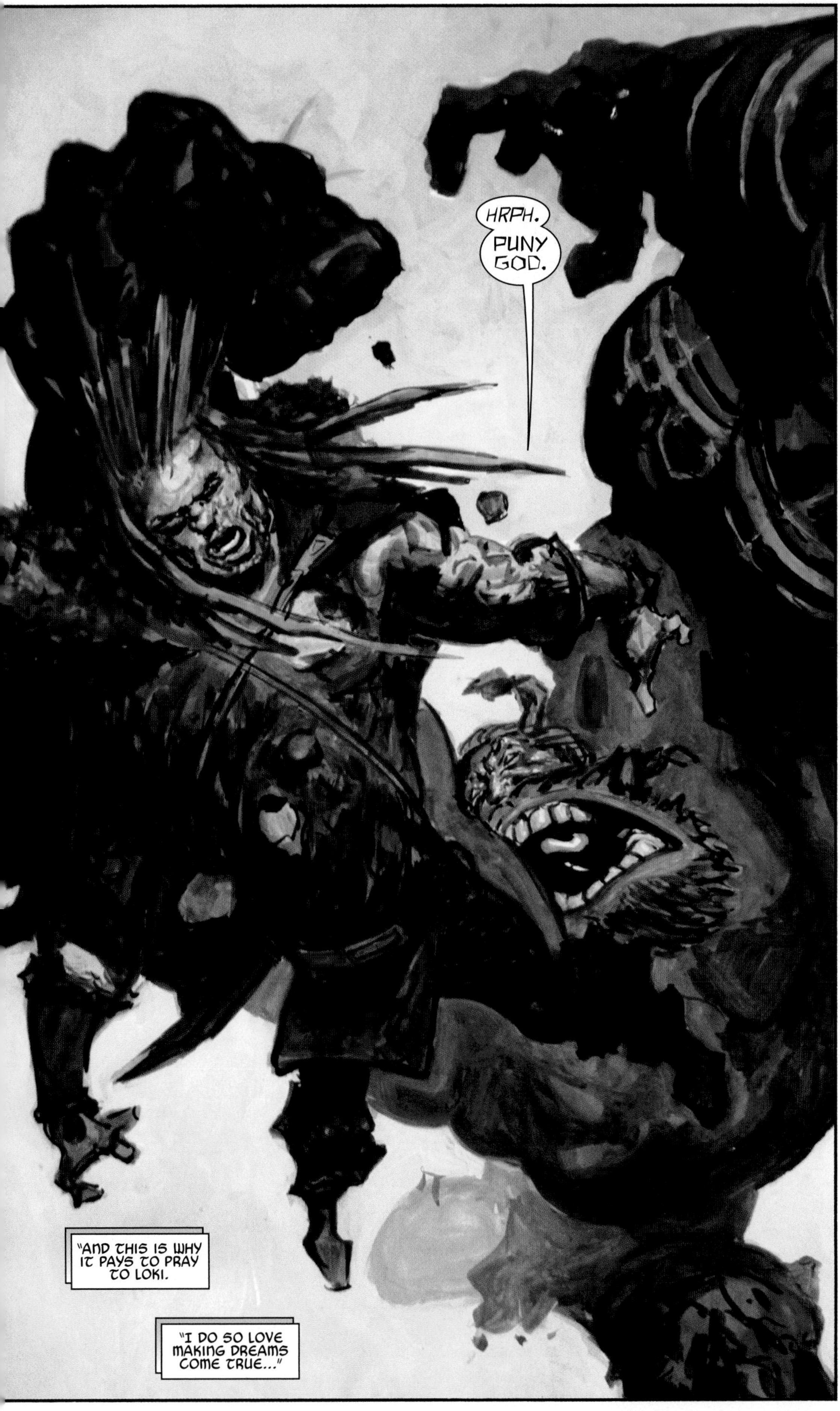
HRPH.
PUNY GOD.
"AND THIS IS WHY IT PAYS TO PRAY TO LOKI.
"I DO SO LOVE MAKING DREAMS COME TRUE..."

7

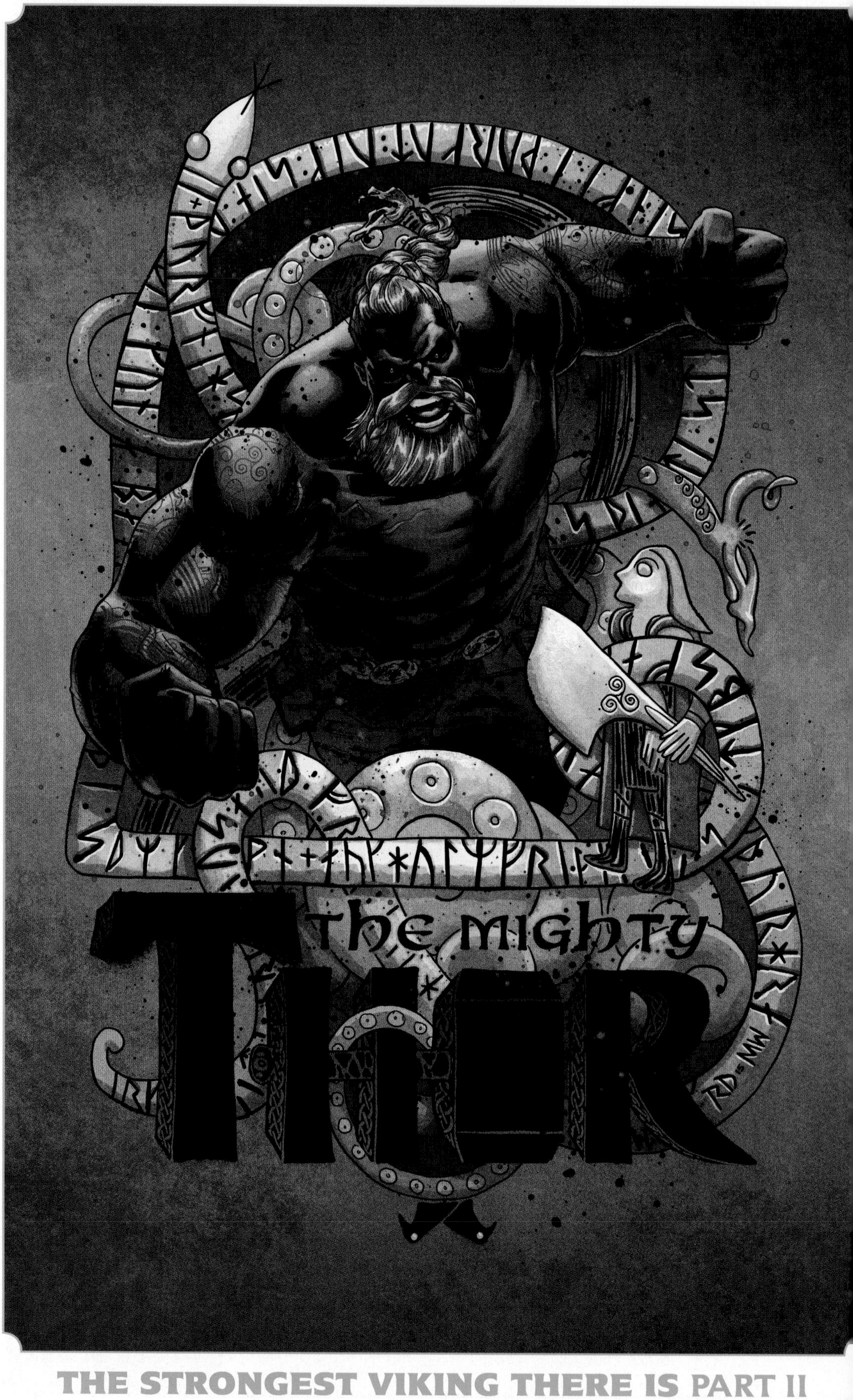
THE MIGHTY
THOR
RD MW

THE STRONGEST VIKING THERE IS PART II

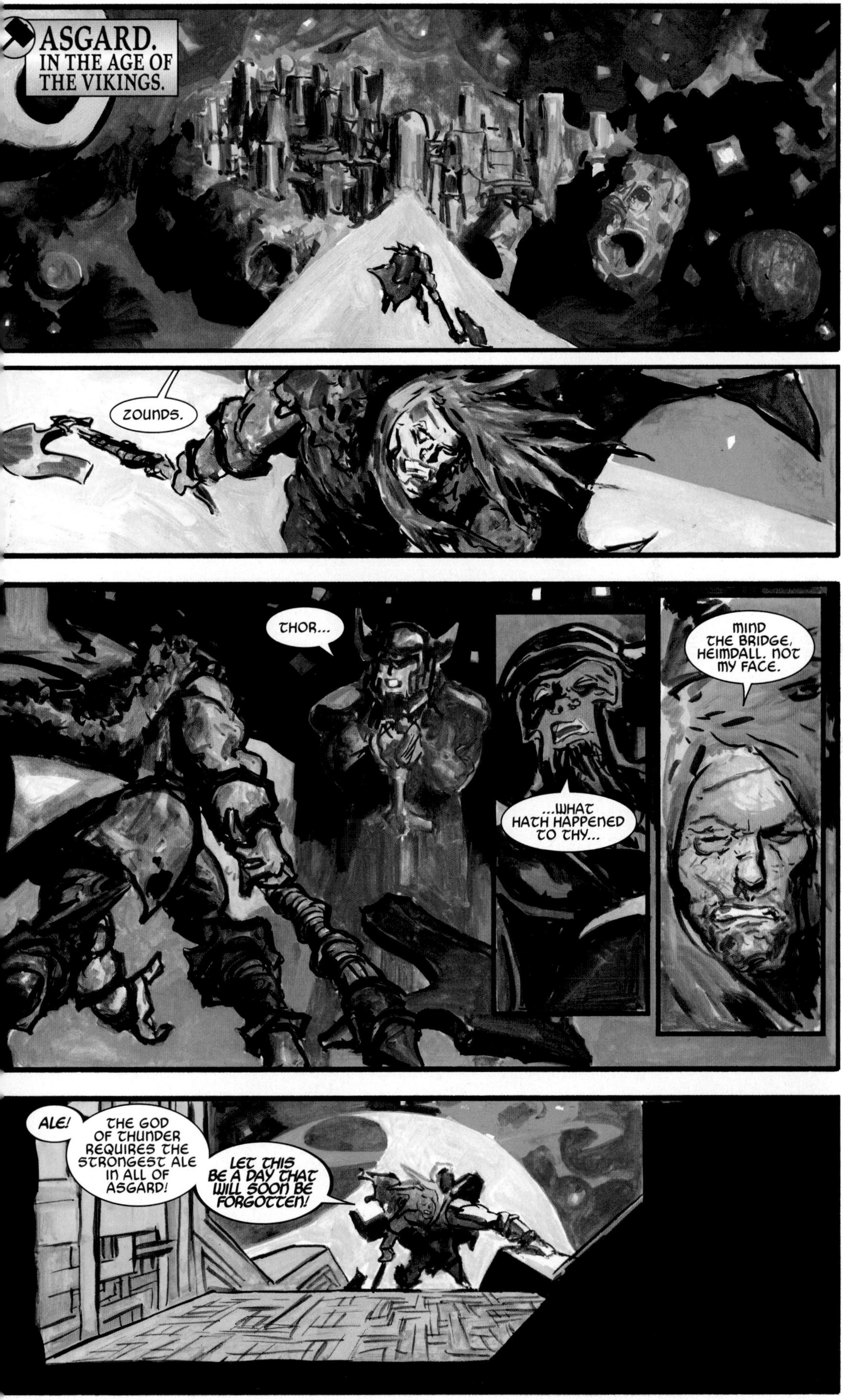
ASGARD.
IN THE AGE OF THE VIKINGS.
ZOUNDS.
THOR...
...WHAT HATH HAPPENED TO THY...
MIND THE BRIDGE, HEIMDALL. NOT MY FACE.
ALE!
THE GOD OF THUNDER REQUIRES THE STRONGEST ALE IN ALL OF ASGARD!
LET THIS BE A DAY THAT WILL SOON BE FORGOTTEN!

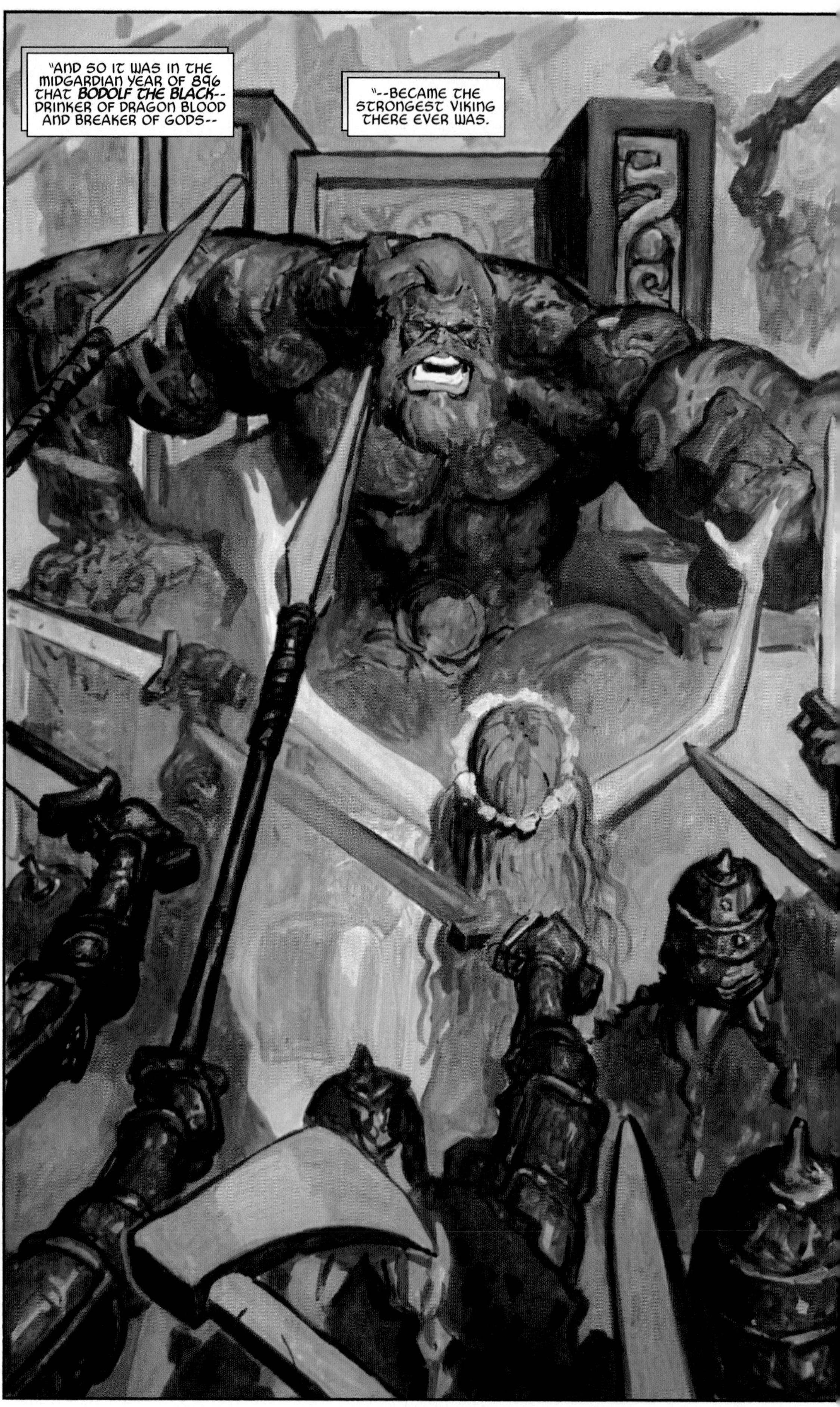
"AND SO IT WAS IN THE MIDGARDIAN YEAR OF 896 THAT **BODOLF THE BLACK**-- DRINKER OF DRAGON BLOOD AND BREAKER OF GODS--
"--BECAME THE STRONGEST VIKING THERE EVER WAS.

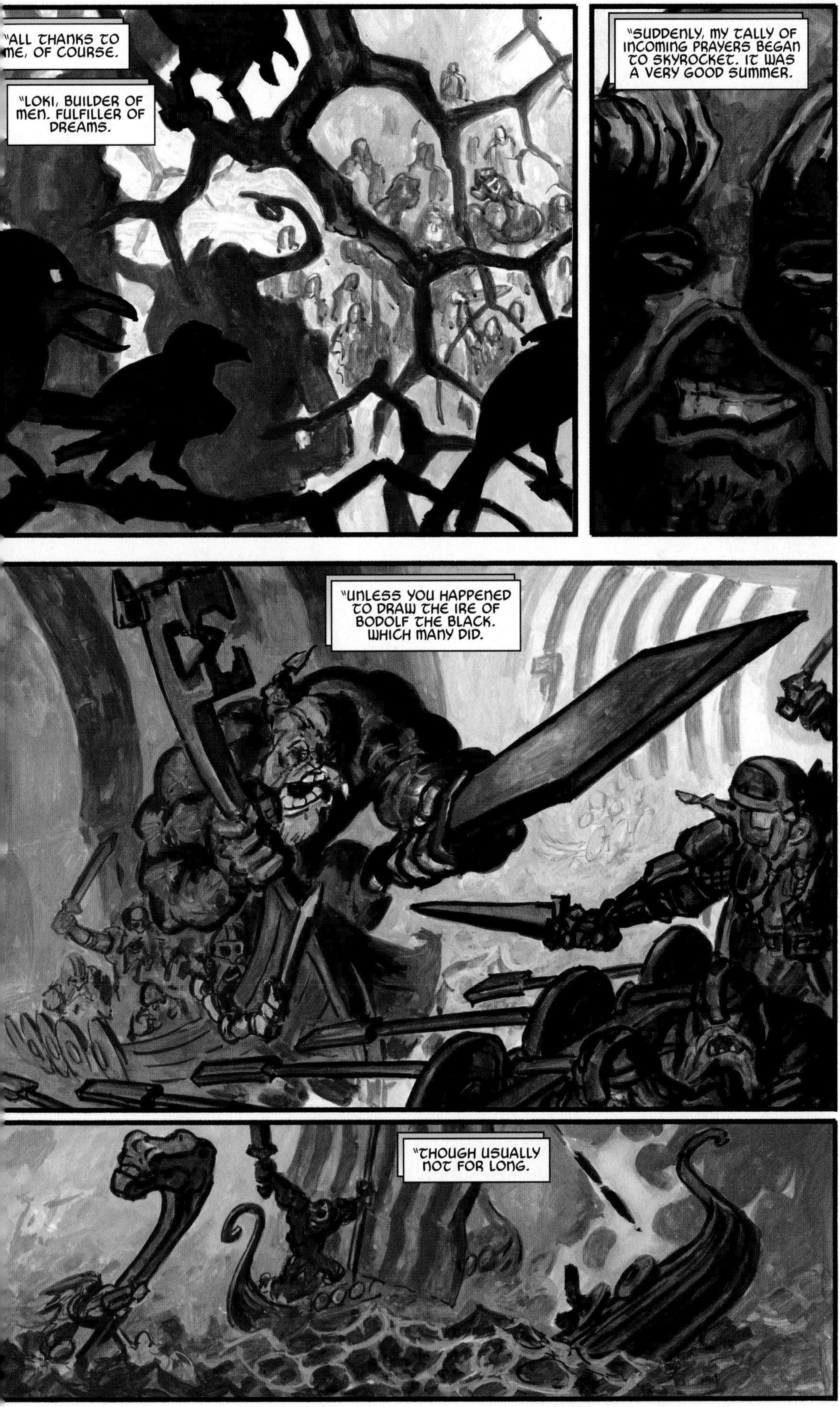
"ALL THANKS TO ME, OF COURSE.
"LOKI, BUILDER OF MEN. FULFILLER OF DREAMS.
"SUDDENLY, MY TALLY OF INCOMING PRAYERS BEGAN TO SKYROCKET. IT WAS A VERY GOOD SUMMER.
"UNLESS YOU HAPPENED TO DRAW THE IRE OF BODOLF THE BLACK. WHICH MANY DID.
"THOUGH USUALLY NOT FOR LONG.

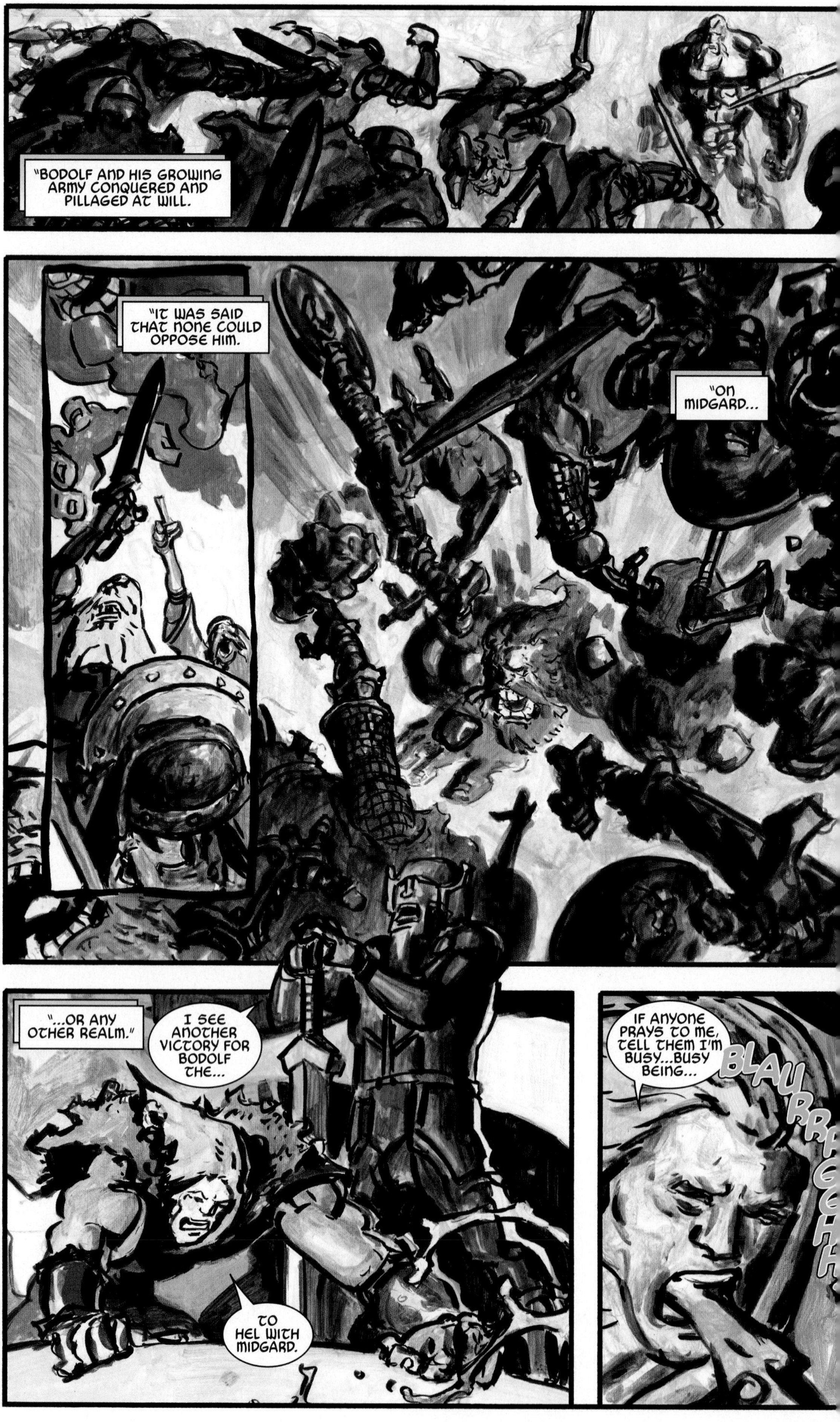
"BODOLF AND HIS GROWING ARMY CONQUERED AND PILLAGED AT WILL.
"IT WAS SAID THAT NONE COULD OPPOSE HIM.
"ON MIDGARD...
"...OR ANY OTHER REALM."
I SEE ANOTHER VICTORY FOR BODOLF THE...
TO HEL WITH MIDGARD.
IF ANYONE PRAYS TO ME, TELL THEM I'M BUSY...BUSY BEING...
BLAURRRGGHH

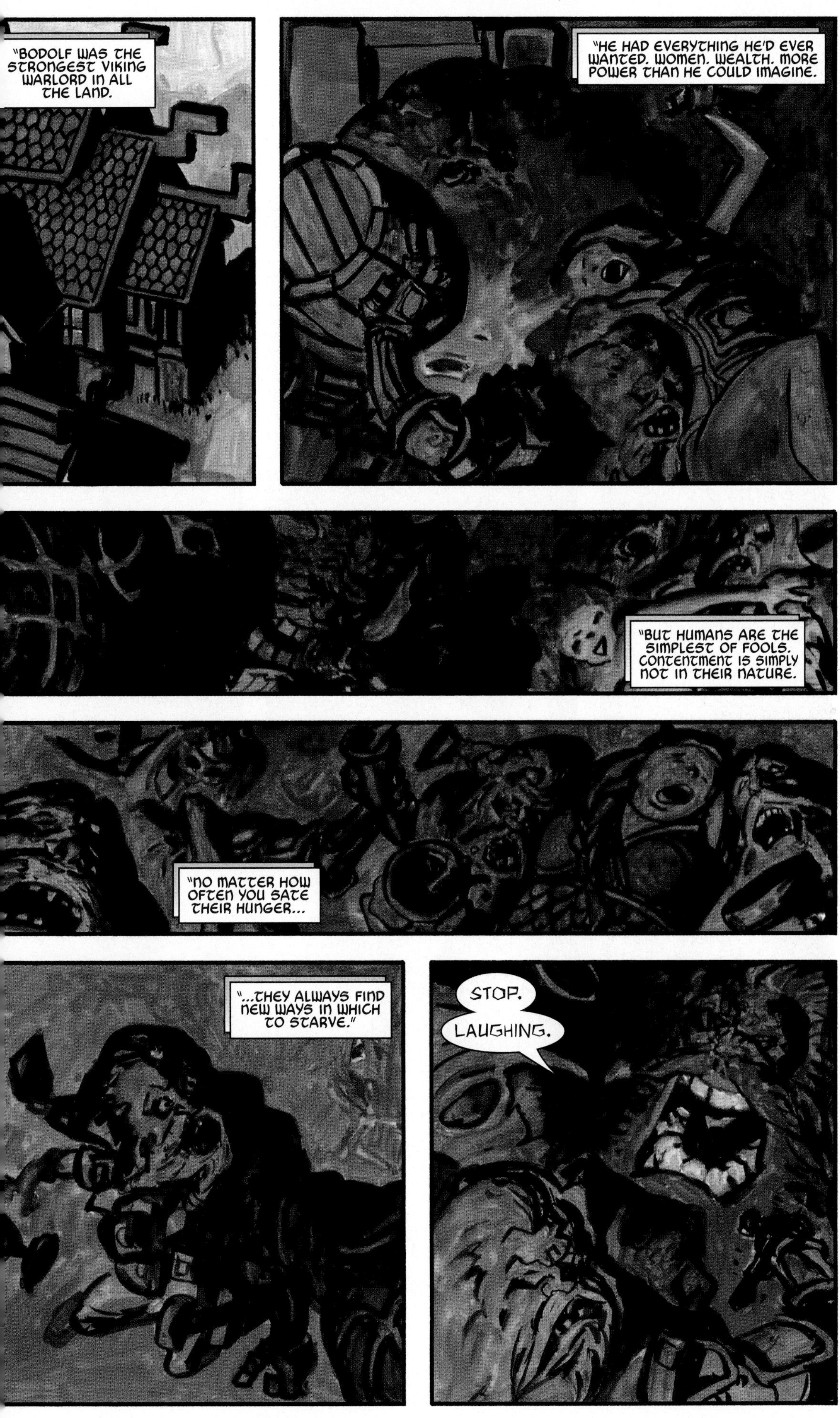
"BODOLF WAS THE STRONGEST VIKING WARLORD IN ALL THE LAND.
"HE HAD EVERYTHING HE'D EVER WANTED. WOMEN. WEALTH. MORE POWER THAN HE COULD IMAGINE.
"BUT HUMANS ARE THE SIMPLEST OF FOOLS. CONTENTMENT IS SIMPLY NOT IN THEIR NATURE.
"NO MATTER HOW OFTEN YOU SATE THEIR HUNGER...
"...THEY ALWAYS FIND NEW WAYS IN WHICH TO STARVE."
STOP.
LAUGHING.

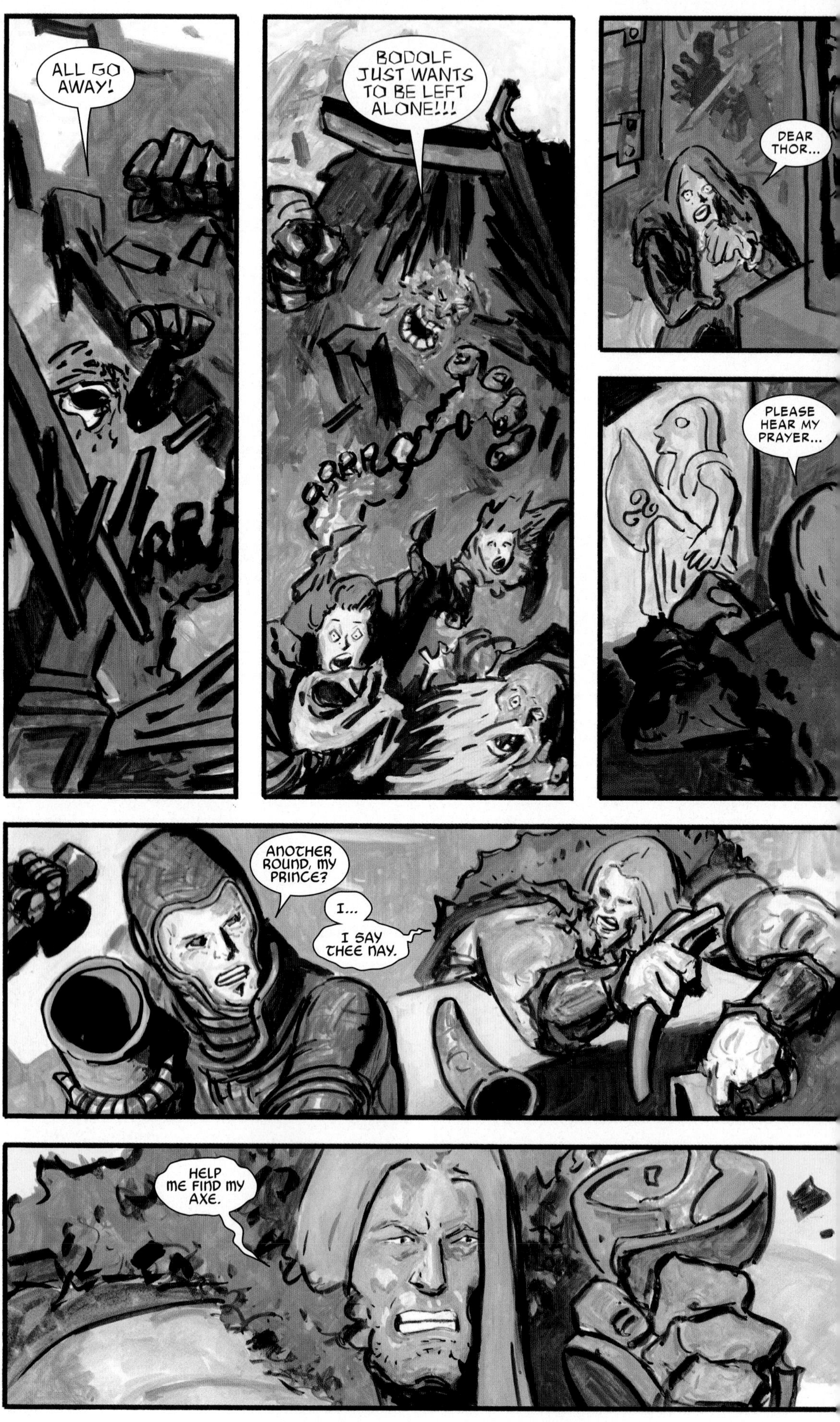
ALL GO AWAY!
BODOLF JUST WANTS TO BE LEFT ALONE!!!
DEAR THOR...
PLEASE HEAR MY PRAYER...
ANOTHER ROUND, MY PRINCE?
I...
I SAY THEE NAY.
HELP ME FIND MY AXE.

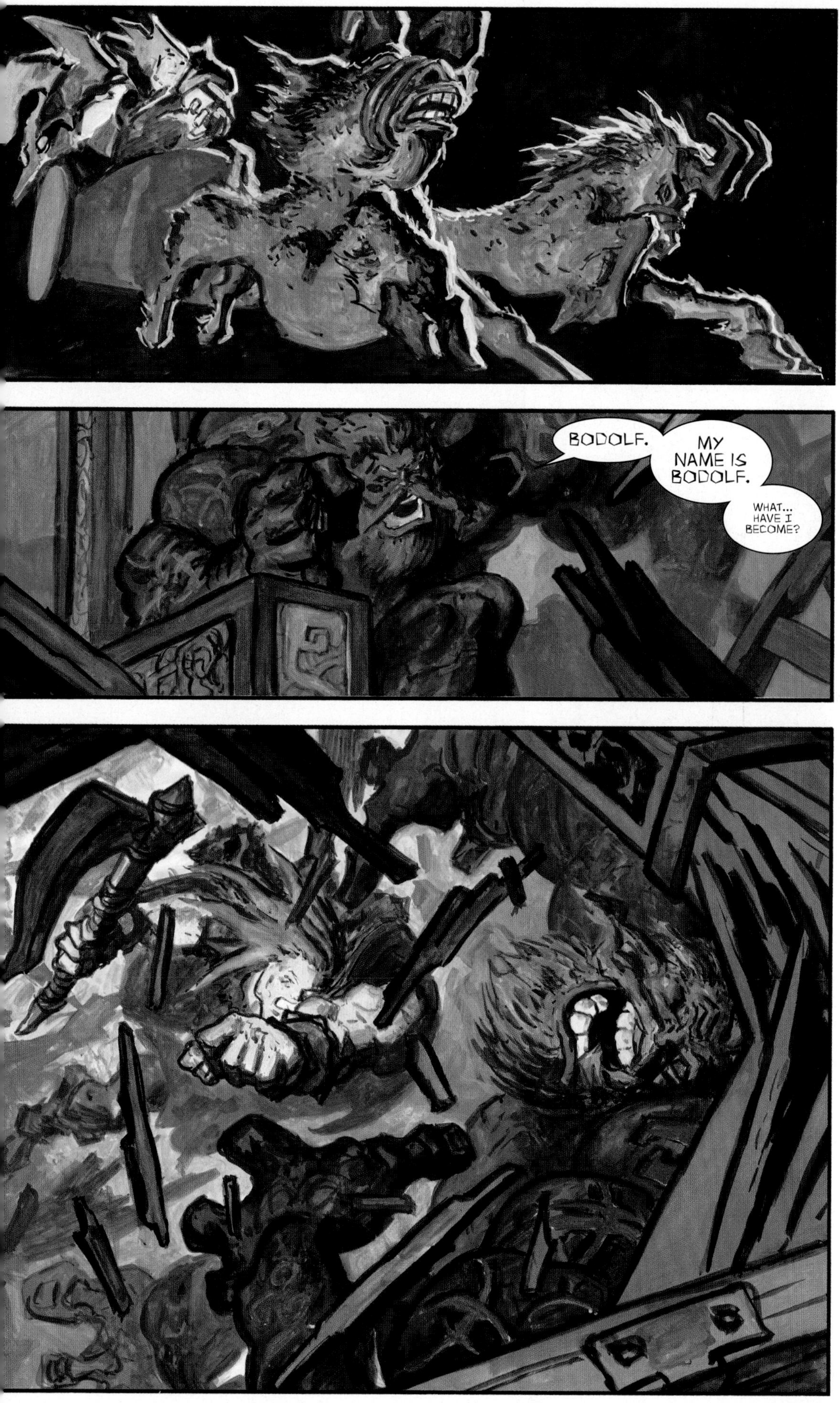
BODOLF.
MY NAME IS BODOLF.
WHAT... HAVE I BECOME?

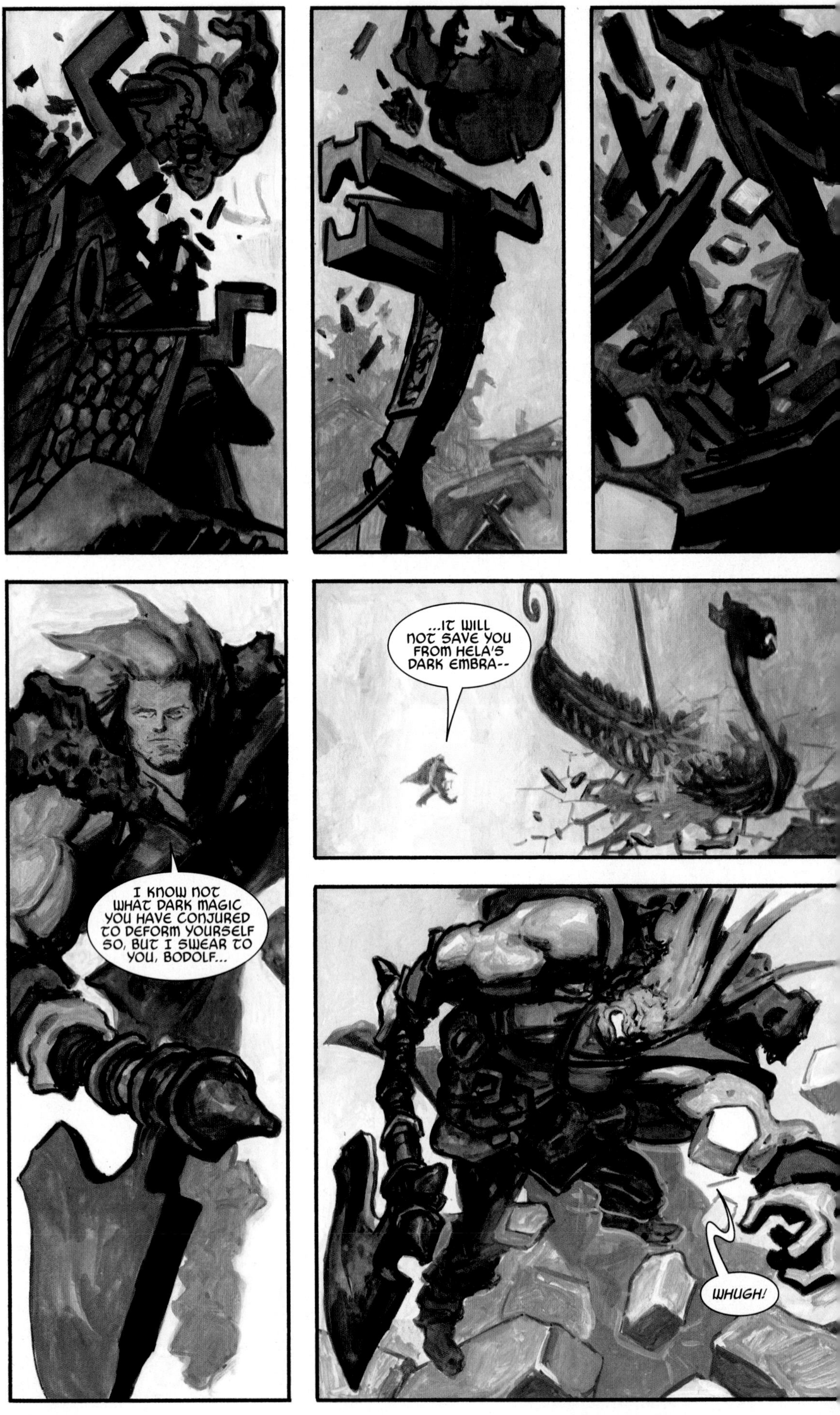
I KNOW NOT WHAT DARK MAGIC YOU HAVE CONJURED TO DEFORM YOURSELF SO, BUT I SWEAR TO YOU, BODOLF...
...IT WILL NOT SAVE YOU FROM HELA'S DARK EMBRA--
WHUGH!

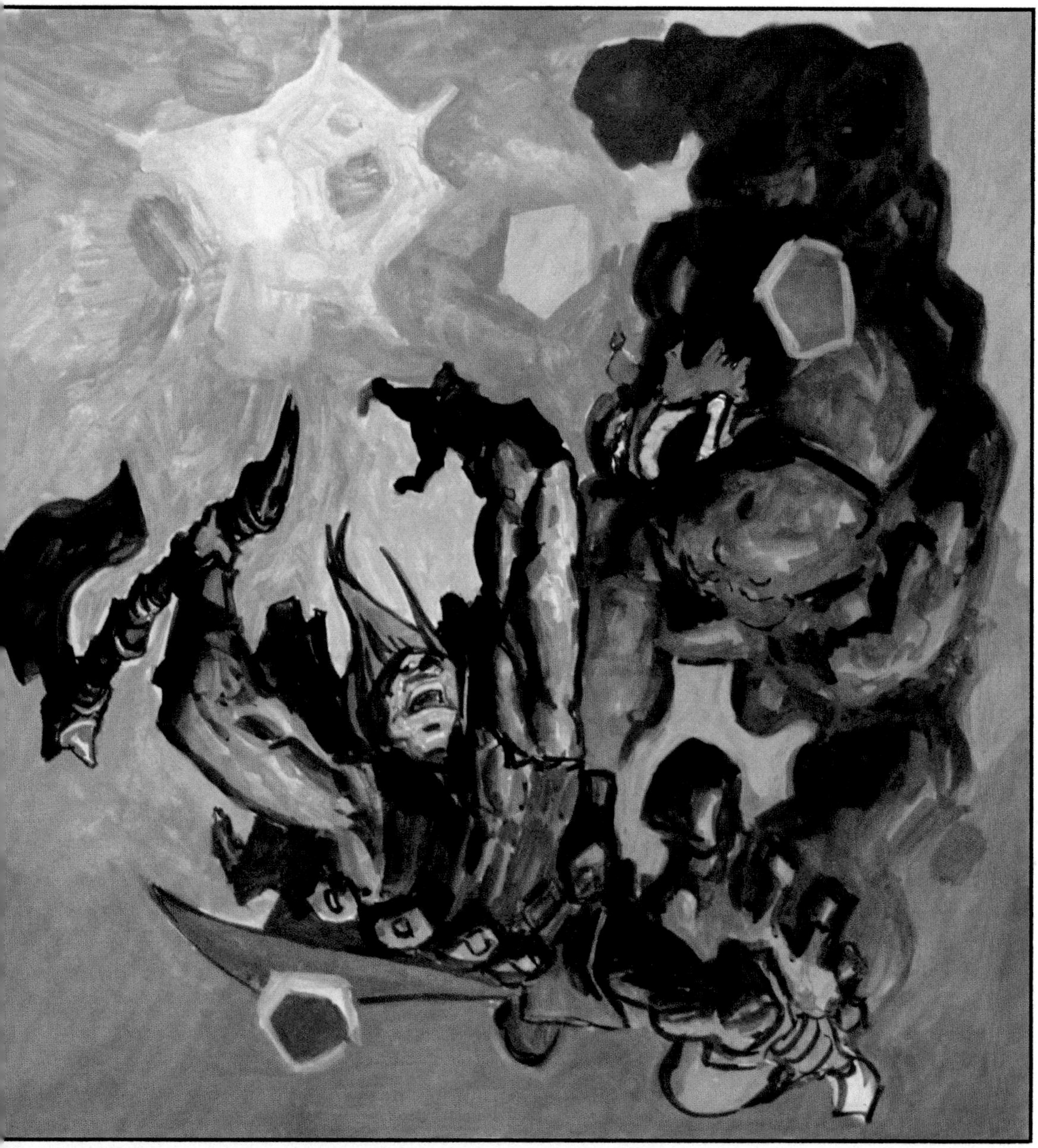

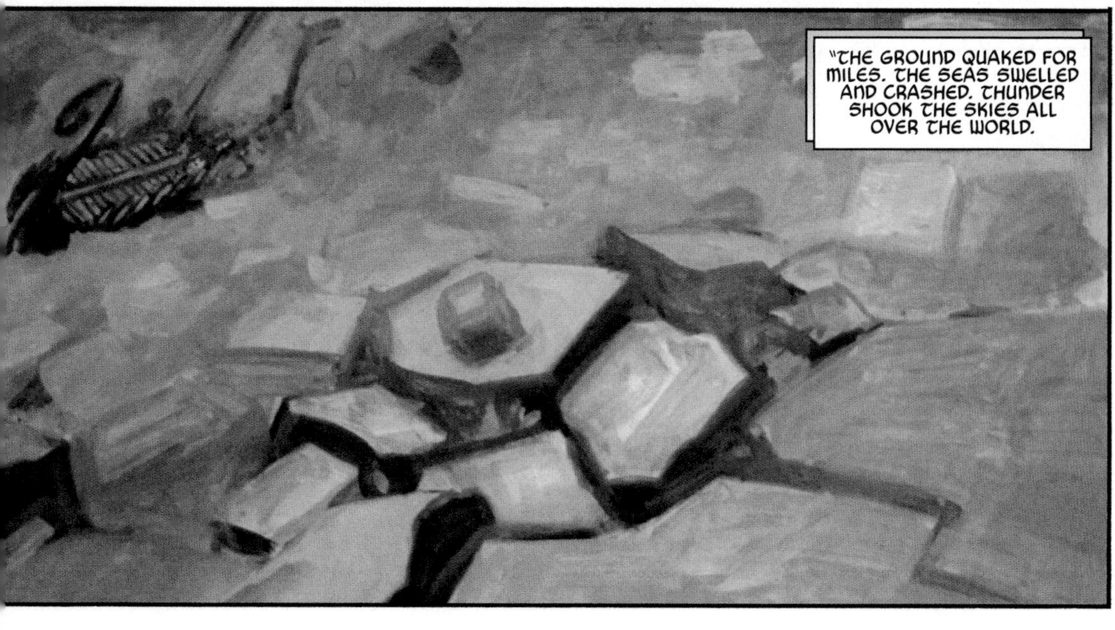
"THE GROUND QUAKED FOR MILES. THE SEAS SWELLED AND CRASHED. THUNDER SHOOK THE SKIES ALL OVER THE WORLD.

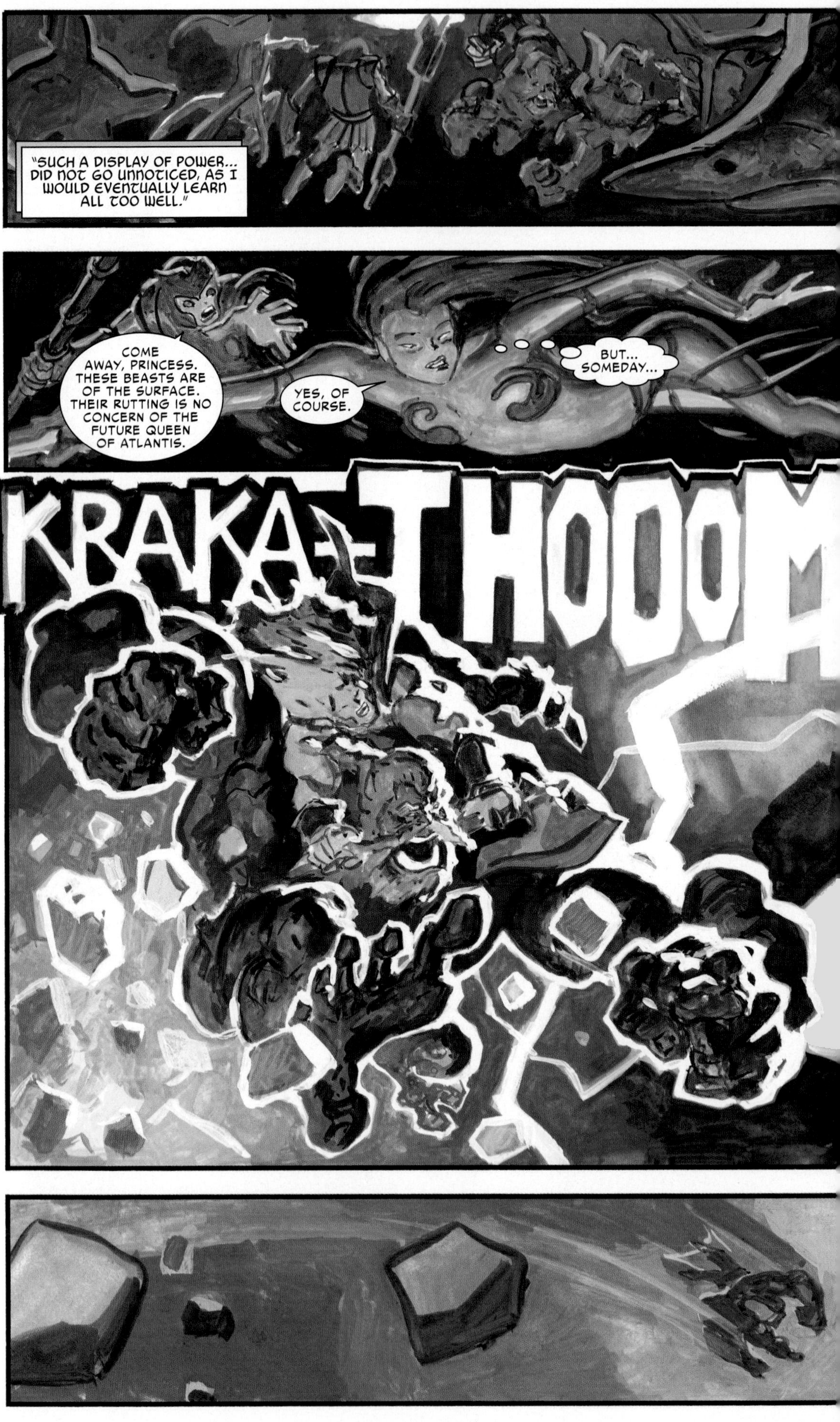
"SUCH A DISPLAY OF POWER... DID NOT GO UNNOTICED, AS I WOULD EVENTUALLY LEARN ALL TOO WELL."
COME AWAY, PRINCESS. THESE BEASTS ARE OF THE SURFACE. THEIR RUTTING IS NO CONCERN OF THE FUTURE QUEEN OF ATLANTIS.
YES, OF COURSE.
BUT... SOMEDAY...
KRAKA-THOOOM

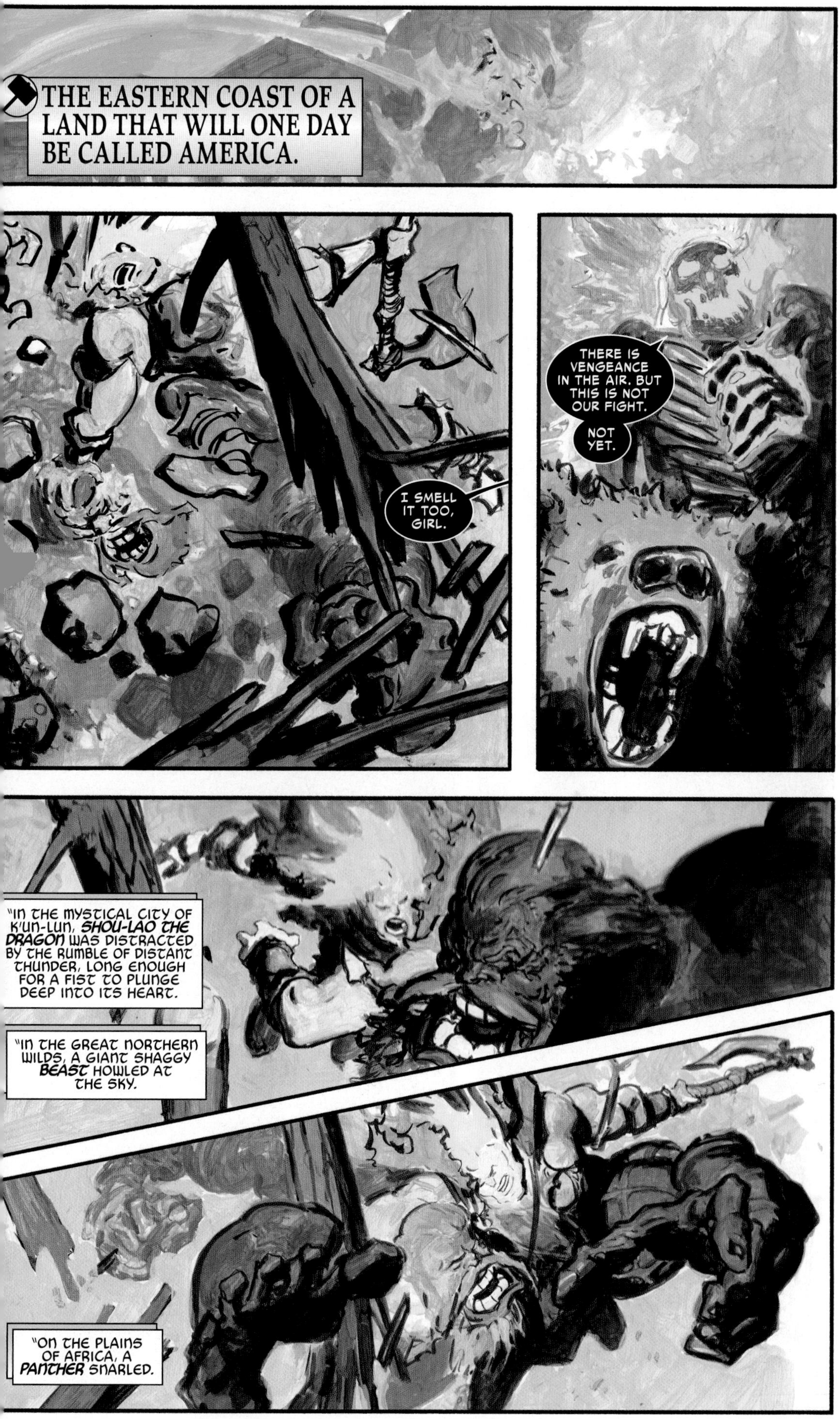
THE EASTERN COAST OF A LAND THAT WILL ONE DAY BE CALLED AMERICA.
I SMELL IT TOO, GIRL.
THERE IS VENGEANCE IN THE AIR. BUT THIS IS NOT OUR FIGHT.
NOT YET.
"IN THE MYSTICAL CITY OF K'UN-LUN, SHOU-LAO THE DRAGON WAS DISTRACTED BY THE RUMBLE OF DISTANT THUNDER, LONG ENOUGH FOR A FIST TO PLUNGE DEEP INTO ITS HEART.
"IN THE GREAT NORTHERN WILDS, A GIANT SHAGGY BEAST HOWLED AT THE SKY.
"ON THE PLAINS OF AFRICA, A PANTHER SNARLED.

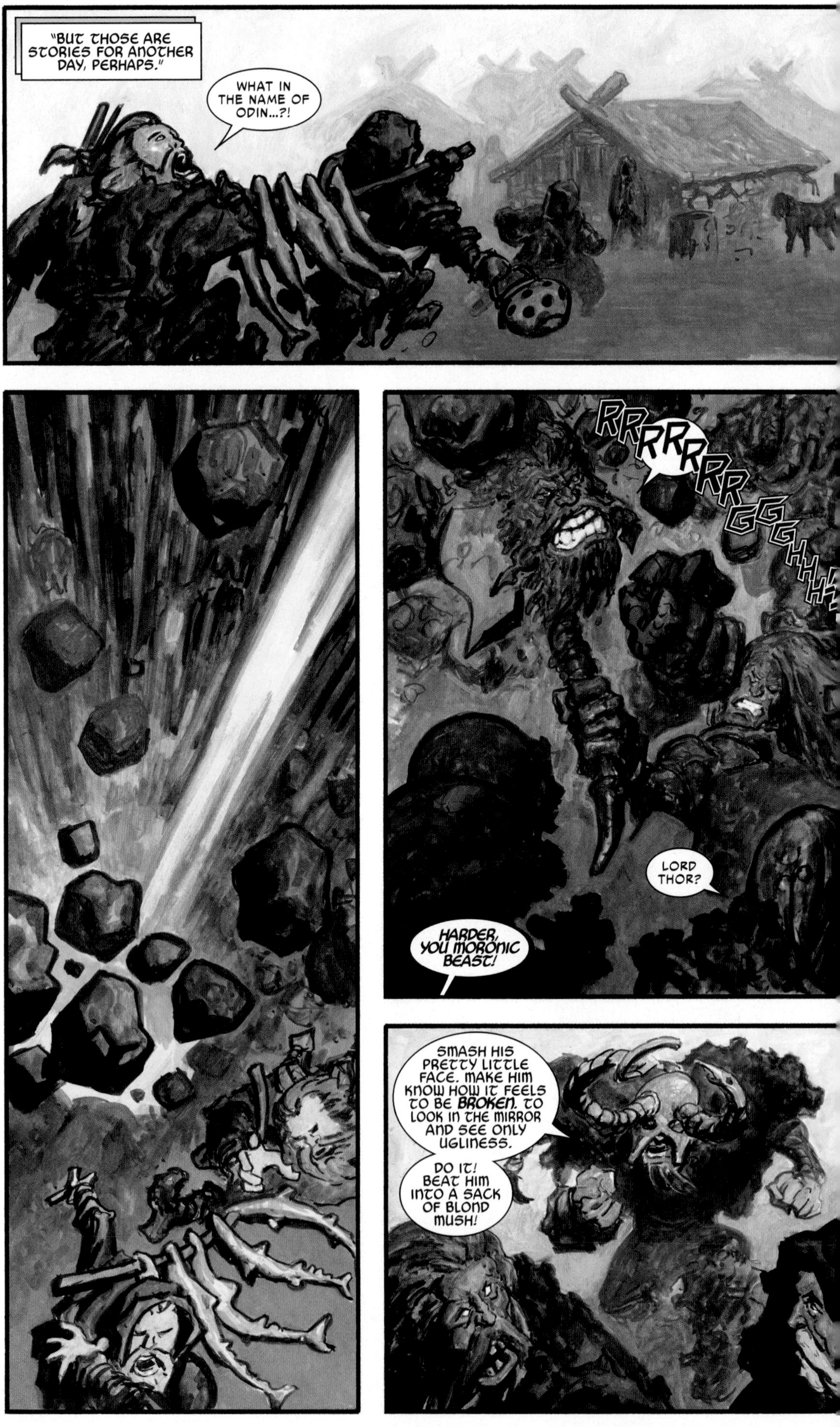
"BUT THOSE ARE STORIES FOR ANOTHER DAY, PERHAPS."
WHAT IN THE NAME OF ODIN...?!
RRRRRRRGGGHHH
LORD THOR?
HARDER, YOU MORONIC BEAST!
SMASH HIS PRETTY LITTLE FACE. MAKE HIM KNOW HOW IT FEELS TO BE BROKEN. TO LOOK IN THE MIRROR AND SEE ONLY UGLINESS.
DO IT! BEAT HIM INTO A SACK OF BLOND MUSH!

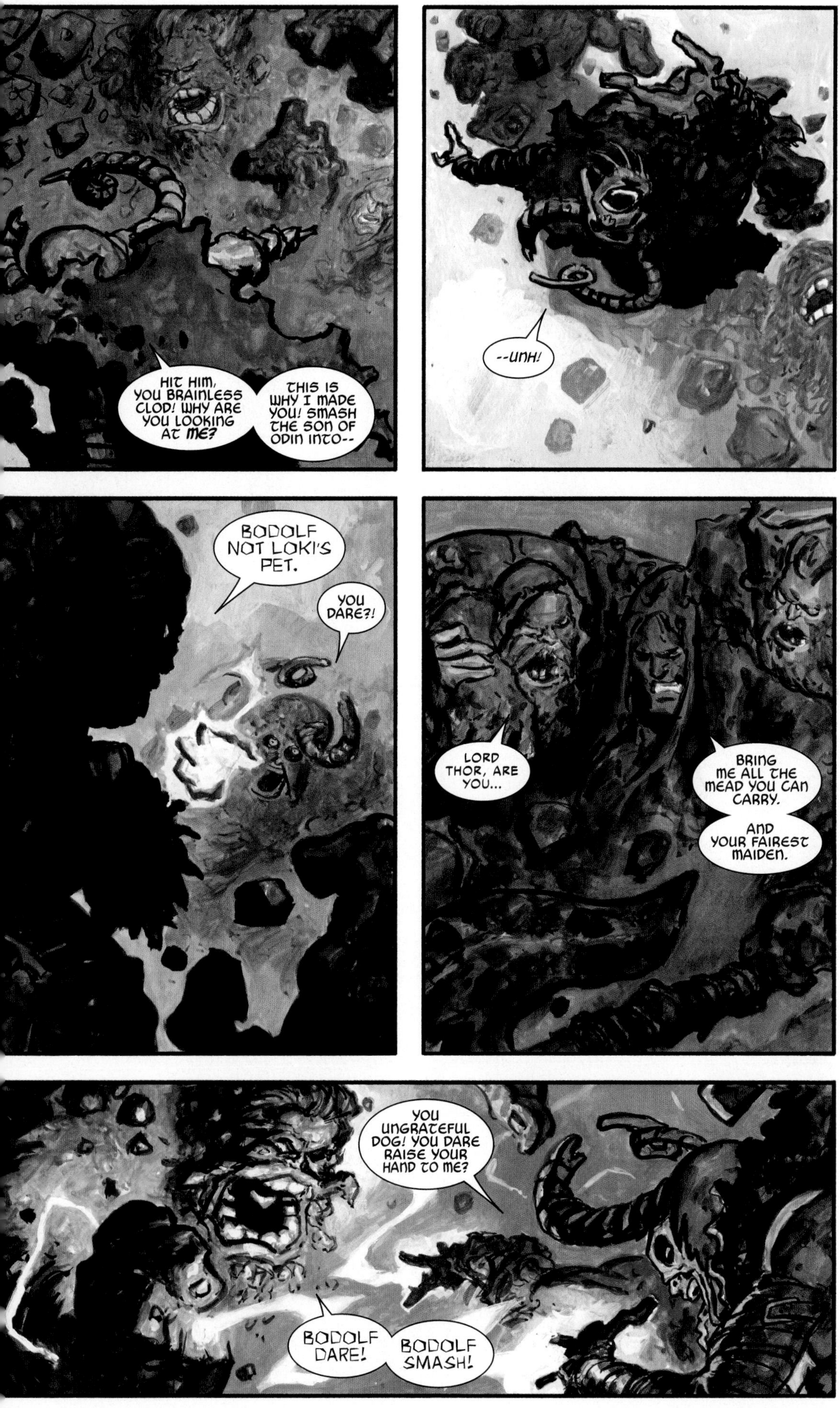
HIT HIM, YOU BRAINLESS CLOD! WHY ARE YOU LOOKING AT *ME*?
THIS IS WHY I MADE YOU! SMASH THE SON OF ODIN INTO--
--UNH!
BODOLF NOT LOKI'S PET.
YOU DARE?!
LORD THOR, ARE YOU...
BRING ME ALL THE MEAD YOU CAN CARRY.
AND YOUR FAIREST MAIDEN.
YOU UNGRATEFUL DOG! YOU DARE RAISE YOUR HAND TO ME?
BODOLF DARE!
BODOLF SMASH!

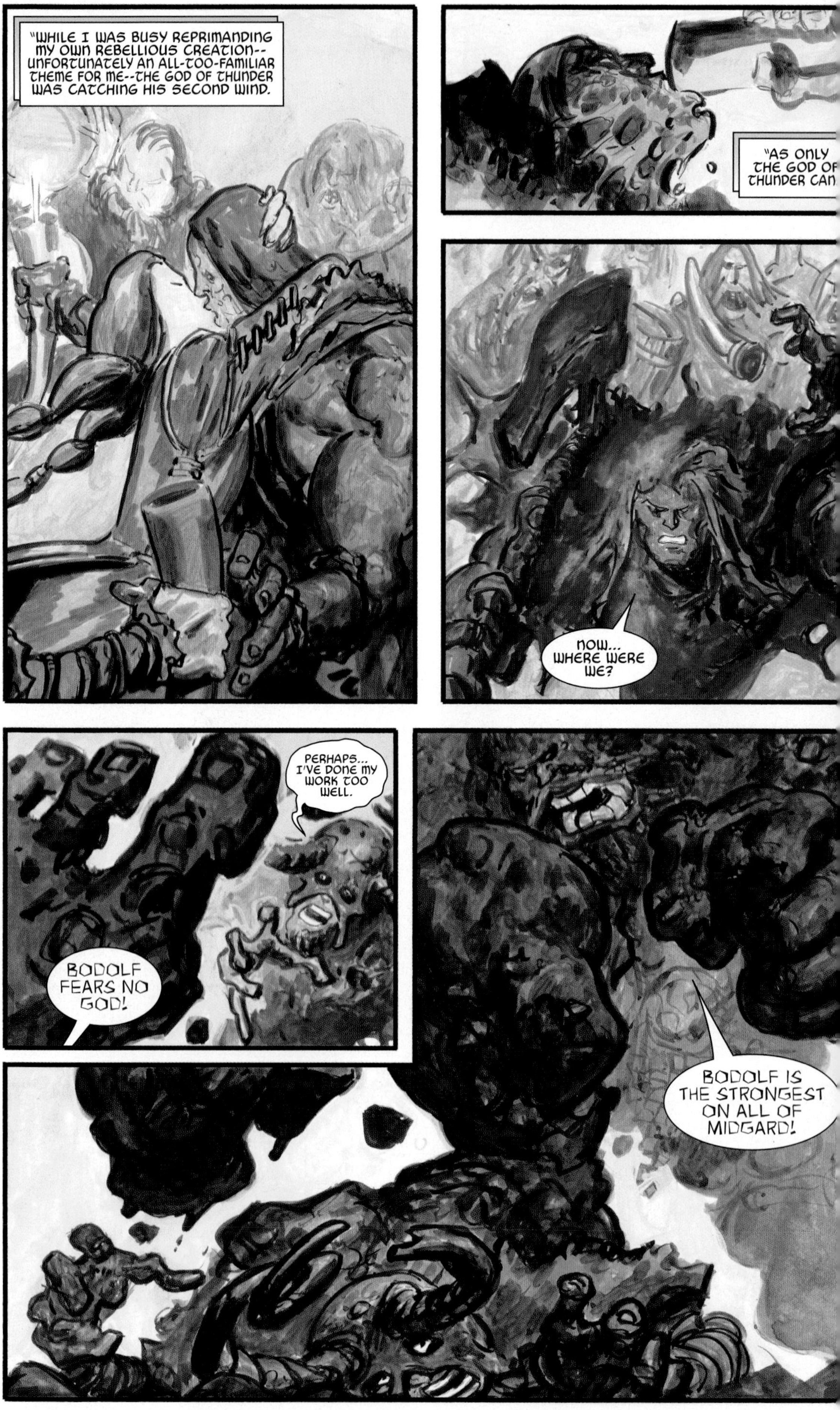
"WHILE I WAS BUSY REPRIMANDING MY OWN REBELLIOUS CREATION--UNFORTUNATELY AN ALL-TOO-FAMILIAR THEME FOR ME--THE GOD OF THUNDER WAS CATCHING HIS SECOND WIND.
"AS ONLY THE GOD OF THUNDER CAN
NOW... WHERE WERE WE?
PERHAPS... I'VE DONE MY WORK TOO WELL.
BODOLF FEARS NO GOD!
BODOLF IS THE STRONGEST ON ALL OF MIDGARD!

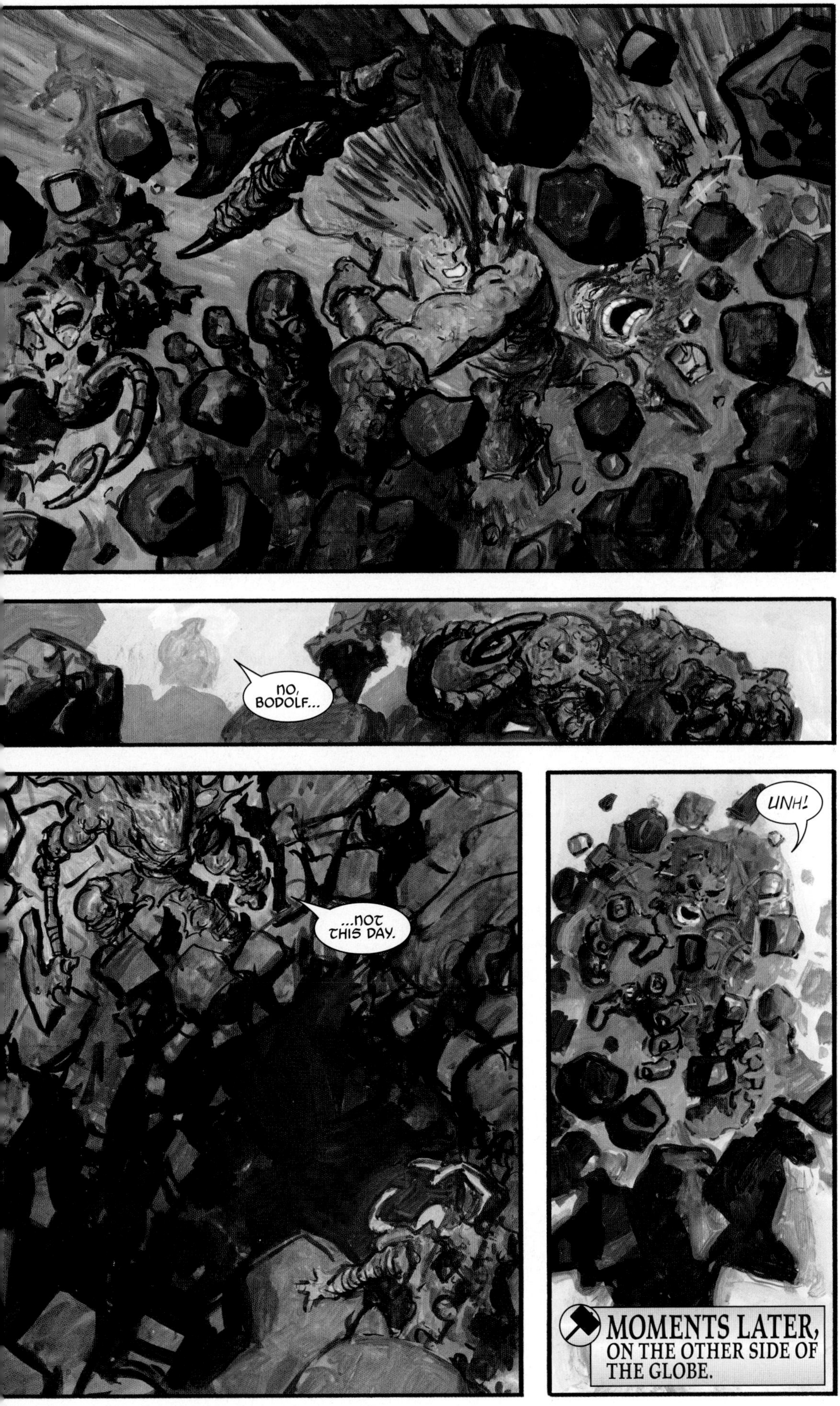

NO, BODOLF...
...NOT THIS DAY.
UNH!
MOMENTS LATER, ON THE OTHER SIDE OF THE GLOBE.

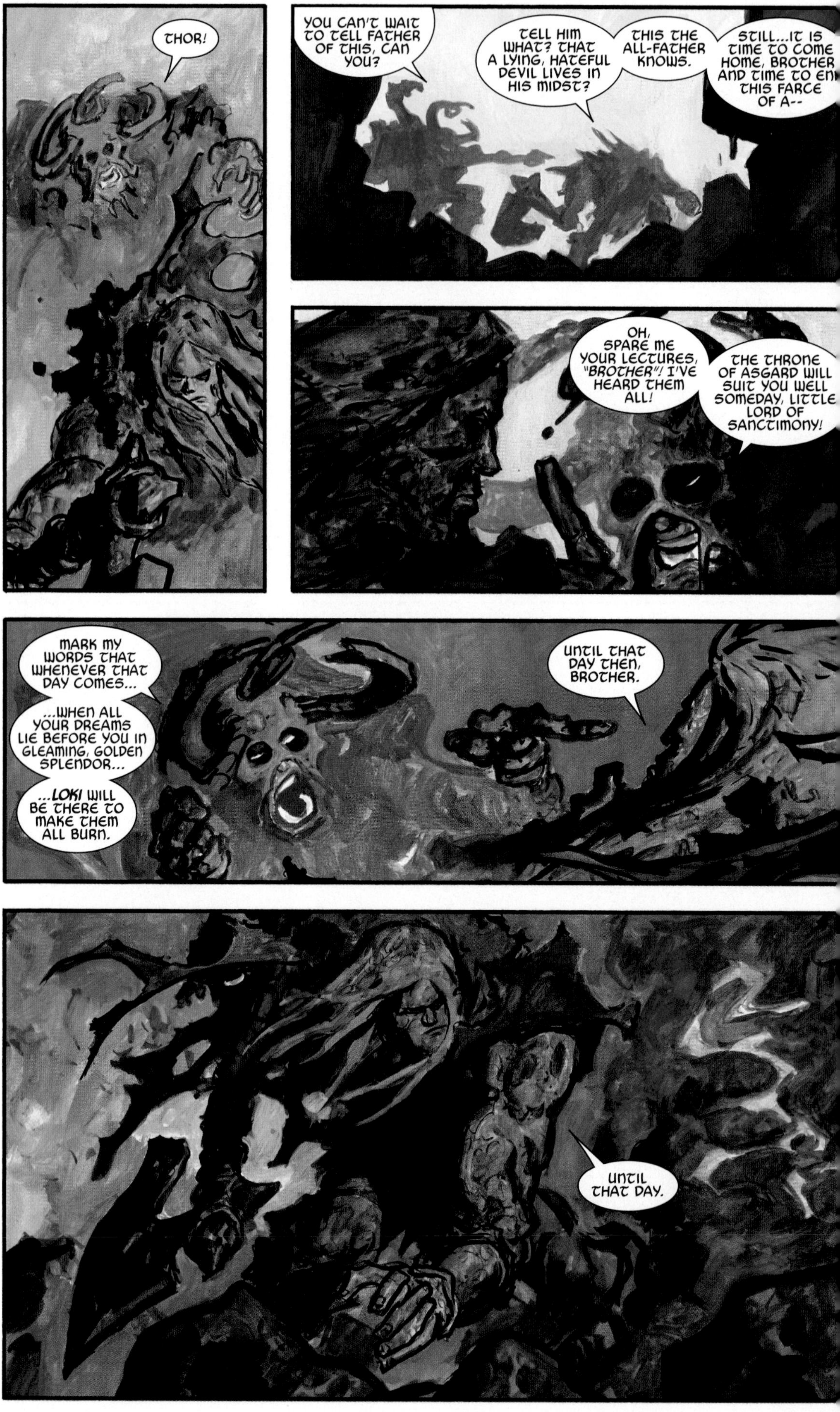
THOR!
YOU CAN'T WAIT TO TELL FATHER OF THIS, CAN YOU?
TELL HIM WHAT? THAT A LYING, HATEFUL DEVIL LIVES IN HIS MIDST?
THIS THE ALL-FATHER KNOWS.
STILL...IT IS TIME TO COME HOME, BROTHER AND TIME TO EN THIS FARCE OF A--
OH, SPARE ME YOUR LECTURES, "BROTHER"! I'VE HEARD THEM ALL!
THE THRONE OF ASGARD WILL SUIT YOU WELL SOMEDAY, LITTLE LORD OF SANCTIMONY!
MARK MY WORDS THAT WHENEVER THAT DAY COMES...
...WHEN ALL YOUR DREAMS LIE BEFORE YOU IN GLEAMING, GOLDEN SPLENDOR...
...LOKI WILL BE THERE TO MAKE THEM ALL BURN.
UNTIL THAT DAY THEN, BROTHER.
UNTIL THAT DAY.

"AND SO WE REACH THE END OF MY TALE, THOUGH IN TRUTH, STORIES NEVER TRULY END, DO THEY? ONE MERELY BLEEDS INTO THE NEXT.

"SO THE SAGA OF THE EPIC BATTLE BETWEEN THOR AND BODOLF THE BLACK...BECOMES THE STORY OF A LONELY VIKING, WANDERING THE EARTH, FIGHTING TO SUPPRESS THE MONSTER INSIDE HIM."

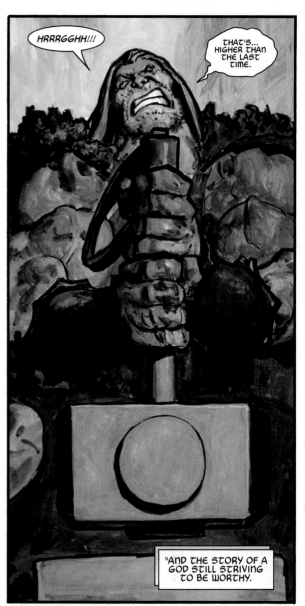

HRRRGGHH!!!

THAT'S... HIGHER THAN THE LAST TIME.

"AND THE STORY OF A GOD STILL STRIVING TO BE WORTHY.

"AND OF A LOKI WHO WOULD SOMEDAY...

"WELL...SOME STORIES ARE STILL YET TO BE WRITTEN."

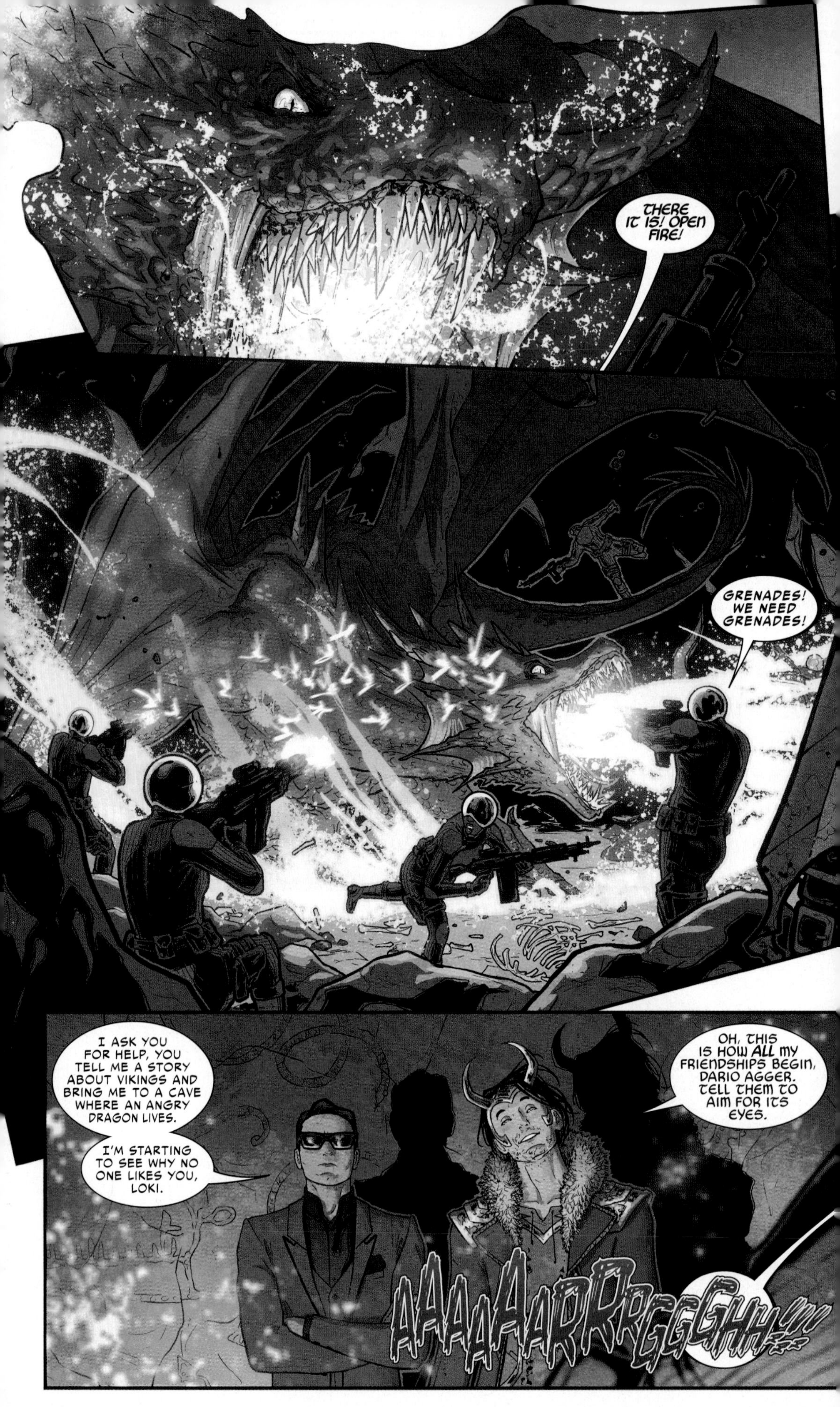

THERE IT IS! OPEN FIRE!
GRENADES! WE NEED GRENADES!
I ASK YOU FOR HELP, YOU TELL ME A STORY ABOUT VIKINGS AND BRING ME TO A CAVE WHERE AN ANGRY DRAGON LIVES.
I'M STARTING TO SEE WHY NO ONE LIKES YOU, LOKI.
OH, THIS IS HOW ALL MY FRIENDSHIPS BEGIN, DARIO AGGER. TELL THEM TO AIM FOR ITS EYES.
AAAAAARRRGGGHH!!!

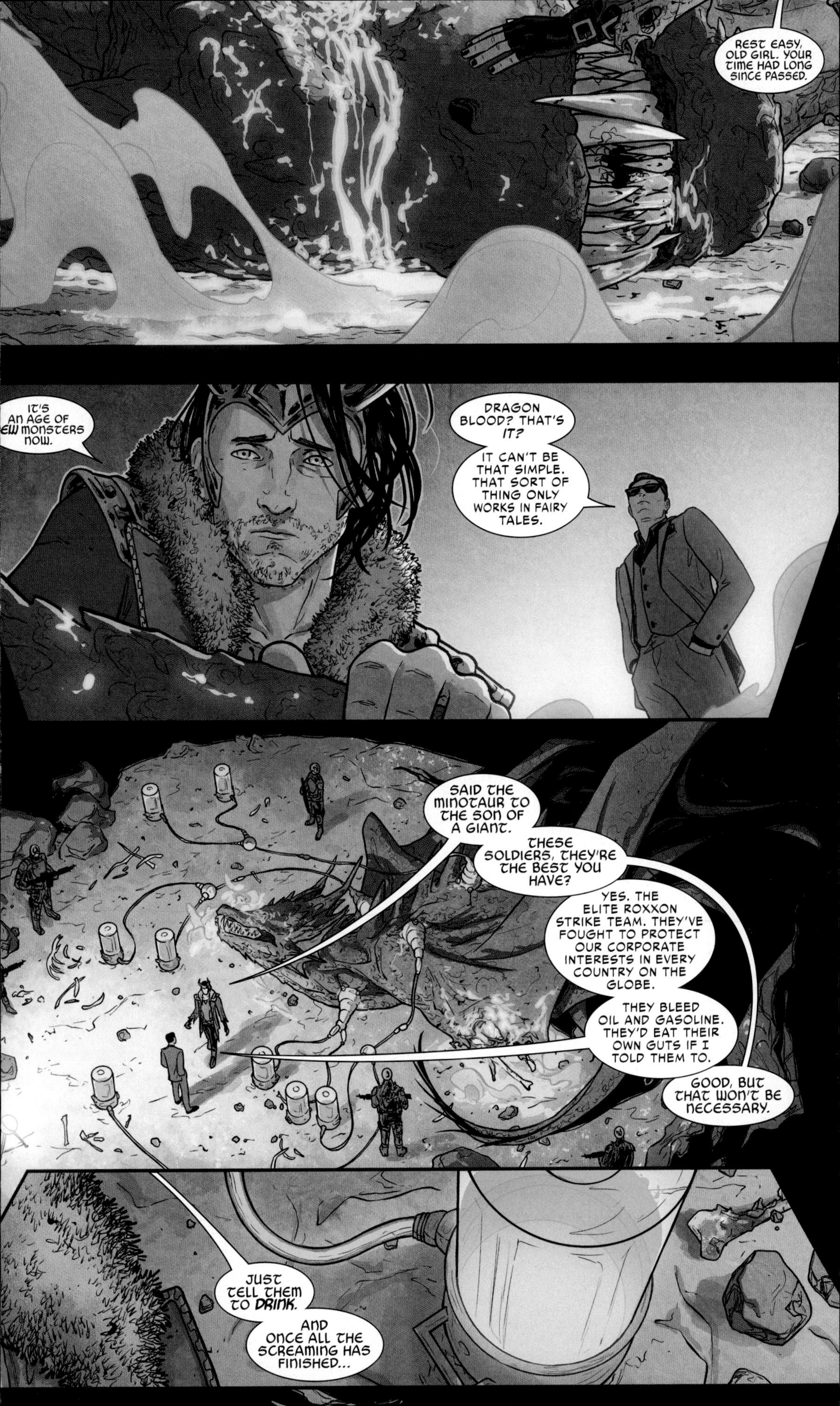
REST EASY, OLD GIRL. YOUR TIME HAD LONG SINCE PASSED.
IT'S AN AGE OF NEW MONSTERS NOW.
DRAGON BLOOD? THAT'S IT?
IT CAN'T BE THAT SIMPLE. THAT SORT OF THING ONLY WORKS IN FAIRY TALES.
SAID THE MINOTAUR TO THE SON OF A GIANT.
THESE SOLDIERS, THEY'RE THE BEST YOU HAVE?
YES. THE ELITE ROXXON STRIKE TEAM. THEY'VE FOUGHT TO PROTECT OUR CORPORATE INTERESTS IN EVERY COUNTRY ON THE GLOBE.
THEY BLEED OIL AND GASOLINE. THEY'D EAT THEIR OWN GUTS IF I TOLD THEM TO.
GOOD, BUT THAT WON'T BE NECESSARY.
JUST TELL THEM TO DRINK.
AND ONCE ALL THE SCREAMING HAS FINISHED...

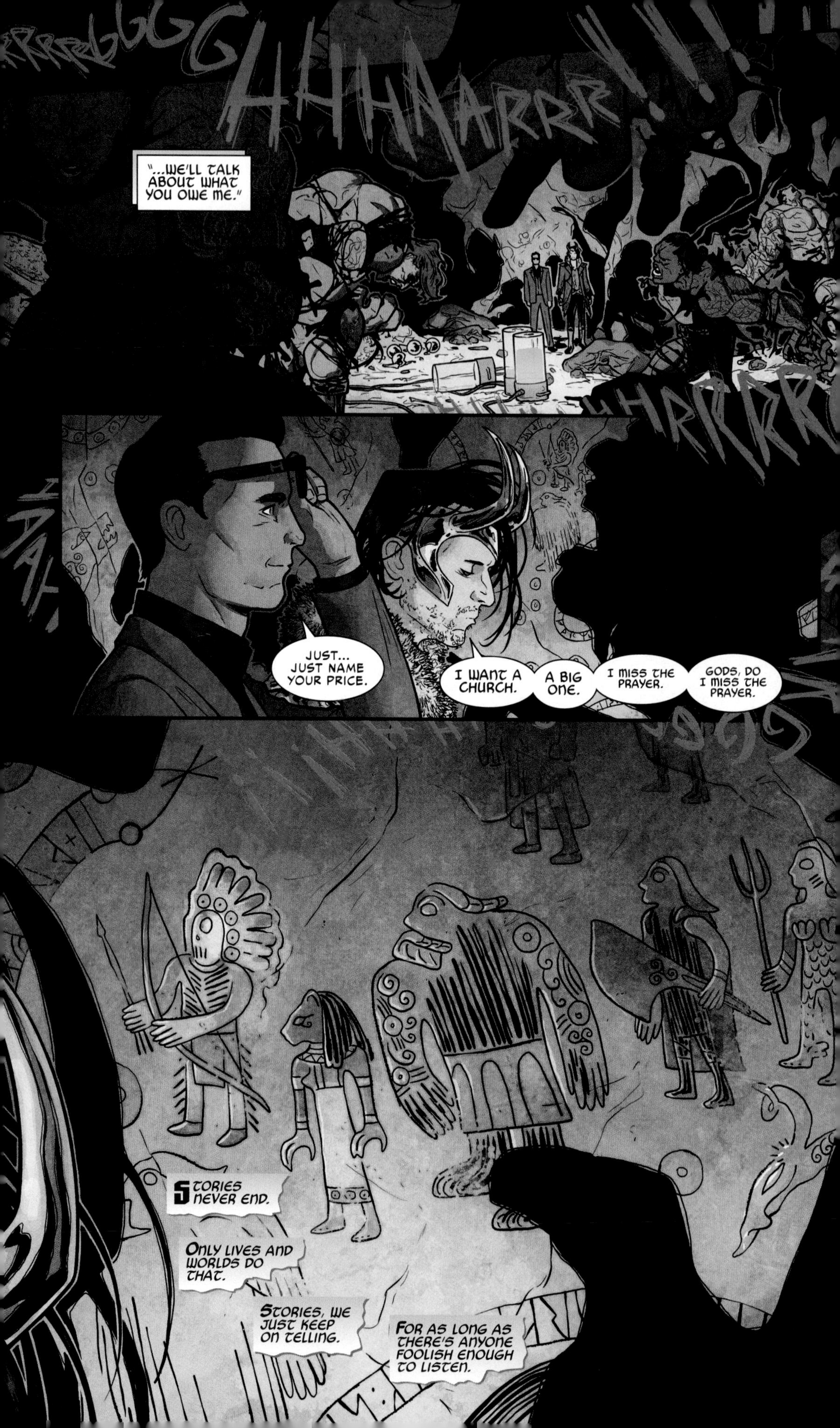

RRRRGGG AHHHARRR!!!
"...WE'LL TALK ABOUT WHAT YOU OWE ME."
HRRRRR
JUST... JUST NAME YOUR PRICE.
I WANT A CHURCH.
A BIG ONE.
I MISS THE PRAYER.
GODS, DO I MISS THE PRAYER.
STORIES NEVER END.
ONLY LIVES AND WORLDS DO THAT.
STORIES, WE JUST KEEP ON TELLING.
FOR AS LONG AS THERE'S ANYONE FOOLISH ENOUGH TO LISTEN.

8

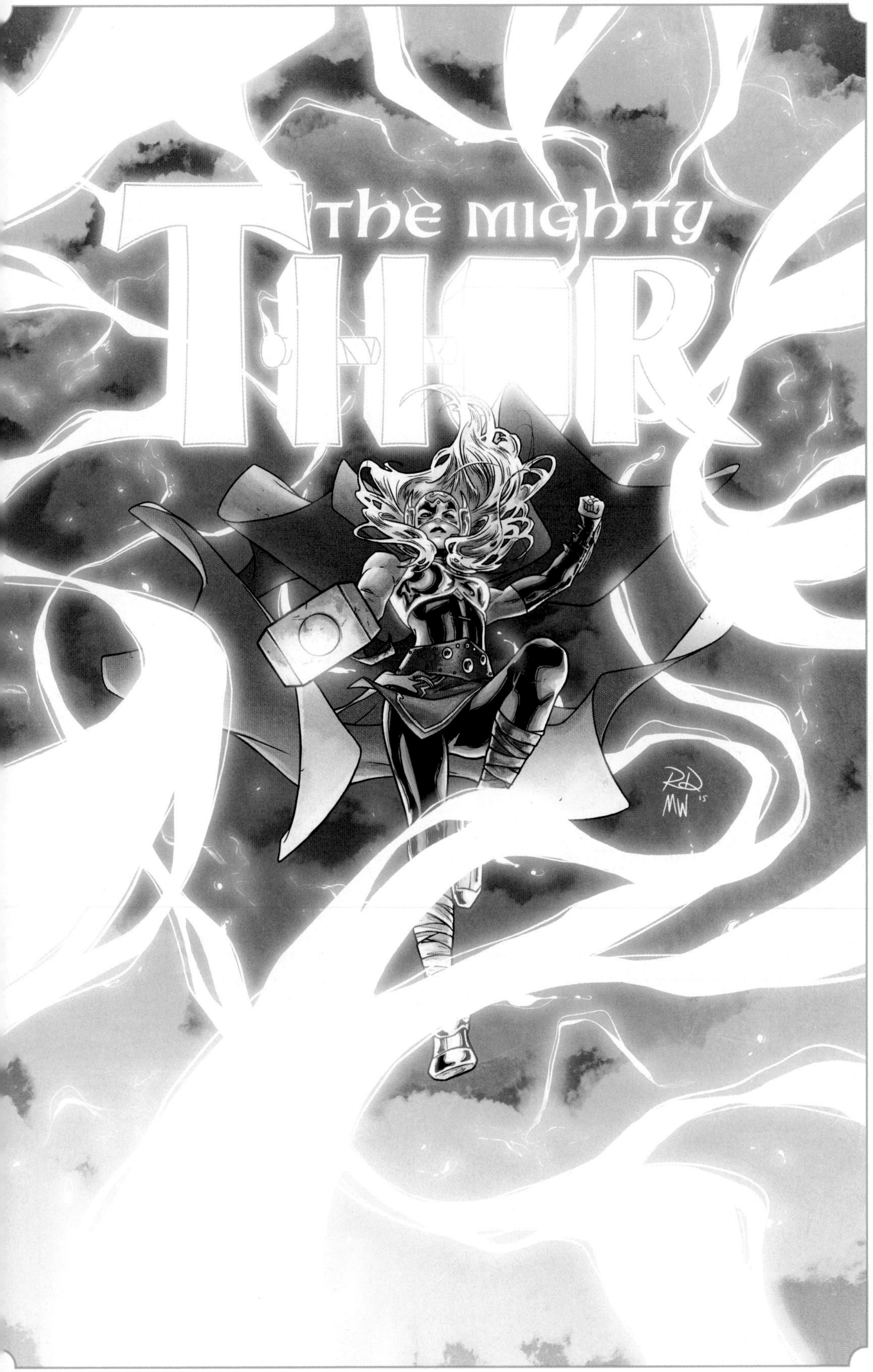
THE MIGHTY
THOR

LORDS OF MIDGARD

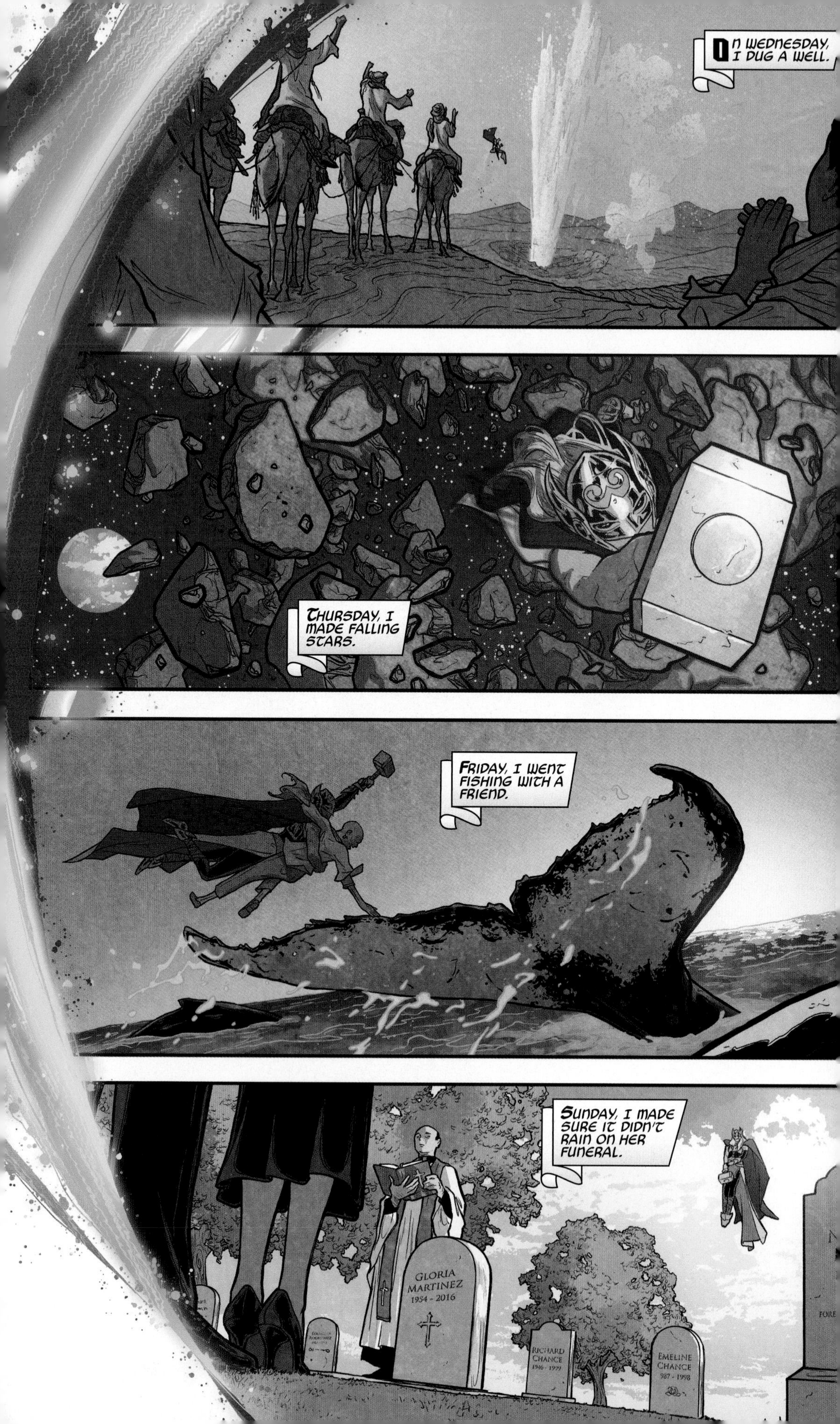

On Wednesday, I dug a well.
Thursday, I made falling stars.
Friday, I went fishing with a friend.
Sunday, I made sure it didn't rain on her funeral.
GLORIA MARTINEZ 1954 - 2016
RICHARD CHANCE 1946 - 1999
EMELINE CHANCE 987 - 1998

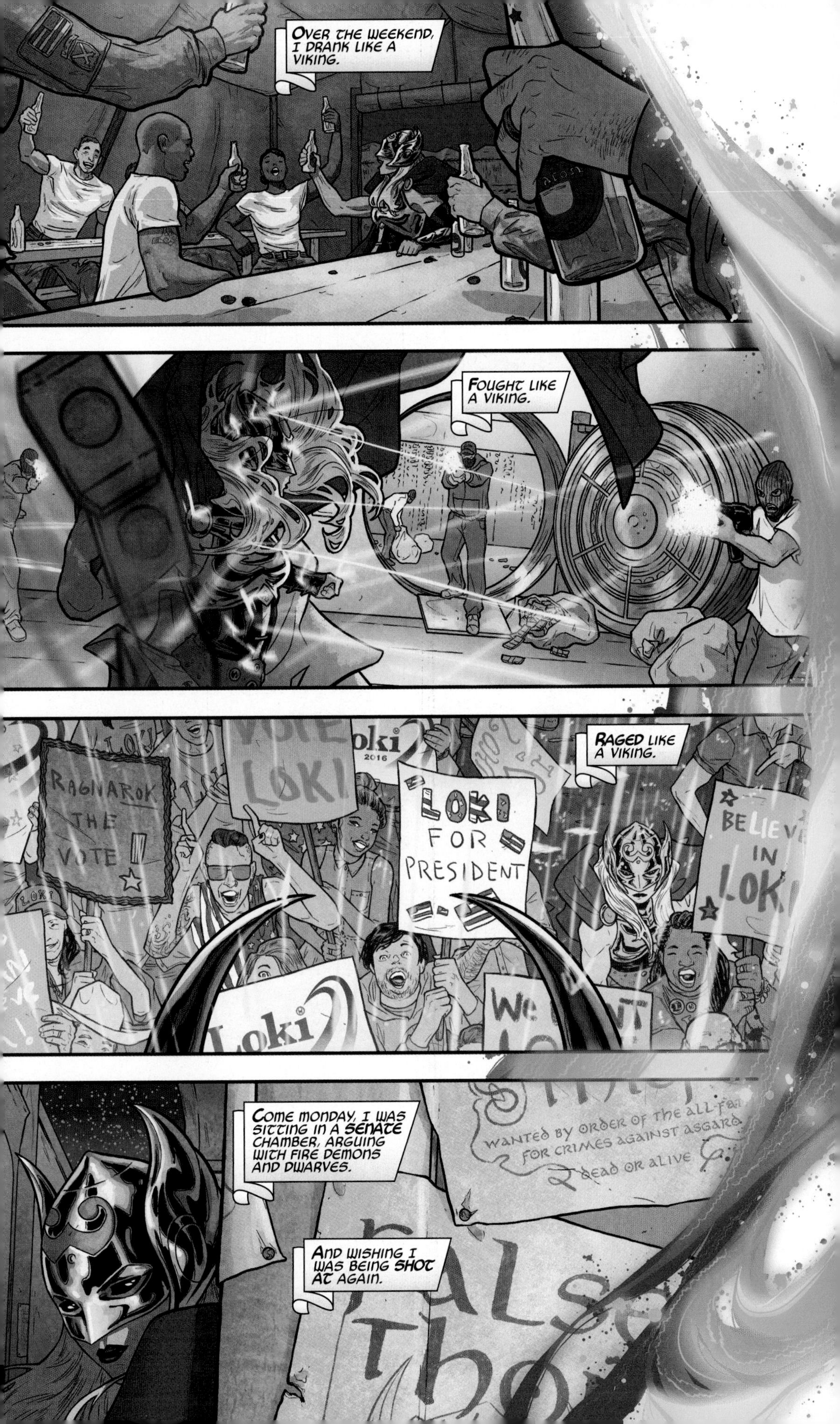

Over the weekend, I drank like a viking.
Fought like a viking.
Raged like a viking.
Ragnarok the vote!
Vote Loki
Loki 2016
Loki for President
Believe in Loki
Loki
Come monday, I was sitting in a SENATE chamber, arguing with fire demons and dwarves.
wanted by order of the all-fa
for crimes against asgard
dead or alive
And wishing I was being SHOT AT again.

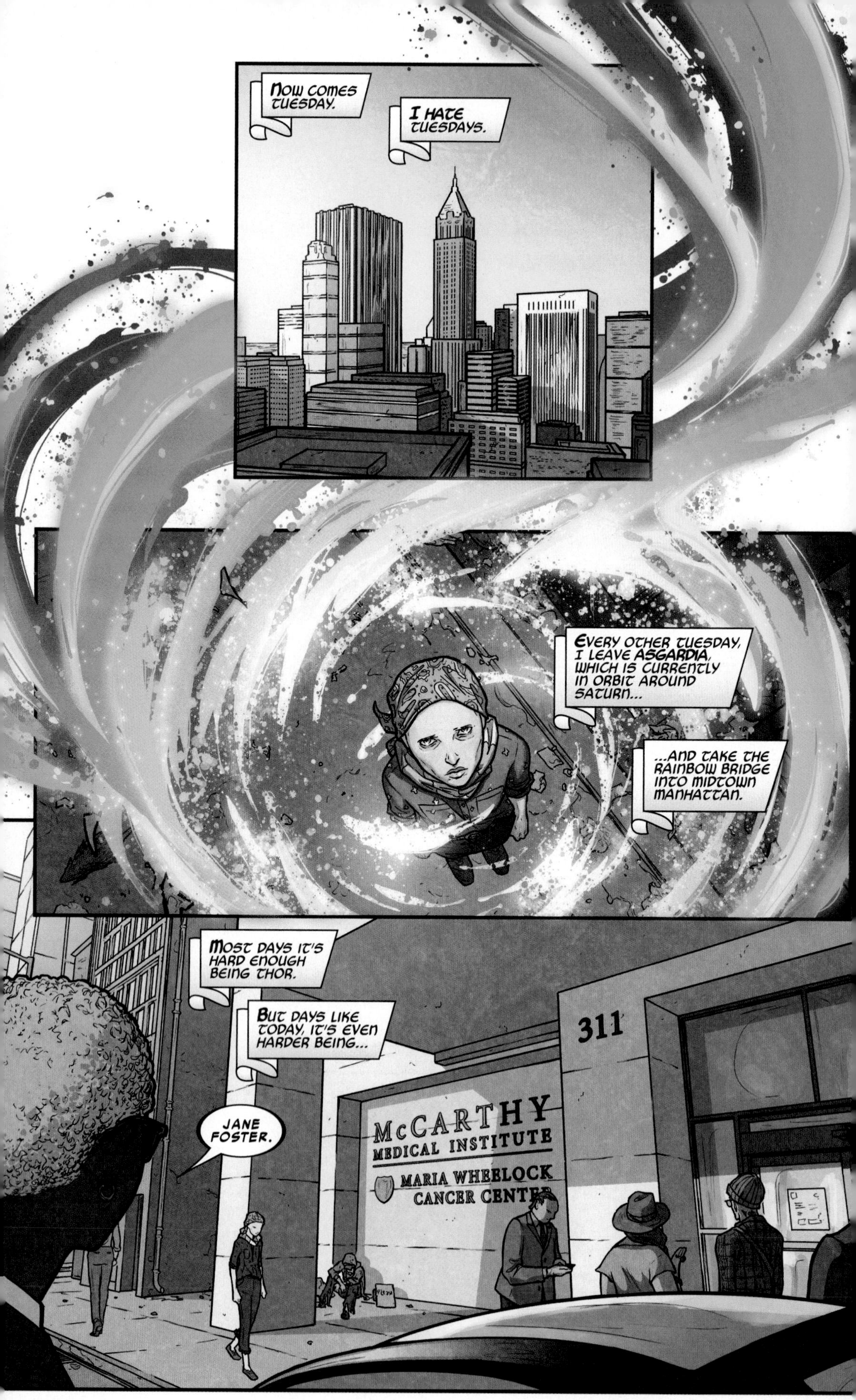
NOW COMES TUESDAY.
I HATE TUESDAYS.
EVERY OTHER TUESDAY, I LEAVE ASGARDIA, WHICH IS CURRENTLY IN ORBIT AROUND SATURN...
...AND TAKE THE RAINBOW BRIDGE INTO MIDTOWN MANHATTAN.
MOST DAYS IT'S HARD ENOUGH BEING THOR.
BUT DAYS LIKE TODAY, IT'S EVEN HARDER BEING...
JANE FOSTER.
311
McCARTHY MEDICAL INSTITUTE
MARIA WHEELOCK CANCER CENTER

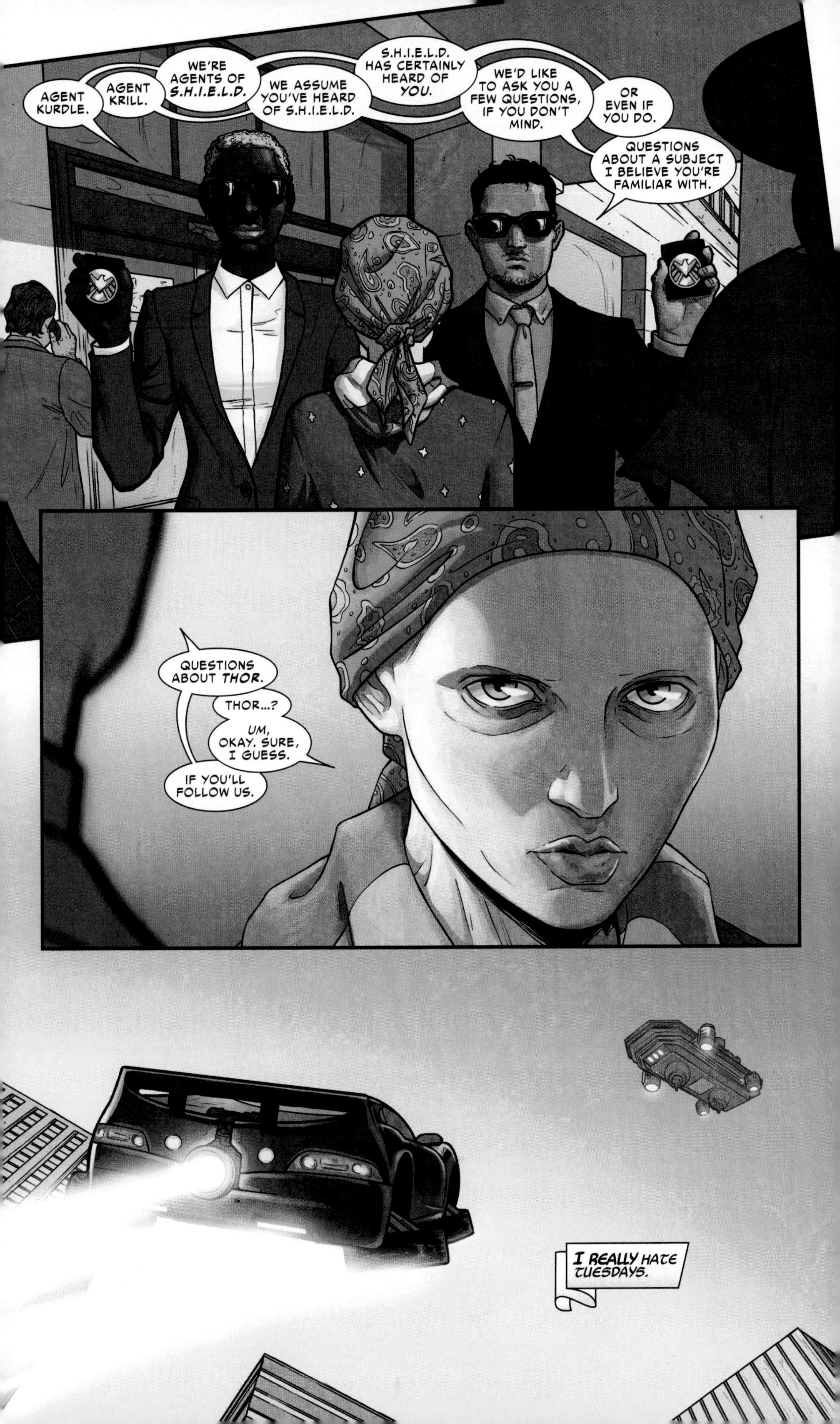
AGENT KURDLE.
AGENT KRILL.
WE'RE AGENTS OF S.H.I.E.L.D.
WE ASSUME YOU'VE HEARD OF S.H.I.E.L.D.
S.H.I.E.L.D. HAS CERTAINLY HEARD OF YOU.
WE'D LIKE TO ASK YOU A FEW QUESTIONS, IF YOU DON'T MIND.
OR EVEN IF YOU DO.
QUESTIONS ABOUT A SUBJECT I BELIEVE YOU'RE FAMILIAR WITH.
QUESTIONS ABOUT THOR.
THOR...?
UM, OKAY. SURE, I GUESS.
IF YOU'LL FOLLOW US.
I REALLY HATE TUESDAYS.

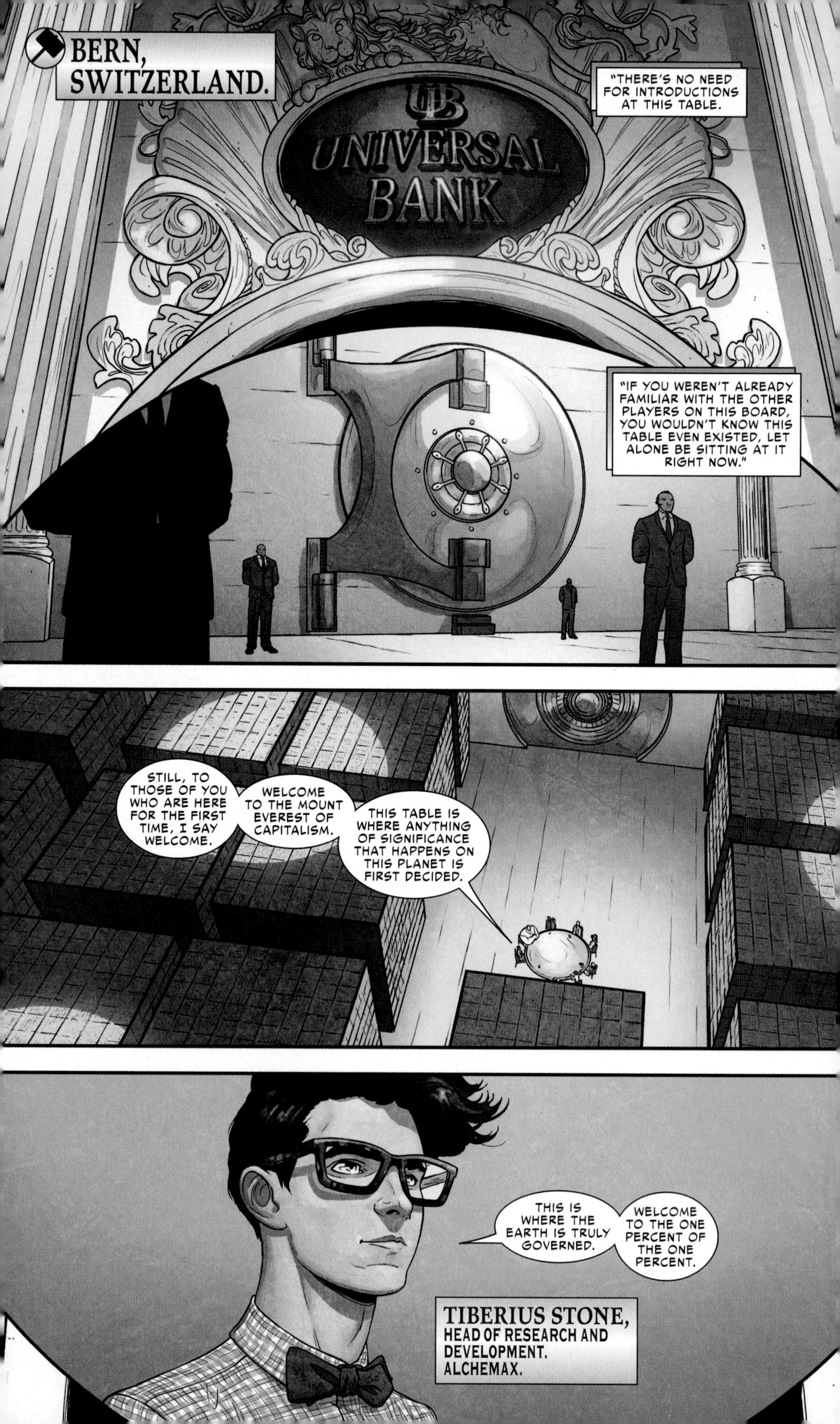
BERN, SWITZERLAND.
UB UNIVERSAL BANK
"THERE'S NO NEED FOR INTRODUCTIONS AT THIS TABLE.
"IF YOU WEREN'T ALREADY FAMILIAR WITH THE OTHER PLAYERS ON THIS BOARD, YOU WOULDN'T KNOW THIS TABLE EVEN EXISTED, LET ALONE BE SITTING AT IT RIGHT NOW."
STILL, TO THOSE OF YOU WHO ARE HERE FOR THE FIRST TIME, I SAY WELCOME.
WELCOME TO THE MOUNT EVEREST OF CAPITALISM.
THIS TABLE IS WHERE ANYTHING OF SIGNIFICANCE THAT HAPPENS ON THIS PLANET IS FIRST DECIDED.
THIS IS WHERE THE EARTH IS TRULY GOVERNED.
WELCOME TO THE ONE PERCENT OF THE ONE PERCENT.
TIBERIUS STONE, HEAD OF RESEARCH AND DEVELOPMENT. ALCHEMAX.

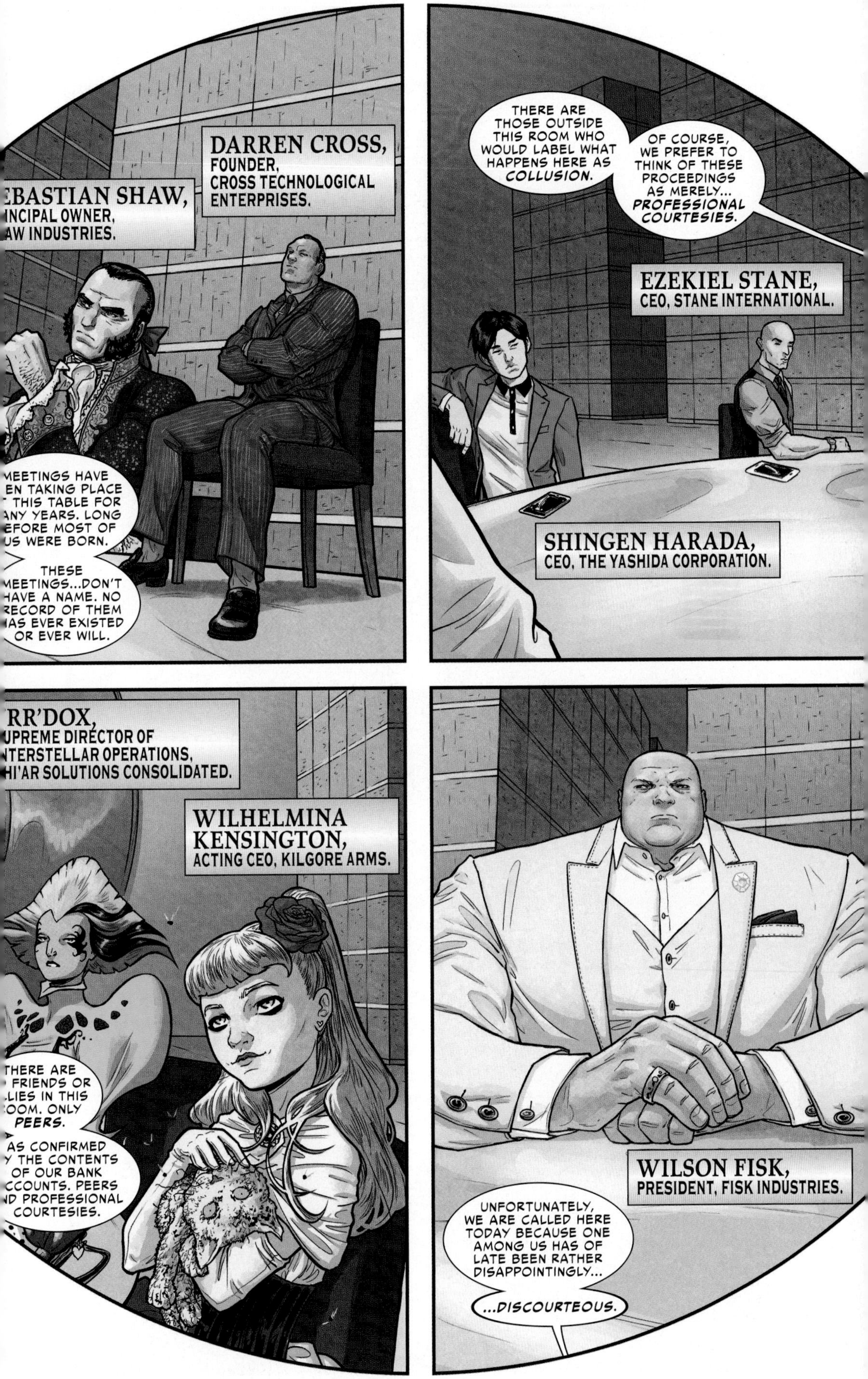

EBASTIAN SHAW,
INCIPAL OWNER,
AW INDUSTRIES.
DARREN CROSS,
FOUNDER,
CROSS TECHNOLOGICAL ENTERPRISES.
MEETINGS HAVE EN TAKING PLACE T THIS TABLE FOR ANY YEARS. LONG EFORE MOST OF US WERE BORN.
THESE MEETINGS...DON'T HAVE A NAME. NO RECORD OF THEM IAS EVER EXISTED OR EVER WILL.
THERE ARE THOSE OUTSIDE THIS ROOM WHO WOULD LABEL WHAT HAPPENS HERE AS *COLLUSION*.
OF COURSE, WE PREFER TO THINK OF THESE PROCEEDINGS AS MERELY... *PROFESSIONAL COURTESIES*.
EZEKIEL STANE,
CEO, STANE INTERNATIONAL.
SHINGEN HARADA,
CEO, THE YASHIDA CORPORATION.
RR'DOX,
UPREME DIRECTOR OF
NTERSTELLAR OPERATIONS,
HI'AR SOLUTIONS CONSOLIDATED.
WILHELMINA KENSINGTON,
ACTING CEO, KILGORE ARMS.
THERE ARE FRIENDS OR LIES IN THIS OOM. ONLY *PEERS*.
AS CONFIRMED Y THE CONTENTS OF OUR BANK CCOUNTS. PEERS ND PROFESSIONAL COURTESIES.
WILSON FISK,
PRESIDENT, FISK INDUSTRIES.
UNFORTUNATELY, WE ARE CALLED HERE TODAY BECAUSE ONE AMONG US HAS OF LATE BEEN RATHER DISAPPOINTINGLY...
...*DISCOURTEOUS*.

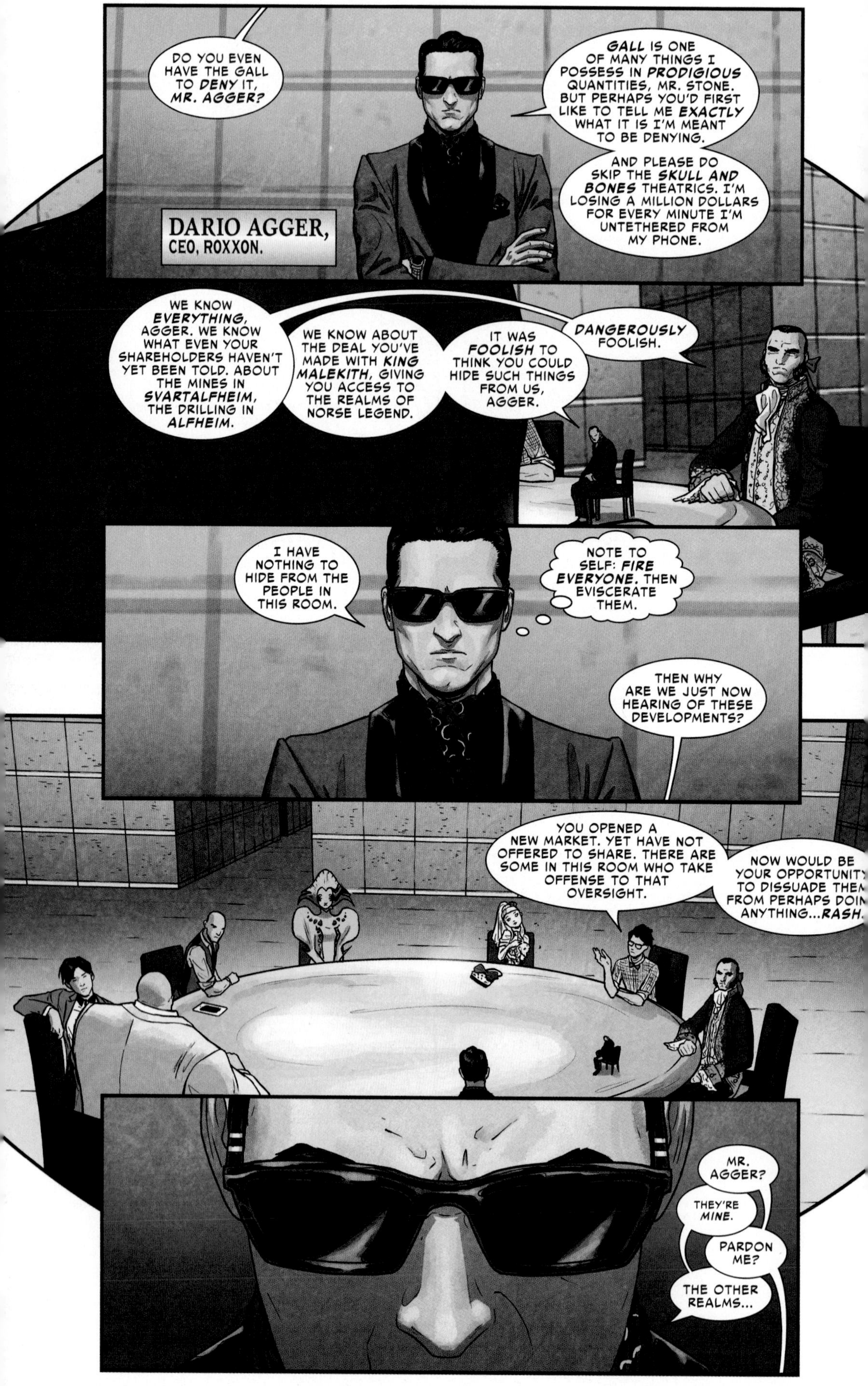

DO YOU EVEN HAVE THE GALL TO *DENY* IT, *MR. AGGER?*
GALL IS ONE OF MANY THINGS I POSSESS IN *PRODIGIOUS* QUANTITIES, MR. STONE. BUT PERHAPS YOU'D FIRST LIKE TO TELL ME *EXACTLY* WHAT IT IS I'M MEANT TO BE DENYING.
AND PLEASE DO SKIP THE *SKULL AND BONES* THEATRICS. I'M LOSING A MILLION DOLLARS FOR EVERY MINUTE I'M UNTETHERED FROM MY PHONE.
DARIO AGGER,
CEO, ROXXON.
WE KNOW *EVERYTHING*, AGGER. WE KNOW WHAT EVEN YOUR SHAREHOLDERS HAVEN'T YET BEEN TOLD. ABOUT THE MINES IN *SVARTALFHEIM*, THE DRILLING IN *ALFHEIM*.
WE KNOW ABOUT THE DEAL YOU'VE MADE WITH *KING MALEKITH*, GIVING YOU ACCESS TO THE REALMS OF NORSE LEGEND.
IT WAS *FOOLISH* TO THINK YOU COULD HIDE SUCH THINGS FROM US, AGGER.
DANGEROUSLY FOOLISH.
I HAVE NOTHING TO HIDE FROM THE PEOPLE IN THIS ROOM.
NOTE TO SELF: *FIRE EVERYONE*. THEN EVISCERATE THEM.
THEN WHY ARE WE JUST NOW HEARING OF THESE DEVELOPMENTS?
YOU OPENED A NEW MARKET. YET HAVE NOT OFFERED TO SHARE. THERE ARE SOME IN THIS ROOM WHO TAKE OFFENSE TO THAT OVERSIGHT.
NOW WOULD BE YOUR OPPORTUNITY TO DISSUADE THEM FROM PERHAPS DOIN ANYTHING...*RASH*.
MR. AGGER?
THEY'RE *MINE*.
PARDON ME?
THE OTHER REALMS...

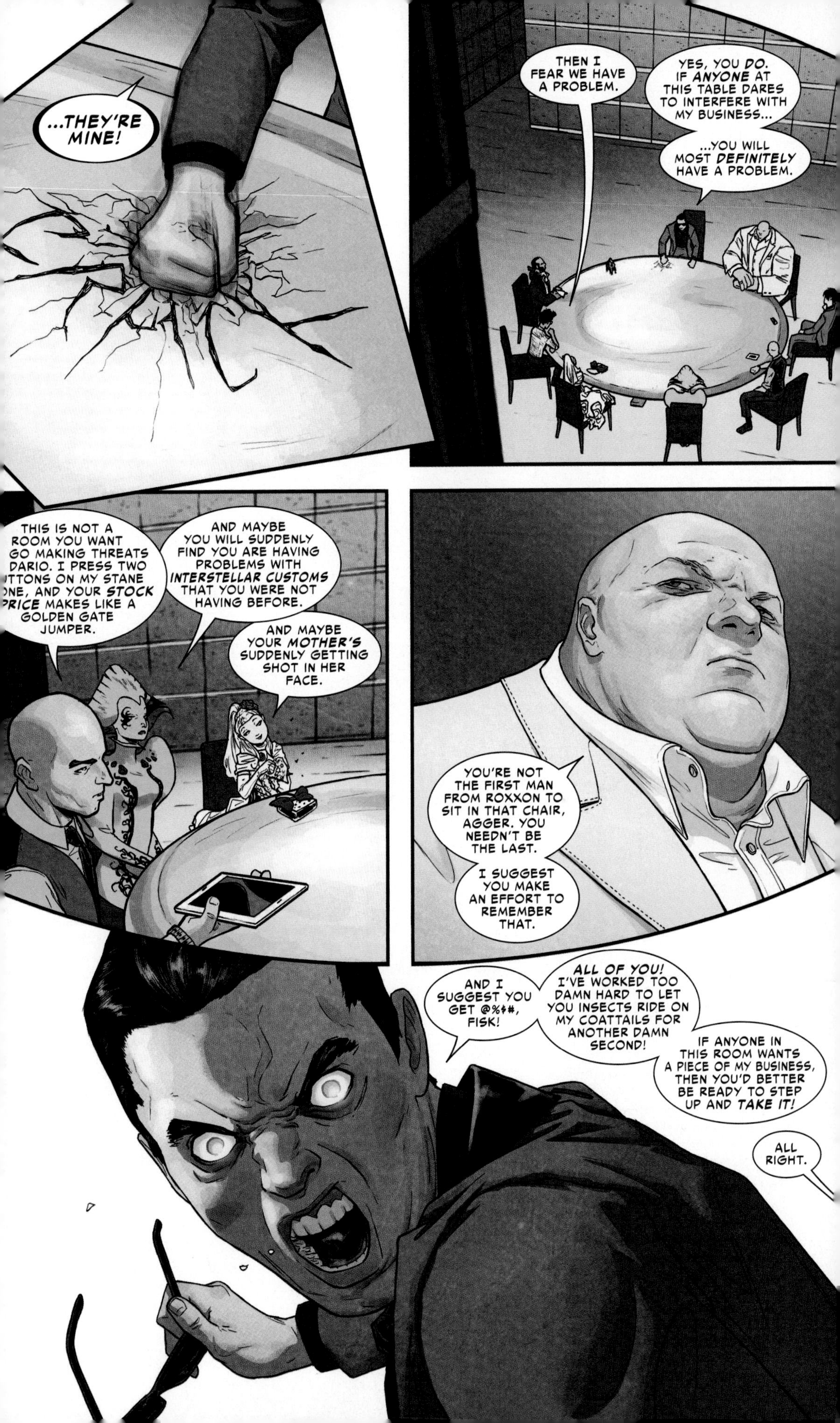
...THEY'RE MINE!
THEN I FEAR WE HAVE A PROBLEM.
YES, YOU DO. IF ANYONE AT THIS TABLE DARES TO INTERFERE WITH MY BUSINESS...
...YOU WILL MOST DEFINITELY HAVE A PROBLEM.
THIS IS NOT A ROOM YOU WANT GO MAKING THREATS DARIO. I PRESS TWO UTTONS ON MY STANE ONE, AND YOUR STOCK PRICE MAKES LIKE A GOLDEN GATE JUMPER.
AND MAYBE YOU WILL SUDDENLY FIND YOU ARE HAVING PROBLEMS WITH INTERSTELLAR CUSTOMS THAT YOU WERE NOT HAVING BEFORE.
AND MAYBE YOUR MOTHER'S SUDDENLY GETTING SHOT IN HER FACE.
YOU'RE NOT THE FIRST MAN FROM ROXXON TO SIT IN THAT CHAIR, AGGER. YOU NEEDN'T BE THE LAST.
I SUGGEST YOU MAKE AN EFFORT TO REMEMBER THAT.
AND I SUGGEST YOU GET @%$#, FISK!
ALL OF YOU! I'VE WORKED TOO DAMN HARD TO LET YOU INSECTS RIDE ON MY COATTAILS FOR ANOTHER DAMN SECOND!
IF ANYONE IN THIS ROOM WANTS A PIECE OF MY BUSINESS, THEN YOU'D BETTER BE READY TO STEP UP AND TAKE IT!
ALL RIGHT.

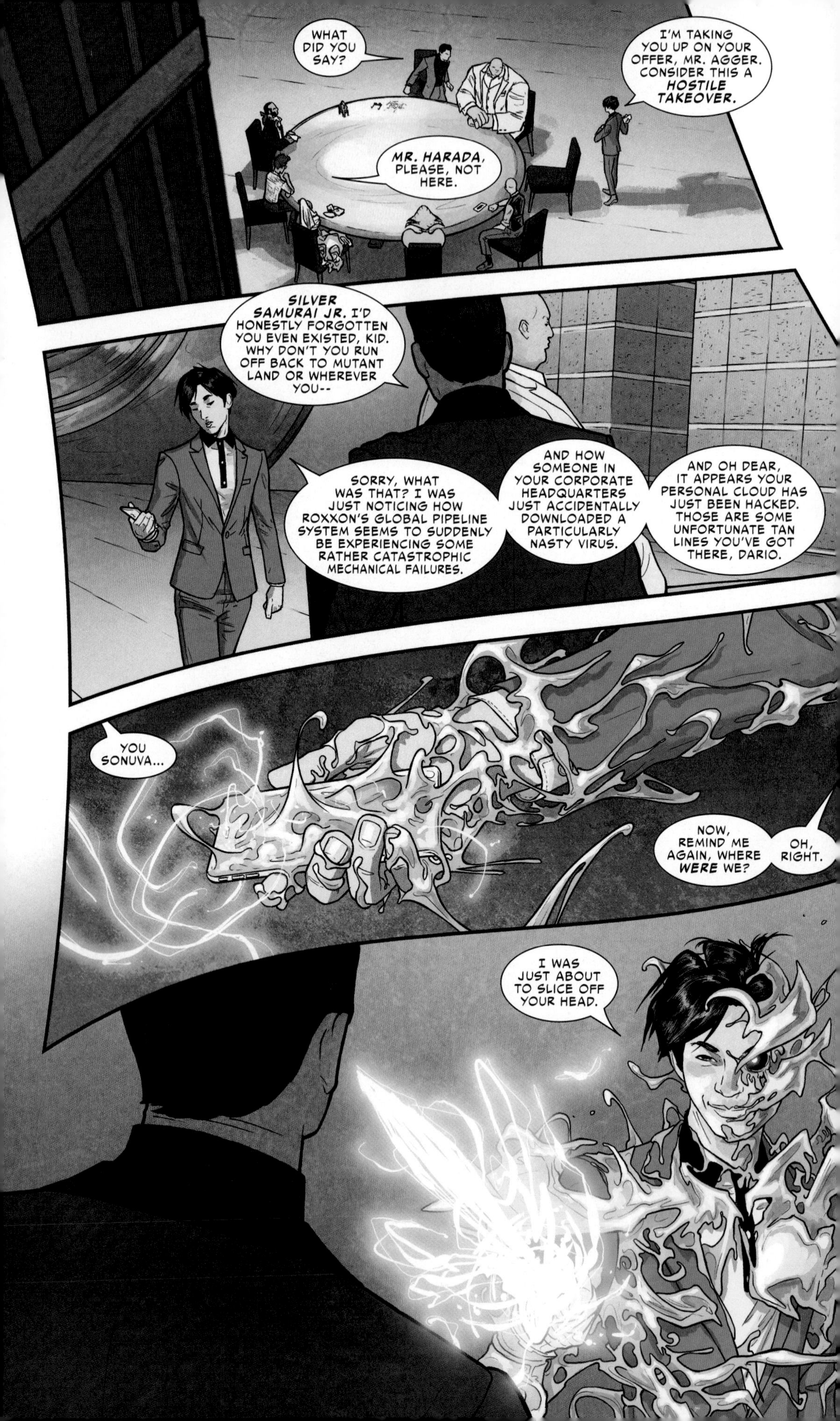
WHAT DID YOU SAY?
I'M TAKING YOU UP ON YOUR OFFER, MR. AGGER. CONSIDER THIS A HOSTILE TAKEOVER.
MR. HARADA, PLEASE, NOT HERE.
SILVER SAMURAI JR. I'D HONESTLY FORGOTTEN YOU EVEN EXISTED, KID. WHY DON'T YOU RUN OFF BACK TO MUTANT LAND OR WHEREVER YOU--
SORRY, WHAT WAS THAT? I WAS JUST NOTICING HOW ROXXON'S GLOBAL PIPELINE SYSTEM SEEMS TO SUDDENLY BE EXPERIENCING SOME RATHER CATASTROPHIC MECHANICAL FAILURES.
AND HOW SOMEONE IN YOUR CORPORATE HEADQUARTERS JUST ACCIDENTALLY DOWNLOADED A PARTICULARLY NASTY VIRUS.
AND OH DEAR, IT APPEARS YOUR PERSONAL CLOUD HAS JUST BEEN HACKED. THOSE ARE SOME UNFORTUNATE TAN LINES YOU'VE GOT THERE, DARIO.
YOU SONUVA...
NOW, REMIND ME AGAIN, WHERE WERE WE?
OH, RIGHT.
I WAS JUST ABOUT TO SLICE OFF YOUR HEAD.

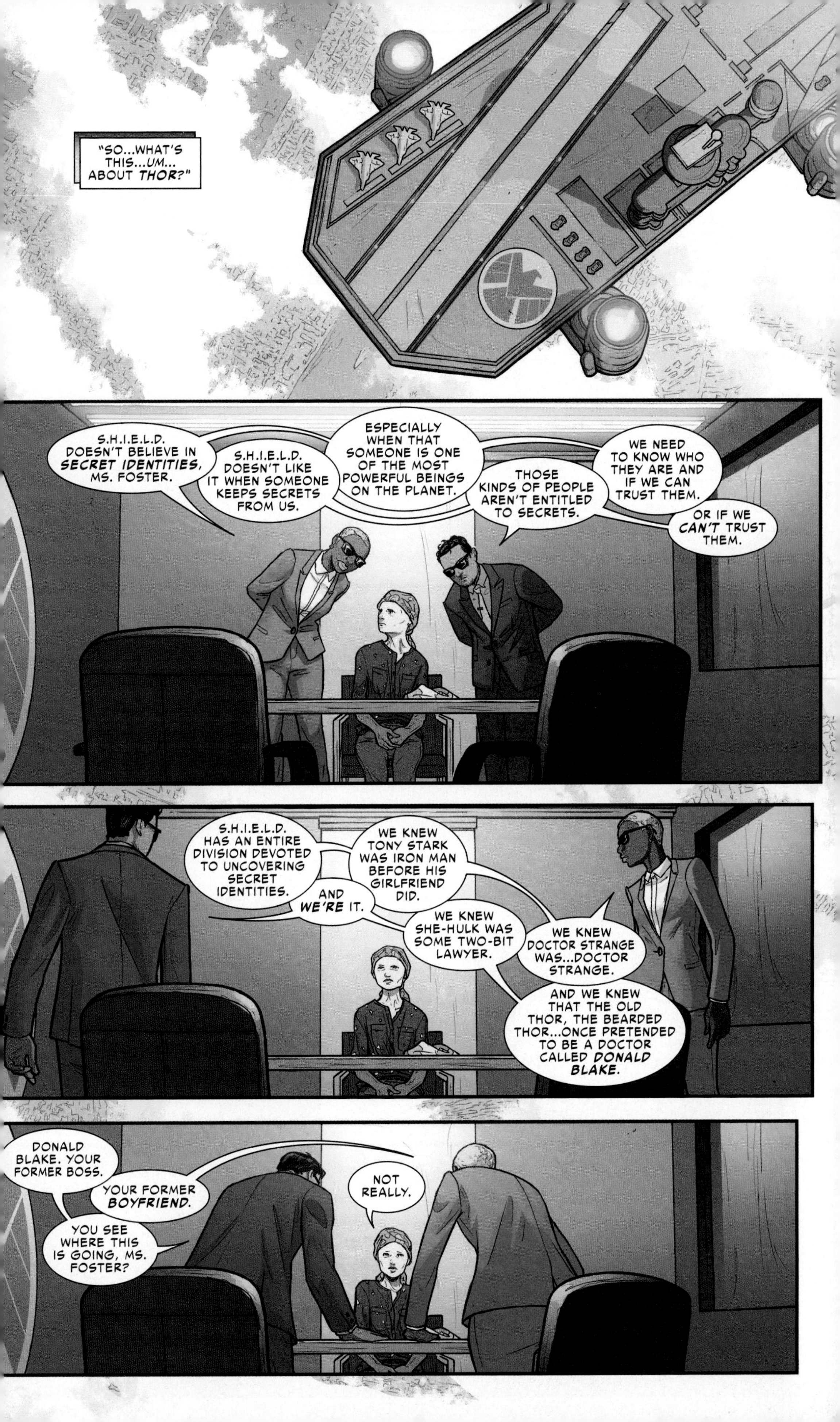
"SO...WHAT'S THIS...UM... ABOUT THOR?"
S.H.I.E.L.D. DOESN'T BELIEVE IN SECRET IDENTITIES, MS. FOSTER.
S.H.I.E.L.D. DOESN'T LIKE IT WHEN SOMEONE KEEPS SECRETS FROM US.
ESPECIALLY WHEN THAT SOMEONE IS ONE OF THE MOST POWERFUL BEINGS ON THE PLANET.
THOSE KINDS OF PEOPLE AREN'T ENTITLED TO SECRETS.
WE NEED TO KNOW WHO THEY ARE AND IF WE CAN TRUST THEM.
OR IF WE CAN'T TRUST THEM.
S.H.I.E.L.D. HAS AN ENTIRE DIVISION DEVOTED TO UNCOVERING SECRET IDENTITIES.
AND WE'RE IT.
WE KNEW TONY STARK WAS IRON MAN BEFORE HIS GIRLFRIEND DID.
WE KNEW SHE-HULK WAS SOME TWO-BIT LAWYER.
WE KNEW DOCTOR STRANGE WAS...DOCTOR STRANGE.
AND WE KNEW THAT THE OLD THOR, THE BEARDED THOR...ONCE PRETENDED TO BE A DOCTOR CALLED DONALD BLAKE.
DONALD BLAKE. YOUR FORMER BOSS.
YOUR FORMER BOYFRIEND.
NOT REALLY.
YOU SEE WHERE THIS IS GOING, MS. FOSTER?

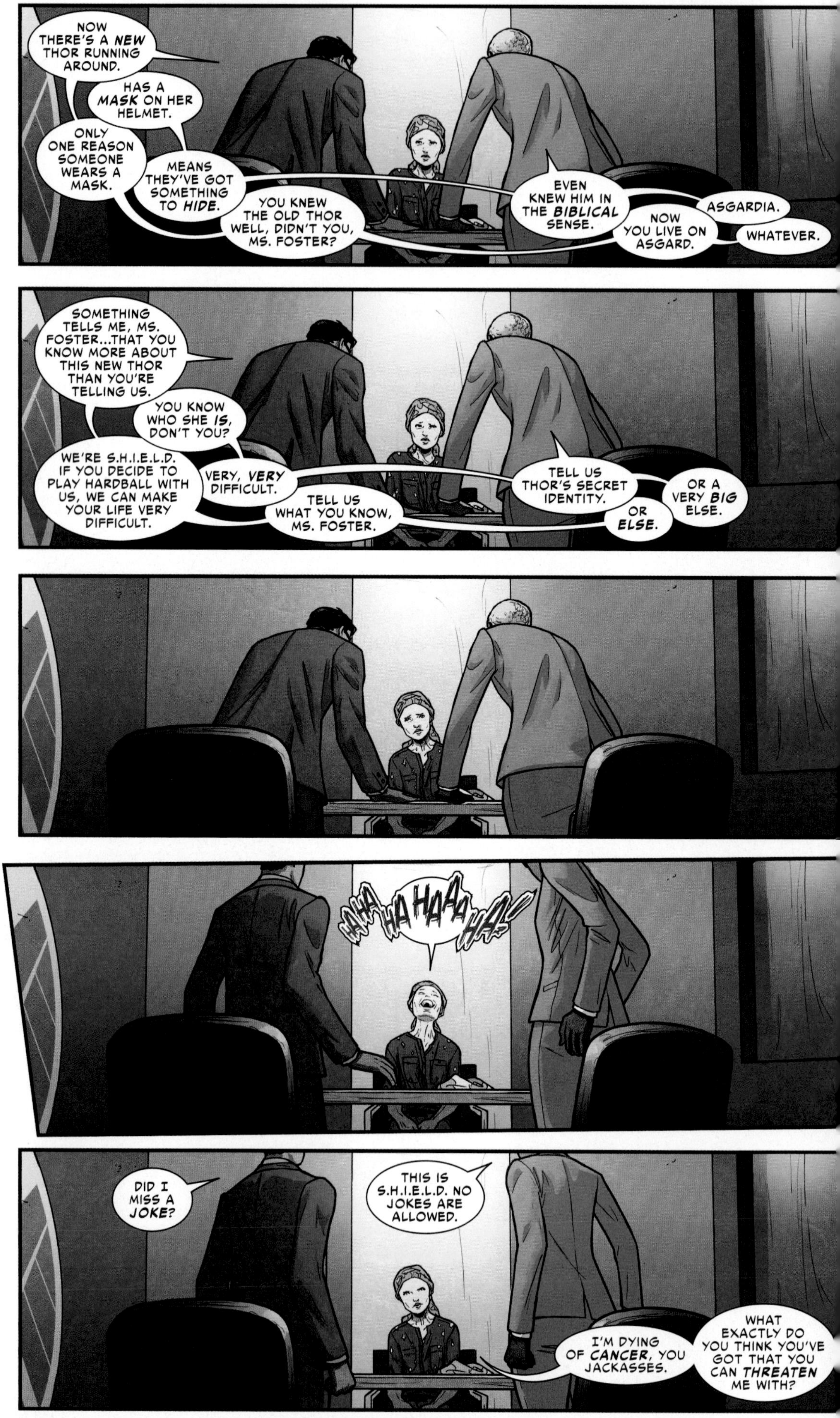
NOW THERE'S A NEW THOR RUNNING AROUND.
HAS A MASK ON HER HELMET.
ONLY ONE REASON SOMEONE WEARS A MASK.
MEANS THEY'VE GOT SOMETHING TO HIDE.
YOU KNEW THE OLD THOR WELL, DIDN'T YOU, MS. FOSTER?
EVEN KNEW HIM IN THE BIBLICAL SENSE.
NOW YOU LIVE ON ASGARD.
ASGARDIA.
WHATEVER.
SOMETHING TELLS ME, MS. FOSTER...THAT YOU KNOW MORE ABOUT THIS NEW THOR THAN YOU'RE TELLING US.
YOU KNOW WHO SHE IS, DON'T YOU?
WE'RE S.H.I.E.L.D. IF YOU DECIDE TO PLAY HARDBALL WITH US, WE CAN MAKE YOUR LIFE VERY DIFFICULT.
VERY, VERY DIFFICULT.
TELL US WHAT YOU KNOW, MS. FOSTER.
TELL US THOR'S SECRET IDENTITY.
OR ELSE.
OR A VERY BIG ELSE.
HAHA HA HAAAA HA!
DID I MISS A JOKE?
THIS IS S.H.I.E.L.D. NO JOKES ARE ALLOWED.
I'M DYING OF CANCER, YOU JACKASSES.
WHAT EXACTLY DO YOU THINK YOU'VE GOT THAT YOU CAN THREATEN ME WITH?

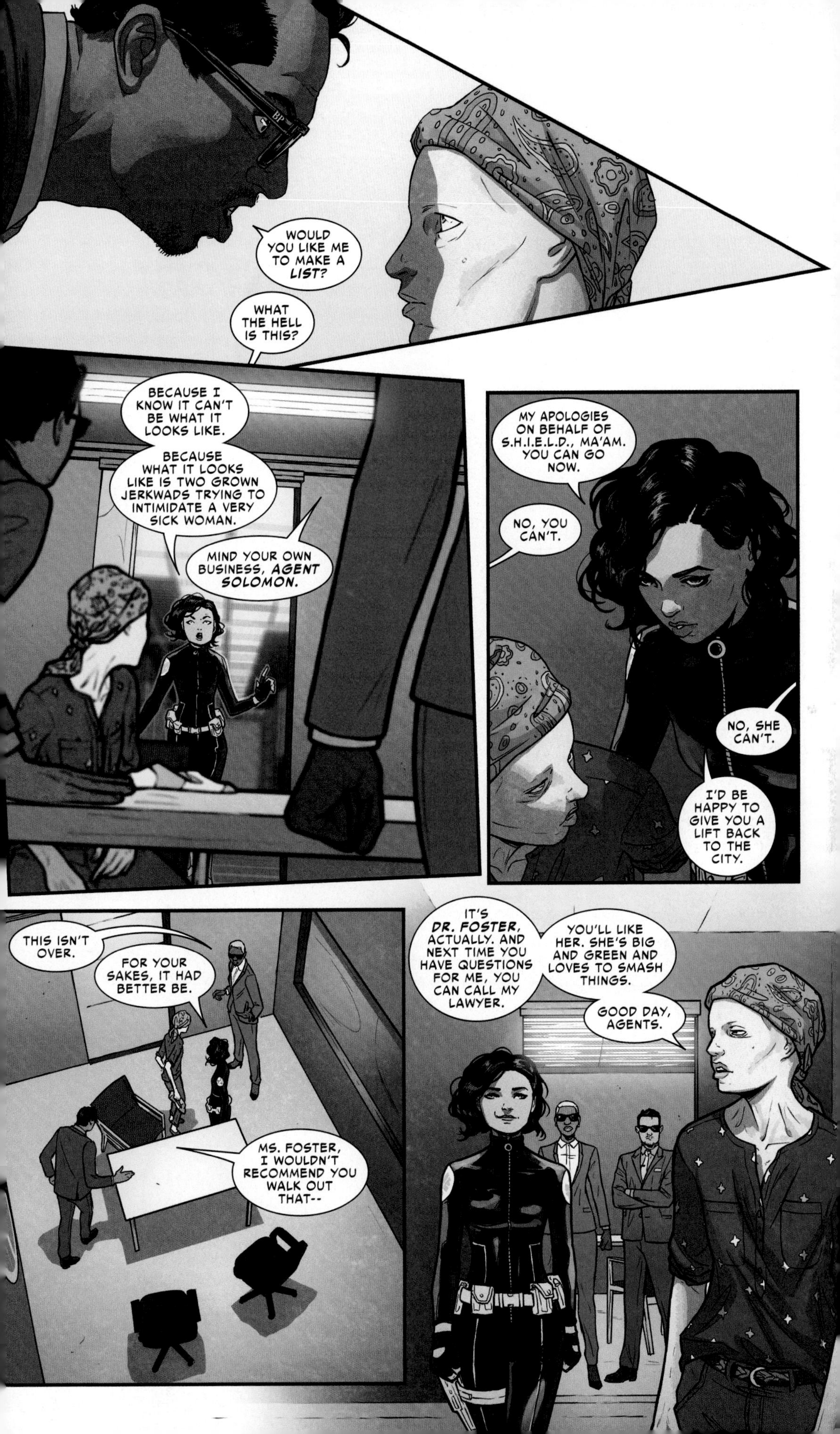

WOULD YOU LIKE ME TO MAKE A *LIST?*
WHAT THE HELL IS THIS?
BECAUSE I KNOW IT CAN'T BE WHAT IT LOOKS LIKE.
BECAUSE WHAT IT LOOKS LIKE IS TWO GROWN JERKWADS TRYING TO INTIMIDATE A VERY SICK WOMAN.
MIND YOUR OWN BUSINESS, *AGENT SOLOMON.*
MY APOLOGIES ON BEHALF OF S.H.I.E.L.D., MA'AM. YOU CAN GO NOW.
NO, YOU CAN'T.
NO, SHE CAN'T.
I'D BE HAPPY TO GIVE YOU A LIFT BACK TO THE CITY.
THIS ISN'T OVER.
FOR YOUR SAKES, IT HAD BETTER BE.
MS. FOSTER, I WOULDN'T RECOMMEND YOU WALK OUT THAT--
IT'S *DR. FOSTER,* ACTUALLY. AND NEXT TIME YOU HAVE QUESTIONS FOR ME, YOU CAN CALL MY LAWYER.
YOU'LL LIKE HER. SHE'S BIG AND GREEN AND LOVES TO SMASH THINGS.
GOOD DAY, AGENTS.

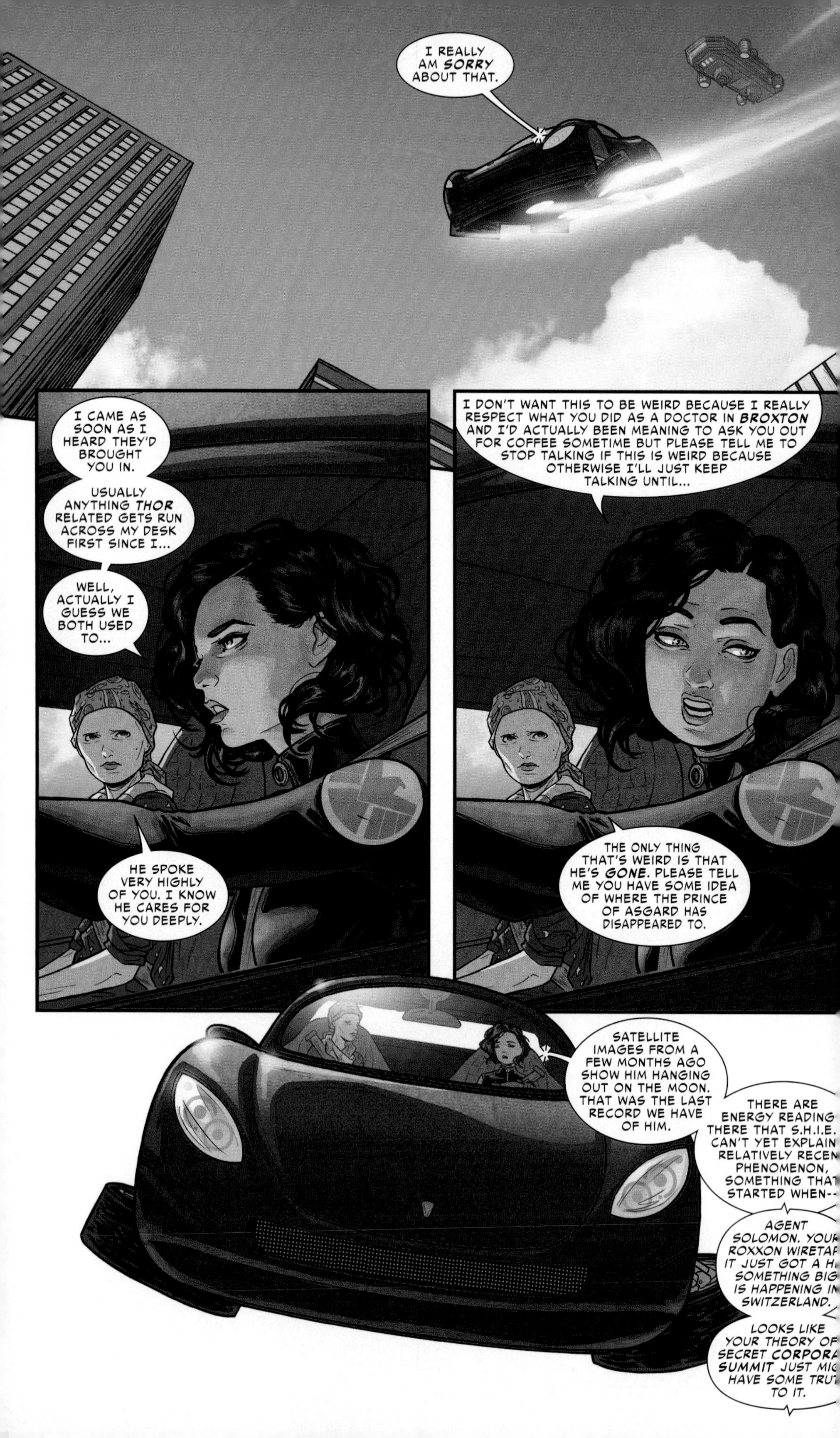
I REALLY AM SORRY ABOUT THAT.
I CAME AS SOON AS I HEARD THEY'D BROUGHT YOU IN.
USUALLY ANYTHING THOR RELATED GETS RUN ACROSS MY DESK FIRST SINCE I...
WELL, ACTUALLY I GUESS WE BOTH USED TO...
HE SPOKE VERY HIGHLY OF YOU. I KNOW HE CARES FOR YOU DEEPLY.
I DON'T WANT THIS TO BE WEIRD BECAUSE I REALLY RESPECT WHAT YOU DID AS A DOCTOR IN BROXTON AND I'D ACTUALLY BEEN MEANING TO ASK YOU OUT FOR COFFEE SOMETIME BUT PLEASE TELL ME TO STOP TALKING IF THIS IS WEIRD BECAUSE OTHERWISE I'LL JUST KEEP TALKING UNTIL...
THE ONLY THING THAT'S WEIRD IS THAT HE'S GONE. PLEASE TELL ME YOU HAVE SOME IDEA OF WHERE THE PRINCE OF ASGARD HAS DISAPPEARED TO.
SATELLITE IMAGES FROM A FEW MONTHS AGO SHOW HIM HANGING OUT ON THE MOON. THAT WAS THE LAST RECORD WE HAVE OF HIM.
THERE ARE ENERGY READING THERE THAT S.H.I.E. CAN'T YET EXPLAIN RELATIVELY RECEN PHENOMENON, SOMETHING THAT STARTED WHEN--
AGENT SOLOMON. YOUR ROXXON WIRETAP IT JUST GOT A H SOMETHING BIG IS HAPPENING IN SWITZERLAND.
LOOKS LIKE YOUR THEORY OF SECRET CORPORA SUMMIT JUST MIG HAVE SOME TRUT TO IT.

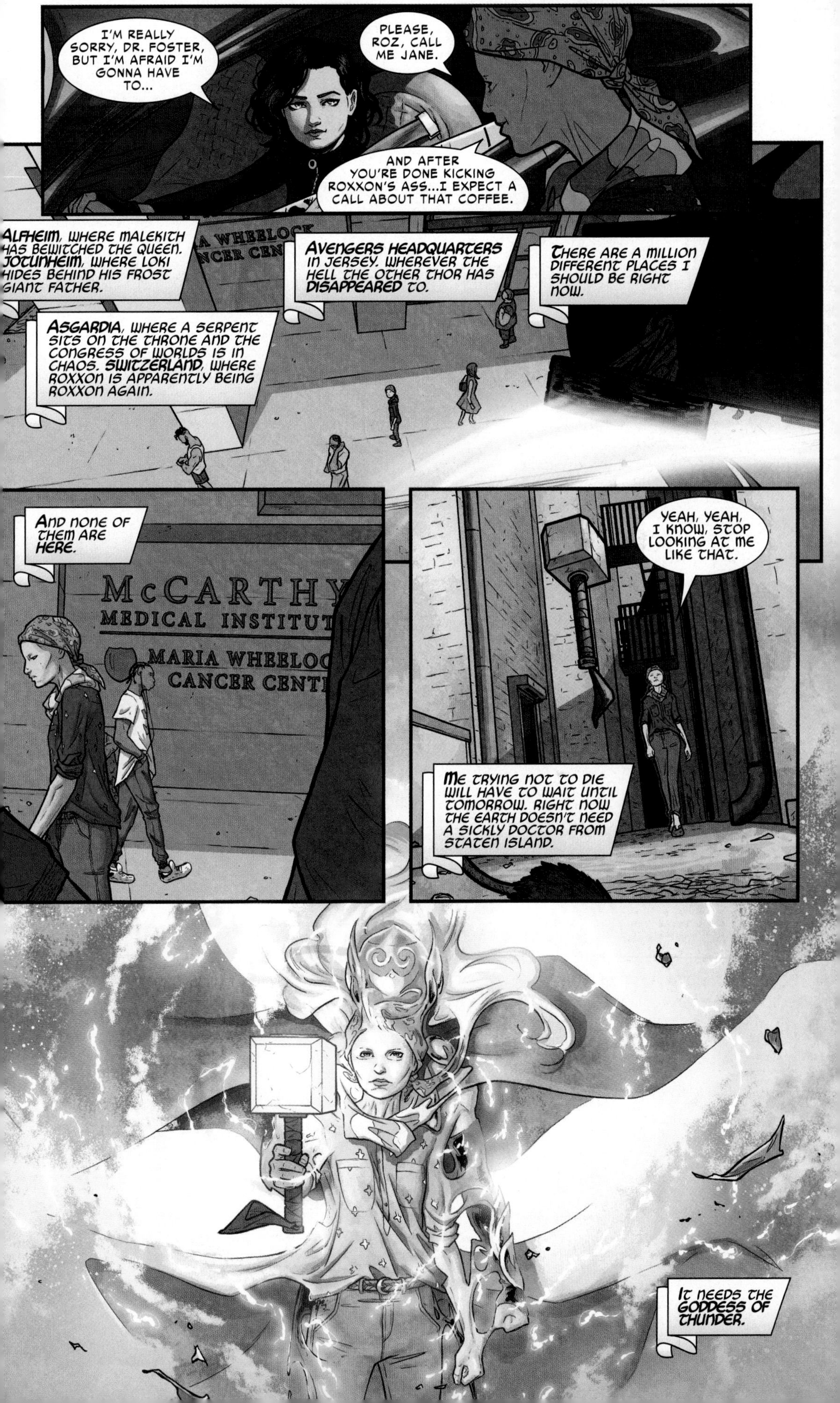
I'M REALLY SORRY, DR. FOSTER, BUT I'M AFRAID I'M GONNA HAVE TO...
PLEASE, ROZ, CALL ME JANE.
AND AFTER YOU'RE DONE KICKING ROXXON'S ASS...I EXPECT A CALL ABOUT THAT COFFEE.
ALFHEIM, WHERE MALEKITH HAS BEWITCHED THE QUEEN. JOTUNHEIM, WHERE LOKI HIDES BEHIND HIS FROST GIANT FATHER.
AVENGERS HEADQUARTERS IN JERSEY. WHEREVER THE HELL THE OTHER THOR HAS DISAPPEARED TO.
THERE ARE A MILLION DIFFERENT PLACES I SHOULD BE RIGHT NOW.
ASGARDIA, WHERE A SERPENT SITS ON THE THRONE AND THE CONGRESS OF WORLDS IS IN CHAOS. SWITZERLAND, WHERE ROXXON IS APPARENTLY BEING ROXXON AGAIN.
AND NONE OF THEM ARE HERE.
McCARTHY MEDICAL INSTITUT
MARIA WHEELOC CANCER CENT
YEAH, YEAH, I KNOW, STOP LOOKING AT ME LIKE THAT.
ME TRYING NOT TO DIE WILL HAVE TO WAIT UNTIL TOMORROW. RIGHT NOW THE EARTH DOESN'T NEED A SICKLY DOCTOR FROM STATEN ISLAND.
IT NEEDS THE GODDESS OF THUNDER.

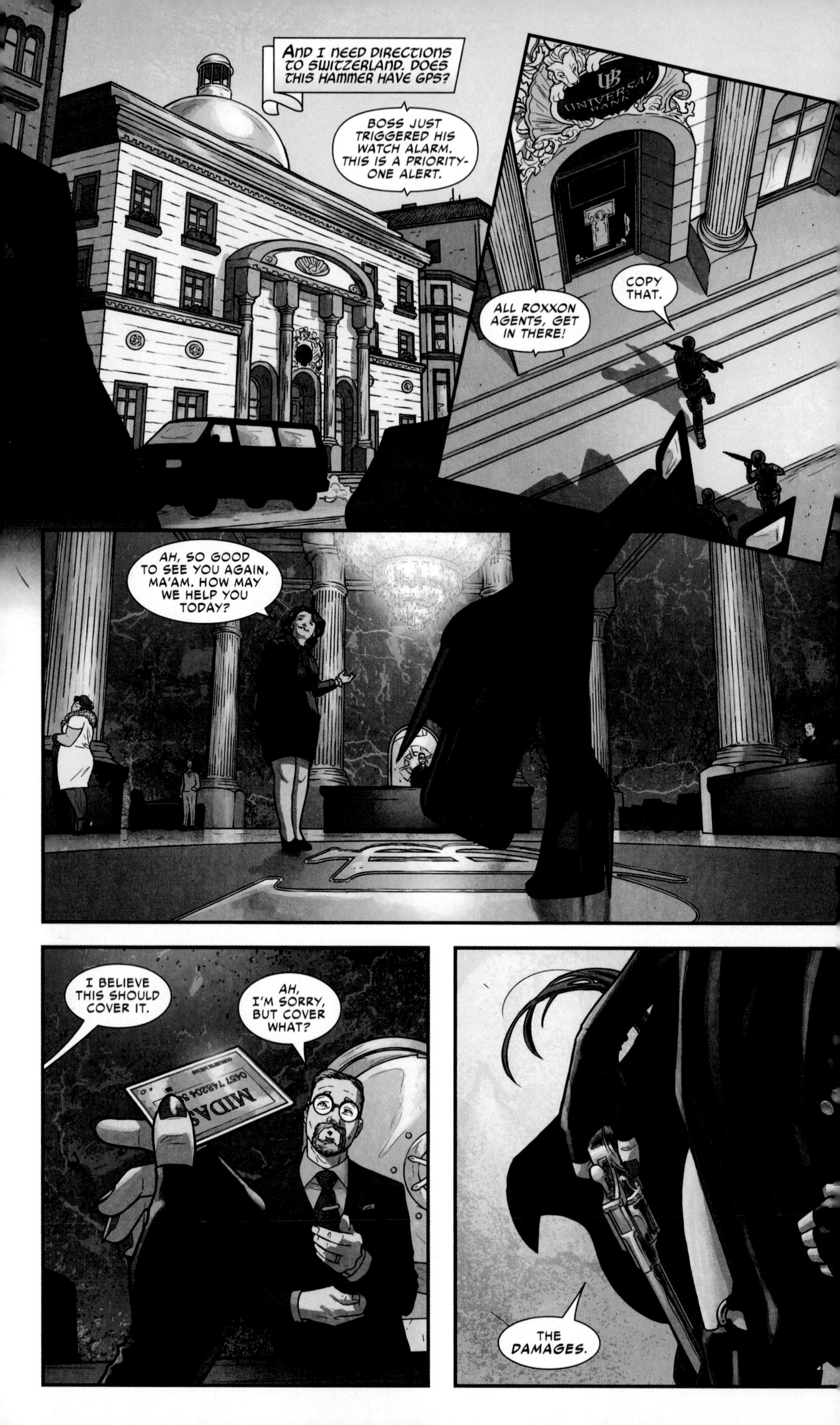
AND I NEED DIRECTIONS TO SWITZERLAND. DOES THIS HAMMER HAVE GPS?
BOSS JUST TRIGGERED HIS WATCH ALARM. THIS IS A PRIORITY-ONE ALERT.
UNIVERSAL BANK
ALL ROXXON AGENTS, GET IN THERE!
COPY THAT.
AH, SO GOOD TO SEE YOU AGAIN, MA'AM. HOW MAY WE HELP YOU TODAY?
I BELIEVE THIS SHOULD COVER IT.
AH, I'M SORRY, BUT COVER WHAT?
MIDAS
THE DAMAGES.

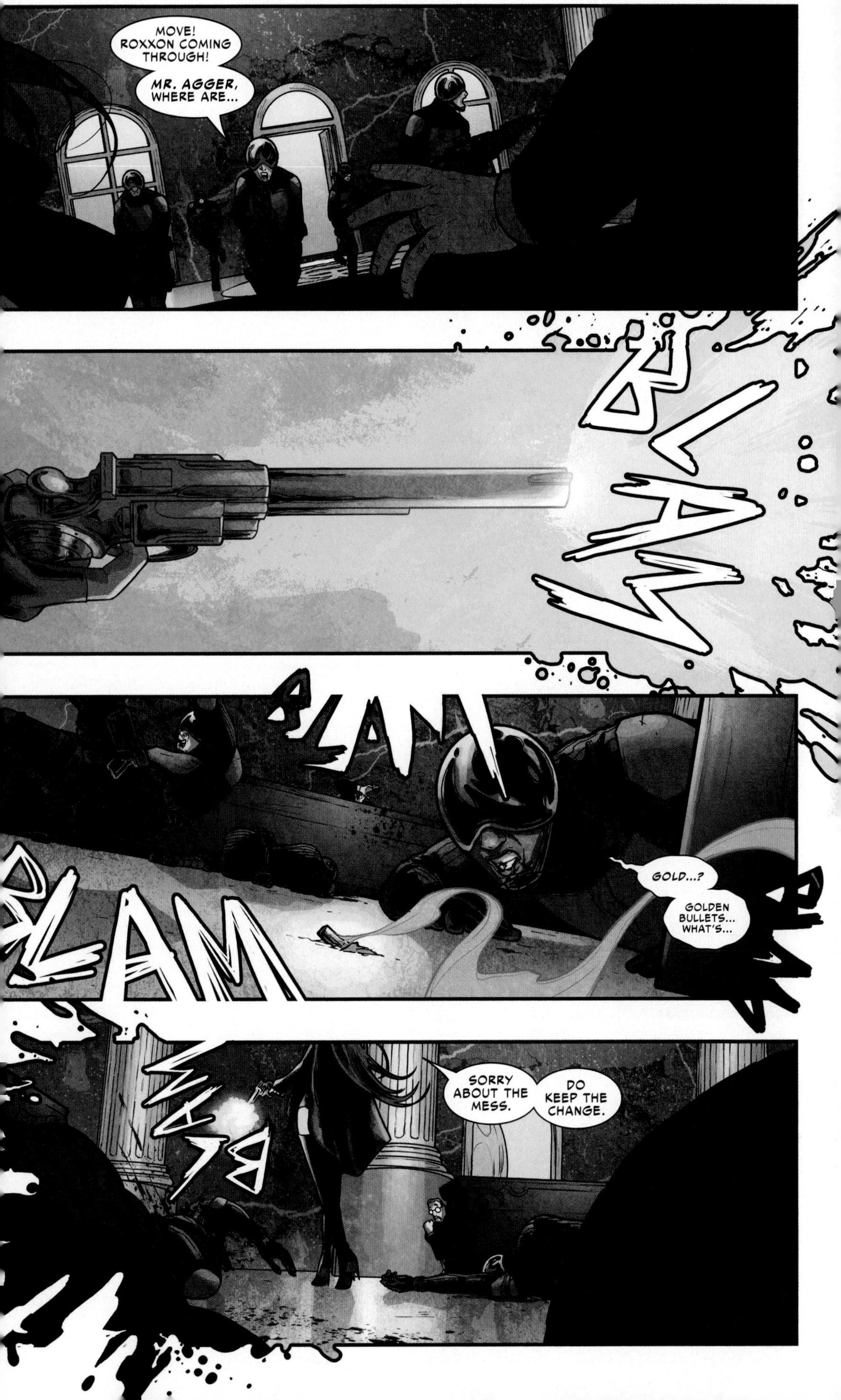
MOVE! ROXXON COMING THROUGH!
MR. AGGER, WHERE ARE...
BLAM
BLAM
GOLD...?
GOLDEN BULLETS... WHAT'S...
BLAM
SORRY ABOUT THE MESS.
DO KEEP THE CHANGE.
BLAM

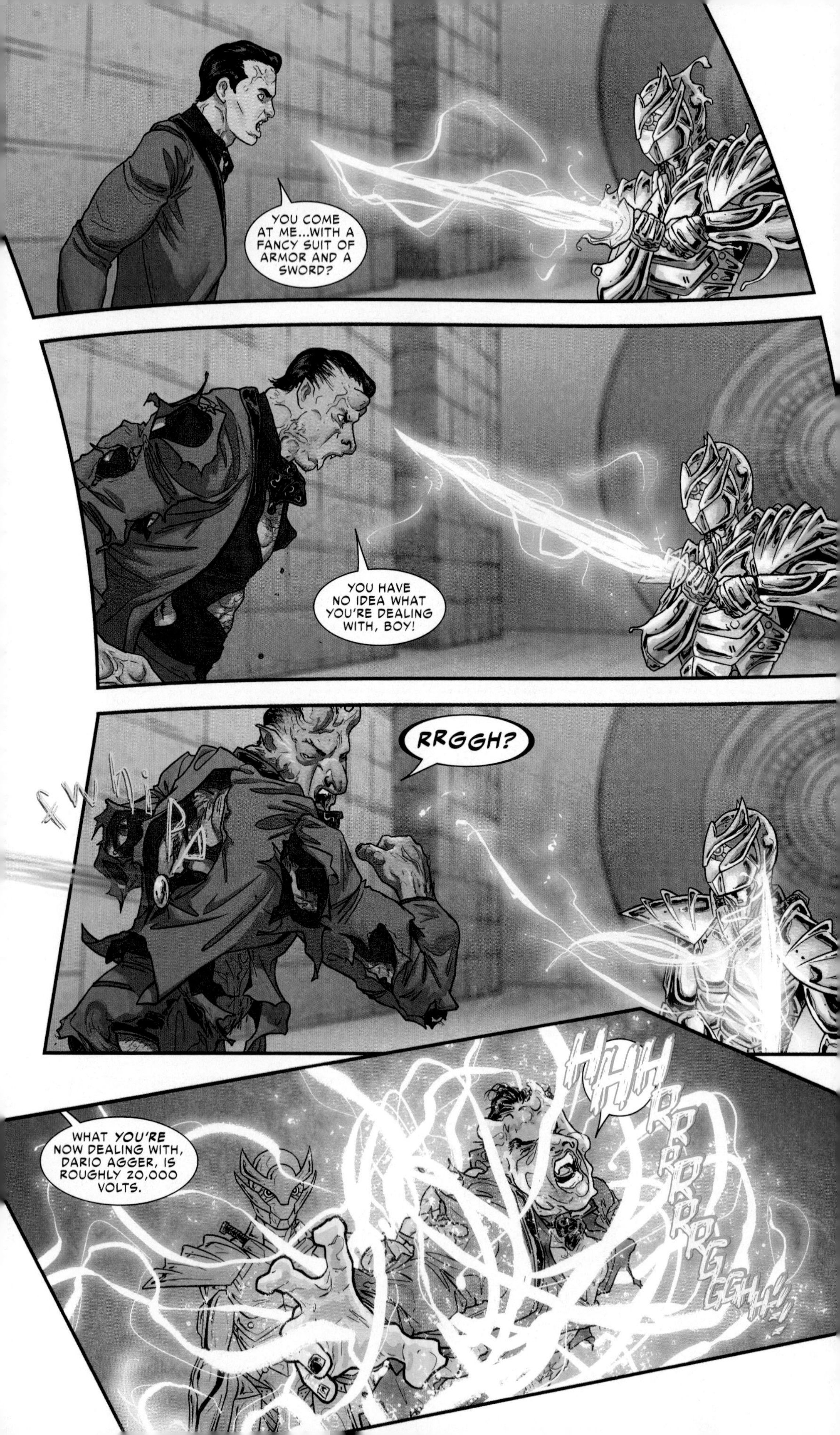
YOU COME AT ME...WITH A FANCY SUIT OF ARMOR AND A SWORD?
YOU HAVE NO IDEA WHAT YOU'RE DEALING WITH, BOY!
fwhiPA
RRGGH?
HHHRRRRRRRGGHH!
WHAT *YOU'RE* NOW DEALING WITH, DARIO AGGER, IS ROUGHLY 20,000 VOLTS.

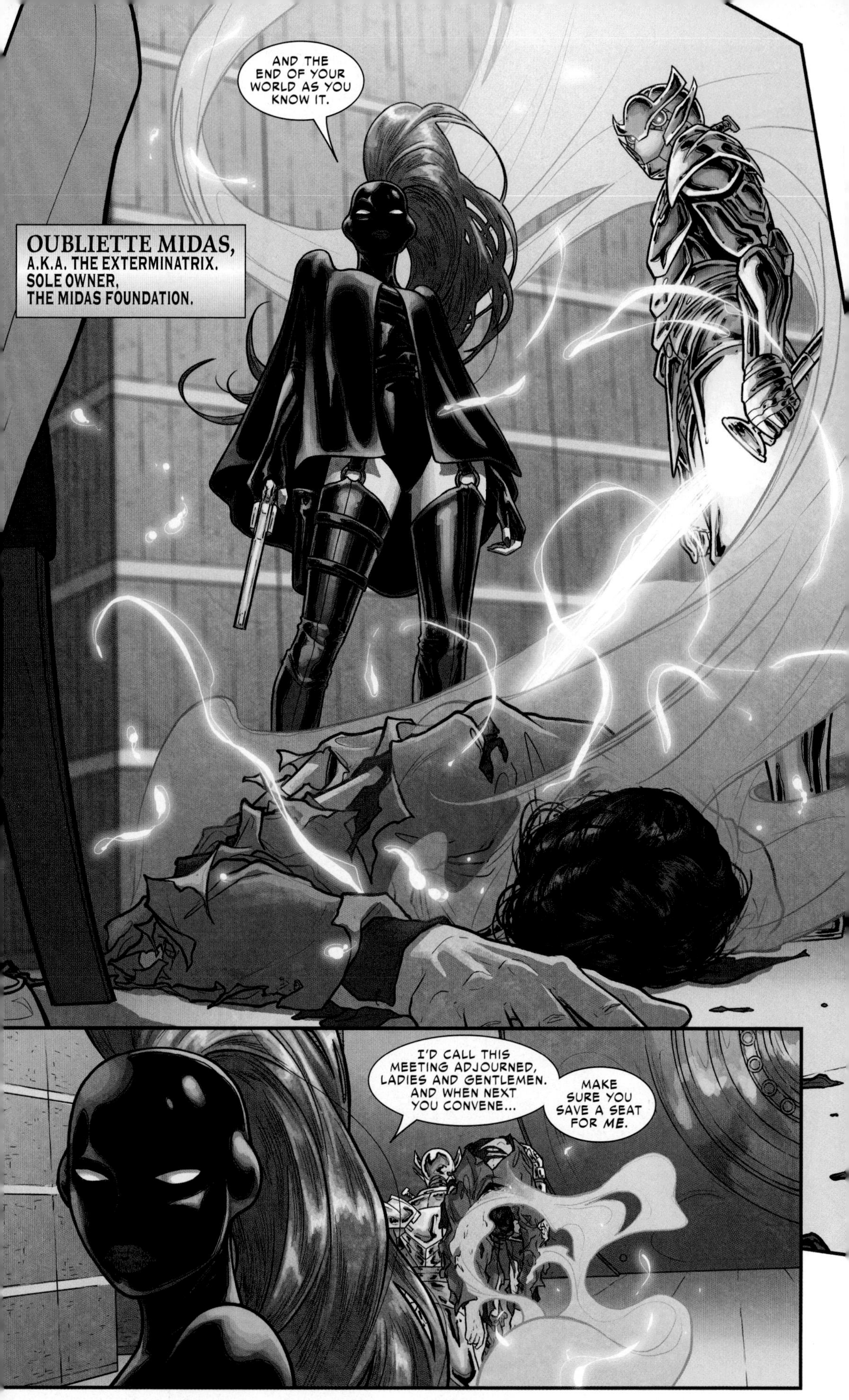
AND THE END OF YOUR WORLD AS YOU KNOW IT.
OUBLIETTE MIDAS, A.K.A. THE EXTERMINATRIX. SOLE OWNER, THE MIDAS FOUNDATION.
I'D CALL THIS MEETING ADJOURNED, LADIES AND GENTLEMEN. AND WHEN NEXT YOU CONVENE...
MAKE SURE YOU SAVE A SEAT FOR *ME*.

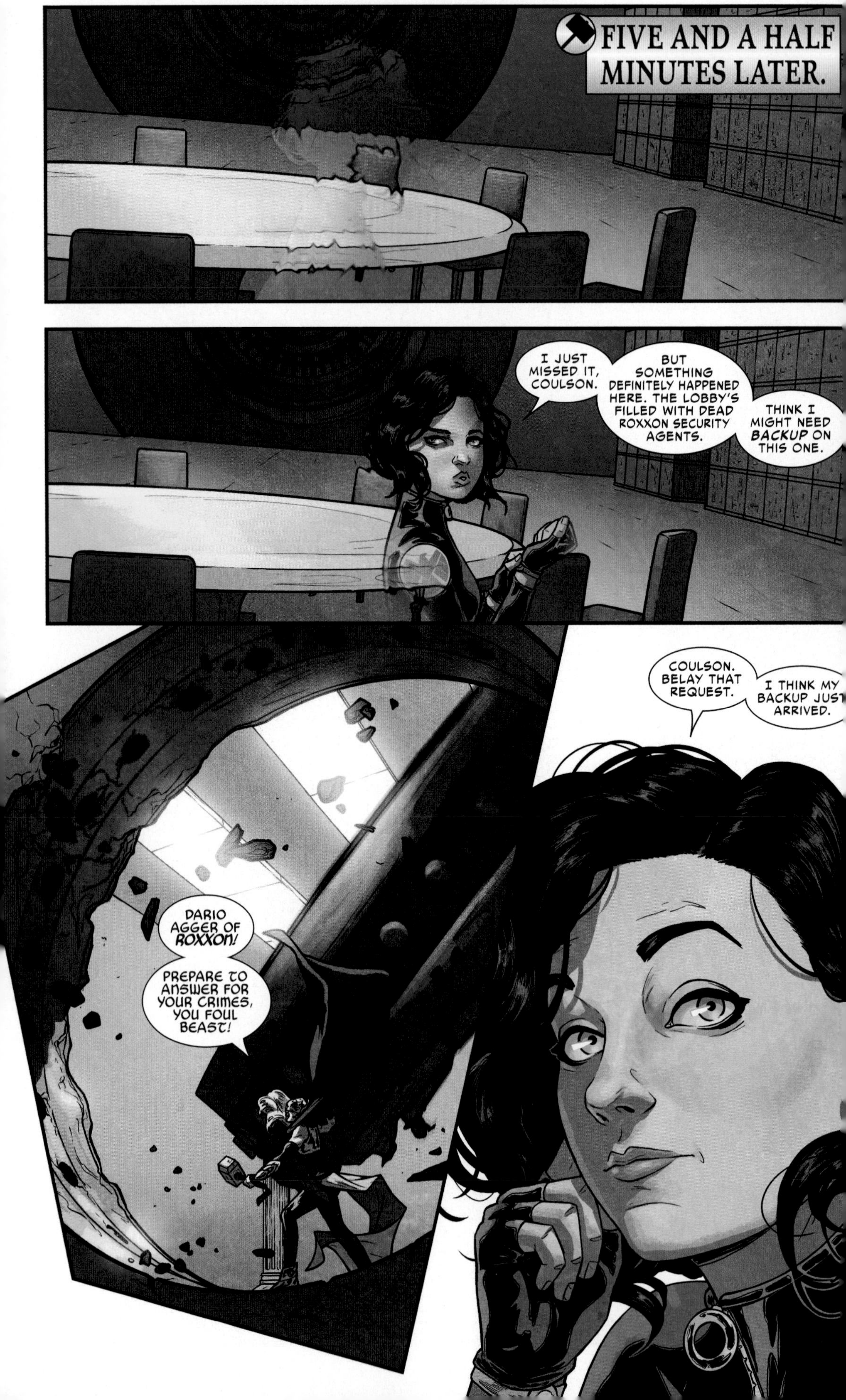
FIVE AND A HALF MINUTES LATER.
I JUST MISSED IT, COULSON.
BUT SOMETHING DEFINITELY HAPPENED HERE. THE LOBBY'S FILLED WITH DEAD ROXXON SECURITY AGENTS.
THINK I MIGHT NEED BACKUP ON THIS ONE.
COULSON. BELAY THAT REQUEST.
I THINK MY BACKUP JUST ARRIVED.
DARIO AGGER OF ROXXON!
PREPARE TO ANSWER FOR YOUR CRIMES, YOU FOUL BEAST!

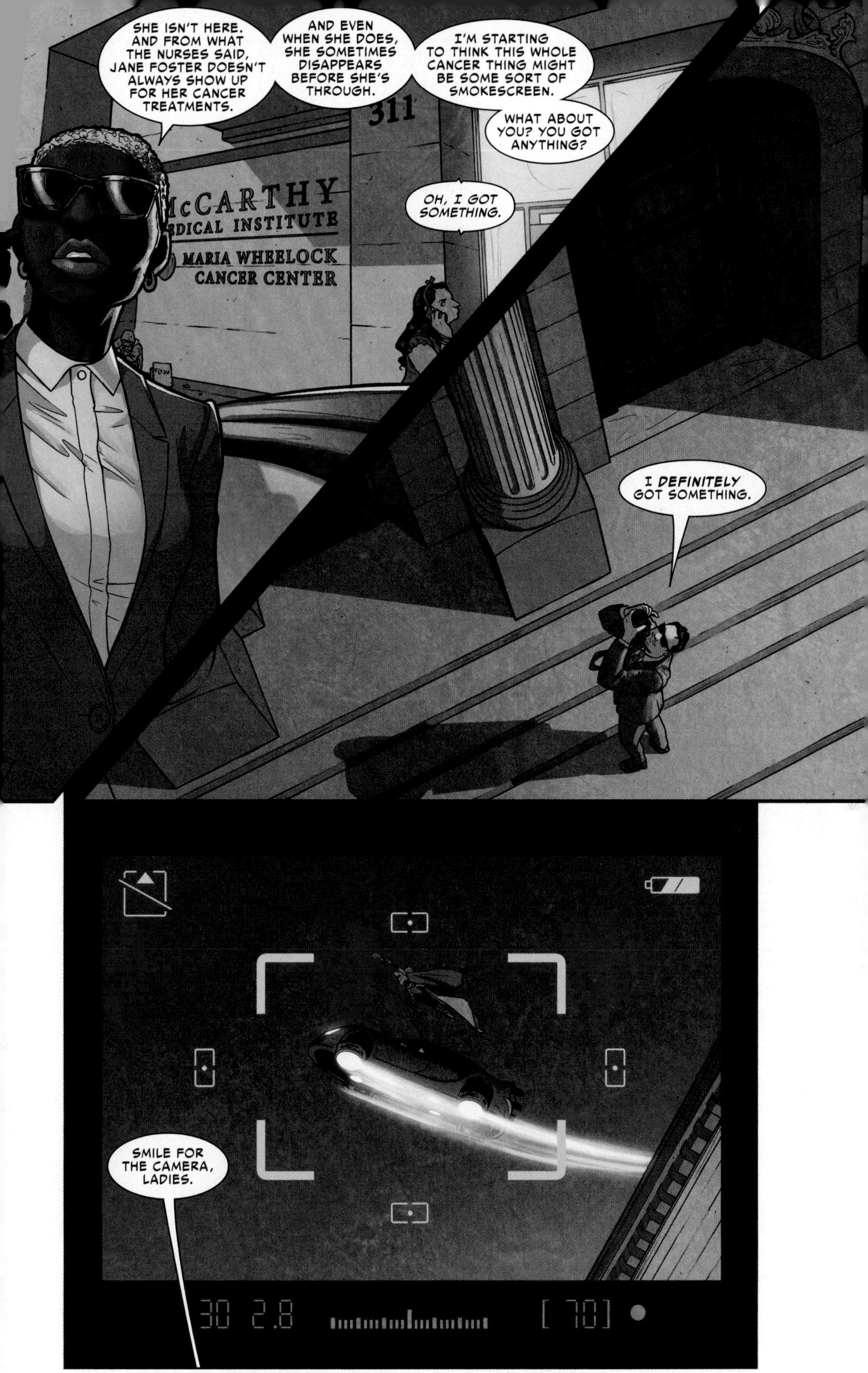
SHE ISN'T HERE. AND FROM WHAT THE NURSES SAID, JANE FOSTER DOESN'T ALWAYS SHOW UP FOR HER CANCER TREATMENTS.
AND EVEN WHEN SHE DOES, SHE SOMETIMES DISAPPEARS BEFORE SHE'S THROUGH.
I'M STARTING TO THINK THIS WHOLE CANCER THING MIGHT BE SOME SORT OF SMOKESCREEN.
WHAT ABOUT YOU? YOU GOT ANYTHING?
311
McCARTHY
MEDICAL INSTITUTE
MARIA WHEELOCK
CANCER CENTER
OH, I GOT SOMETHING.
I DEFINITELY GOT SOMETHING.
SMILE FOR THE CAMERA, LADIES.
30 2.8
[70]

9

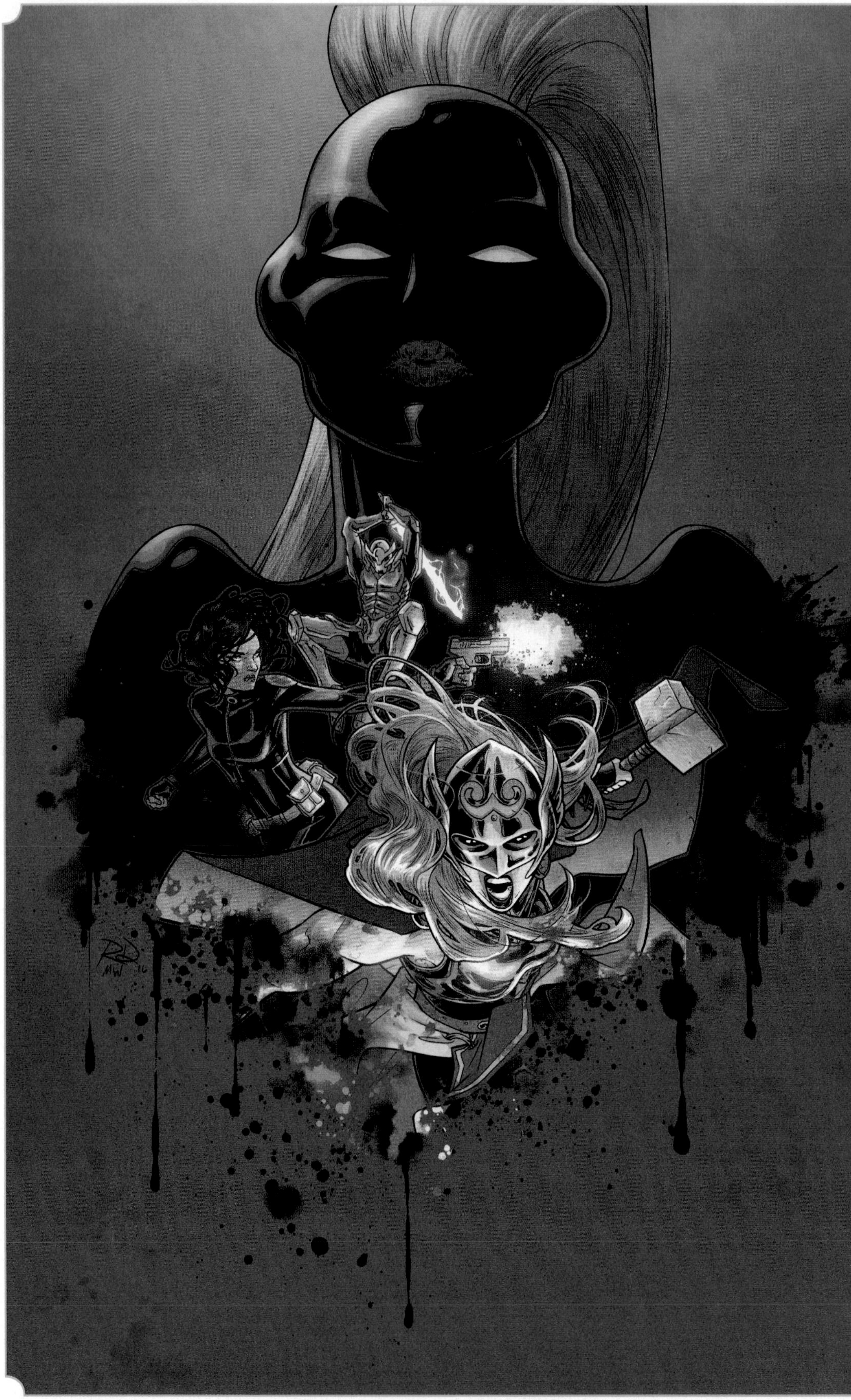

THE AGGER IMPERATIVE

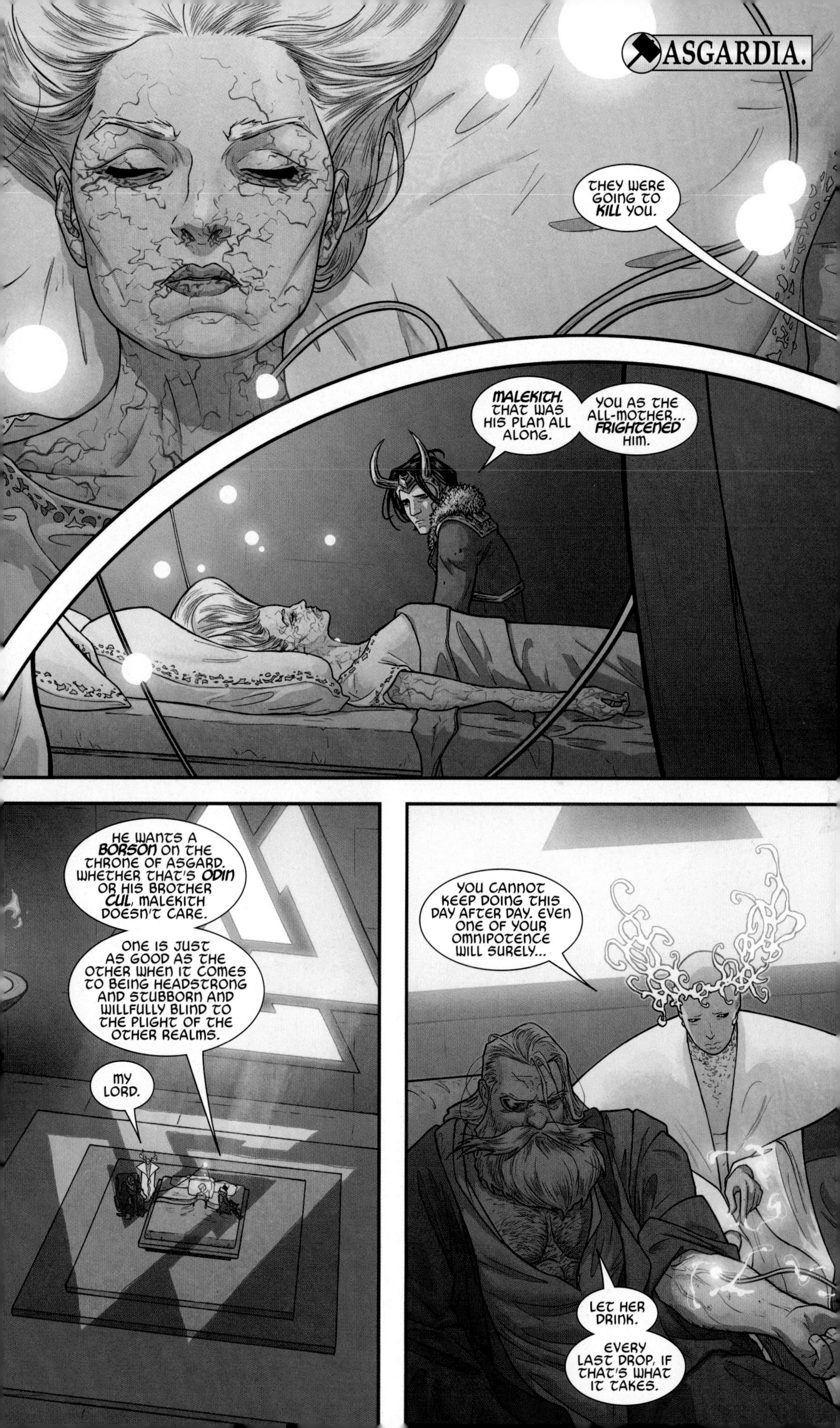
ASGARDIA.
THEY WERE GOING TO KILL YOU.
MALEKITH. THAT WAS HIS PLAN ALL ALONG.
YOU AS THE ALL-MOTHER... FRIGHTENED HIM.
HE WANTS A BORSON ON THE THRONE OF ASGARD. WHETHER THAT'S ODIN OR HIS BROTHER CUL, MALEKITH DOESN'T CARE.
ONE IS JUST AS GOOD AS THE OTHER WHEN IT COMES TO BEING HEADSTRONG AND STUBBORN AND WILLFULLY BLIND TO THE PLIGHT OF THE OTHER REALMS.
MY LORD.
YOU CANNOT KEEP DOING THIS DAY AFTER DAY. EVEN ONE OF YOUR OMNIPOTENCE WILL SURELY...
LET HER DRINK.
EVERY LAST DROP, IF THAT'S WHAT IT TAKES.

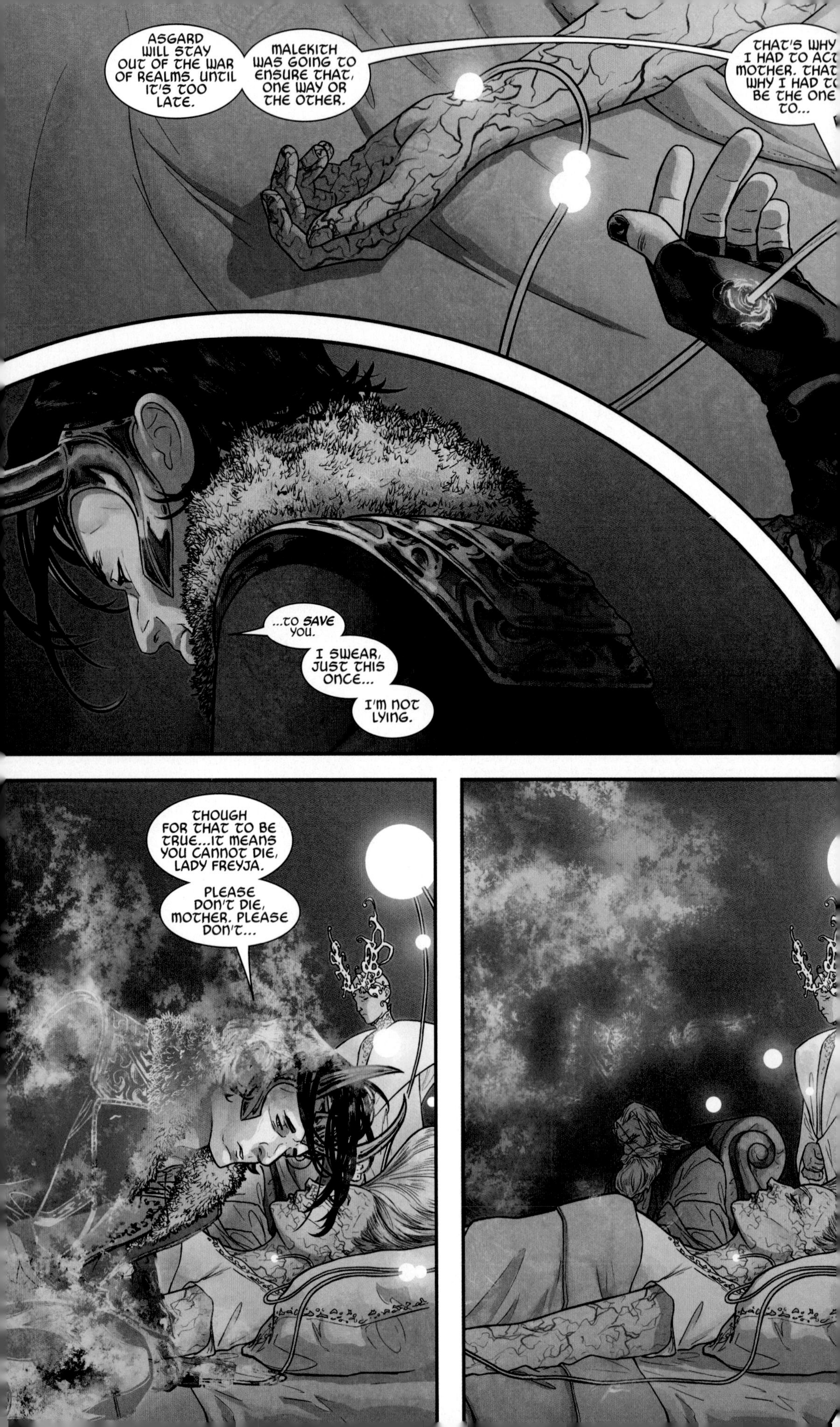
ASGARD WILL STAY OUT OF THE WAR OF REALMS. UNTIL IT'S TOO LATE.
MALEKITH WAS GOING TO ENSURE THAT, ONE WAY OR THE OTHER.
THAT'S WHY I HAD TO ACT, MOTHER. THAT'S WHY I HAD TO BE THE ONE TO...
...TO SAVE YOU.
I SWEAR, JUST THIS ONCE...
I'M NOT LYING.
THOUGH FOR THAT TO BE TRUE...IT MEANS YOU CANNOT DIE, LADY FREYJA.
PLEASE DON'T DIE, MOTHER. PLEASE DON'T...

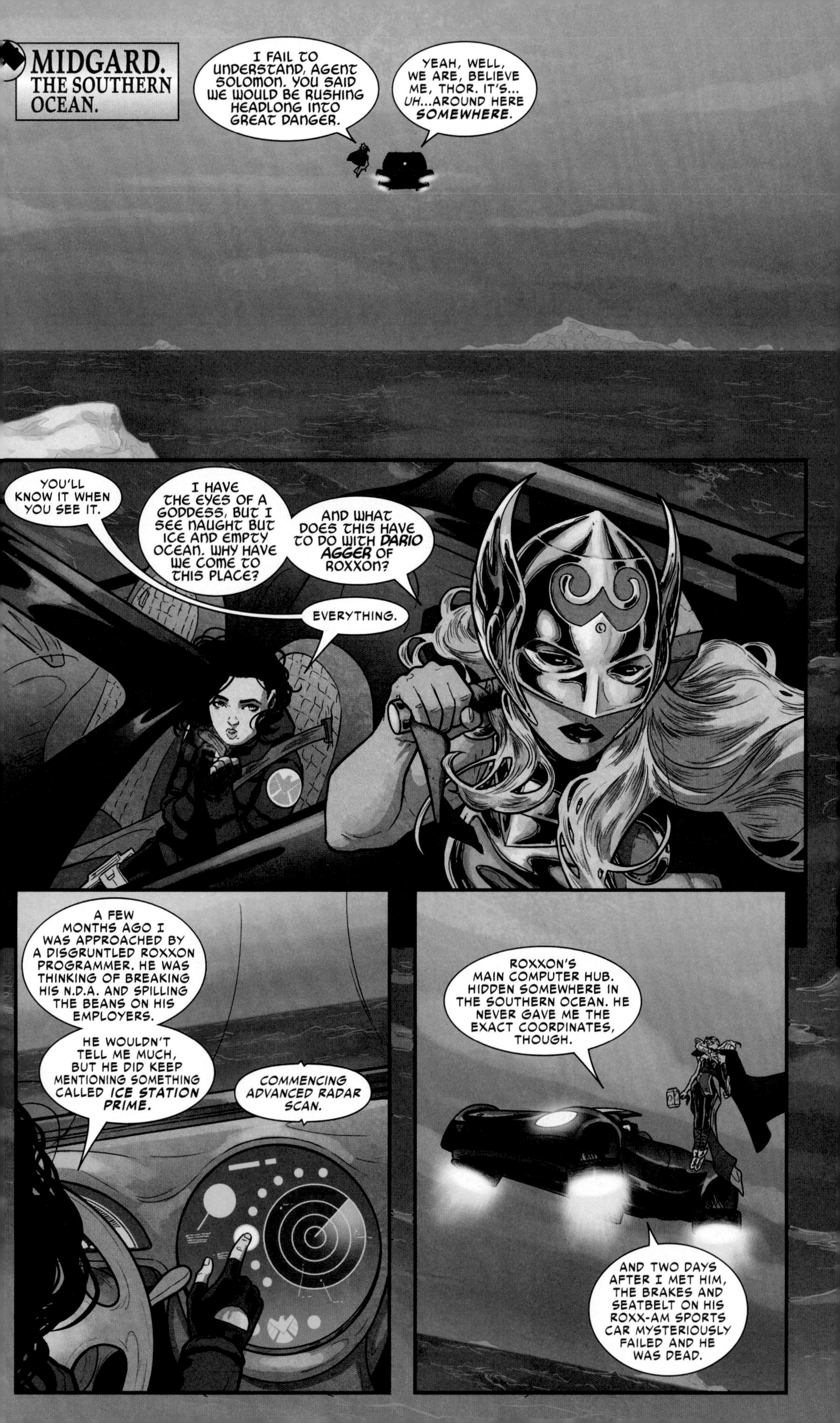
MIDGARD. THE SOUTHERN OCEAN.
I FAIL TO UNDERSTAND, AGENT SOLOMON. YOU SAID WE WOULD BE RUSHING HEADLONG INTO GREAT DANGER.
YEAH, WELL, WE ARE, BELIEVE ME, THOR. IT'S... UH...AROUND HERE *SOMEWHERE*.
I HAVE THE EYES OF A GODDESS, BUT I SEE NAUGHT BUT ICE AND EMPTY OCEAN. WHY HAVE WE COME TO THIS PLACE?
YOU'LL KNOW IT WHEN YOU SEE IT.
AND WHAT DOES THIS HAVE TO DO WITH *DARIO AGGER* OF ROXXON?
EVERYTHING.
A FEW MONTHS AGO I WAS APPROACHED BY A DISGRUNTLED ROXXON PROGRAMMER. HE WAS THINKING OF BREAKING HIS N.D.A. AND SPILLING THE BEANS ON HIS EMPLOYERS.
HE WOULDN'T TELL ME MUCH, BUT HE DID KEEP MENTIONING SOMETHING CALLED *ICE STATION PRIME*.
COMMENCING ADVANCED RADAR SCAN.
ROXXON'S MAIN COMPUTER HUB. HIDDEN SOMEWHERE IN THE SOUTHERN OCEAN. HE NEVER GAVE ME THE EXACT COORDINATES, THOUGH.
AND TWO DAYS AFTER I MET HIM, THE BRAKES AND SEATBELT ON HIS ROXX-AM SPORTS CAR MYSTERIOUSLY FAILED AND HE WAS DEAD.

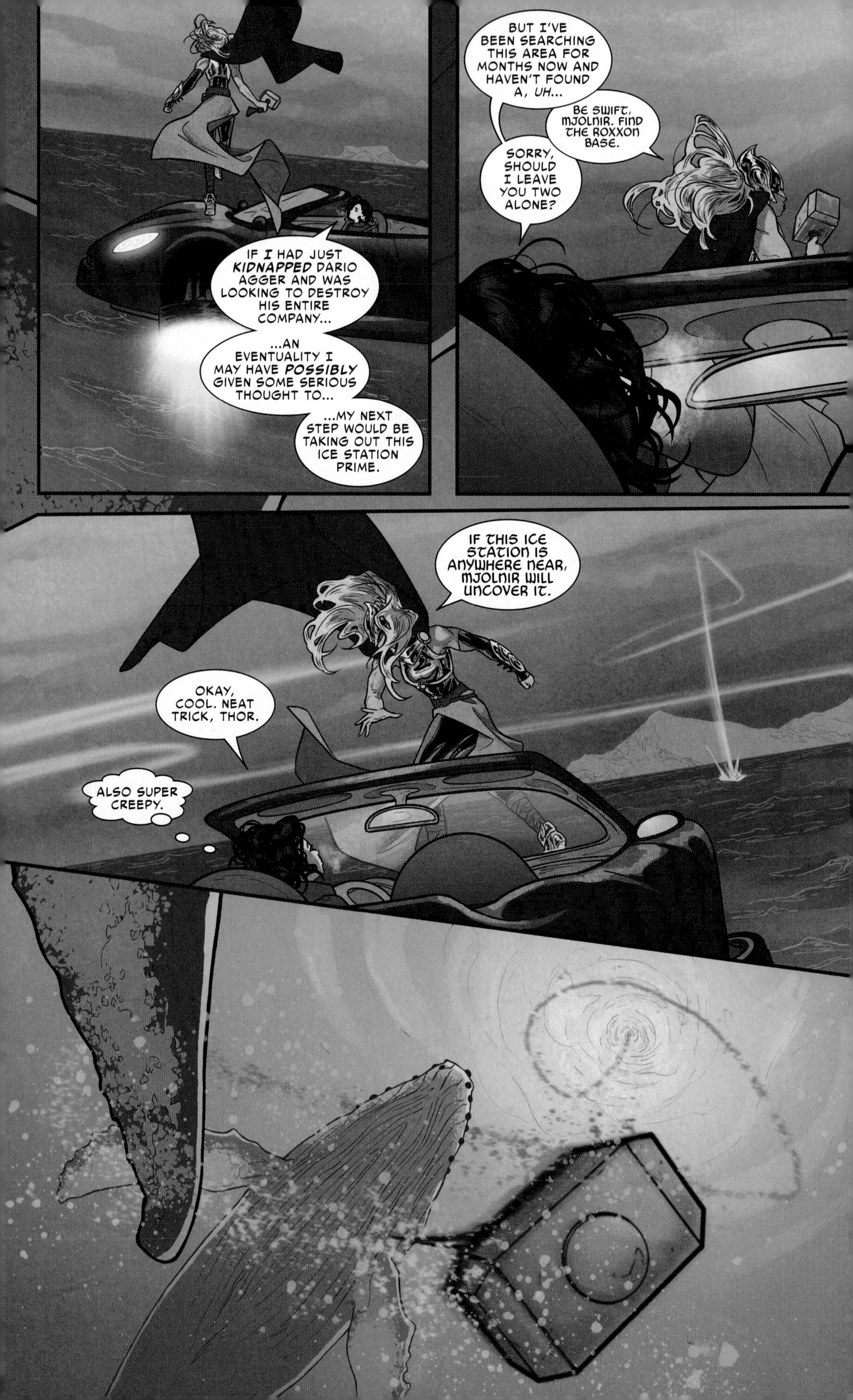
IF I HAD JUST KIDNAPPED DARIO AGGER AND WAS LOOKING TO DESTROY HIS ENTIRE COMPANY...
...AN EVENTUALITY I MAY HAVE POSSIBLY GIVEN SOME SERIOUS THOUGHT TO...
...MY NEXT STEP WOULD BE TAKING OUT THIS ICE STATION PRIME.
BUT I'VE BEEN SEARCHING THIS AREA FOR MONTHS NOW AND HAVEN'T FOUND A, UH...
BE SWIFT, MJOLNIR. FIND THE ROXXON BASE.
SORRY, SHOULD I LEAVE YOU TWO ALONE?
IF THIS ICE STATION IS ANYWHERE NEAR, MJOLNIR WILL UNCOVER IT.
OKAY, COOL. NEAT TRICK, THOR.
ALSO SUPER CREEPY.

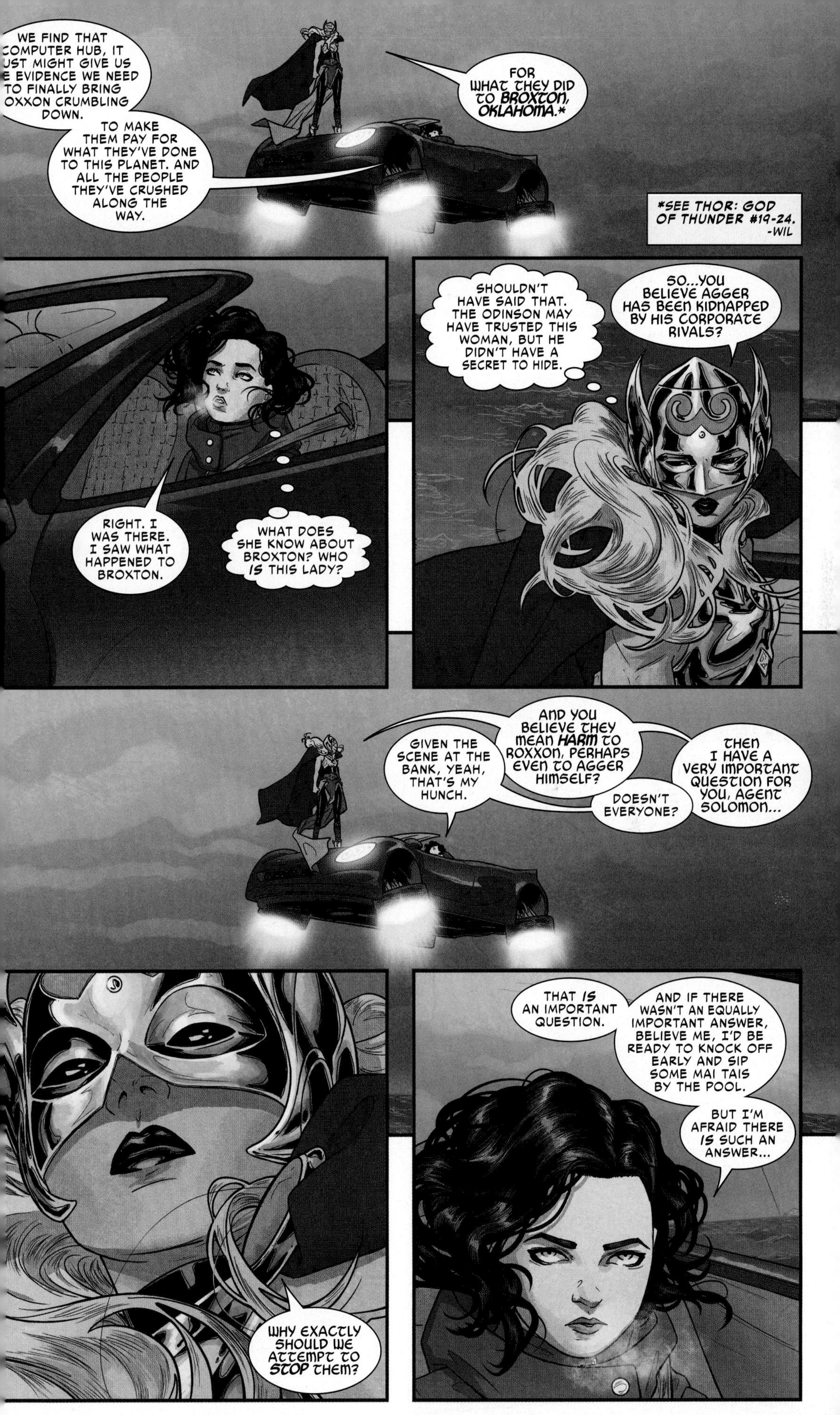
WE FIND THAT COMPUTER HUB, IT UST MIGHT GIVE US E EVIDENCE WE NEED TO FINALLY BRING OXXON CRUMBLING DOWN.
TO MAKE THEM PAY FOR WHAT THEY'VE DONE TO THIS PLANET. AND ALL THE PEOPLE THEY'VE CRUSHED ALONG THE WAY.
FOR WHAT THEY DID TO BROXTON, OKLAHOMA.*
*SEE THOR: GOD OF THUNDER #19-24. -WIL
RIGHT. I WAS THERE. I SAW WHAT HAPPENED TO BROXTON.
WHAT DOES SHE KNOW ABOUT BROXTON? WHO IS THIS LADY?
SHOULDN'T HAVE SAID THAT. THE ODINSON MAY HAVE TRUSTED THIS WOMAN, BUT HE DIDN'T HAVE A SECRET TO HIDE.
SO...YOU BELIEVE AGGER HAS BEEN KIDNAPPED BY HIS CORPORATE RIVALS?
GIVEN THE SCENE AT THE BANK, YEAH, THAT'S MY HUNCH.
AND YOU BELIEVE THEY MEAN HARM TO ROXXON, PERHAPS EVEN TO AGGER HIMSELF?
DOESN'T EVERYONE?
THEN I HAVE A VERY IMPORTANT QUESTION FOR YOU, AGENT SOLOMON...
WHY EXACTLY SHOULD WE ATTEMPT TO STOP THEM?
THAT IS AN IMPORTANT QUESTION.
AND IF THERE WASN'T AN EQUALLY IMPORTANT ANSWER, BELIEVE ME, I'D BE READY TO KNOCK OFF EARLY AND SIP SOME MAI TAIS BY THE POOL.
BUT I'M AFRAID THERE IS SUCH AN ANSWER...

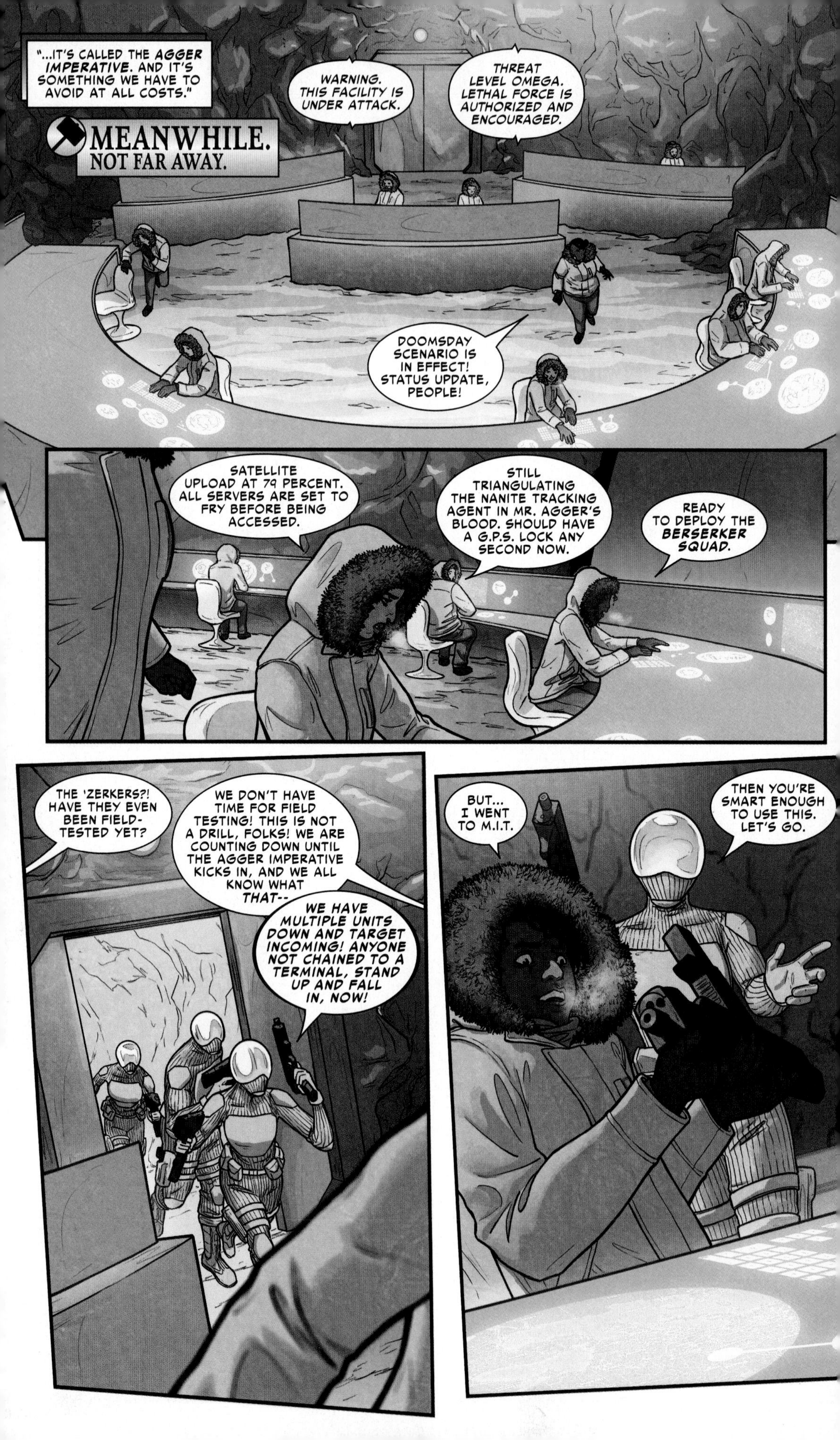
"...IT'S CALLED THE AGGER IMPERATIVE. AND IT'S SOMETHING WE HAVE TO AVOID AT ALL COSTS."
MEANWHILE. NOT FAR AWAY.
WARNING. THIS FACILITY IS UNDER ATTACK.
THREAT LEVEL OMEGA. LETHAL FORCE IS AUTHORIZED AND ENCOURAGED.
DOOMSDAY SCENARIO IS IN EFFECT! STATUS UPDATE, PEOPLE!
SATELLITE UPLOAD AT 79 PERCENT. ALL SERVERS ARE SET TO FRY BEFORE BEING ACCESSED.
STILL TRIANGULATING THE NANITE TRACKING AGENT IN MR. AGGER'S BLOOD. SHOULD HAVE A G.P.S. LOCK ANY SECOND NOW.
READY TO DEPLOY THE BERSERKER SQUAD.
THE 'ZERKERS?! HAVE THEY EVEN BEEN FIELD-TESTED YET?
WE DON'T HAVE TIME FOR FIELD TESTING! THIS IS NOT A DRILL, FOLKS! WE ARE COUNTING DOWN UNTIL THE AGGER IMPERATIVE KICKS IN, AND WE ALL KNOW WHAT THAT--
WE HAVE MULTIPLE UNITS DOWN AND TARGET INCOMING! ANYONE NOT CHAINED TO A TERMINAL, STAND UP AND FALL IN, NOW!
BUT... I WENT TO M.I.T.
THEN YOU'RE SMART ENOUGH TO USE THIS. LET'S GO.

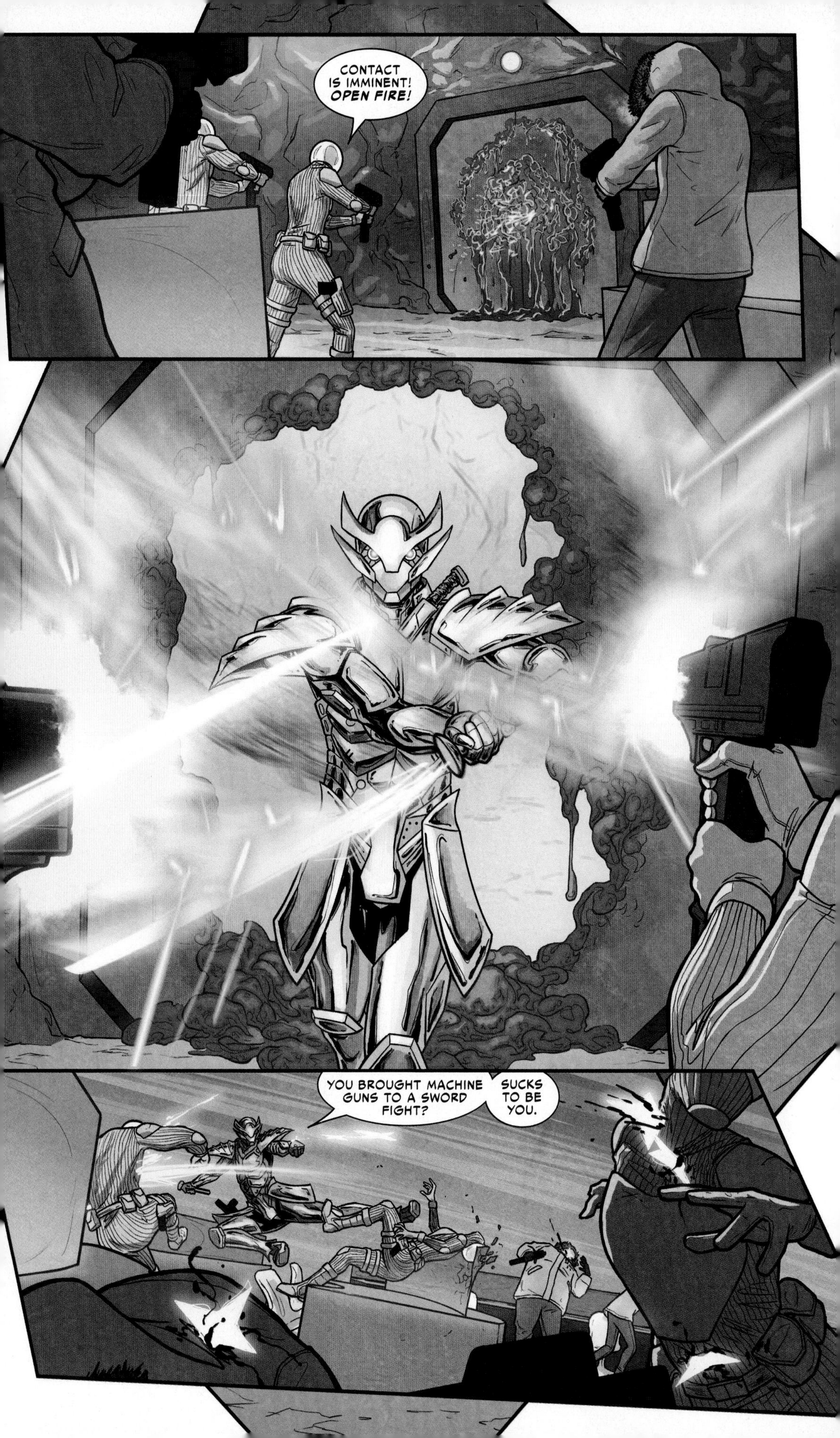
CONTACT IS IMMINENT! OPEN FIRE!
YOU BROUGHT MACHINE GUNS TO A SWORD FIGHT?
SUCKS TO BE YOU.

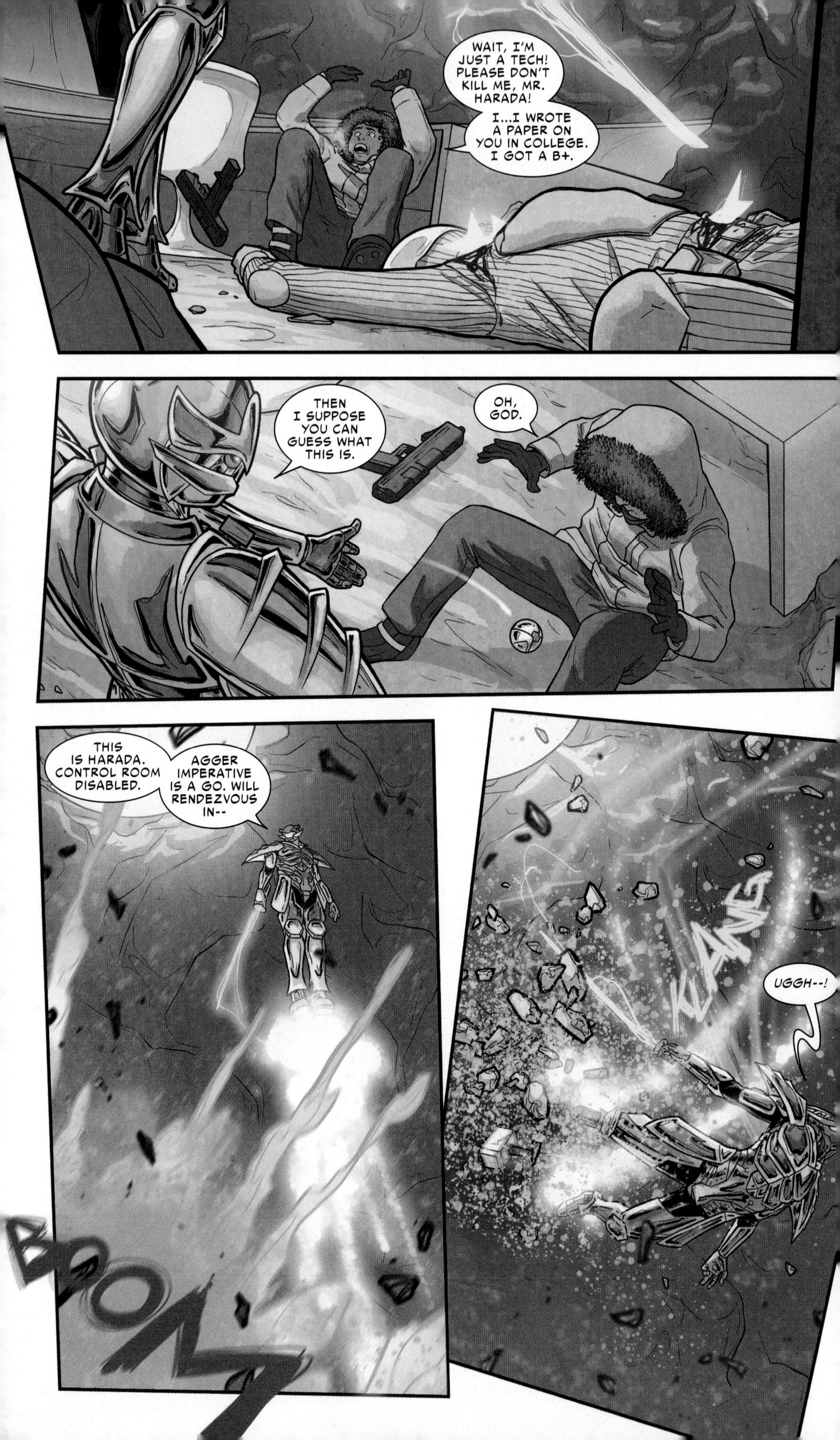
WAIT, I'M JUST A TECH! PLEASE DON'T KILL ME, MR. HARADA!
I...I WROTE A PAPER ON YOU IN COLLEGE. I GOT A B+.
THEN I SUPPOSE YOU CAN GUESS WHAT THIS IS.
OH, GOD.
THIS IS HARADA. CONTROL ROOM DISABLED.
AGGER IMPERATIVE IS A GO. WILL RENDEZVOUS IN--
BOOM
KLANG
UGGH--!

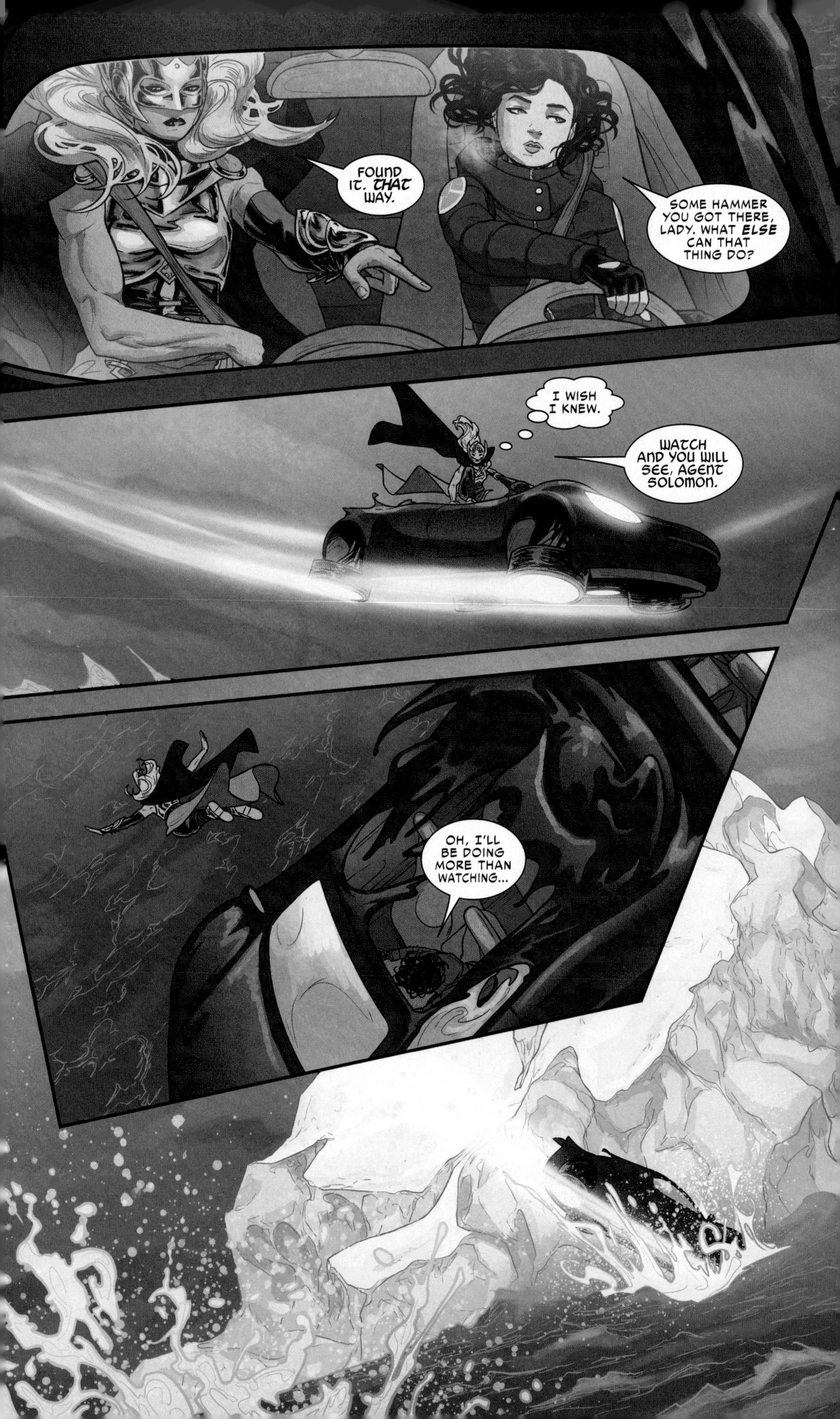
FOUND IT. THAT WAY.
SOME HAMMER YOU GOT THERE, LADY. WHAT ELSE CAN THAT THING DO?
I WISH I KNEW.
WATCH AND YOU WILL SEE, AGENT SOLOMON.
OH, I'LL BE DOING MORE THAN WATCHING...

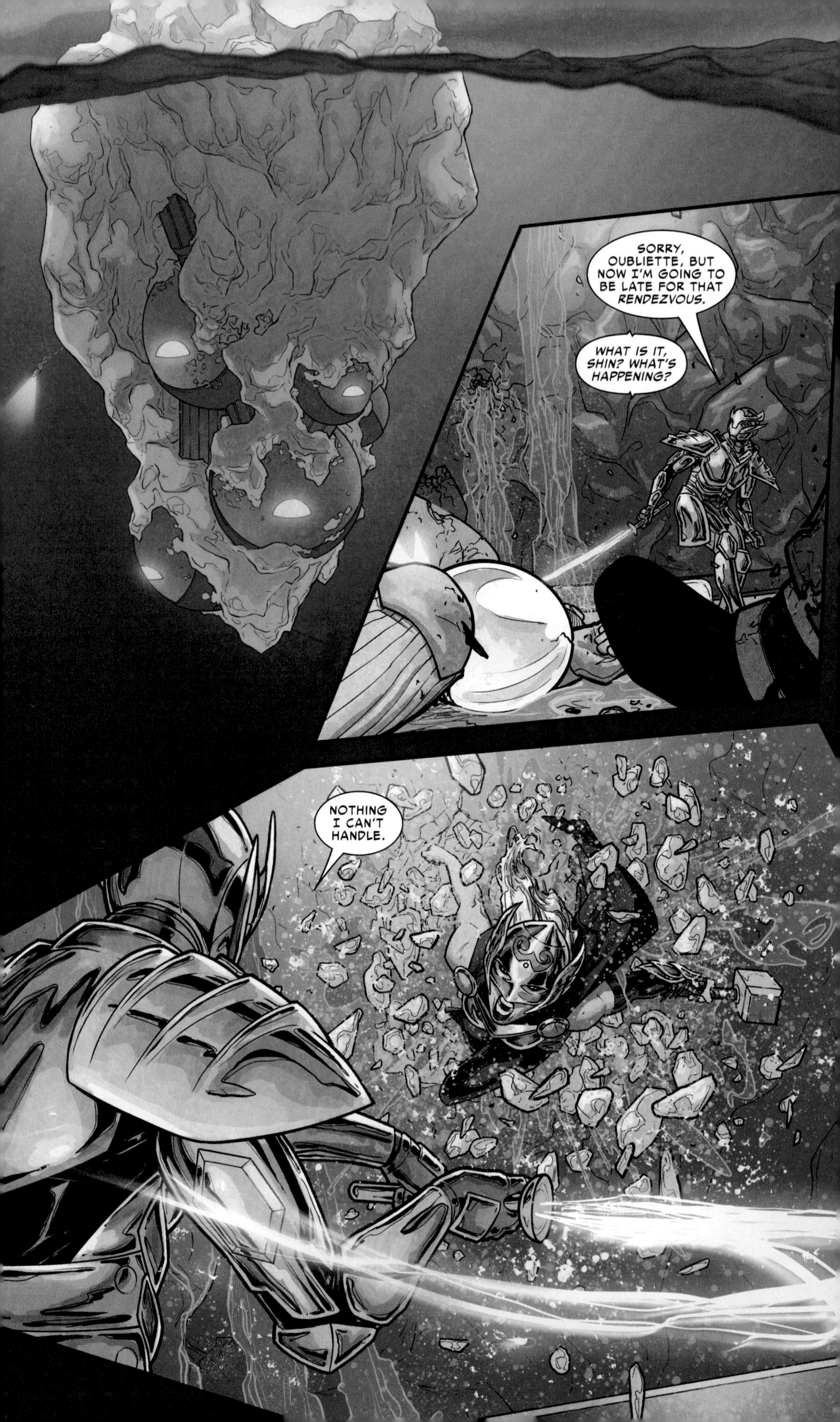
SORRY, OUBLIETTE, BUT NOW I'M GOING TO BE LATE FOR THAT RENDEZVOUS.
WHAT IS IT, SHIN? WHAT'S HAPPENING?
NOTHING I CAN'T HANDLE.

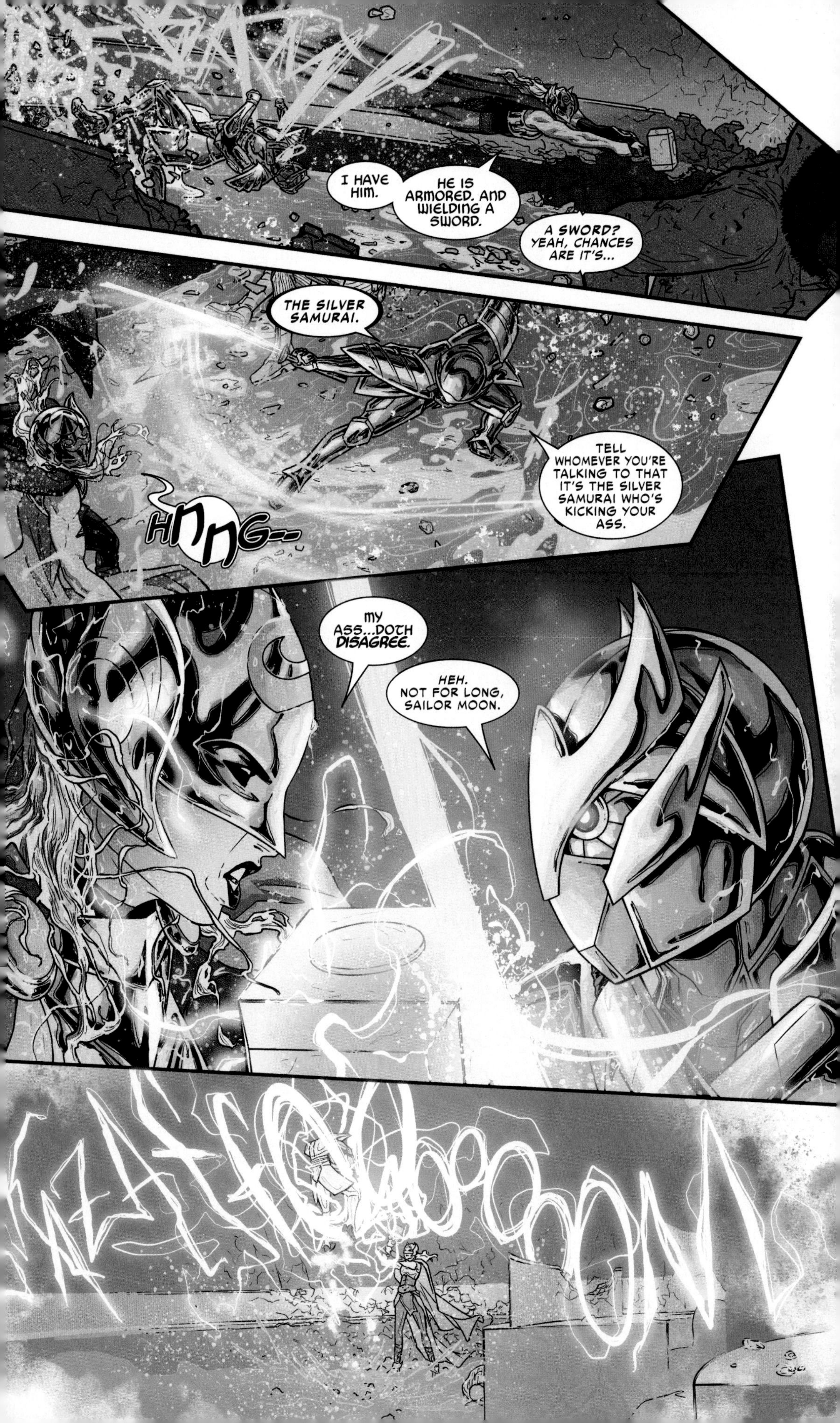
I HAVE HIM.
HE IS ARMORED. AND WIELDING A SWORD.
A SWORD? YEAH, CHANCES ARE IT'S...
THE SILVER SAMURAI.
TELL WHOMEVER YOU'RE TALKING TO THAT IT'S THE SILVER SAMURAI WHO'S KICKING YOUR ASS.
HNNG--
MY ASS...DOTH DISAGREE.
HEH. NOT FOR LONG, SAILOR MOON.

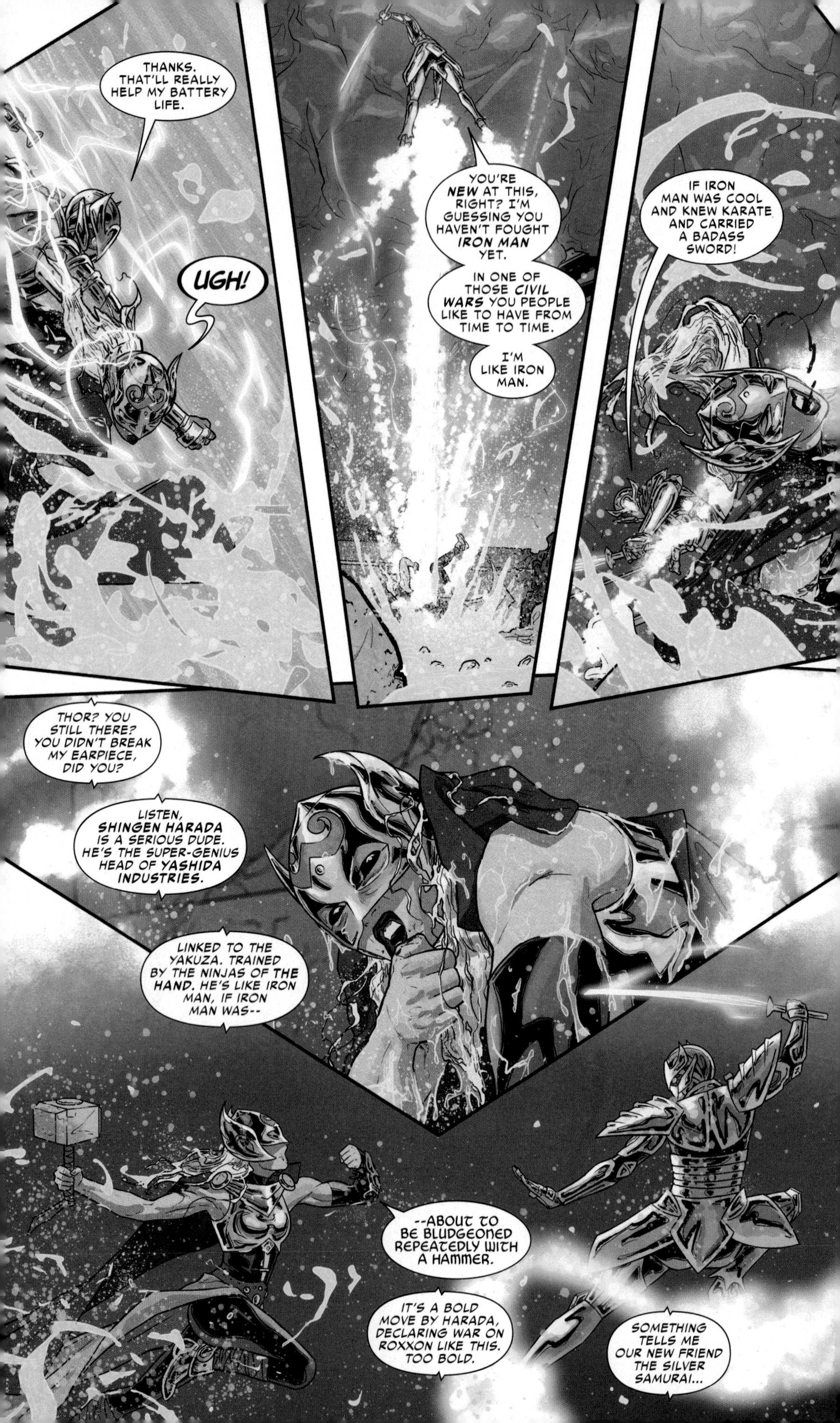
THANKS. THAT'LL REALLY HELP MY BATTERY LIFE.
UGH!
YOU'RE NEW AT THIS, RIGHT? I'M GUESSING YOU HAVEN'T FOUGHT IRON MAN YET.
IN ONE OF THOSE CIVIL WARS YOU PEOPLE LIKE TO HAVE FROM TIME TO TIME.
I'M LIKE IRON MAN.
IF IRON MAN WAS COOL AND KNEW KARATE AND CARRIED A BADASS SWORD!
THOR? YOU STILL THERE? YOU DIDN'T BREAK MY EARPIECE, DID YOU?
LISTEN, SHINGEN HARADA IS A SERIOUS DUDE. HE'S THE SUPER-GENIUS HEAD OF YASHIDA INDUSTRIES.
LINKED TO THE YAKUZA. TRAINED BY THE NINJAS OF THE HAND. HE'S LIKE IRON MAN, IF IRON MAN WAS--
--ABOUT TO BE BLUDGEONED REPEATEDLY WITH A HAMMER.
IT'S A BOLD MOVE BY HARADA, DECLARING WAR ON ROXXON LIKE THIS. TOO BOLD.
SOMETHING TELLS ME OUR NEW FRIEND THE SILVER SAMURAI...

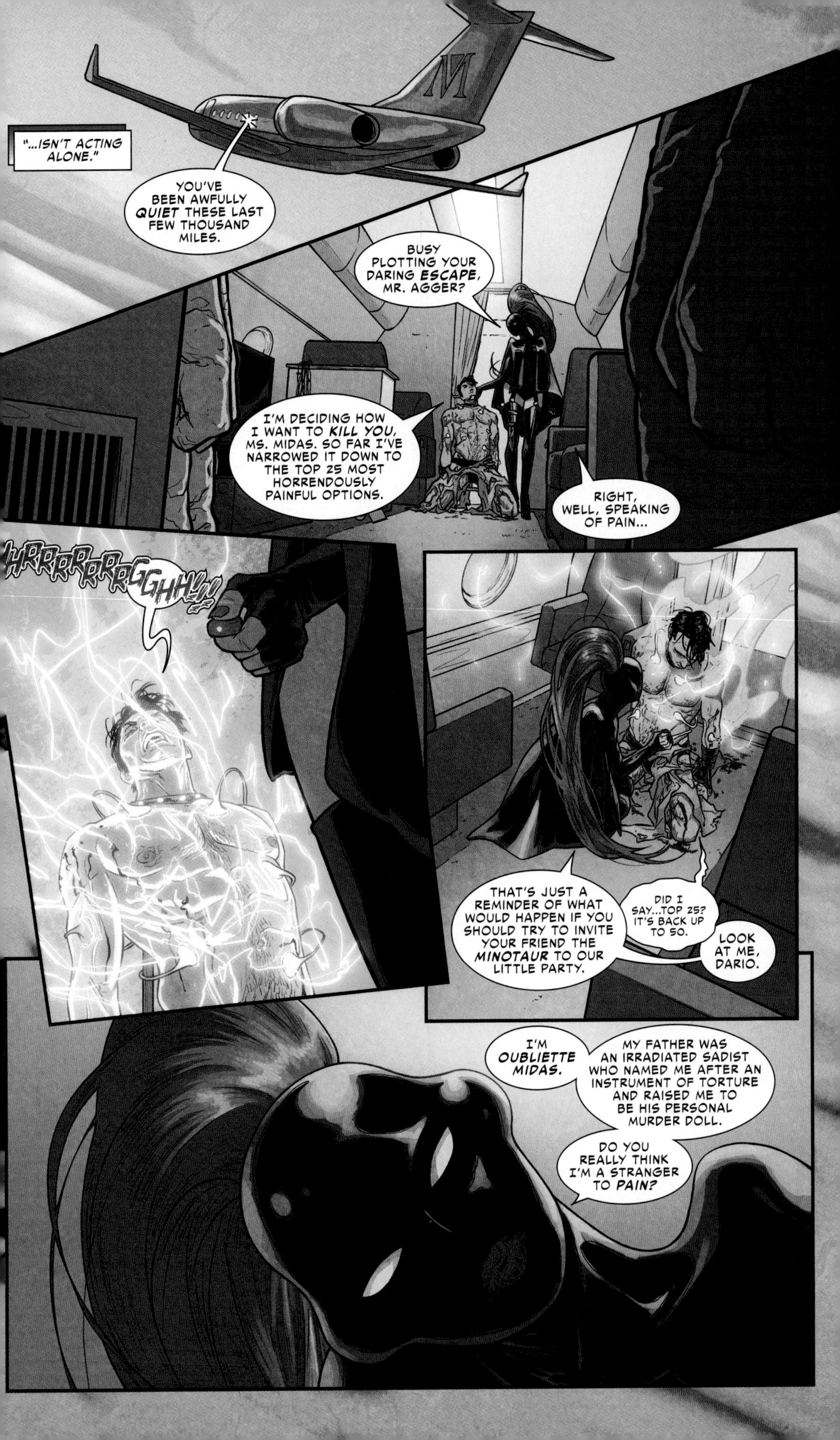
"...ISN'T ACTING ALONE."
YOU'VE BEEN AWFULLY QUIET THESE LAST FEW THOUSAND MILES.
BUSY PLOTTING YOUR DARING ESCAPE, MR. AGGER?
I'M DECIDING HOW I WANT TO KILL YOU, MS. MIDAS. SO FAR I'VE NARROWED IT DOWN TO THE TOP 25 MOST HORRENDOUSLY PAINFUL OPTIONS.
RIGHT, WELL, SPEAKING OF PAIN...
HRRRRRRRGGHH!!!
THAT'S JUST A REMINDER OF WHAT WOULD HAPPEN IF YOU SHOULD TRY TO INVITE YOUR FRIEND THE MINOTAUR TO OUR LITTLE PARTY.
DID I SAY...TOP 25? IT'S BACK UP TO 50.
LOOK AT ME, DARIO.
I'M OUBLIETTE MIDAS.
MY FATHER WAS AN IRRADIATED SADIST WHO NAMED ME AFTER AN INSTRUMENT OF TORTURE AND RAISED ME TO BE HIS PERSONAL MURDER DOLL.
DO YOU REALLY THINK I'M A STRANGER TO PAIN?

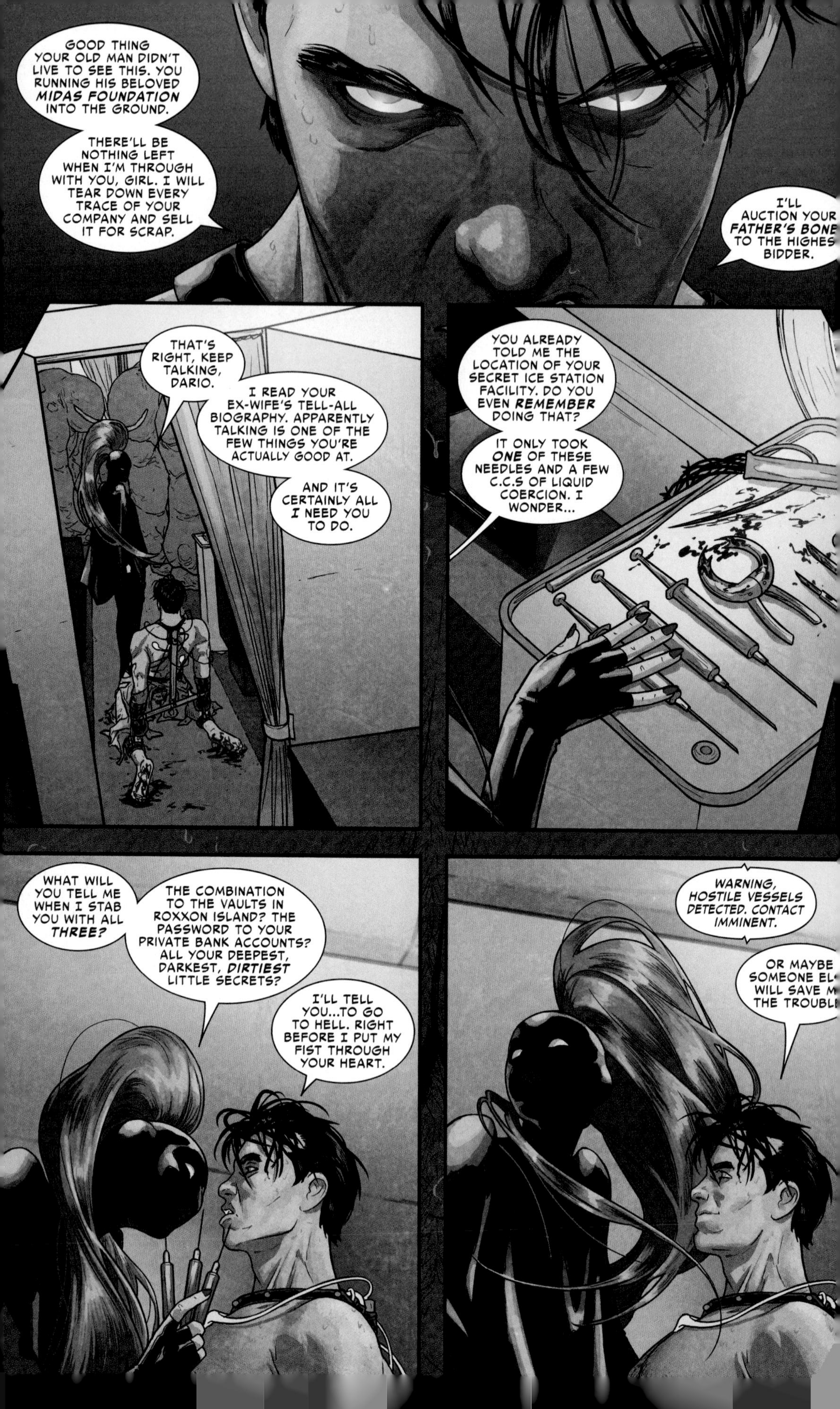
GOOD THING YOUR OLD MAN DIDN'T LIVE TO SEE THIS. YOU RUNNING HIS BELOVED MIDAS FOUNDATION INTO THE GROUND.
THERE'LL BE NOTHING LEFT WHEN I'M THROUGH WITH YOU, GIRL. I WILL TEAR DOWN EVERY TRACE OF YOUR COMPANY AND SELL IT FOR SCRAP.
I'LL AUCTION YOUR FATHER'S BONE TO THE HIGHES BIDDER.
THAT'S RIGHT, KEEP TALKING, DARIO.
I READ YOUR EX-WIFE'S TELL-ALL BIOGRAPHY. APPARENTLY TALKING IS ONE OF THE FEW THINGS YOU'RE ACTUALLY GOOD AT.
AND IT'S CERTAINLY ALL I NEED YOU TO DO.
YOU ALREADY TOLD ME THE LOCATION OF YOUR SECRET ICE STATION FACILITY. DO YOU EVEN REMEMBER DOING THAT?
IT ONLY TOOK ONE OF THESE NEEDLES AND A FEW C.C.S OF LIQUID COERCION. I WONDER...
WHAT WILL YOU TELL ME WHEN I STAB YOU WITH ALL THREE?
THE COMBINATION TO THE VAULTS IN ROXXON ISLAND? THE PASSWORD TO YOUR PRIVATE BANK ACCOUNTS? ALL YOUR DEEPEST, DARKEST, DIRTIEST LITTLE SECRETS?
I'LL TELL YOU...TO GO TO HELL. RIGHT BEFORE I PUT MY FIST THROUGH YOUR HEART.
WARNING, HOSTILE VESSELS DETECTED. CONTACT IMMINENT.
OR MAYBE SOMEONE EL WILL SAVE M THE TROUBL

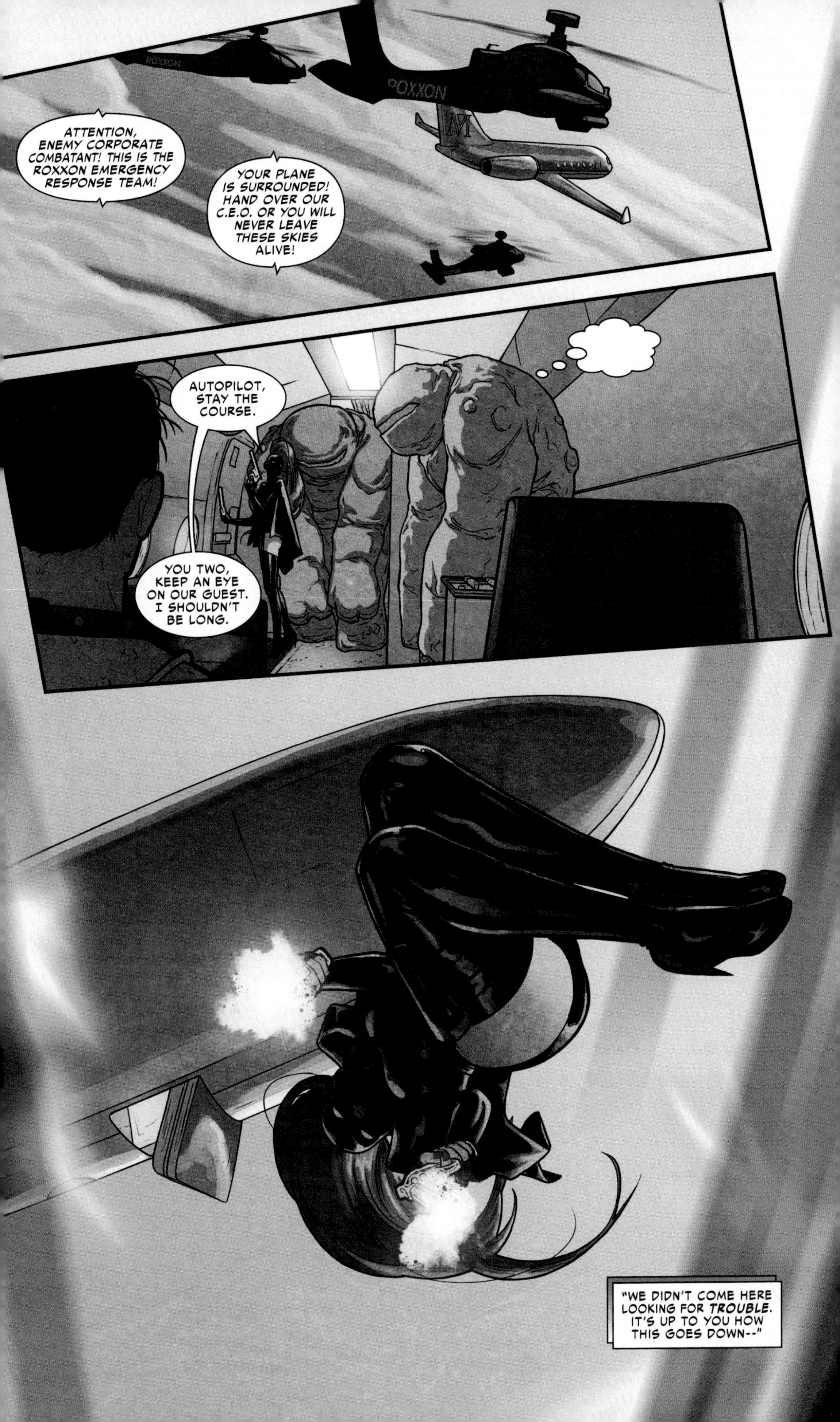
ROXXON
ROXXON
ATTENTION, ENEMY CORPORATE COMBATANT! THIS IS THE ROXXON EMERGENCY RESPONSE TEAM!
YOUR PLANE IS SURROUNDED! HAND OVER OUR C.E.O. OR YOU WILL NEVER LEAVE THESE SKIES ALIVE!
AUTOPILOT, STAY THE COURSE.
YOU TWO, KEEP AN EYE ON OUR GUEST. I SHOULDN'T BE LONG.
"WE DIDN'T COME HERE LOOKING FOR TROUBLE. IT'S UP TO YOU HOW THIS GOES DOWN--"

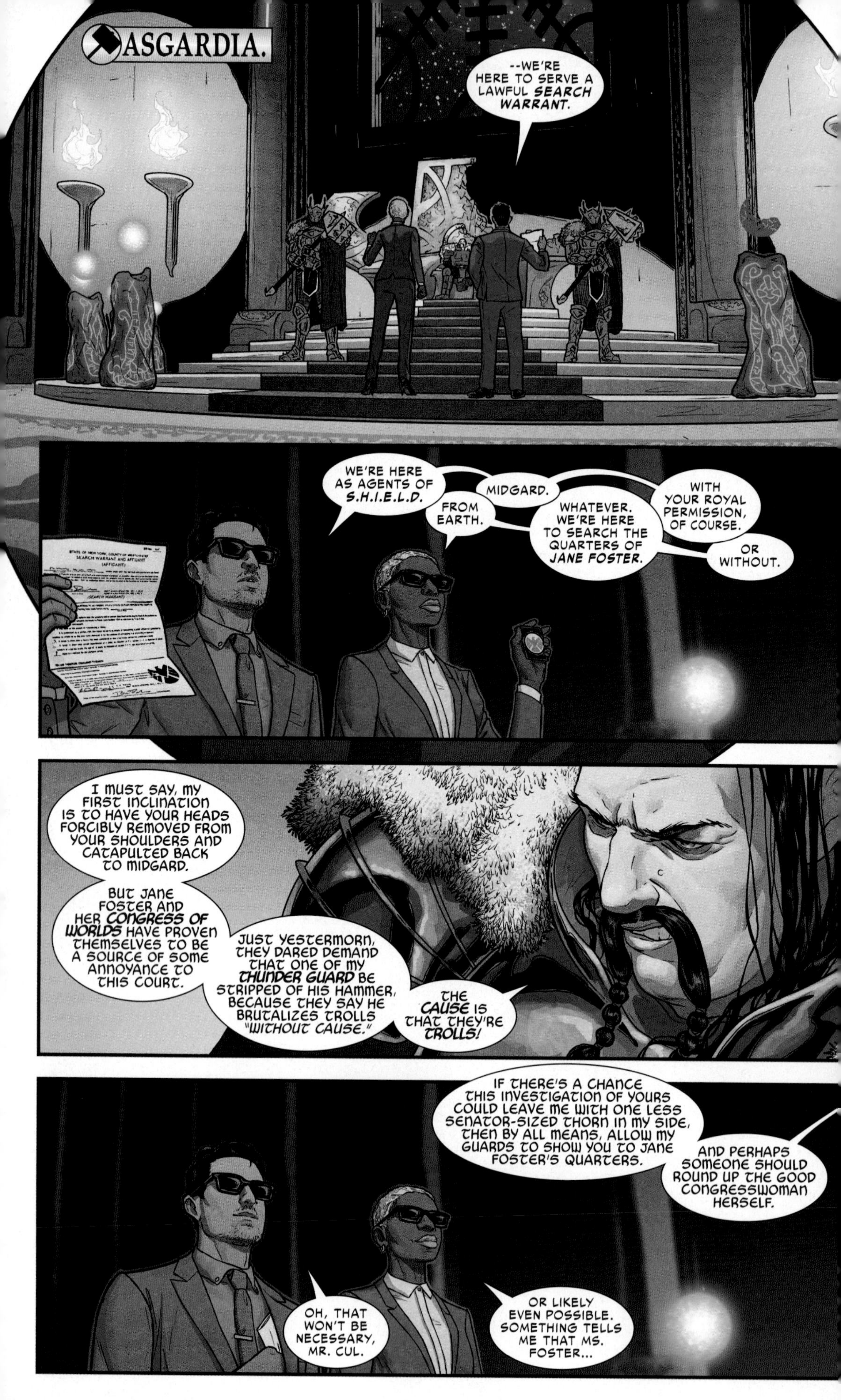
ASGARDIA.
--WE'RE HERE TO SERVE A LAWFUL SEARCH WARRANT.
WE'RE HERE AS AGENTS OF S.H.I.E.L.D.
FROM EARTH.
MIDGARD.
WHATEVER. WE'RE HERE TO SEARCH THE QUARTERS OF JANE FOSTER.
WITH YOUR ROYAL PERMISSION, OF COURSE.
OR WITHOUT.
SEARCH WARRANT AND AFFIDAVIT
I MUST SAY, MY FIRST INCLINATION IS TO HAVE YOUR HEADS FORCIBLY REMOVED FROM YOUR SHOULDERS AND CATAPULTED BACK TO MIDGARD.
BUT JANE FOSTER AND HER CONGRESS OF WORLDS HAVE PROVEN THEMSELVES TO BE A SOURCE OF SOME ANNOYANCE TO THIS COURT.
JUST YESTERMORN, THEY DARED DEMAND THAT ONE OF MY THUNDER GUARD BE STRIPPED OF HIS HAMMER, BECAUSE THEY SAY HE BRUTALIZES TROLLS "WITHOUT CAUSE."
THE CAUSE IS THAT THEY'RE TROLLS!
IF THERE'S A CHANCE THIS INVESTIGATION OF YOURS COULD LEAVE ME WITH ONE LESS SENATOR-SIZED THORN IN MY SIDE, THEN BY ALL MEANS, ALLOW MY GUARDS TO SHOW YOU TO JANE FOSTER'S QUARTERS.
AND PERHAPS SOMEONE SHOULD ROUND UP THE GOOD CONGRESSWOMAN HERSELF.
OH, THAT WON'T BE NECESSARY, MR. CUL.
OR LIKELY EVEN POSSIBLE. SOMETHING TELLS ME THAT MS. FOSTER...

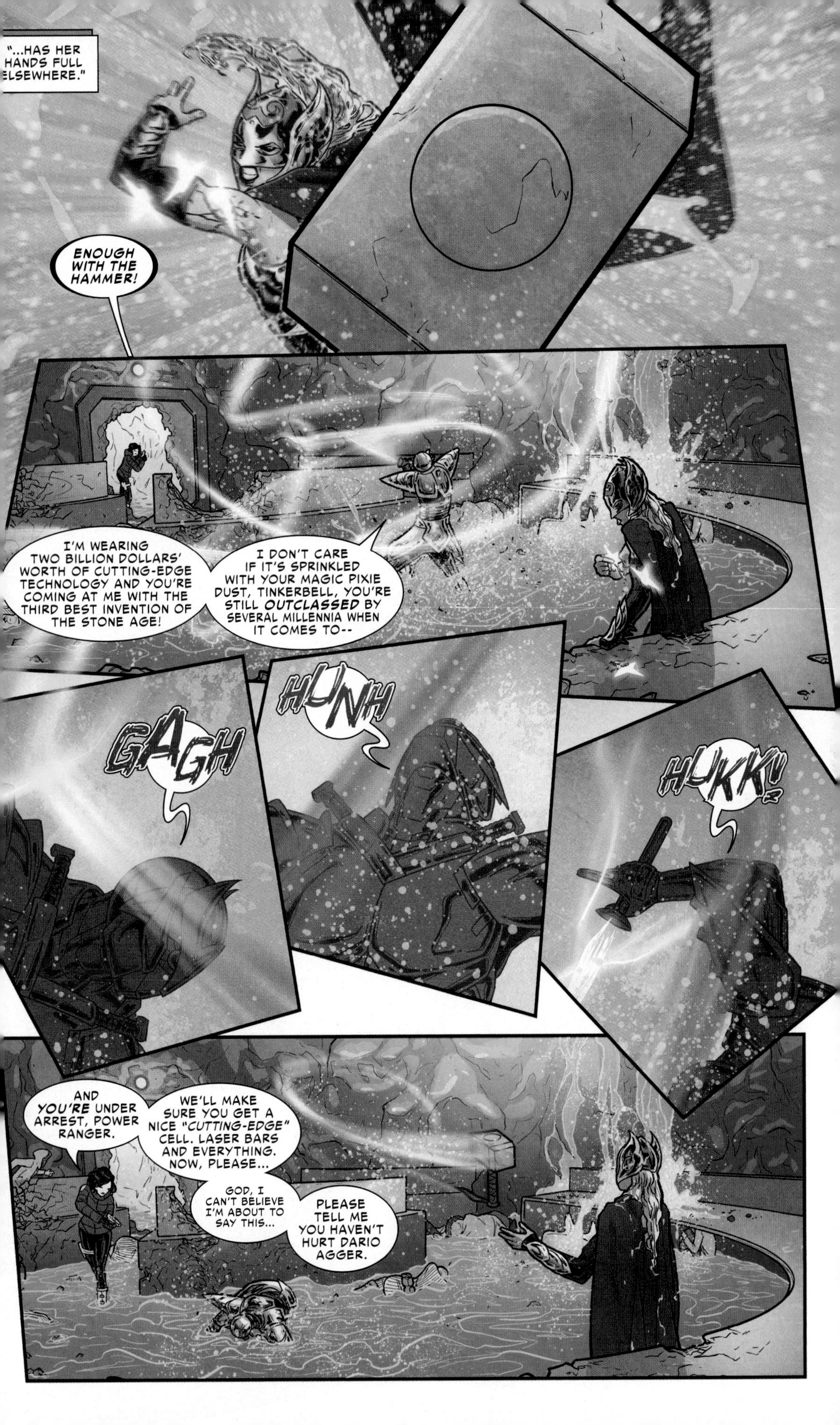
"...HAS HER HANDS FULL ELSEWHERE."
ENOUGH WITH THE HAMMER!
I'M WEARING TWO BILLION DOLLARS' WORTH OF CUTTING-EDGE TECHNOLOGY AND YOU'RE COMING AT ME WITH THE THIRD BEST INVENTION OF THE STONE AGE!
I DON'T CARE IF IT'S SPRINKLED WITH YOUR MAGIC PIXIE DUST, TINKERBELL, YOU'RE STILL *OUTCLASSED* BY SEVERAL MILLENNIA WHEN IT COMES TO--
GAGH
HUNH
HUKK!?
AND *YOU'RE* UNDER ARREST, POWER RANGER.
WE'LL MAKE SURE YOU GET A NICE "*CUTTING-EDGE*" CELL. LASER BARS AND EVERYTHING. NOW, PLEASE...
GOD, I CAN'T BELIEVE I'M ABOUT TO SAY THIS...
PLEASE TELL ME YOU HAVEN'T HURT DARIO AGGER.

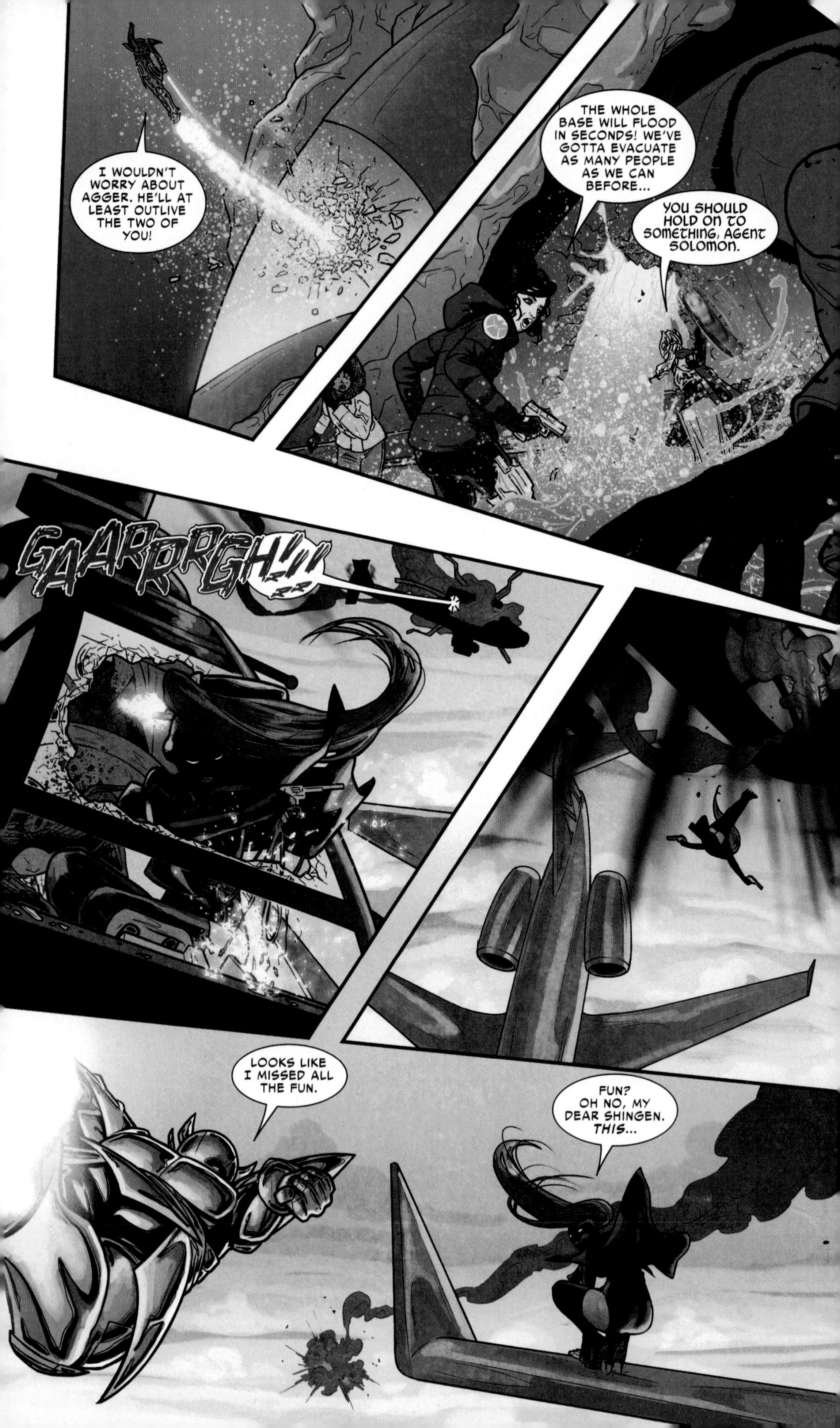
I WOULDN'T WORRY ABOUT AGGER. HE'LL AT LEAST OUTLIVE THE TWO OF YOU!
THE WHOLE BASE WILL FLOOD IN SECONDS! WE'VE GOTTA EVACUATE AS MANY PEOPLE AS WE CAN BEFORE...
YOU SHOULD HOLD ON TO SOMETHING, AGENT SOLOMON.
GAARRRGH!!!
LOOKS LIKE I MISSED ALL THE FUN.
FUN? OH NO, MY DEAR SHINGEN. THIS...

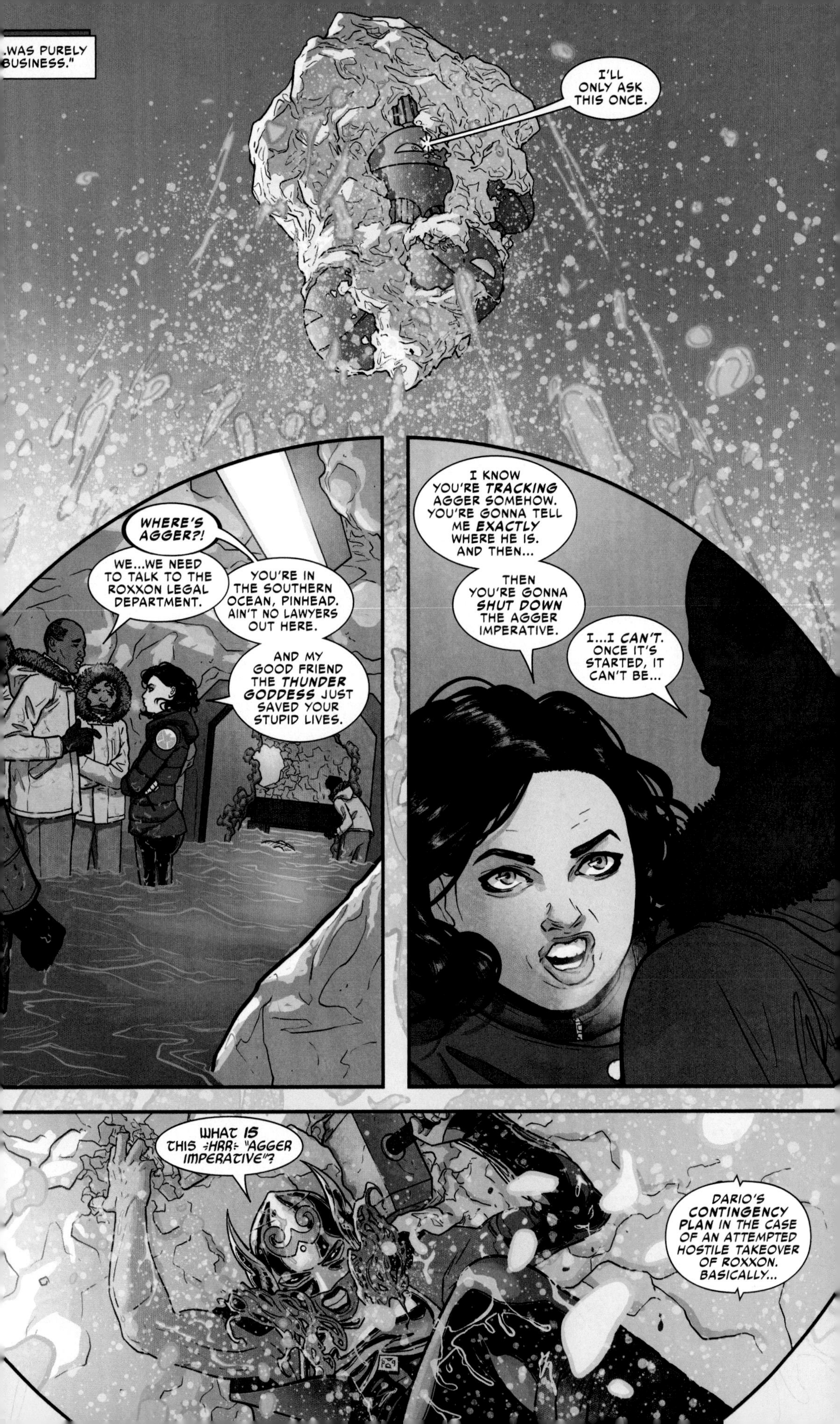
..WAS PURELY BUSINESS."
I'LL ONLY ASK THIS ONCE.
WHERE'S AGGER?!
WE...WE NEED TO TALK TO THE ROXXON LEGAL DEPARTMENT.
YOU'RE IN THE SOUTHERN OCEAN, PINHEAD. AIN'T NO LAWYERS OUT HERE.
AND MY GOOD FRIEND THE THUNDER GODDESS JUST SAVED YOUR STUPID LIVES.
I KNOW YOU'RE TRACKING AGGER SOMEHOW. YOU'RE GONNA TELL ME EXACTLY WHERE HE IS. AND THEN...
THEN YOU'RE GONNA SHUT DOWN THE AGGER IMPERATIVE.
I...I CAN'T. ONCE IT'S STARTED, IT CAN'T BE...
WHAT IS THIS ÷HRR÷ "AGGER IMPERATIVE"?
DARIO'S CONTINGENCY PLAN IN THE CASE OF AN ATTEMPTED HOSTILE TAKEOVER OF ROXXON. BASICALLY...

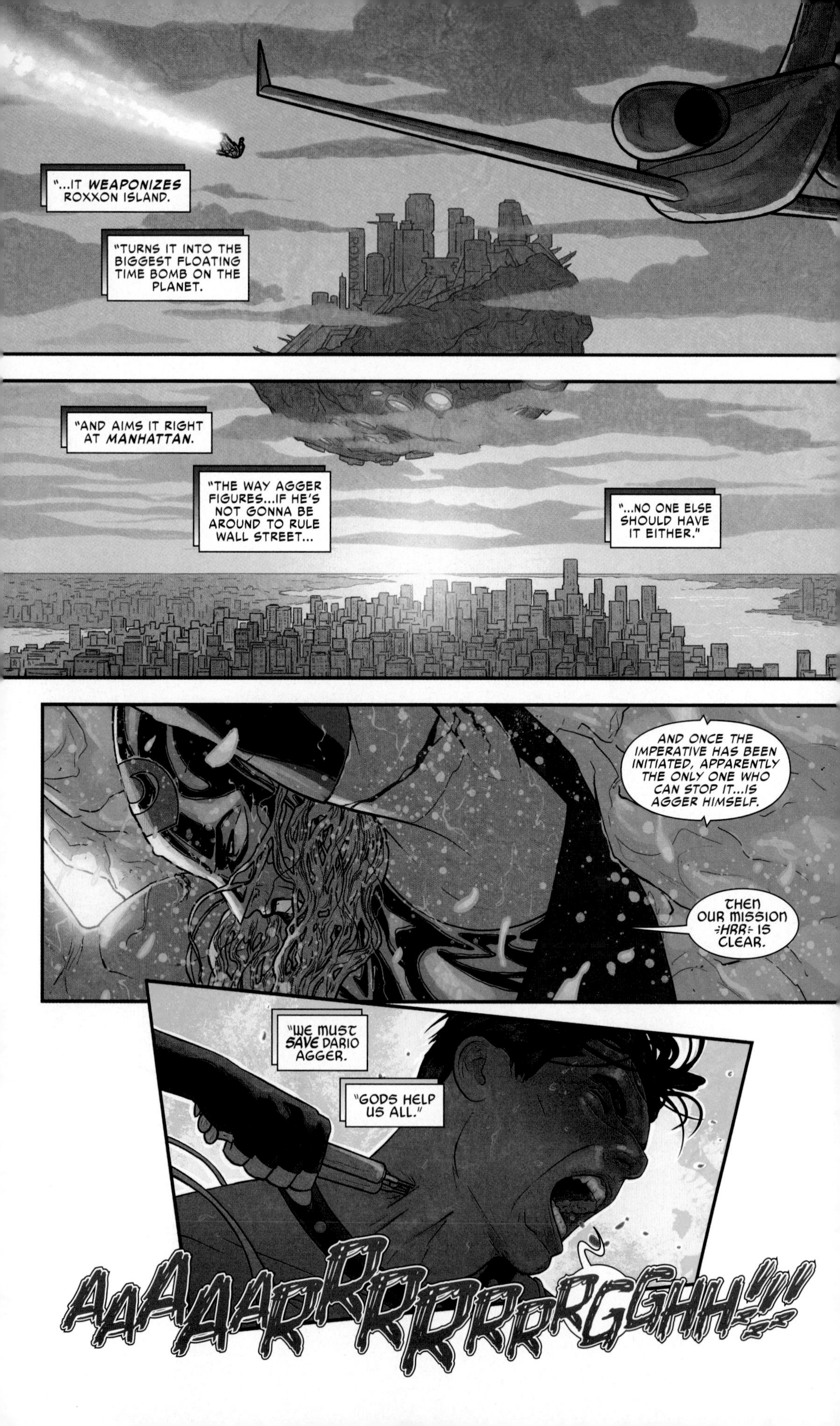
"...IT WEAPONIZES ROXXON ISLAND.
"TURNS IT INTO THE BIGGEST FLOATING TIME BOMB ON THE PLANET.
"AND AIMS IT RIGHT AT MANHATTAN.
"THE WAY AGGER FIGURES...IF HE'S NOT GONNA BE AROUND TO RULE WALL STREET...
"...NO ONE ELSE SHOULD HAVE IT EITHER."
AND ONCE THE IMPERATIVE HAS BEEN INITIATED, APPARENTLY THE ONLY ONE WHO CAN STOP IT...IS AGGER HIMSELF.
THEN OUR MISSION =HRR= IS CLEAR.
"WE MUST SAVE DARIO AGGER.
"GODS HELP US ALL."
AAAAAARRRRRRRGGHH!!!

10

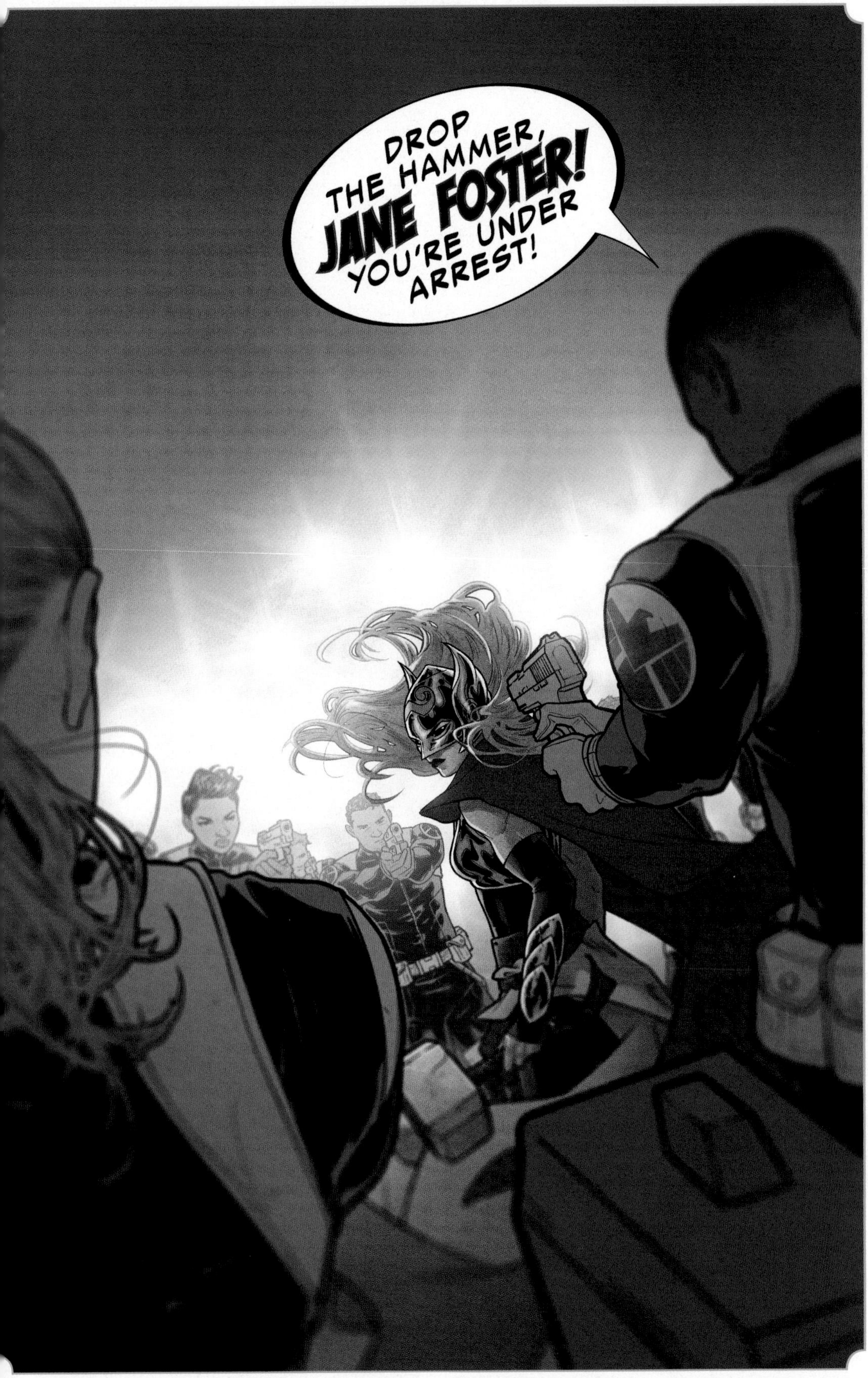
DROP THE HAMMER, JANE FOSTER! YOU'RE UNDER ARREST!

THE BATTLE OF ROXXON ISLAND

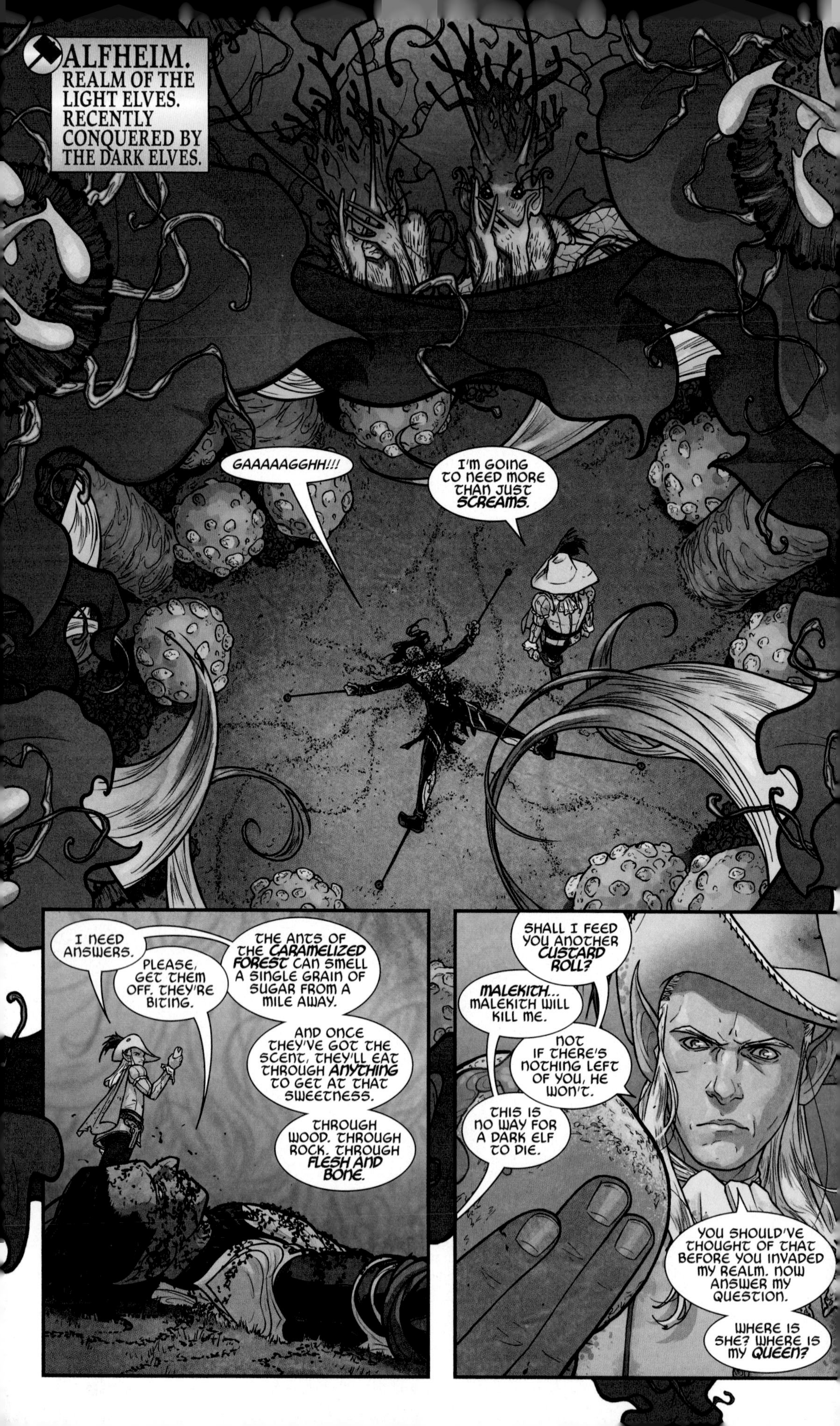

ALFHEIM. REALM OF THE LIGHT ELVES. RECENTLY CONQUERED BY THE DARK ELVES.
GAAAAAGGHH!!!
I'M GOING TO NEED MORE THAN JUST SCREAMS.
I NEED ANSWERS.
PLEASE, GET THEM OFF. THEY'RE BITING.
THE ANTS OF THE CARAMELIZED FOREST CAN SMELL A SINGLE GRAIN OF SUGAR FROM A MILE AWAY.
AND ONCE THEY'VE GOT THE SCENT, THEY'LL EAT THROUGH ANYTHING TO GET AT THAT SWEETNESS.
THROUGH WOOD. THROUGH ROCK. THROUGH FLESH AND BONE.
SHALL I FEED YOU ANOTHER CUSTARD ROLL?
MALEKITH... MALEKITH WILL KILL ME.
NOT IF THERE'S NOTHING LEFT OF YOU, HE WON'T.
THIS IS NO WAY FOR A DARK ELF TO DIE.
YOU SHOULD'VE THOUGHT OF THAT BEFORE YOU INVADED MY REALM. NOW ANSWER MY QUESTION.
WHERE IS SHE? WHERE IS MY QUEEN?

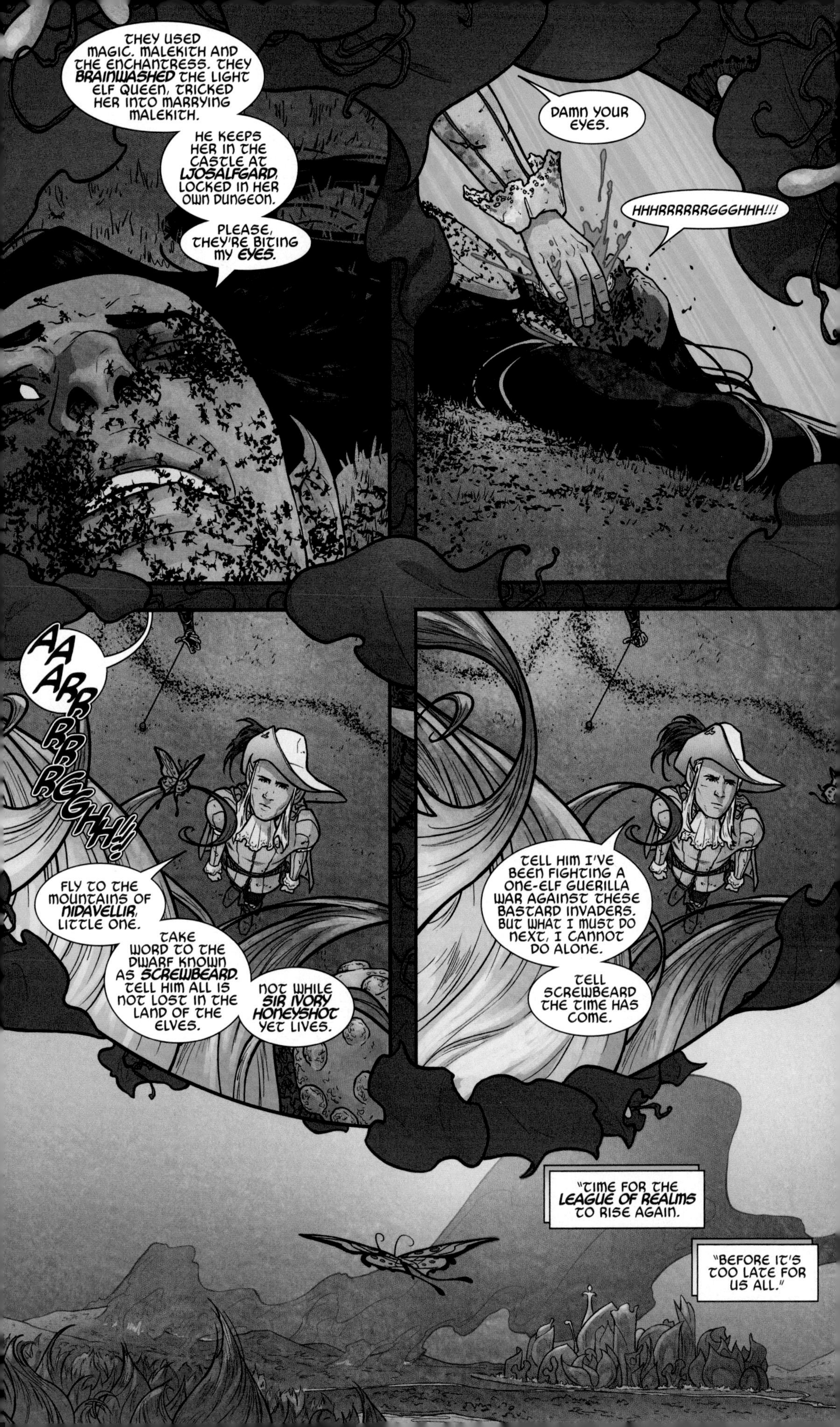

THEY USED MAGIC. MALEKITH AND THE ENCHANTRESS. THEY BRAINWASHED THE LIGHT ELF QUEEN, TRICKED HER INTO MARRYING MALEKITH.
HE KEEPS HER IN THE CASTLE AT LJOSALFGARD, LOCKED IN HER OWN DUNGEON.
PLEASE, THEY'RE BITING MY EYES.
DAMN YOUR EYES.
HHHRRRRRRGGHHH!!!
AAARRRRRRGGHHH!!!
FLY TO THE MOUNTAINS OF NIDAVELLIR, LITTLE ONE.
TAKE WORD TO THE DWARF KNOWN AS SCREWBEARD. TELL HIM ALL IS NOT LOST IN THE LAND OF THE ELVES.
NOT WHILE SIR IVORY HONEYSHOT YET LIVES.
TELL HIM I'VE BEEN FIGHTING A ONE-ELF GUERILLA WAR AGAINST THESE BASTARD INVADERS. BUT WHAT I MUST DO NEXT, I CANNOT DO ALONE.
TELL SCREWBEARD THE TIME HAS COME.
"TIME FOR THE LEAGUE OF REALMS TO RISE AGAIN.
"BEFORE IT'S TOO LATE FOR US ALL."

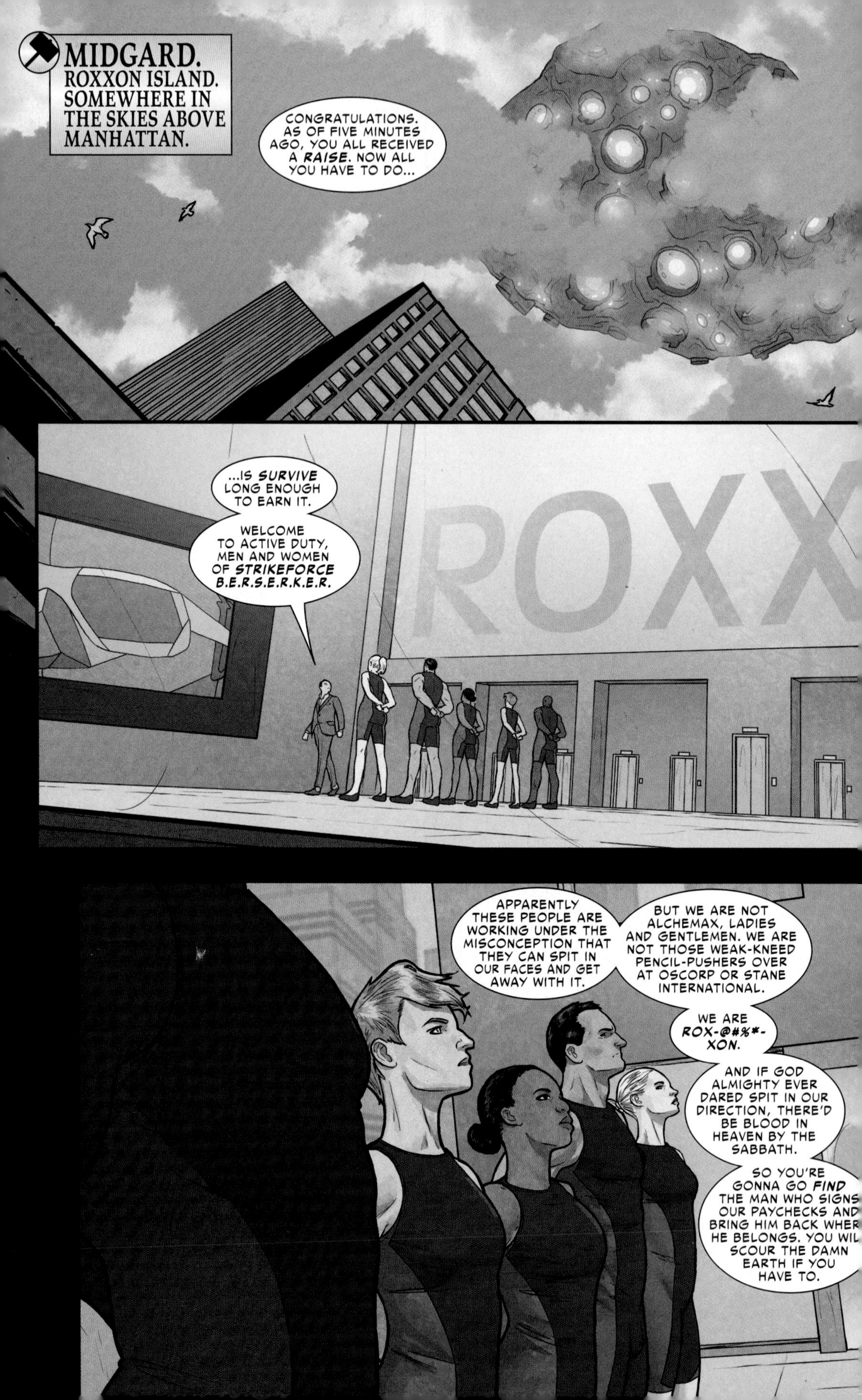
MIDGARD. ROXXON ISLAND. SOMEWHERE IN THE SKIES ABOVE MANHATTAN.
CONGRATULATIONS. AS OF FIVE MINUTES AGO, YOU ALL RECEIVED A RAISE. NOW ALL YOU HAVE TO DO...
...IS SURVIVE LONG ENOUGH TO EARN IT.
WELCOME TO ACTIVE DUTY, MEN AND WOMEN OF STRIKEFORCE B.E.R.S.E.R.K.E.R.
ROXX
APPARENTLY THESE PEOPLE ARE WORKING UNDER THE MISCONCEPTION THAT THEY CAN SPIT IN OUR FACES AND GET AWAY WITH IT.
BUT WE ARE NOT ALCHEMAX, LADIES AND GENTLEMEN. WE ARE NOT THOSE WEAK-KNEED PENCIL-PUSHERS OVER AT OSCORP OR STANE INTERNATIONAL.
WE ARE ROX-@#%*-XON.
AND IF GOD ALMIGHTY EVER DARED SPIT IN OUR DIRECTION, THERE'D BE BLOOD IN HEAVEN BY THE SABBATH.
SO YOU'RE GONNA GO FIND THE MAN WHO SIGNS OUR PAYCHECKS AND BRING HIM BACK WHER HE BELONGS. YOU WIL SCOUR THE DAMN EARTH IF YOU HAVE TO.

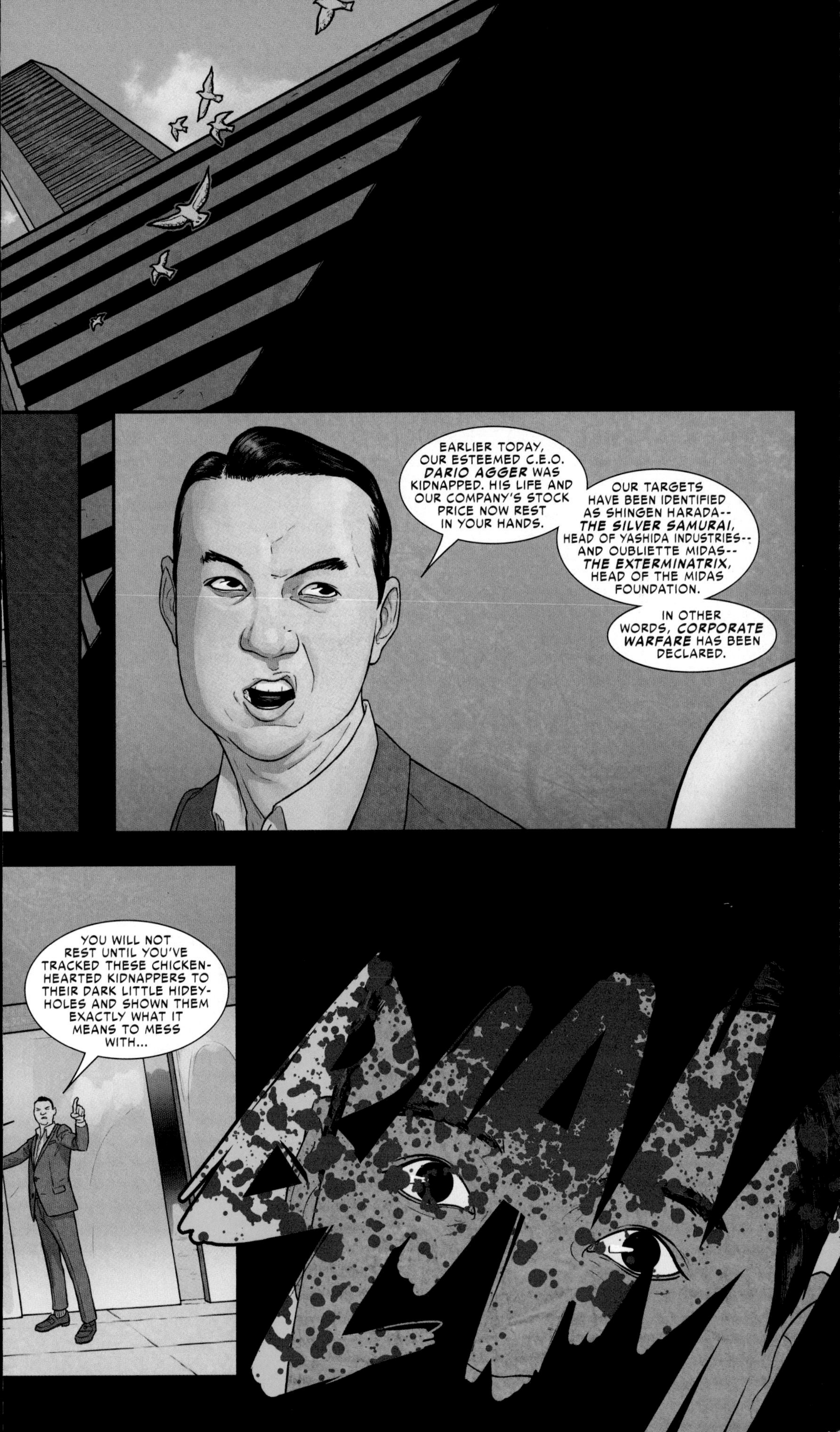
EARLIER TODAY, OUR ESTEEMED C.E.O. DARIO AGGER WAS KIDNAPPED. HIS LIFE AND OUR COMPANY'S STOCK PRICE NOW REST IN YOUR HANDS.
OUR TARGETS HAVE BEEN IDENTIFIED AS SHINGEN HARADA-- THE SILVER SAMURAI, HEAD OF YASHIDA INDUSTRIES-- AND OUBLIETTE MIDAS-- THE EXTERMINATRIX, HEAD OF THE MIDAS FOUNDATION.
IN OTHER WORDS, CORPORATE WARFARE HAS BEEN DECLARED.
YOU WILL NOT REST UNTIL YOU'VE TRACKED THESE CHICKEN-HEARTED KIDNAPPERS TO THEIR DARK LITTLE HIDEY-HOLES AND SHOWN THEM EXACTLY WHAT IT MEANS TO MESS WITH...

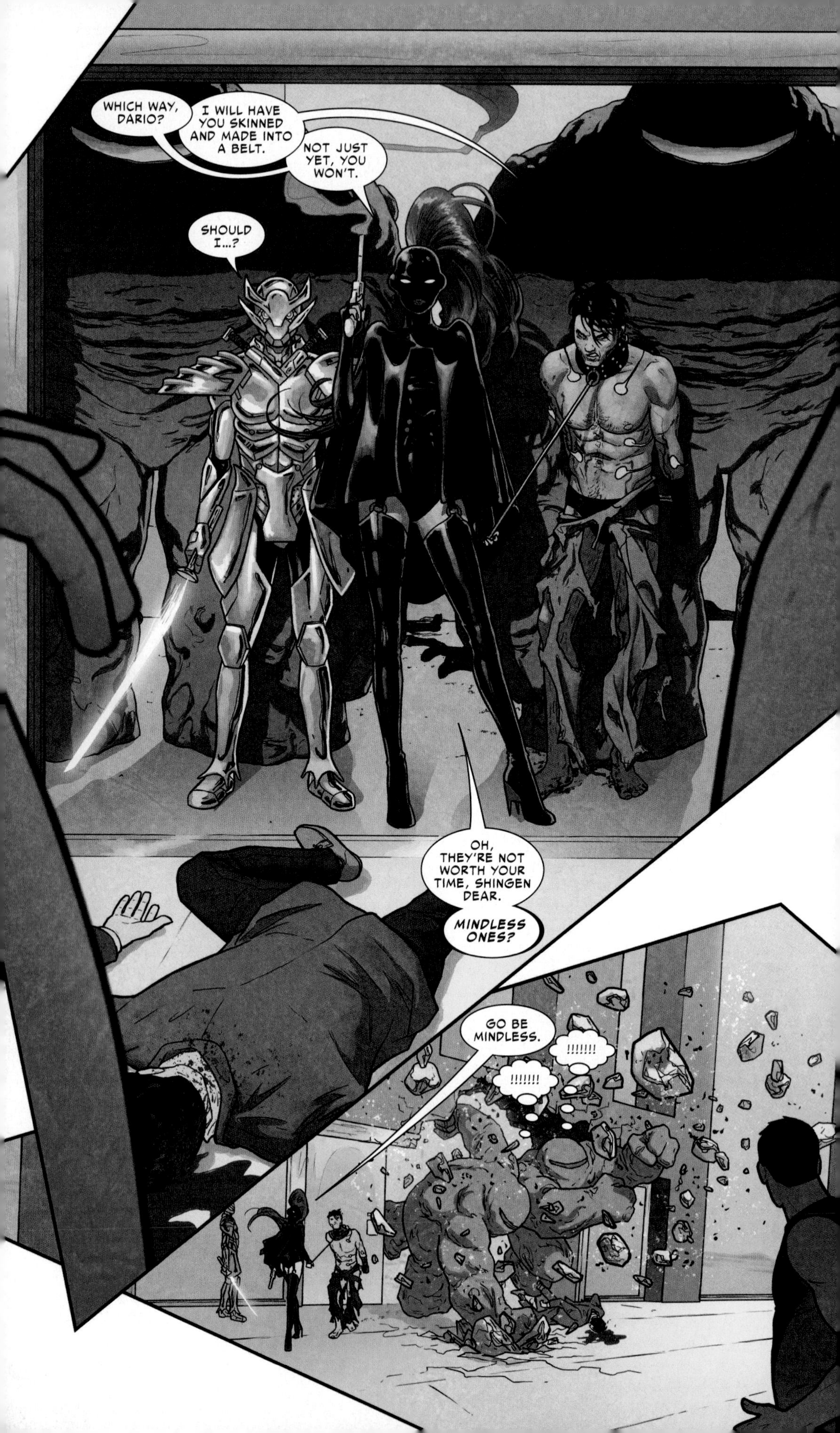
WHICH WAY, DARIO?
I WILL HAVE YOU SKINNED AND MADE INTO A BELT.
NOT JUST YET, YOU WON'T.
SHOULD I...?
OH, THEY'RE NOT WORTH YOUR TIME, SHINGEN DEAR.
MINDLESS ONES?
GO BE MINDLESS.
!!!!!!!
!!!!!!!

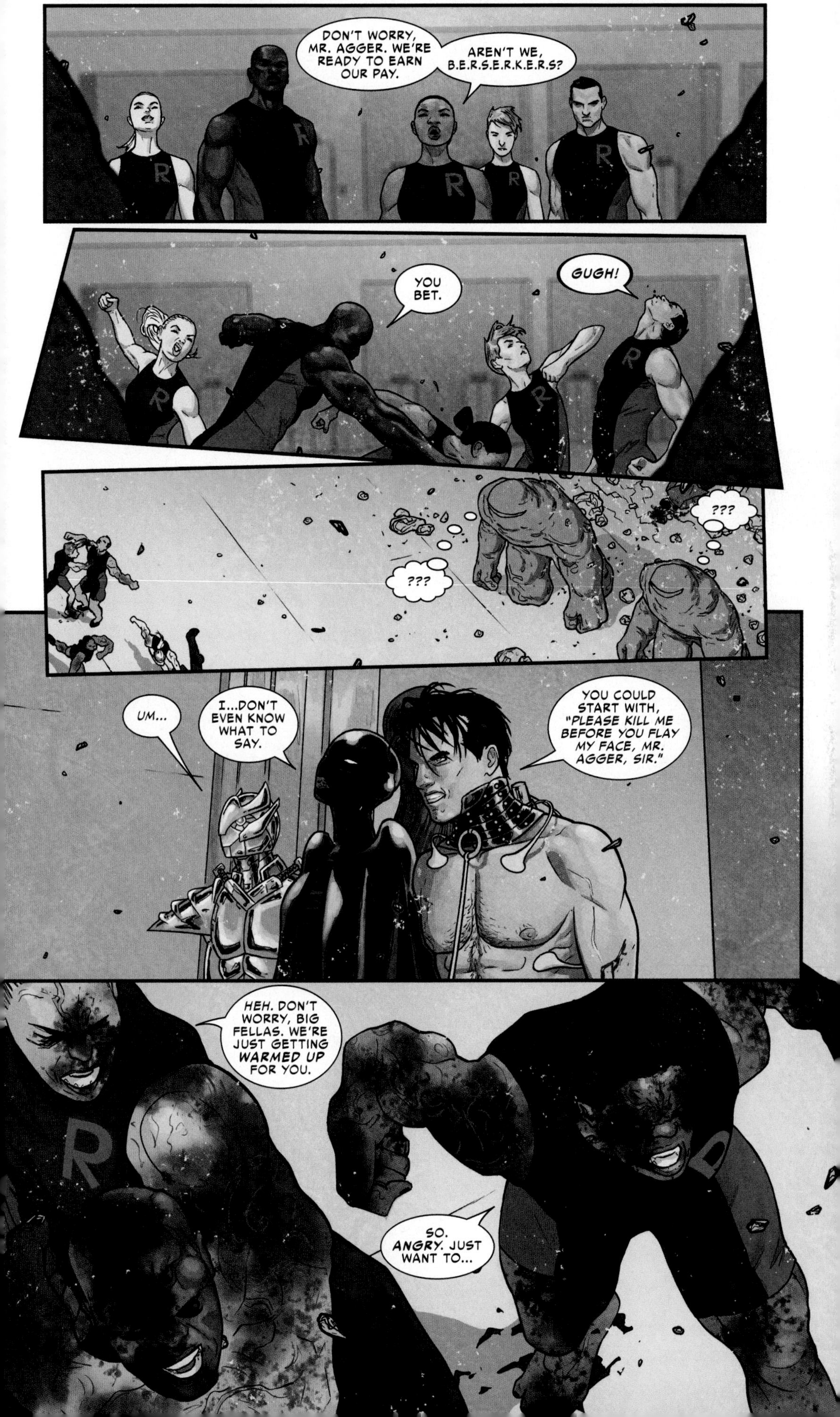
DON'T WORRY, MR. AGGER. WE'RE READY TO EARN OUR PAY.
AREN'T WE, B.E.R.S.E.R.K.E.R.S?
YOU BET.
GUGH!
???
???
UM...
I...DON'T EVEN KNOW WHAT TO SAY.
YOU COULD START WITH, "PLEASE KILL ME BEFORE YOU FLAY MY FACE, MR. AGGER, SIR."
HEH. DON'T WORRY, BIG FELLAS. WE'RE JUST GETTING WARMED UP FOR YOU.
SO. ANGRY. JUST WANT TO...

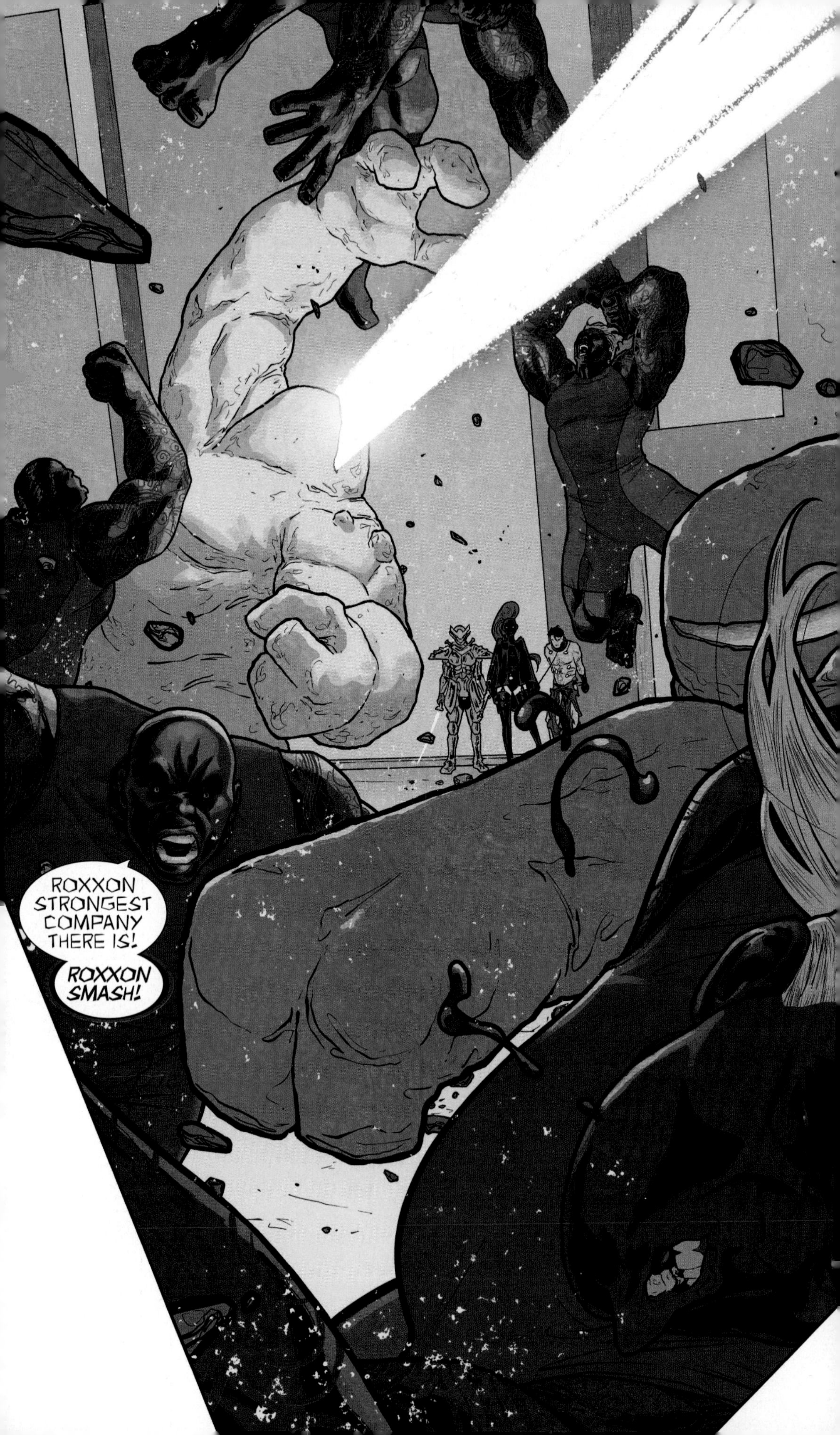
ROXXON STRONGEST COMPANY THERE IS!
ROXXON SMASH!

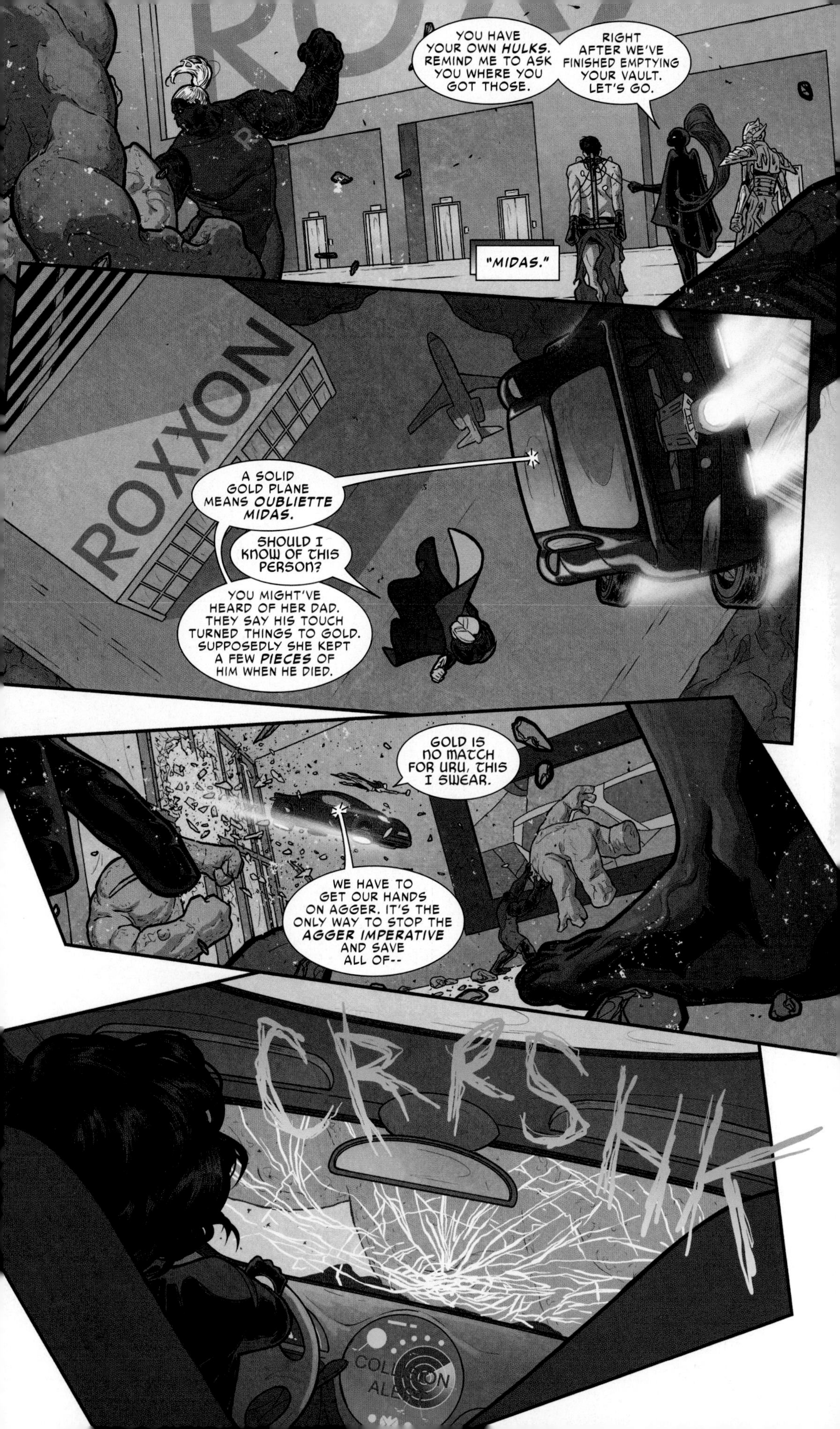
YOU HAVE YOUR OWN HULKS. REMIND ME TO ASK YOU WHERE YOU GOT THOSE.
RIGHT AFTER WE'VE FINISHED EMPTYING YOUR VAULT. LET'S GO.
"MIDAS."
ROXXON
A SOLID GOLD PLANE MEANS OUBLIETTE MIDAS.
SHOULD I KNOW OF THIS PERSON?
YOU MIGHT'VE HEARD OF HER DAD. THEY SAY HIS TOUCH TURNED THINGS TO GOLD. SUPPOSEDLY SHE KEPT A FEW PIECES OF HIM WHEN HE DIED.
GOLD IS NO MATCH FOR URU, THIS I SWEAR.
WE HAVE TO GET OUR HANDS ON AGGER. IT'S THE ONLY WAY TO STOP THE AGGER IMPERATIVE AND SAVE ALL OF--
CRRSHK

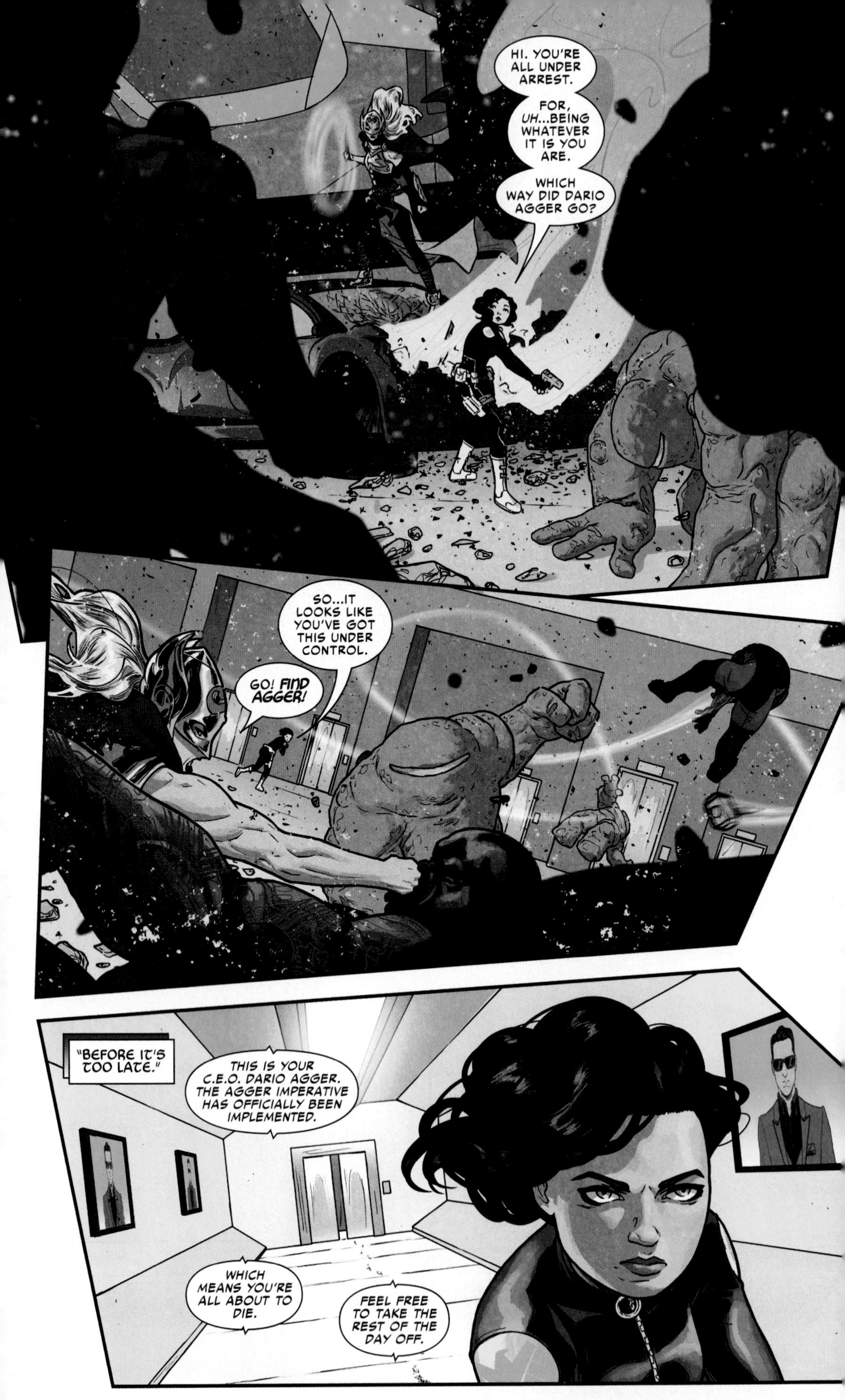
HI. YOU'RE ALL UNDER ARREST.
FOR, *UH*...BEING WHATEVER IT IS YOU ARE.
WHICH WAY DID DARIO AGGER GO?
SO...IT LOOKS LIKE YOU'VE GOT THIS UNDER CONTROL.
GO! **FIND AGGER!**
"BEFORE IT'S TOO LATE."
THIS IS YOUR C.E.O. DARIO AGGER. THE AGGER IMPERATIVE HAS OFFICIALLY BEEN IMPLEMENTED.
WHICH MEANS YOU'RE ALL ABOUT TO DIE.
FEEL FREE TO TAKE THE REST OF THE DAY OFF.

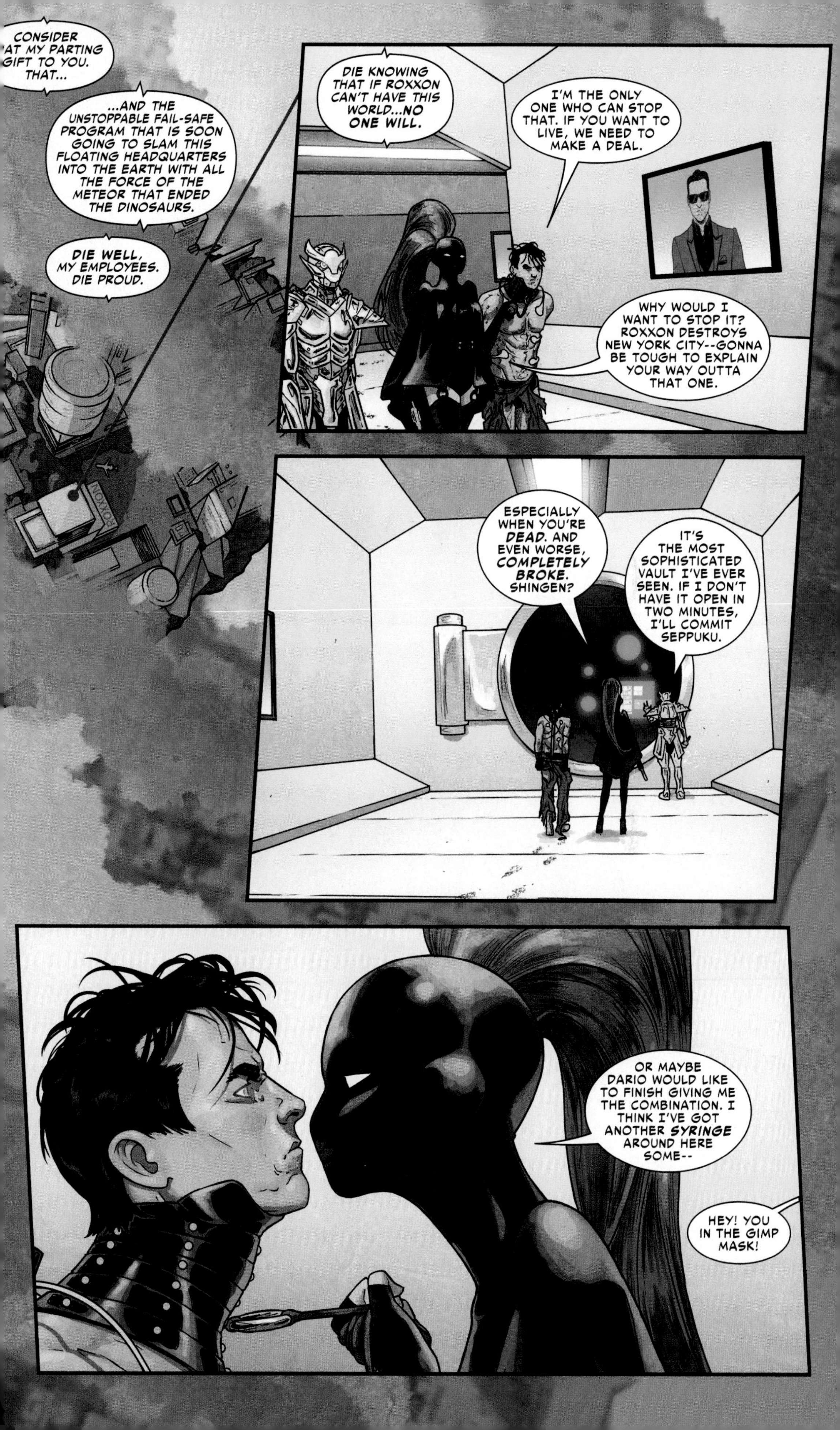

CONSIDER THAT MY PARTING GIFT TO YOU. THAT...
...AND THE UNSTOPPABLE FAIL-SAFE PROGRAM THAT IS SOON GOING TO SLAM THIS FLOATING HEADQUARTERS INTO THE EARTH WITH ALL THE FORCE OF THE METEOR THAT ENDED THE DINOSAURS.
DIE WELL, MY EMPLOYEES. DIE PROUD.
DIE KNOWING THAT IF ROXXON CAN'T HAVE THIS WORLD...NO ONE WILL.
I'M THE ONLY ONE WHO CAN STOP THAT. IF YOU WANT TO LIVE, WE NEED TO MAKE A DEAL.
WHY WOULD I WANT TO STOP IT? ROXXON DESTROYS NEW YORK CITY--GONNA BE TOUGH TO EXPLAIN YOUR WAY OUTTA THAT ONE.
ESPECIALLY WHEN YOU'RE DEAD. AND EVEN WORSE, COMPLETELY BROKE. SHINGEN?
IT'S THE MOST SOPHISTICATED VAULT I'VE EVER SEEN. IF I DON'T HAVE IT OPEN IN TWO MINUTES, I'LL COMMIT SEPPUKU.
OR MAYBE DARIO WOULD LIKE TO FINISH GIVING ME THE COMBINATION. I THINK I'VE GOT ANOTHER SYRINGE AROUND HERE SOME--
HEY! YOU IN THE GIMP MASK!

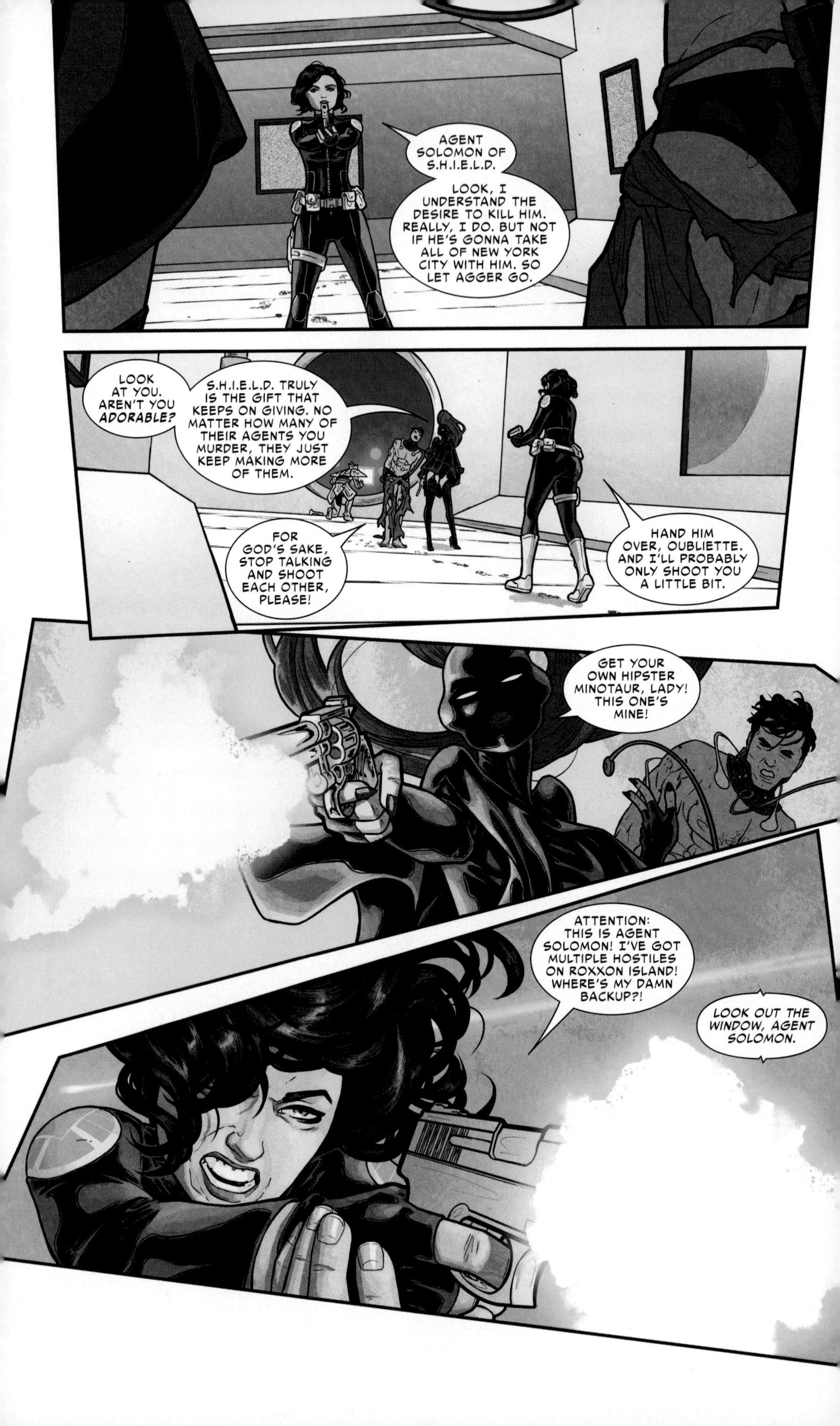
AGENT SOLOMON OF S.H.I.E.L.D.
LOOK, I UNDERSTAND THE DESIRE TO KILL HIM. REALLY, I DO. BUT NOT IF HE'S GONNA TAKE ALL OF NEW YORK CITY WITH HIM. SO LET AGGER GO.
LOOK AT YOU. AREN'T YOU *ADORABLE?*
S.H.I.E.L.D. TRULY IS THE GIFT THAT KEEPS ON GIVING. NO MATTER HOW MANY OF THEIR AGENTS YOU MURDER, THEY JUST KEEP MAKING MORE OF THEM.
FOR GOD'S SAKE, STOP TALKING AND SHOOT EACH OTHER, PLEASE!
HAND HIM OVER, OUBLIETTE. AND I'LL PROBABLY ONLY SHOOT YOU A LITTLE BIT.
GET YOUR OWN HIPSTER MINOTAUR, LADY! THIS ONE'S MINE!
ATTENTION: THIS IS AGENT SOLOMON! I'VE GOT MULTIPLE HOSTILES ON ROXXON ISLAND! WHERE'S MY DAMN BACKUP?!
LOOK OUT THE WINDOW, AGENT SOLOMON.

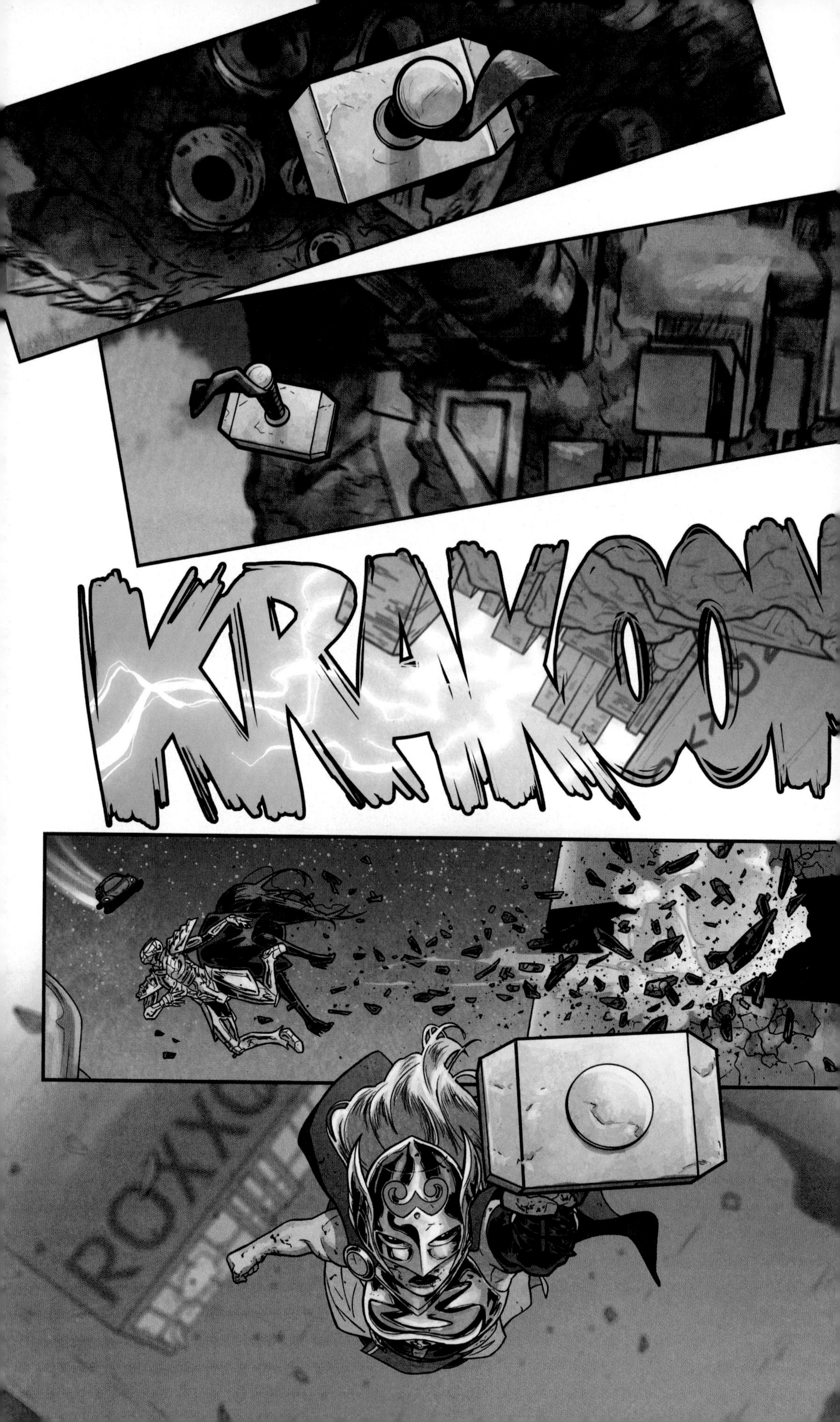
KRAKOOM

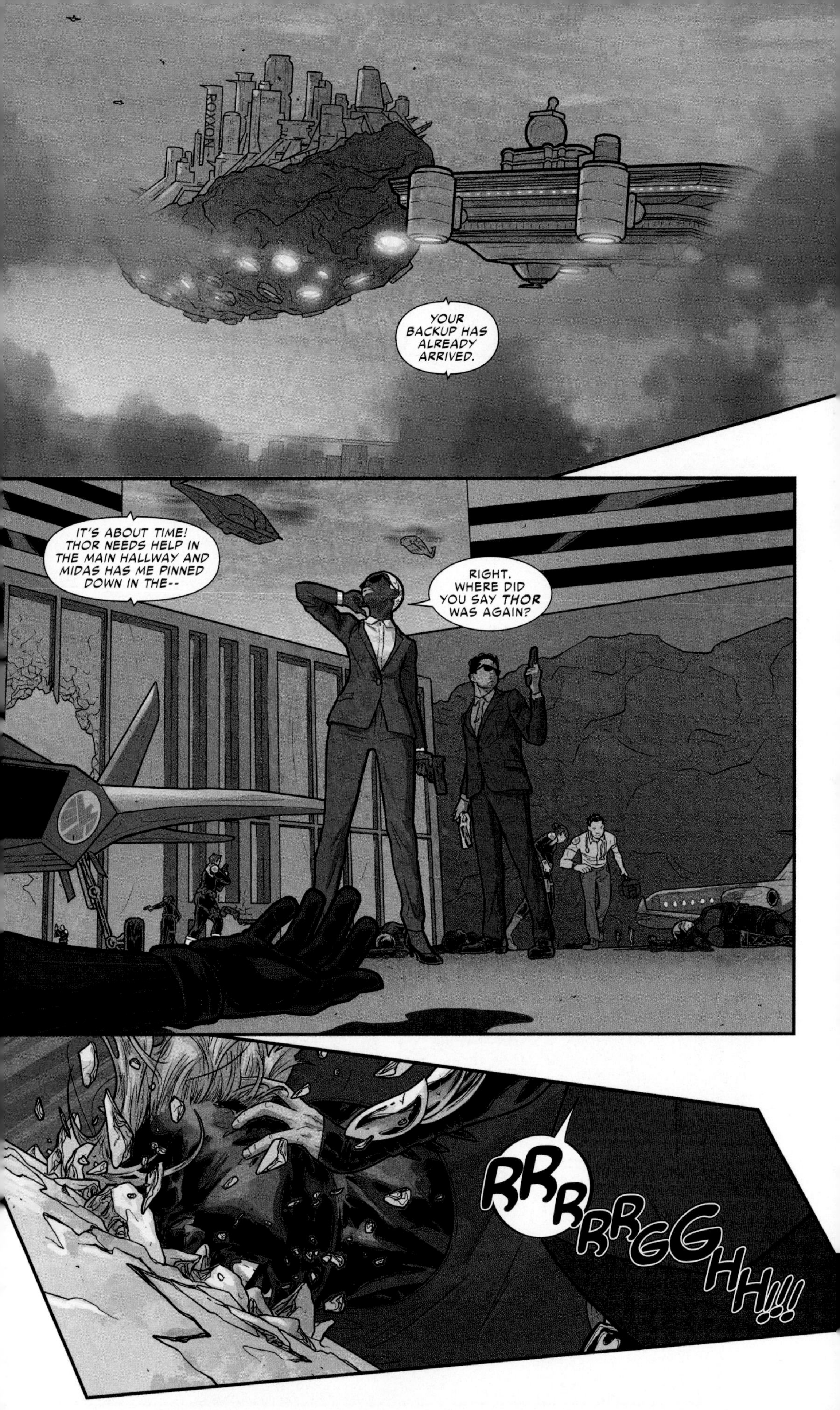
ROXXON
YOUR BACKUP HAS ALREADY ARRIVED.
IT'S ABOUT TIME! THOR NEEDS HELP IN THE MAIN HALLWAY AND MIDAS HAS ME PINNED DOWN IN THE--
RIGHT. WHERE DID YOU SAY THOR WAS AGAIN?
RRRRRGGHH!!!

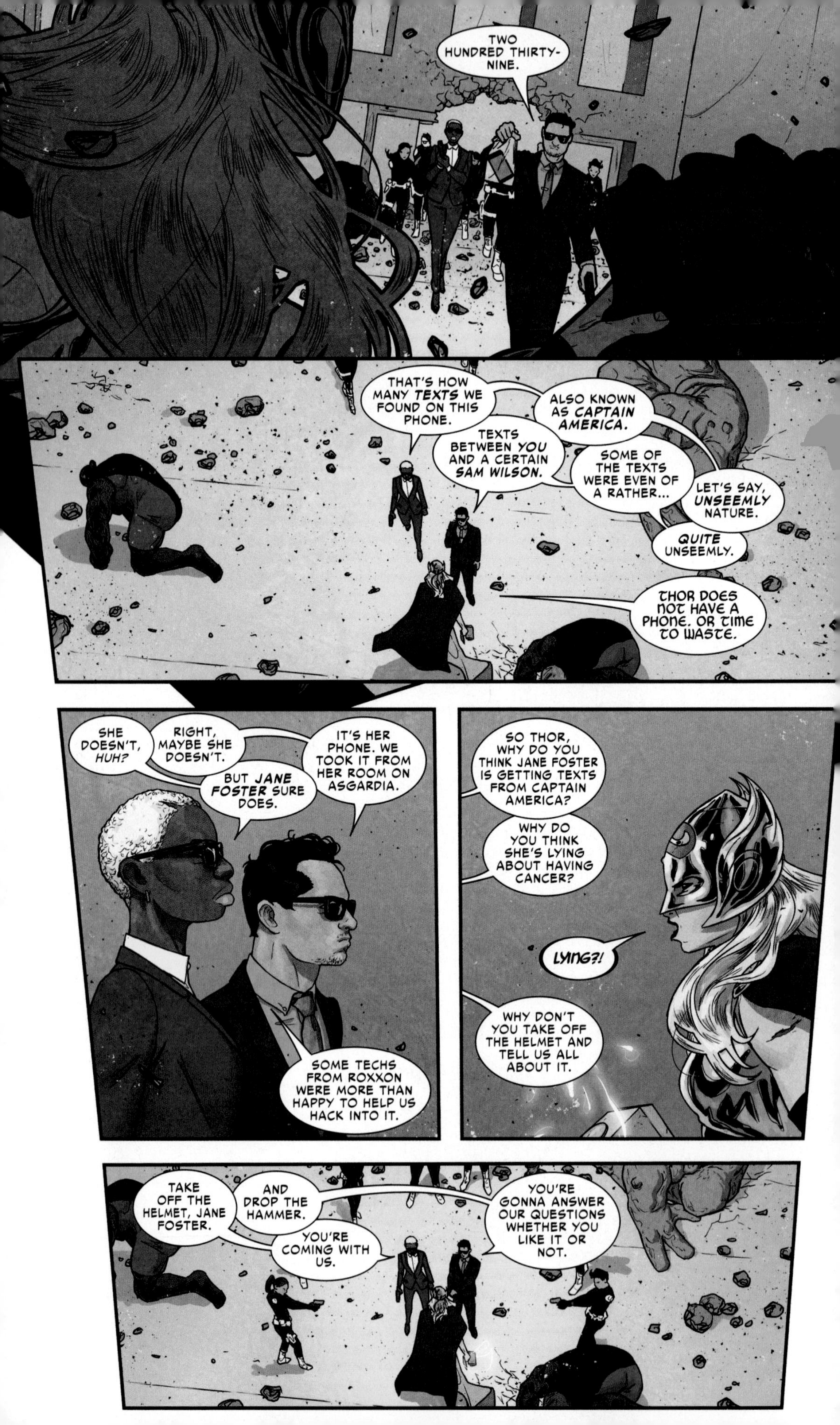

TWO HUNDRED THIRTY-NINE.
THAT'S HOW MANY TEXTS WE FOUND ON THIS PHONE.
TEXTS BETWEEN YOU AND A CERTAIN SAM WILSON.
ALSO KNOWN AS CAPTAIN AMERICA.
SOME OF THE TEXTS WERE EVEN OF A RATHER...
LET'S SAY, UNSEEMLY NATURE.
QUITE UNSEEMLY.
THOR DOES NOT HAVE A PHONE. OR TIME TO WASTE.
SHE DOESN'T, HUH?
RIGHT, MAYBE SHE DOESN'T.
BUT JANE FOSTER SURE DOES.
IT'S HER PHONE. WE TOOK IT FROM HER ROOM ON ASGARDIA.
SOME TECHS FROM ROXXON WERE MORE THAN HAPPY TO HELP US HACK INTO IT.
SO THOR, WHY DO YOU THINK JANE FOSTER IS GETTING TEXTS FROM CAPTAIN AMERICA?
WHY DO YOU THINK SHE'S LYING ABOUT HAVING CANCER?
LYING?!
WHY DON'T YOU TAKE OFF THE HELMET AND TELL US ALL ABOUT IT.
TAKE OFF THE HELMET, JANE FOSTER.
AND DROP THE HAMMER.
YOU'RE COMING WITH US.
YOU'RE GONNA ANSWER OUR QUESTIONS WHETHER YOU LIKE IT OR NOT.

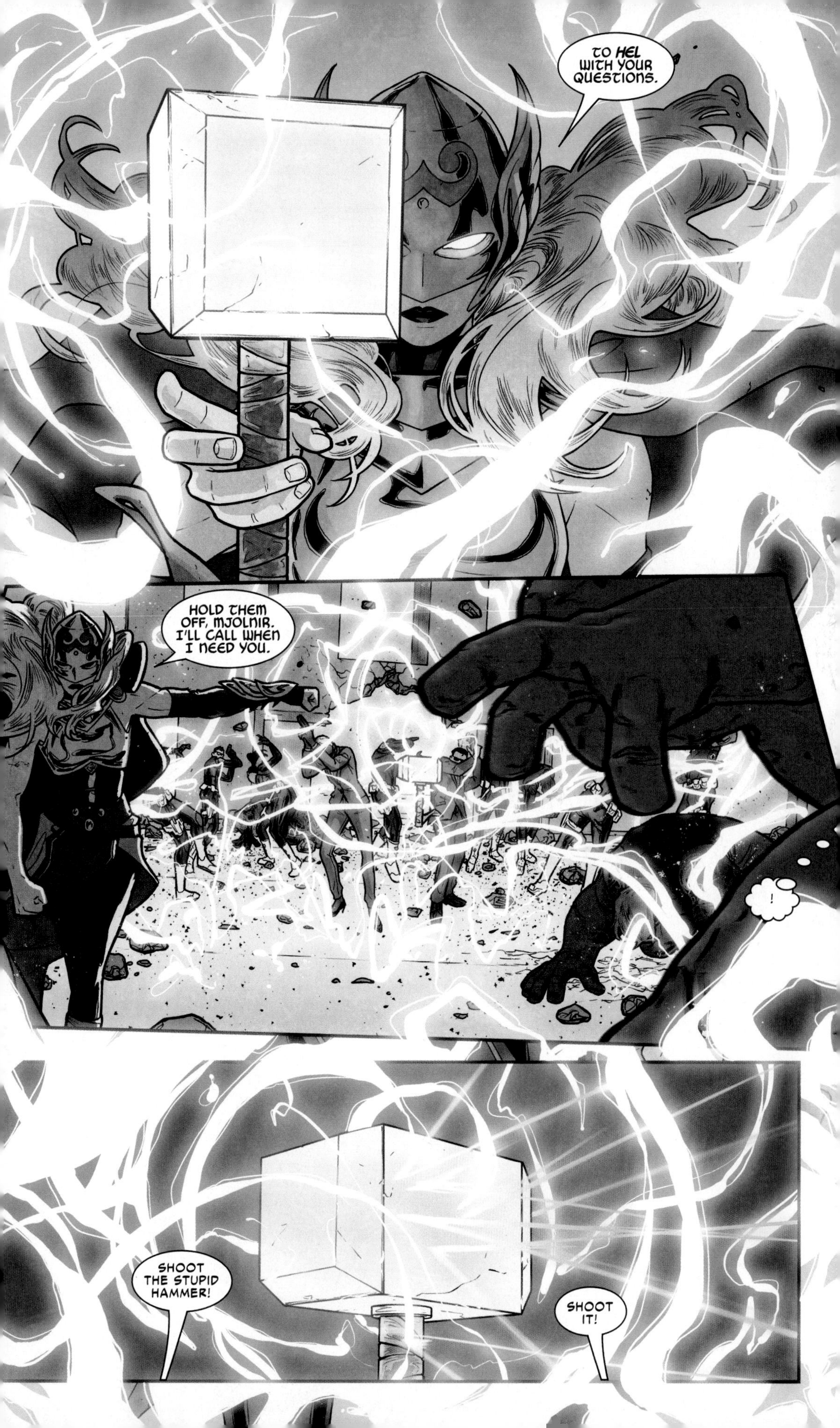
TO HEL WITH YOUR QUESTIONS.
HOLD THEM OFF, MJOLNIR. I'LL CALL WHEN I NEED YOU.
!
SHOOT THE STUPID HAMMER!
SHOOT IT!

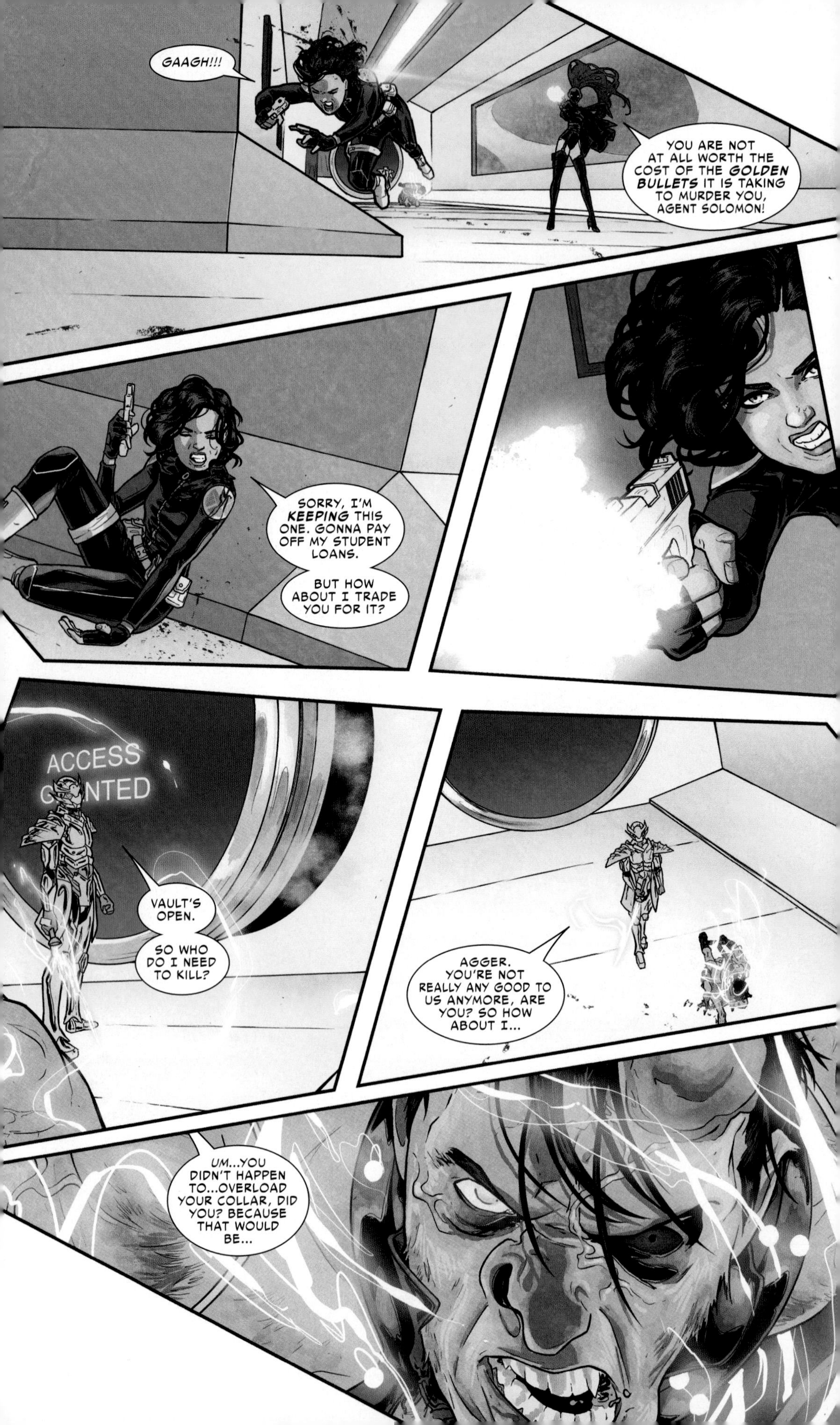
GAAGH!!!
YOU ARE NOT AT ALL WORTH THE COST OF THE GOLDEN BULLETS IT IS TAKING TO MURDER YOU, AGENT SOLOMON!
SORRY, I'M KEEPING THIS ONE. GONNA PAY OFF MY STUDENT LOANS.
BUT HOW ABOUT I TRADE YOU FOR IT?
ACCESS
NTED
VAULT'S OPEN.
SO WHO DO I NEED TO KILL?
AGGER. YOU'RE NOT REALLY ANY GOOD TO US ANYMORE, ARE YOU? SO HOW ABOUT I...
UM...YOU DIDN'T HAPPEN TO...OVERLOAD YOUR COLLAR, DID YOU? BECAUSE THAT WOULD BE...

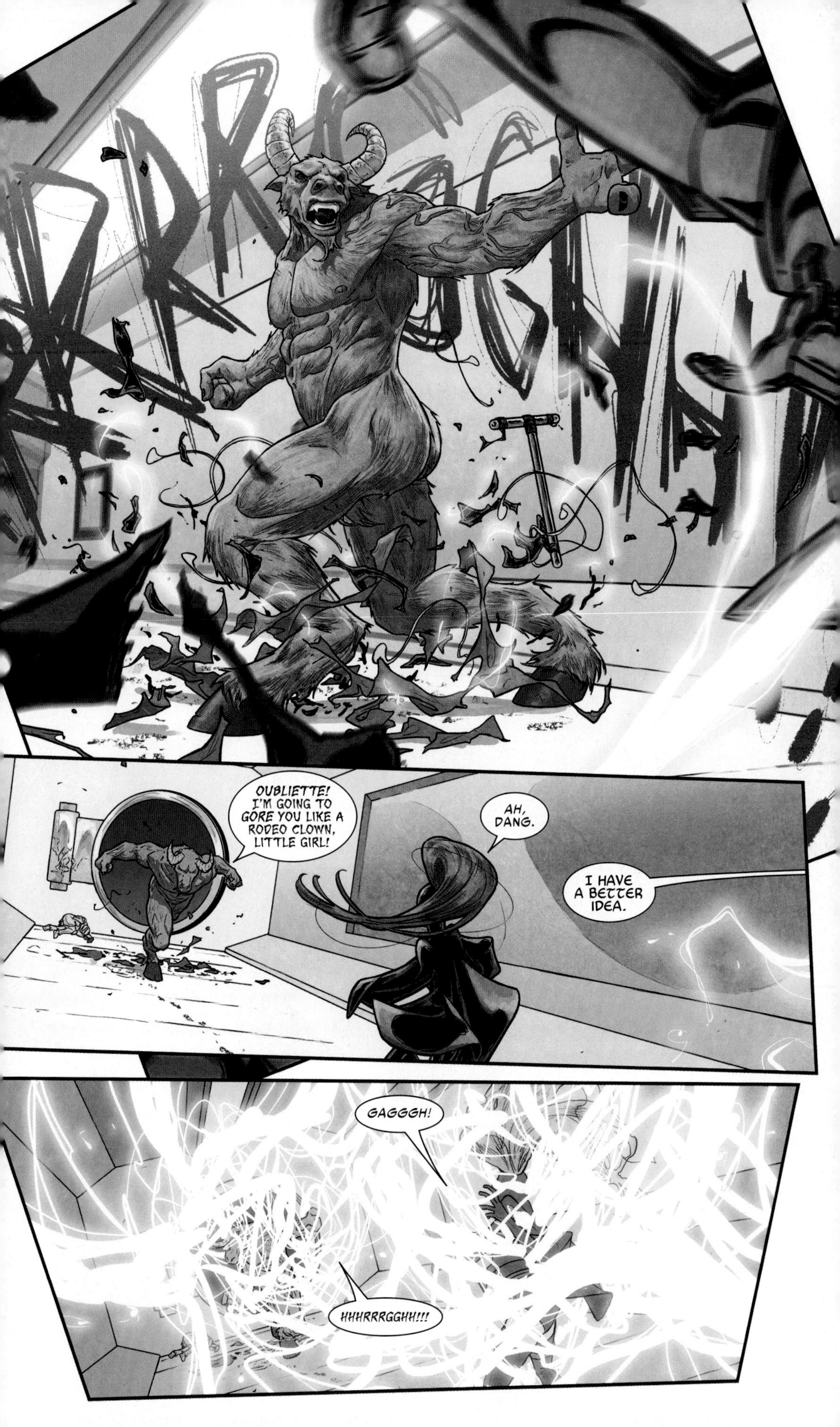
OUBLIETTE! I'M GOING TO GORE YOU LIKE A RODEO CLOWN, LITTLE GIRL!
AH, DANG.
I HAVE A BETTER IDEA.
GAGGGH!
HHHRRRGGHH!!!

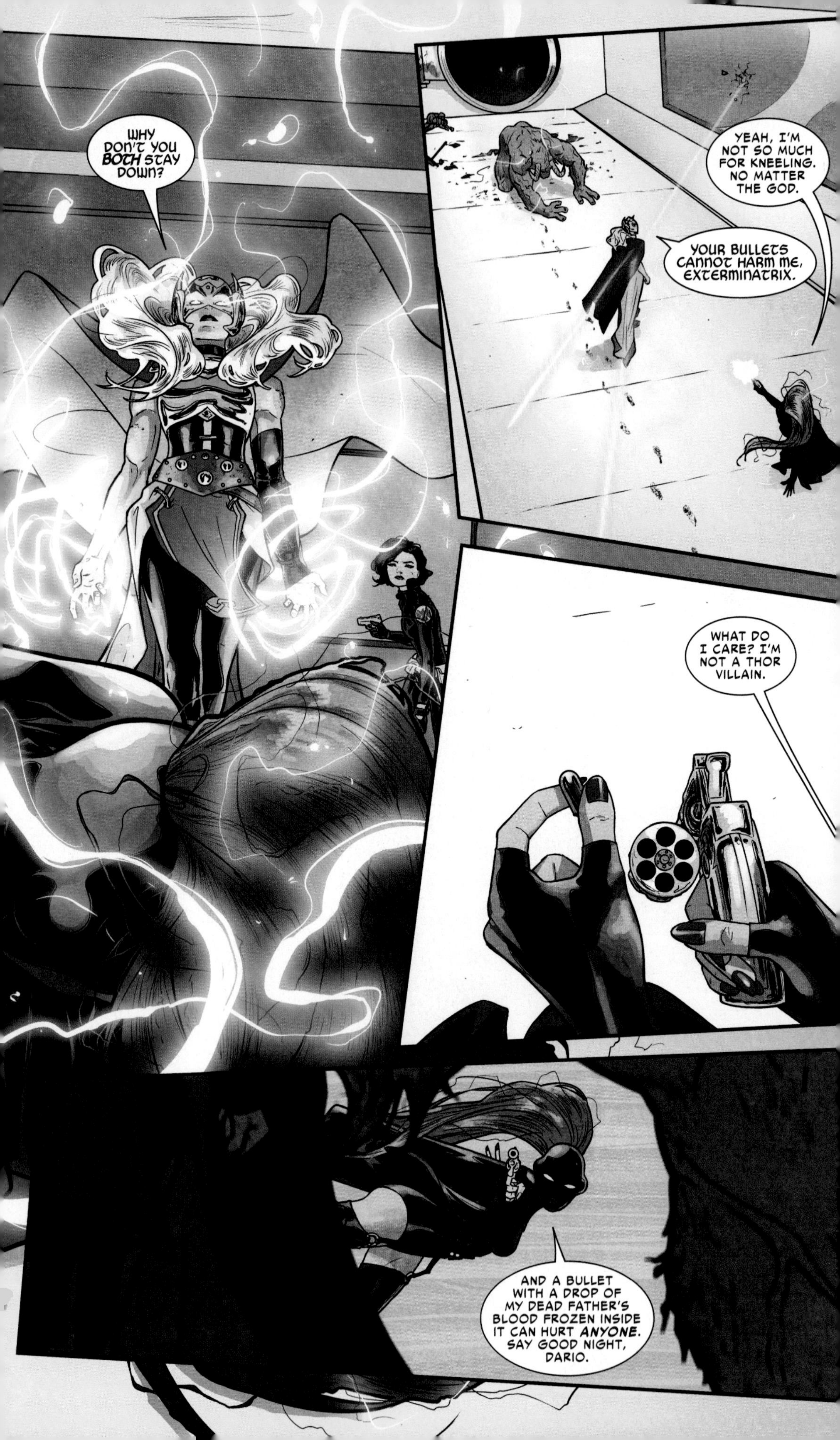
WHY DON'T YOU *BOTH* STAY DOWN?
YEAH, I'M NOT SO MUCH FOR KNEELING. NO MATTER THE GOD.
YOUR BULLETS CANNOT HARM ME, EXTERMINATRIX.
WHAT DO I CARE? I'M NOT A THOR VILLAIN.
AND A BULLET WITH A DROP OF MY DEAD FATHER'S BLOOD FROZEN INSIDE IT CAN HURT *ANYONE*. SAY GOOD NIGHT, DARIO.

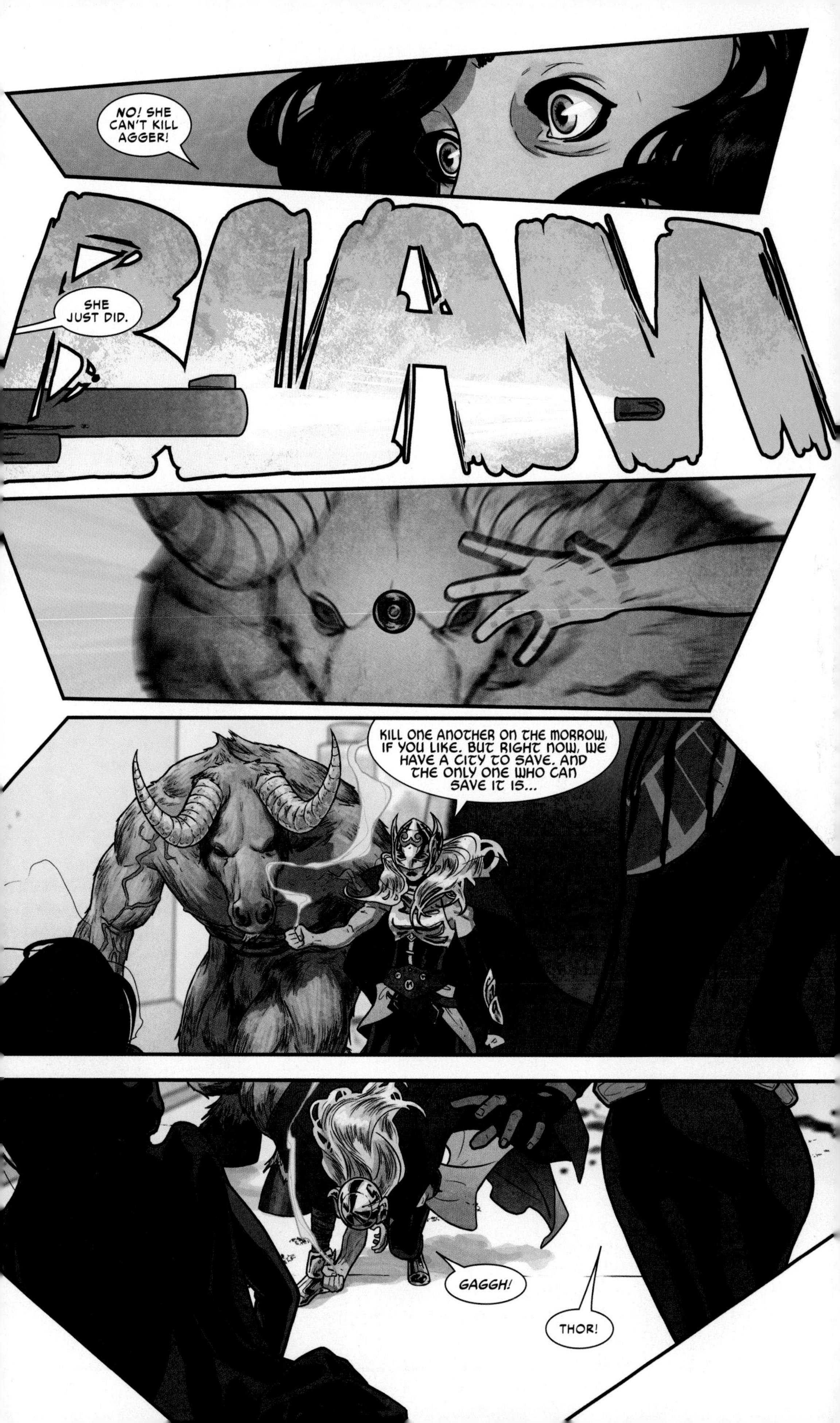
NO! SHE CAN'T KILL AGGER!
BLAM
SHE JUST DID.
KILL ONE ANOTHER ON THE MORROW, IF YOU LIKE. BUT RIGHT NOW, WE HAVE A CITY TO SAVE. AND THE ONLY ONE WHO CAN SAVE IT IS...
GAGGH!
THOR!

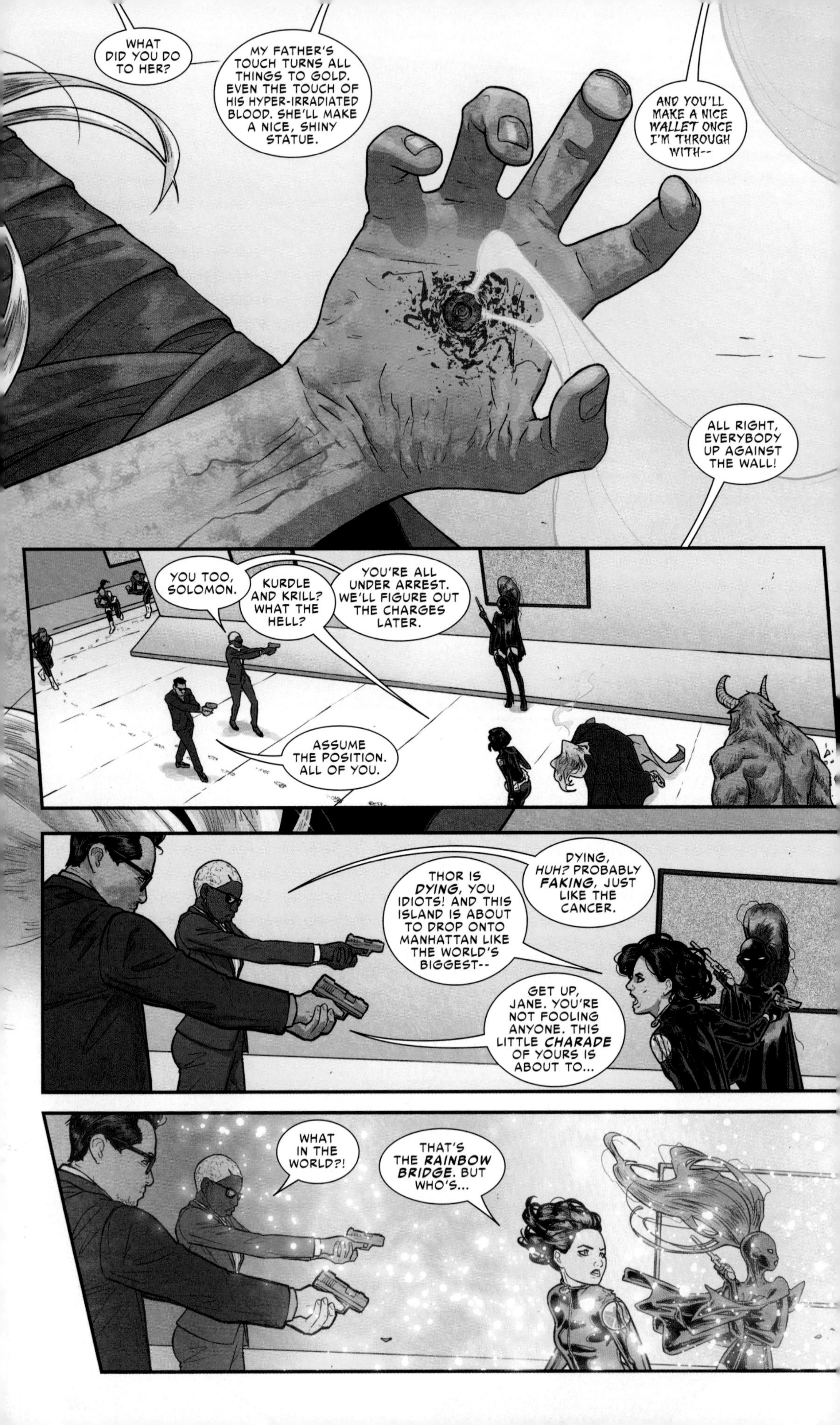
WHAT DID YOU DO TO HER?
MY FATHER'S TOUCH TURNS ALL THINGS TO GOLD. EVEN THE TOUCH OF HIS HYPER-IRRADIATED BLOOD. SHE'LL MAKE A NICE, SHINY STATUE.
AND YOU'LL MAKE A NICE WALLET ONCE I'M THROUGH WITH--
ALL RIGHT, EVERYBODY UP AGAINST THE WALL!
YOU TOO, SOLOMON.
KURDLE AND KRILL? WHAT THE HELL?
YOU'RE ALL UNDER ARREST. WE'LL FIGURE OUT THE CHARGES LATER.
ASSUME THE POSITION. ALL OF YOU.
THOR IS DYING, YOU IDIOTS! AND THIS ISLAND IS ABOUT TO DROP ONTO MANHATTAN LIKE THE WORLD'S BIGGEST--
DYING, HUH? PROBABLY FAKING, JUST LIKE THE CANCER.
GET UP, JANE. YOU'RE NOT FOOLING ANYONE. THIS LITTLE CHARADE OF YOURS IS ABOUT TO...
WHAT IN THE WORLD?!
THAT'S THE RAINBOW BRIDGE. BUT WHO'S...

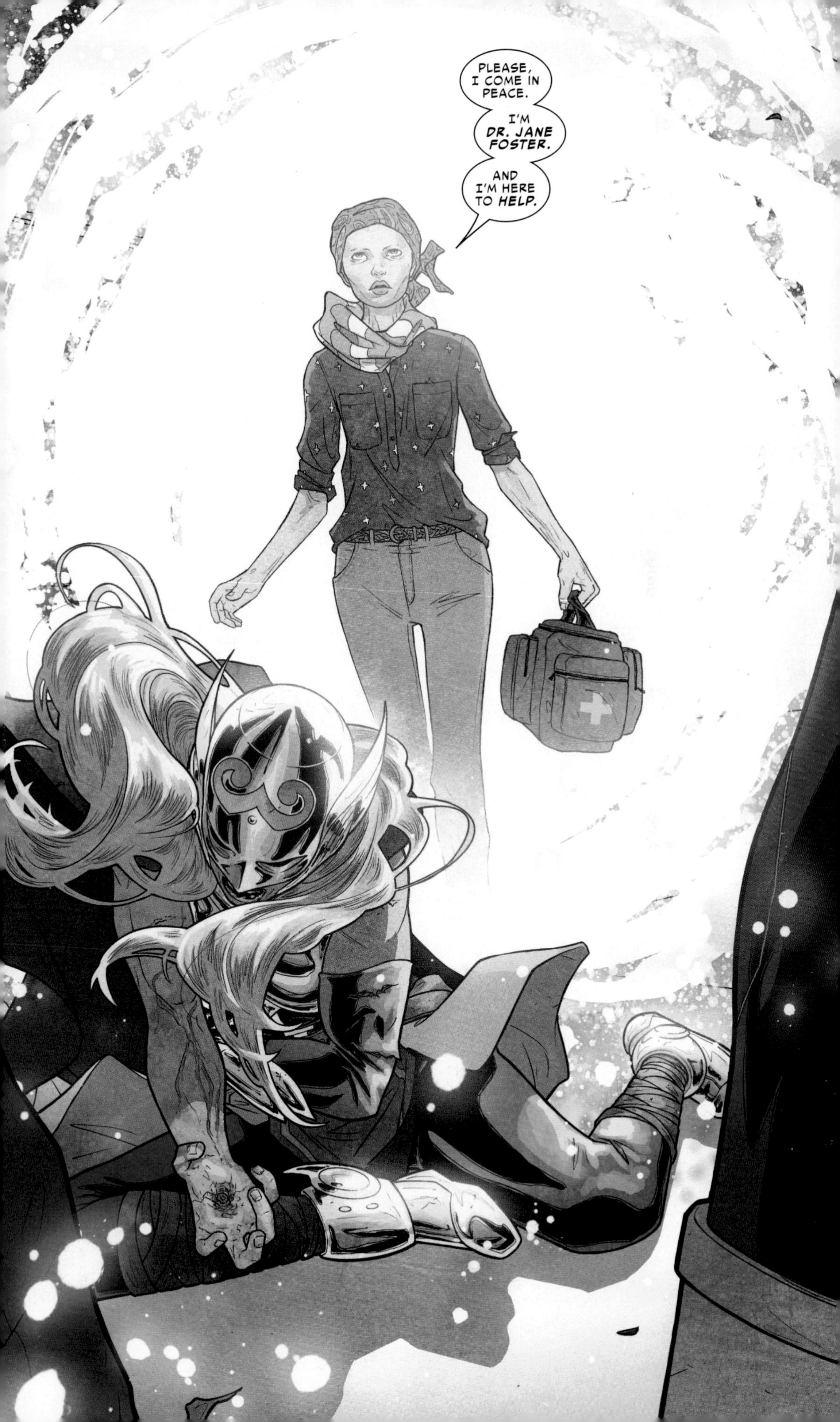
PLEASE, I COME IN PEACE.
I'M DR. JANE FOSTER.
AND I'M HERE TO HELP.

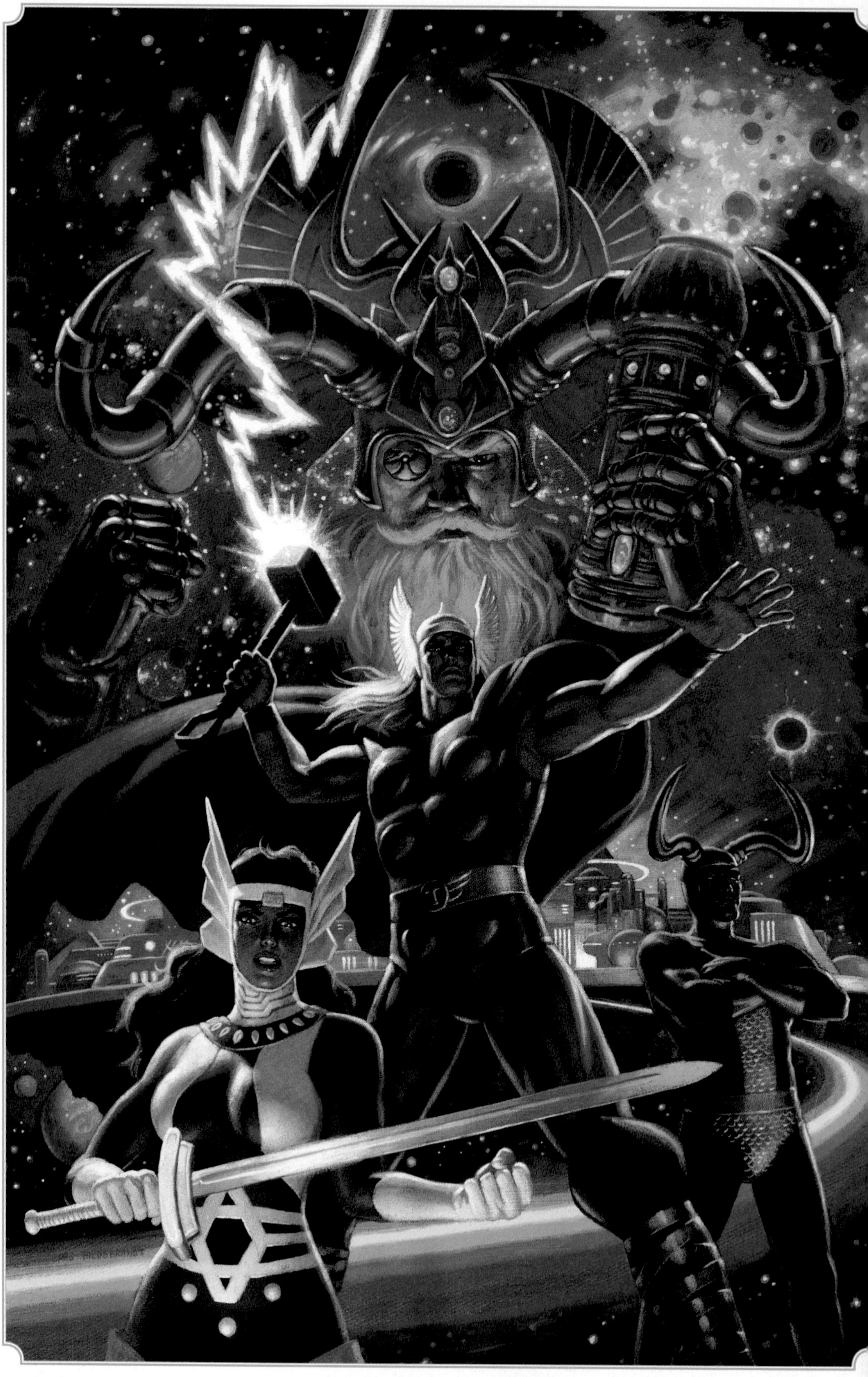

MIGHTY THOR # 8 VARIANT
BY **GREG HILDEBRANDT**

11

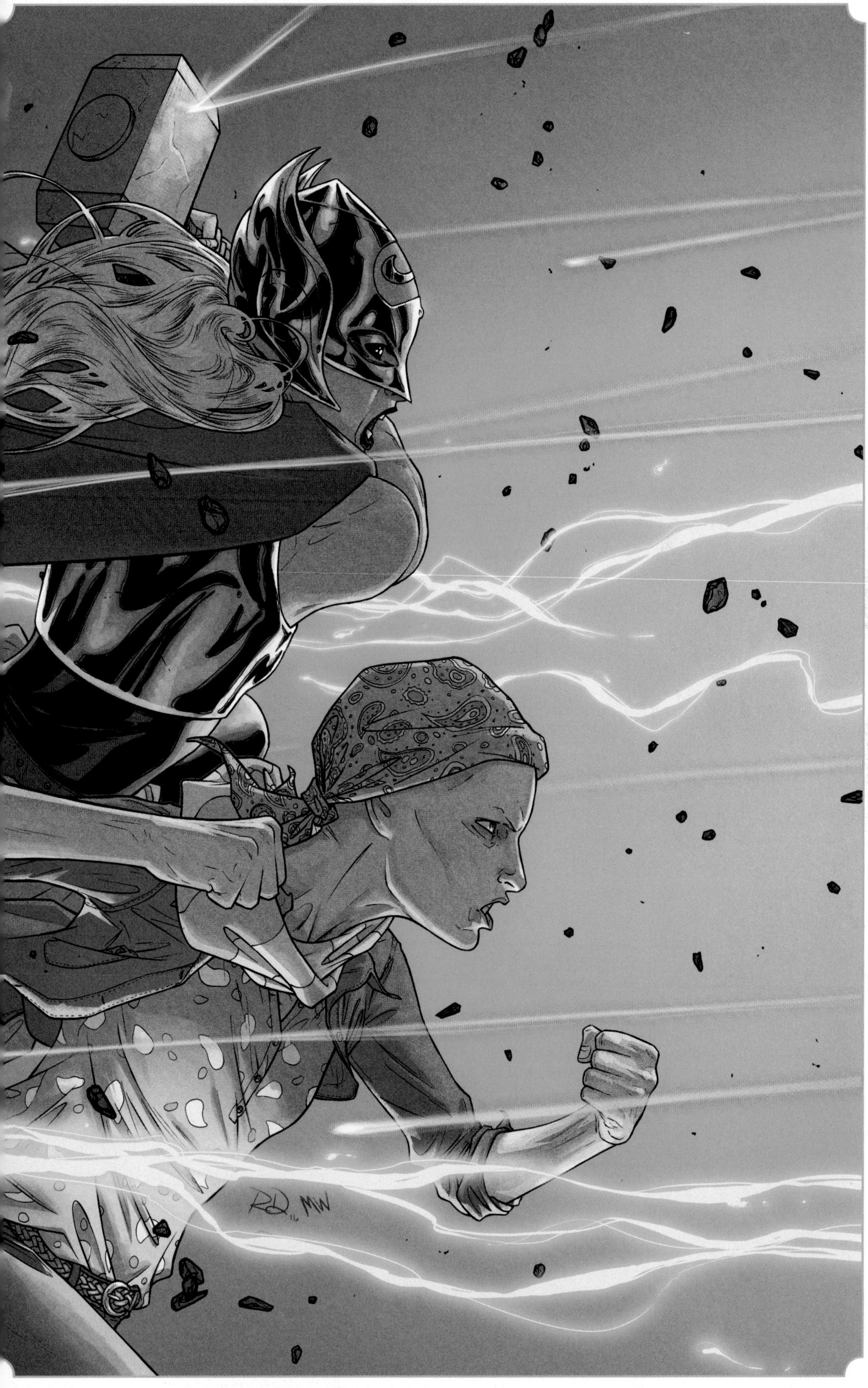

RD 16 MW

THOR'S BEST FRIEND

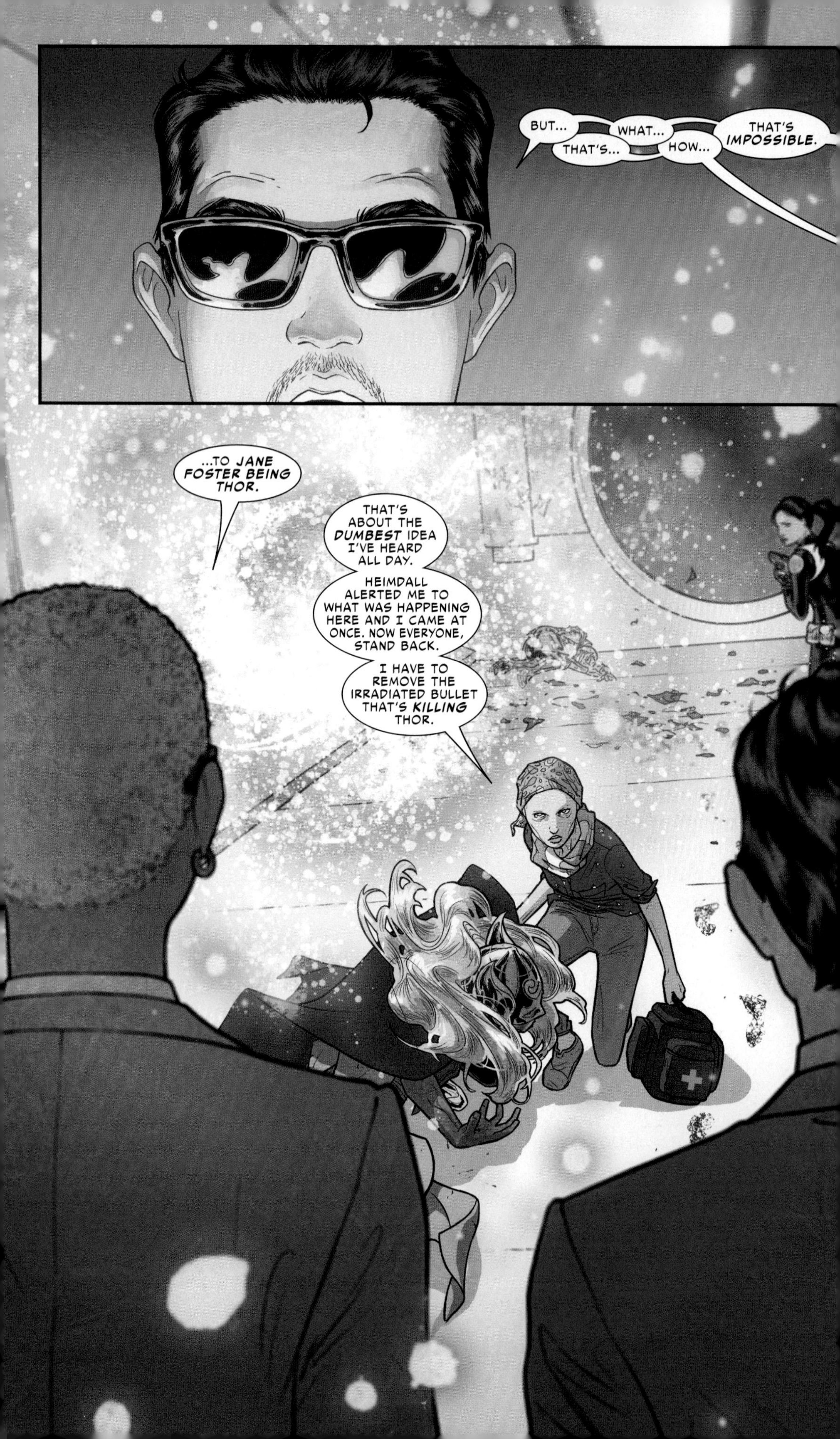

BUT...
THAT'S...
WHAT...
HOW...
THAT'S IMPOSSIBLE.
...TO JANE FOSTER BEING THOR.
THAT'S ABOUT THE DUMBEST IDEA I'VE HEARD ALL DAY.
HEIMDALL ALERTED ME TO WHAT WAS HAPPENING HERE AND I CAME AT ONCE. NOW EVERYONE, STAND BACK.
I HAVE TO REMOVE THE IRRADIATED BULLET THAT'S KILLING THOR.

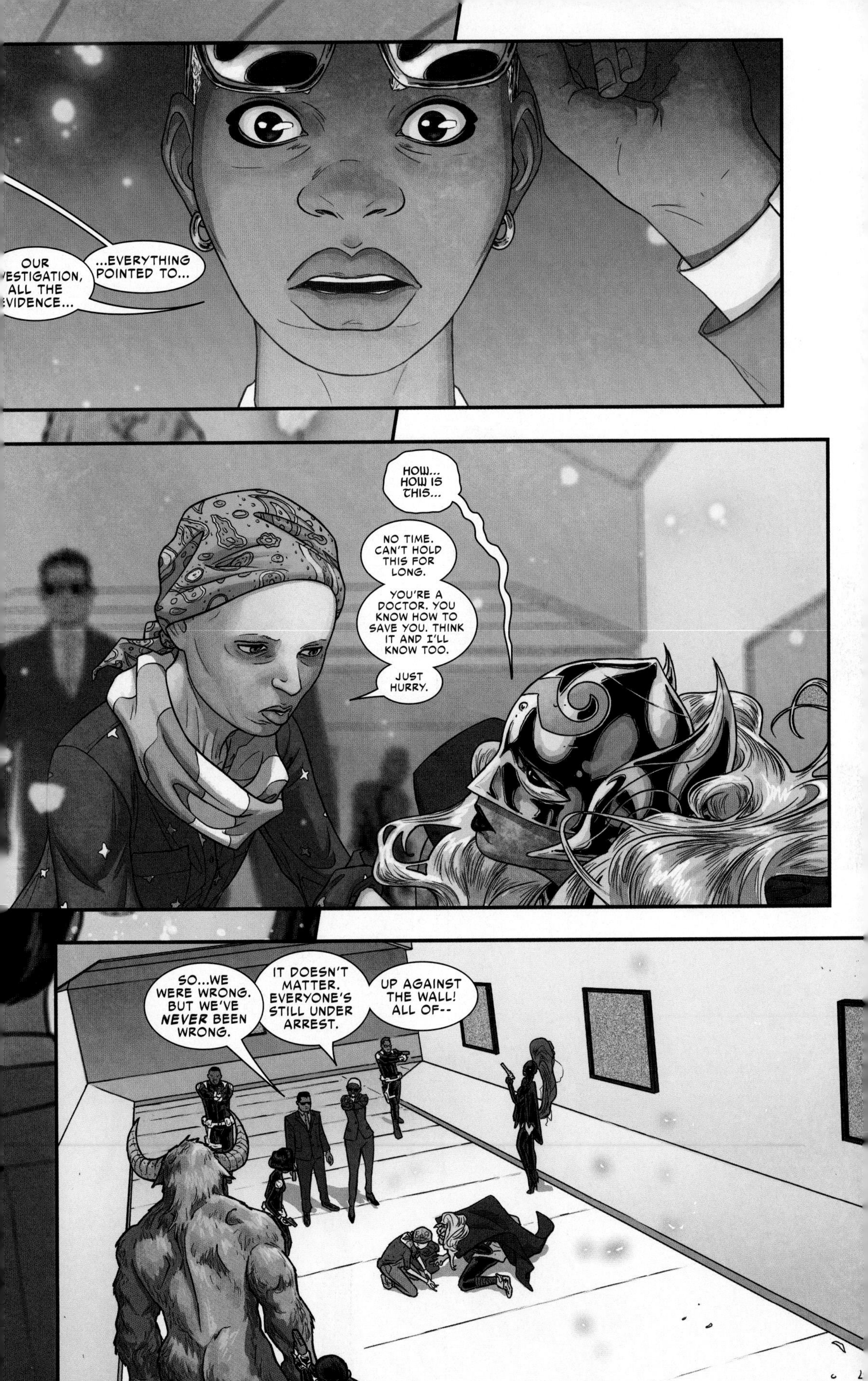
OUR VESTIGATION, ALL THE VIDENCE...
...EVERYTHING POINTED TO...
HOW... HOW IS THIS...
NO TIME. CAN'T HOLD THIS FOR LONG.
YOU'RE A DOCTOR. YOU KNOW HOW TO SAVE YOU. THINK IT AND I'LL KNOW TOO.
JUST HURRY.
SO...WE WERE WRONG. BUT WE'VE *NEVER* BEEN WRONG.
IT DOESN'T MATTER. EVERYONE'S STILL UNDER ARREST.
UP AGAINST THE WALL! ALL OF--

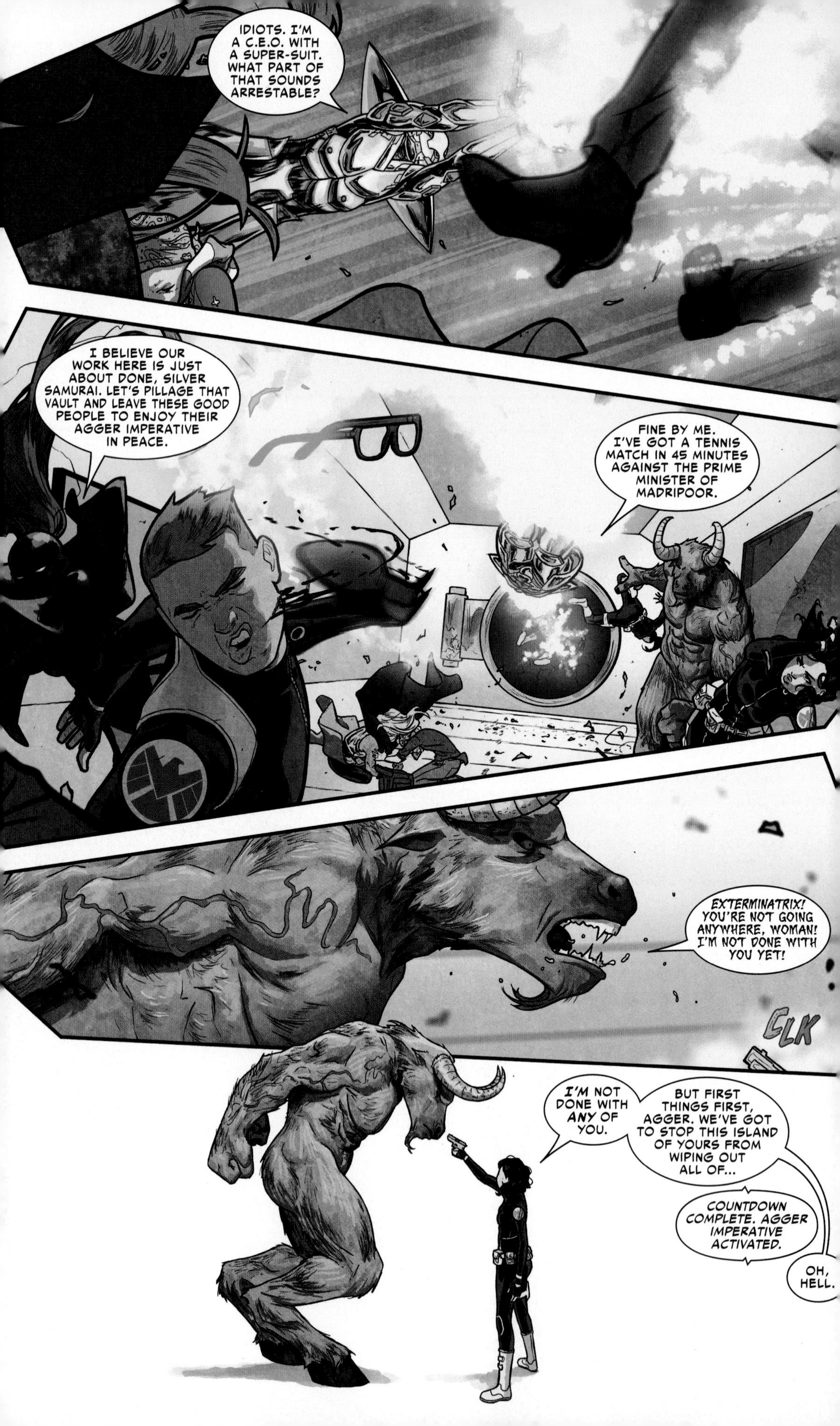
IDIOTS. I'M A C.E.O. WITH A SUPER-SUIT. WHAT PART OF THAT SOUNDS ARRESTABLE?
I BELIEVE OUR WORK HERE IS JUST ABOUT DONE, SILVER SAMURAI. LET'S PILLAGE THAT VAULT AND LEAVE THESE GOOD PEOPLE TO ENJOY THEIR AGGER IMPERATIVE IN PEACE.
FINE BY ME. I'VE GOT A TENNIS MATCH IN 45 MINUTES AGAINST THE PRIME MINISTER OF MADRIPOOR.
EXTERMINATRIX! YOU'RE NOT GOING ANYWHERE, WOMAN! I'M NOT DONE WITH YOU YET!
CLK
I'M NOT DONE WITH ANY OF YOU.
BUT FIRST THINGS FIRST, AGGER. WE'VE GOT TO STOP THIS ISLAND OF YOURS FROM WIPING OUT ALL OF...
COUNTDOWN COMPLETE. AGGER IMPERATIVE ACTIVATED.
OH, HELL.

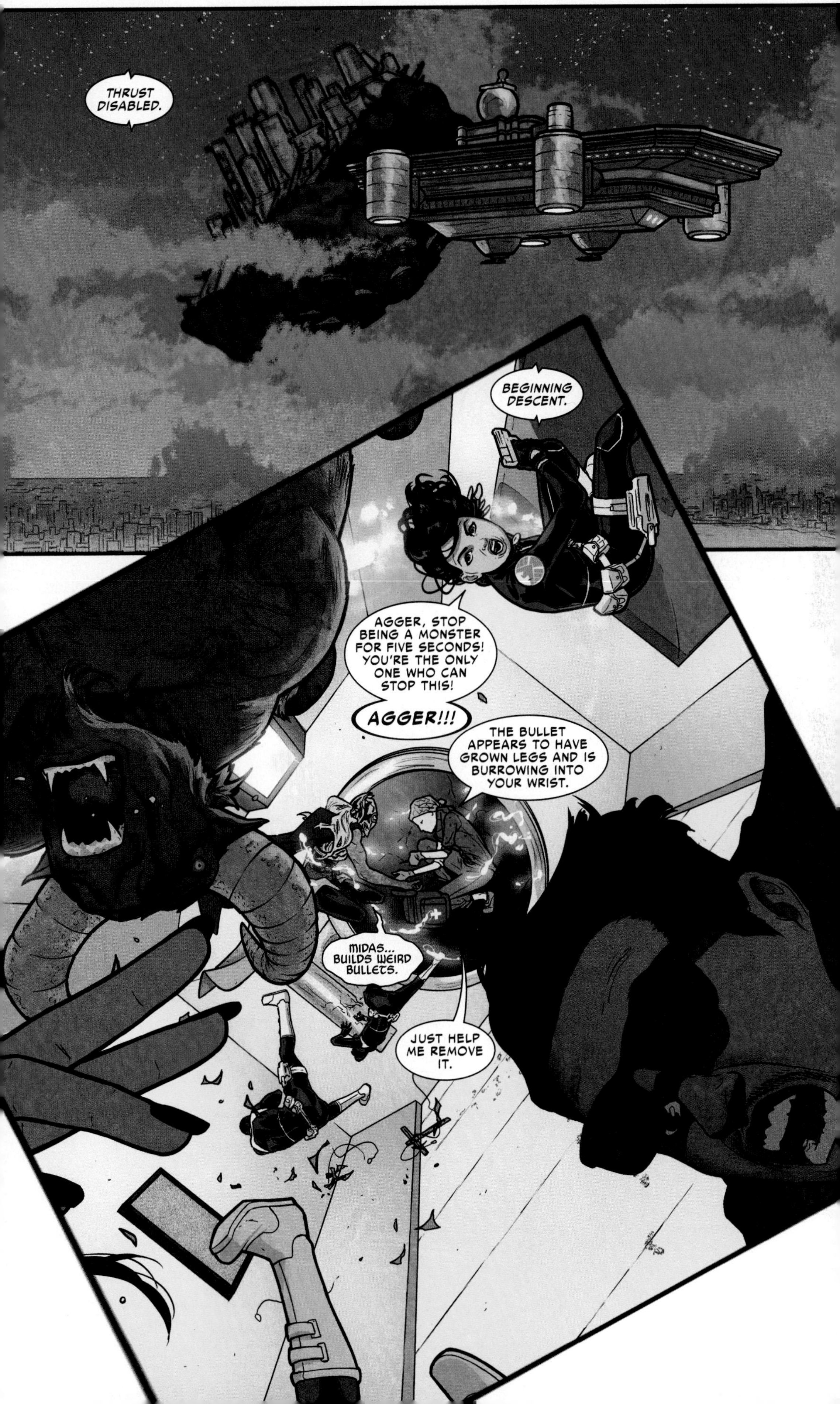
THRUST DISABLED.
BEGINNING DESCENT.
AGGER, STOP BEING A MONSTER FOR FIVE SECONDS! YOU'RE THE ONLY ONE WHO CAN STOP THIS!
AGGER!!!
THE BULLET APPEARS TO HAVE GROWN LEGS AND IS BURROWING INTO YOUR WRIST.
MIDAS... BUILDS WEIRD BULLETS.
JUST HELP ME REMOVE IT.

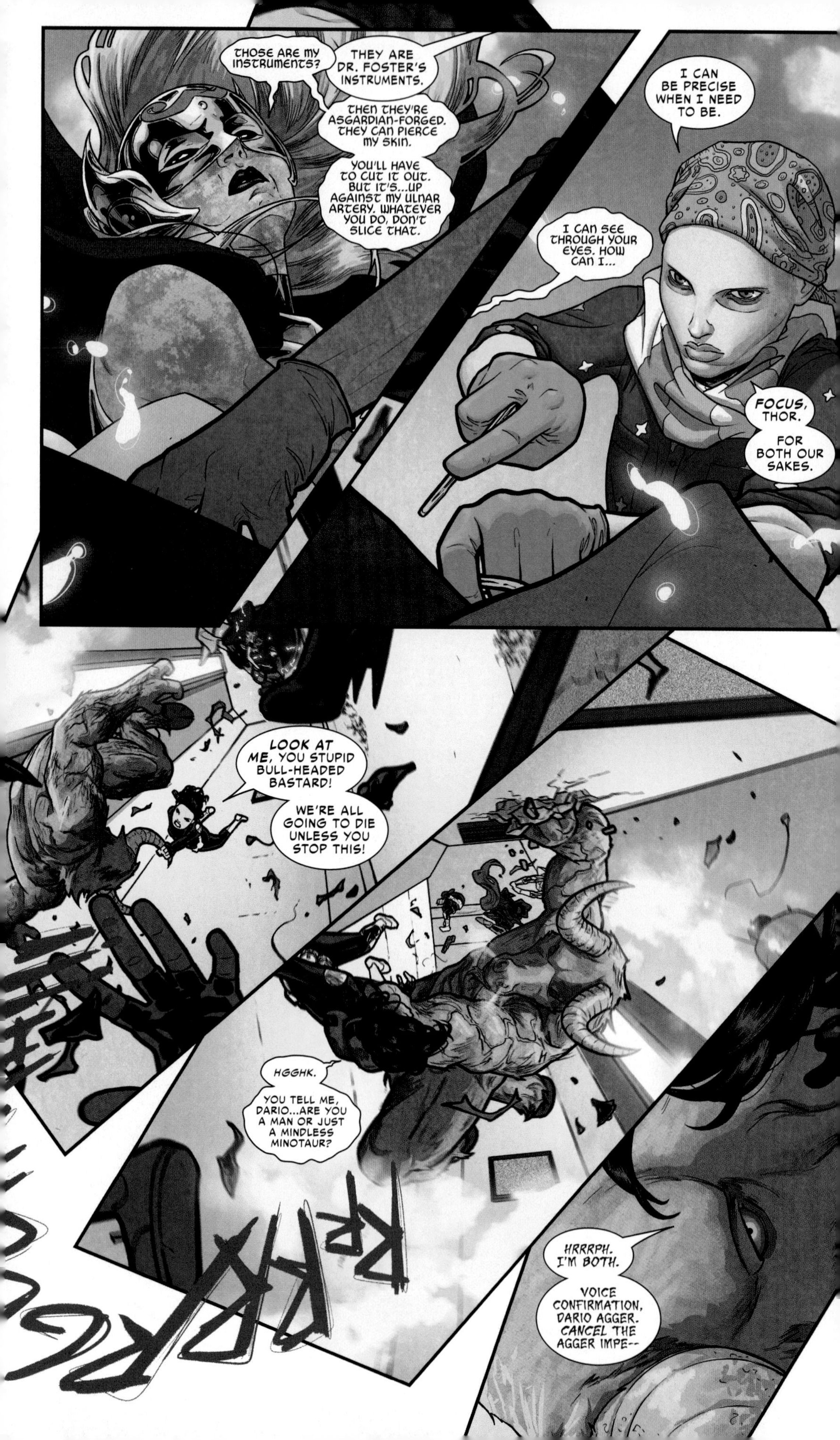
THOSE ARE MY INSTRUMENTS?
THEY ARE DR. FOSTER'S INSTRUMENTS.
THEN THEY'RE ASGARDIAN-FORGED. THEY CAN PIERCE MY SKIN.
YOU'LL HAVE TO CUT IT OUT. BUT IT'S...UP AGAINST MY ULNAR ARTERY. WHATEVER YOU DO, DON'T SLICE THAT.
I CAN BE PRECISE WHEN I NEED TO BE.
I CAN SEE THROUGH YOUR EYES. HOW CAN I...
FOCUS, THOR.
FOR BOTH OUR SAKES.
LOOK AT ME, YOU STUPID BULL-HEADED BASTARD!
WE'RE ALL GOING TO DIE UNLESS YOU STOP THIS!
HGGHK.
YOU TELL ME, DARIO...ARE YOU A MAN OR JUST A MINDLESS MINOTAUR?
HRRRPH. I'M BOTH.
VOICE CONFIRMATION, DARIO AGGER. CANCEL THE AGGER IMPE--

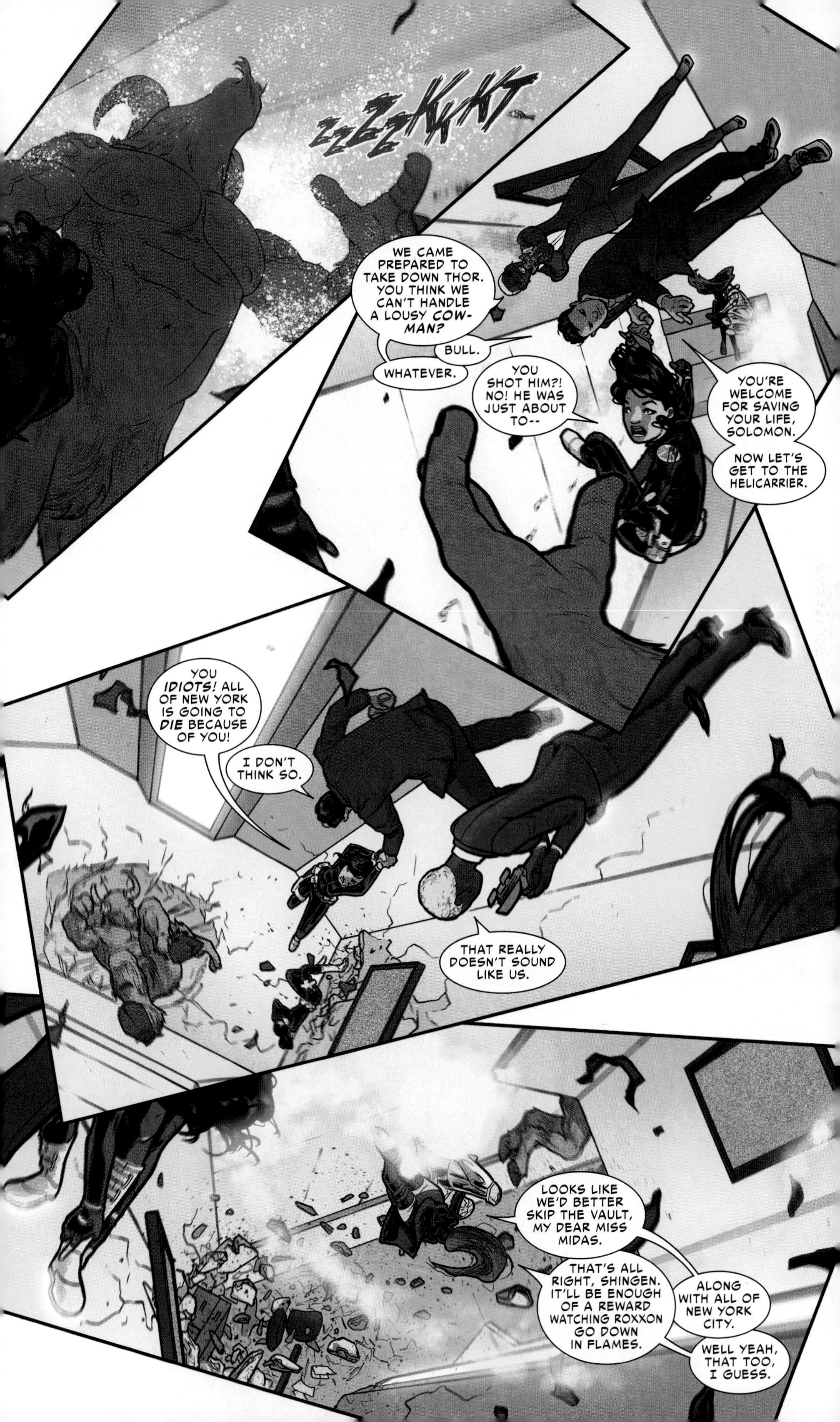
ZZZZZKKKT
WE CAME PREPARED TO TAKE DOWN THOR. YOU THINK WE CAN'T HANDLE A LOUSY COW-MAN?
BULL.
WHATEVER.
YOU SHOT HIM?! NO! HE WAS JUST ABOUT TO--
YOU'RE WELCOME FOR SAVING YOUR LIFE, SOLOMON.
NOW LET'S GET TO THE HELICARRIER.
YOU IDIOTS! ALL OF NEW YORK IS GOING TO DIE BECAUSE OF YOU!
I DON'T THINK SO.
THAT REALLY DOESN'T SOUND LIKE US.
LOOKS LIKE WE'D BETTER SKIP THE VAULT, MY DEAR MISS MIDAS.
THAT'S ALL RIGHT, SHINGEN. IT'LL BE ENOUGH OF A REWARD WATCHING ROXXON GO DOWN IN FLAMES.
ALONG WITH ALL OF NEW YORK CITY.
WELL YEAH, THAT TOO, I GUESS.

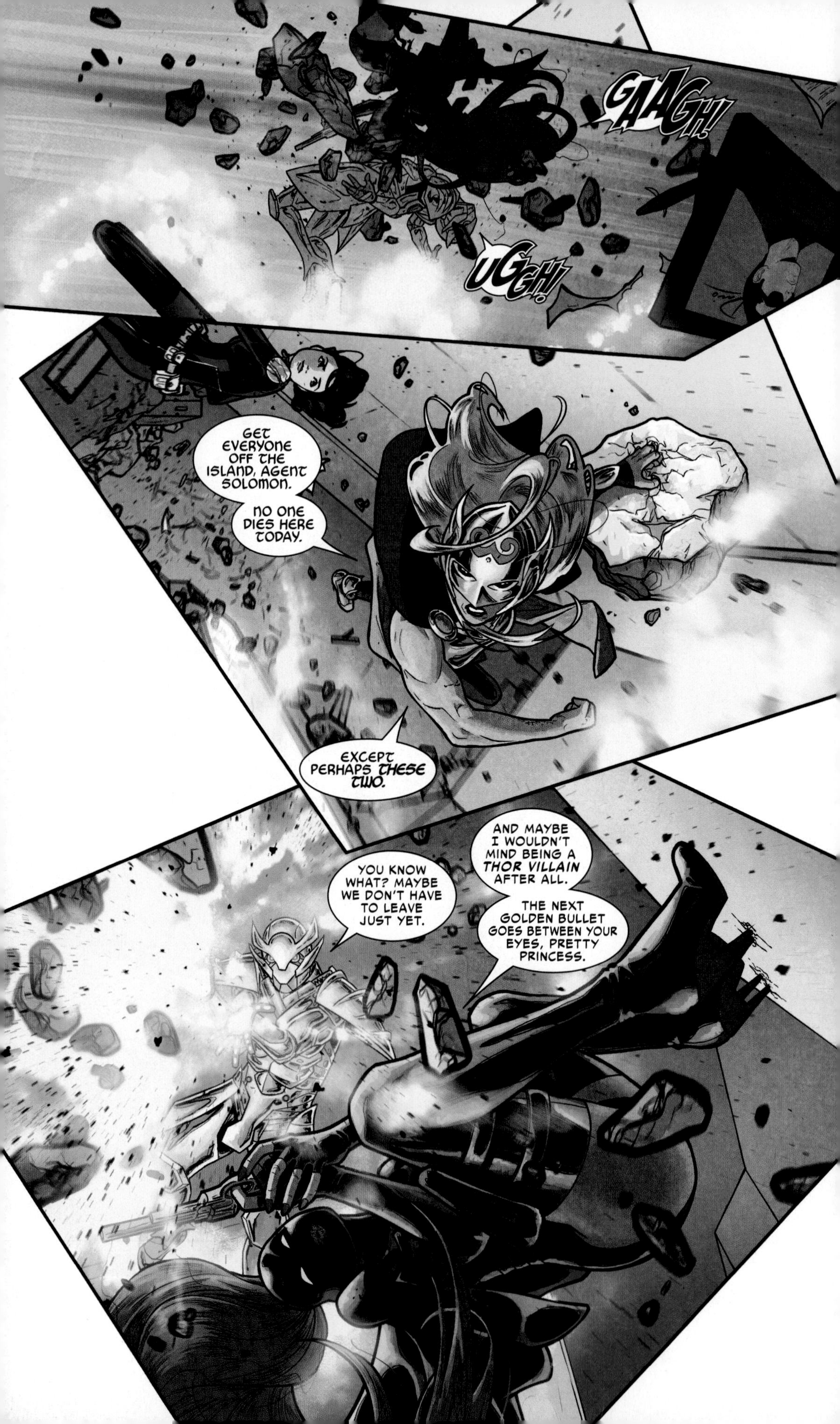
GAAAGH!
UGGH!
GET EVERYONE OFF THE ISLAND, AGENT SOLOMON.
NO ONE DIES HERE TODAY.
EXCEPT PERHAPS *THESE TWO.*
YOU KNOW WHAT? MAYBE WE DON'T HAVE TO LEAVE JUST YET.
AND MAYBE I WOULDN'T MIND BEING A *THOR VILLAIN* AFTER ALL.
THE NEXT GOLDEN BULLET GOES BETWEEN YOUR EYES, PRETTY PRINCESS.

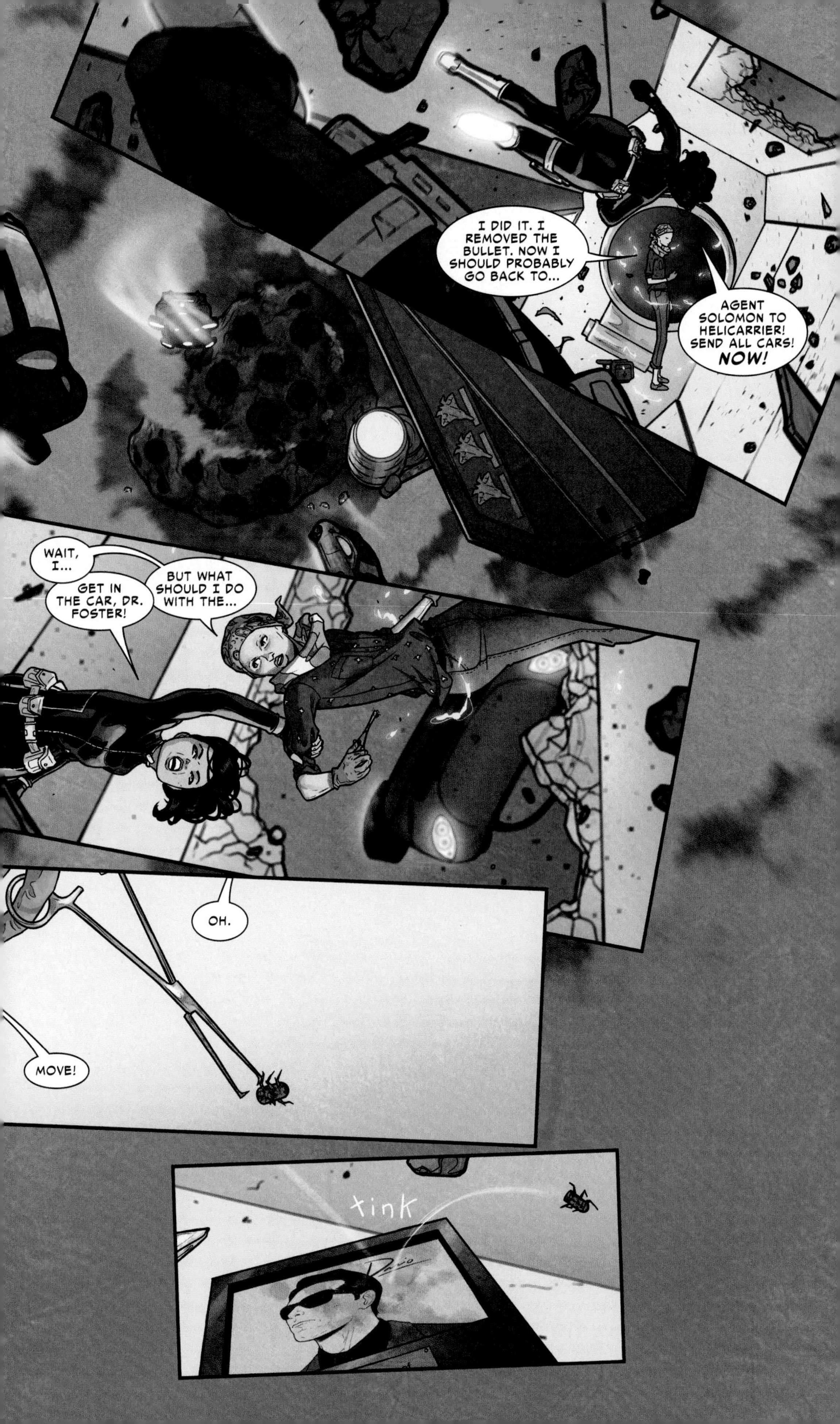
I DID IT. I REMOVED THE BULLET. NOW I SHOULD PROBABLY GO BACK TO...
AGENT SOLOMON TO HELICARRIER! SEND ALL CARS! NOW!
WAIT, I...
GET IN THE CAR, DR. FOSTER!
BUT WHAT SHOULD I DO WITH THE...
OH.
MOVE!
tink

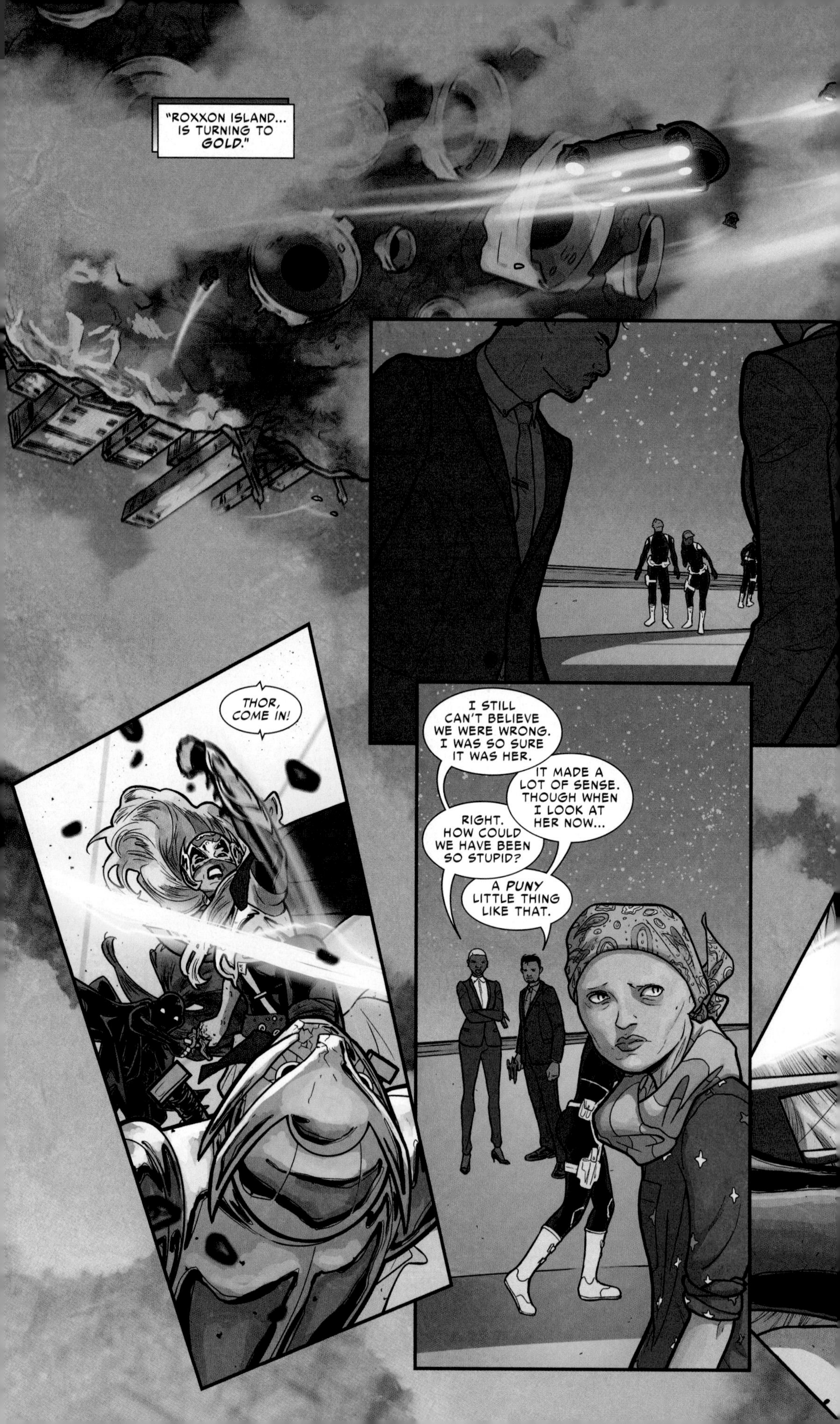
"ROXXON ISLAND... IS TURNING TO GOLD."
THOR, COME IN!
I STILL CAN'T BELIEVE WE WERE WRONG. I WAS SO SURE IT WAS HER.
IT MADE A LOT OF SENSE. THOUGH WHEN I LOOK AT HER NOW...
RIGHT. HOW COULD WE HAVE BEEN SO STUPID?
A PUNY LITTLE THING LIKE THAT.

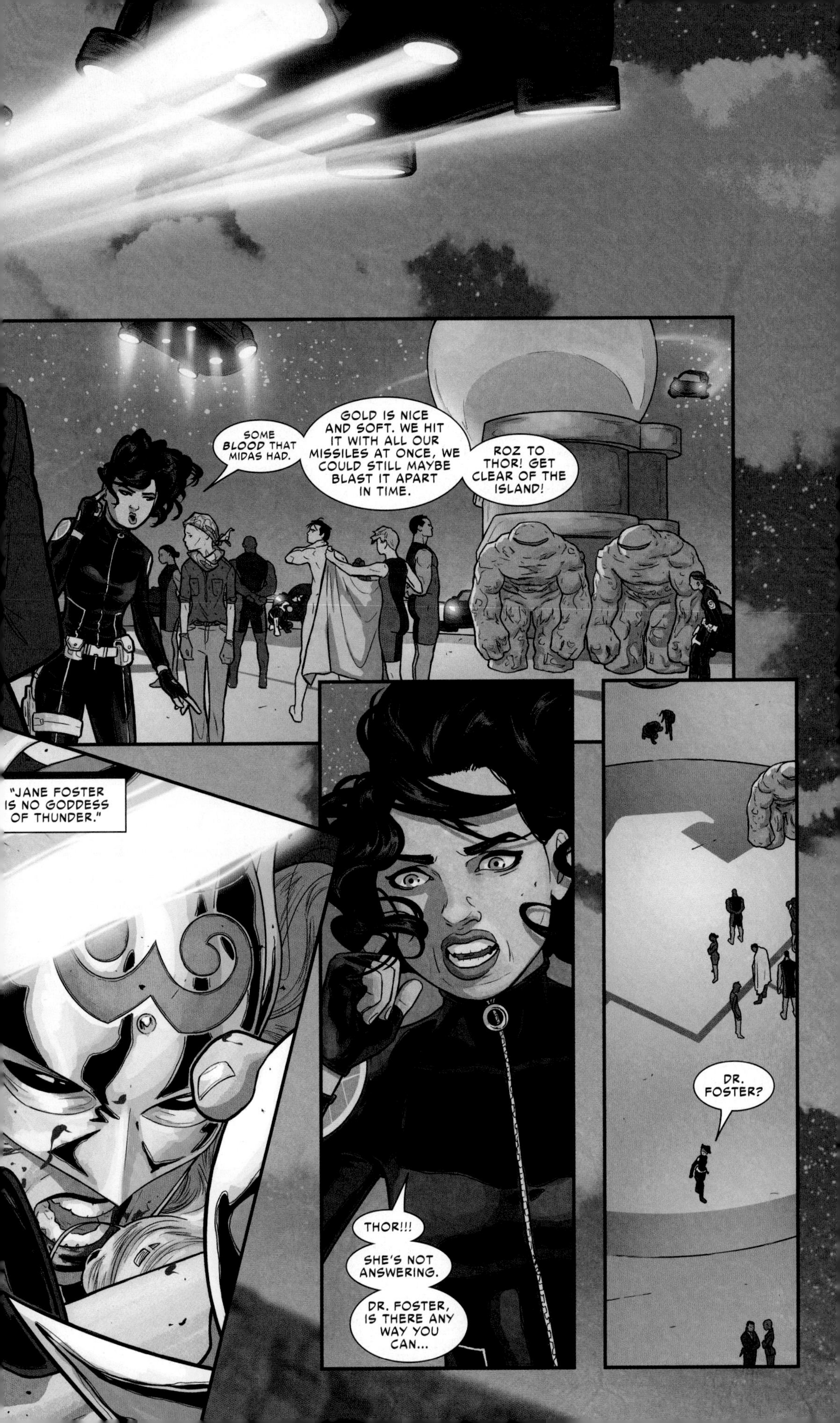
SOME BLOOD THAT MIDAS HAD.
GOLD IS NICE AND SOFT. WE HIT IT WITH ALL OUR MISSILES AT ONCE, WE COULD STILL MAYBE BLAST IT APART IN TIME.
ROZ TO THOR! GET CLEAR OF THE ISLAND!
"JANE FOSTER IS NO GODDESS OF THUNDER."
THOR!!!
SHE'S NOT ANSWERING.
DR. FOSTER, IS THERE ANY WAY YOU CAN...
DR. FOSTER?

LORD ODIN?

IT IS...

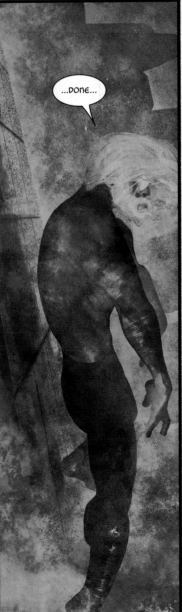

...DONE...

THE ALL-FATHER HAD *TRAPPED* THE *STORM INSIDE* THE URU. THROUGH WHAT DARK AND PRIMAL MAGIC, EVEN HE COULD NOT SAY.

THOUGH HE KNEW EXACTLY WHAT TO DO NEXT.

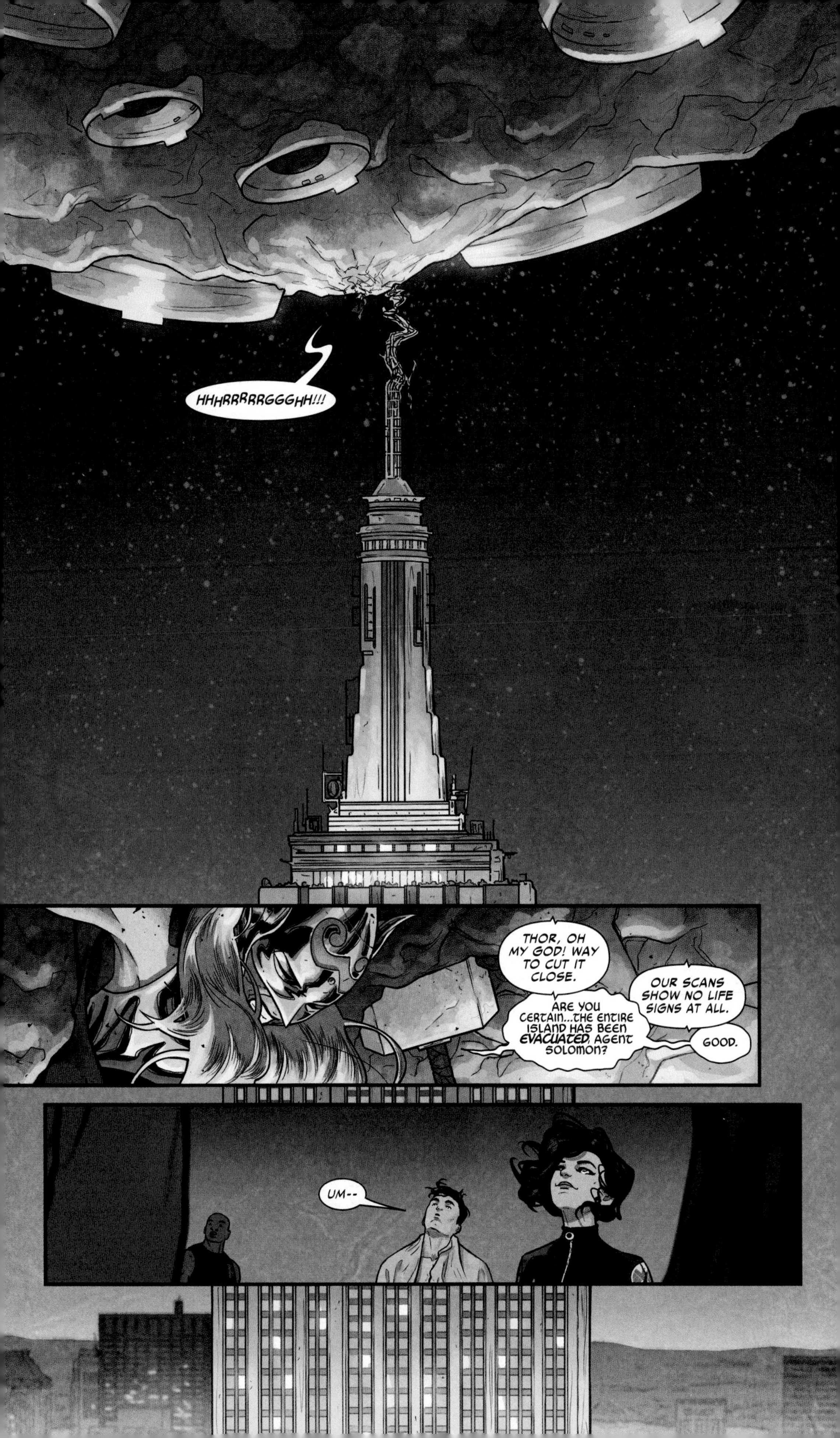
HHHRRRRRGGGHH!!!
THOR, OH MY GOD! WAY TO CUT IT CLOSE.
ARE YOU CERTAIN...THE ENTIRE ISLAND HAS BEEN EVACUATED, AGENT SOLOMON?
OUR SCANS SHOW NO LIFE SIGNS AT ALL.
GOOD.
UM--

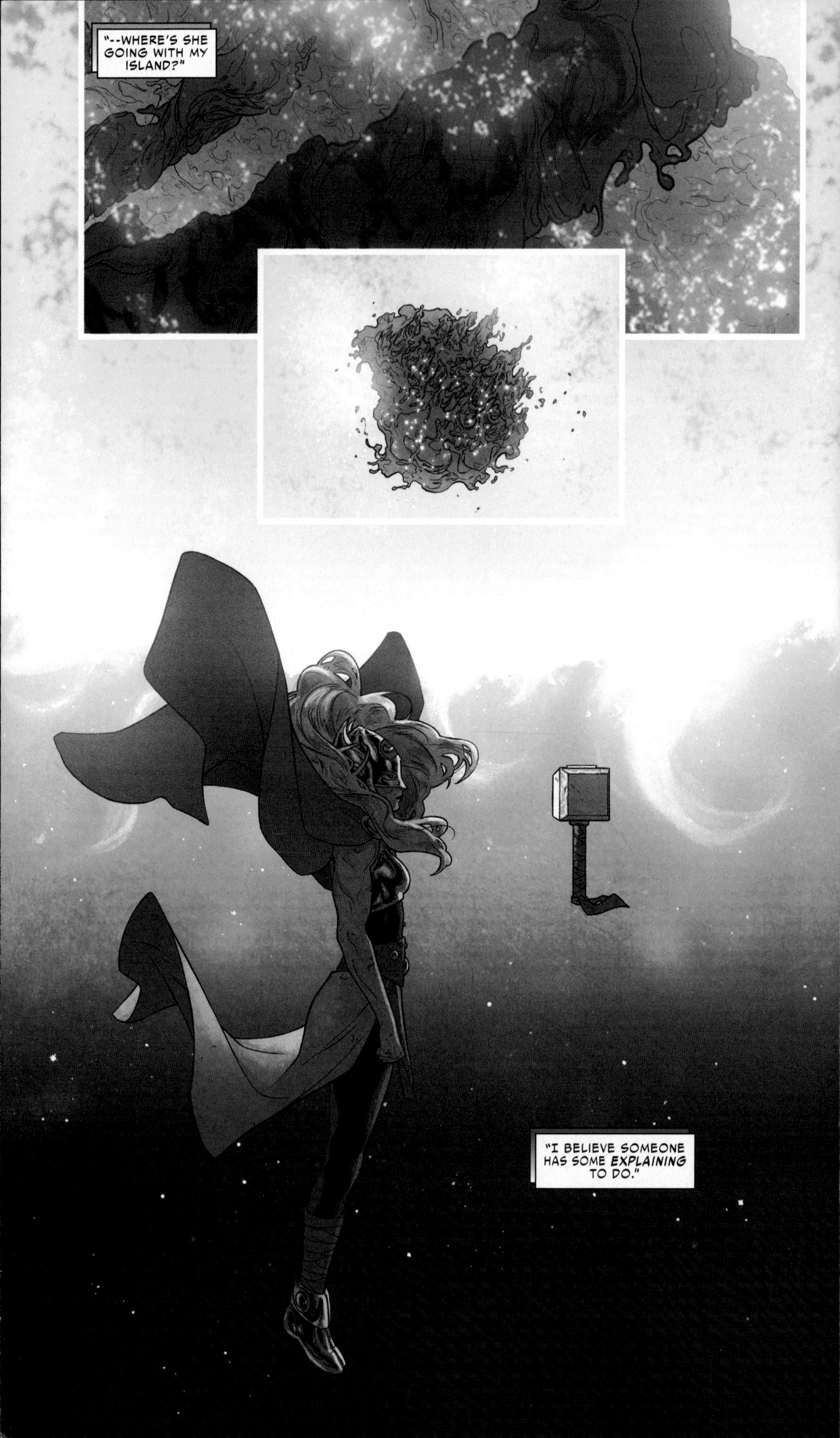
"--WHERE'S SHE GOING WITH MY ISLAND?"
"I BELIEVE SOMEONE HAS SOME EXPLAINING TO DO."

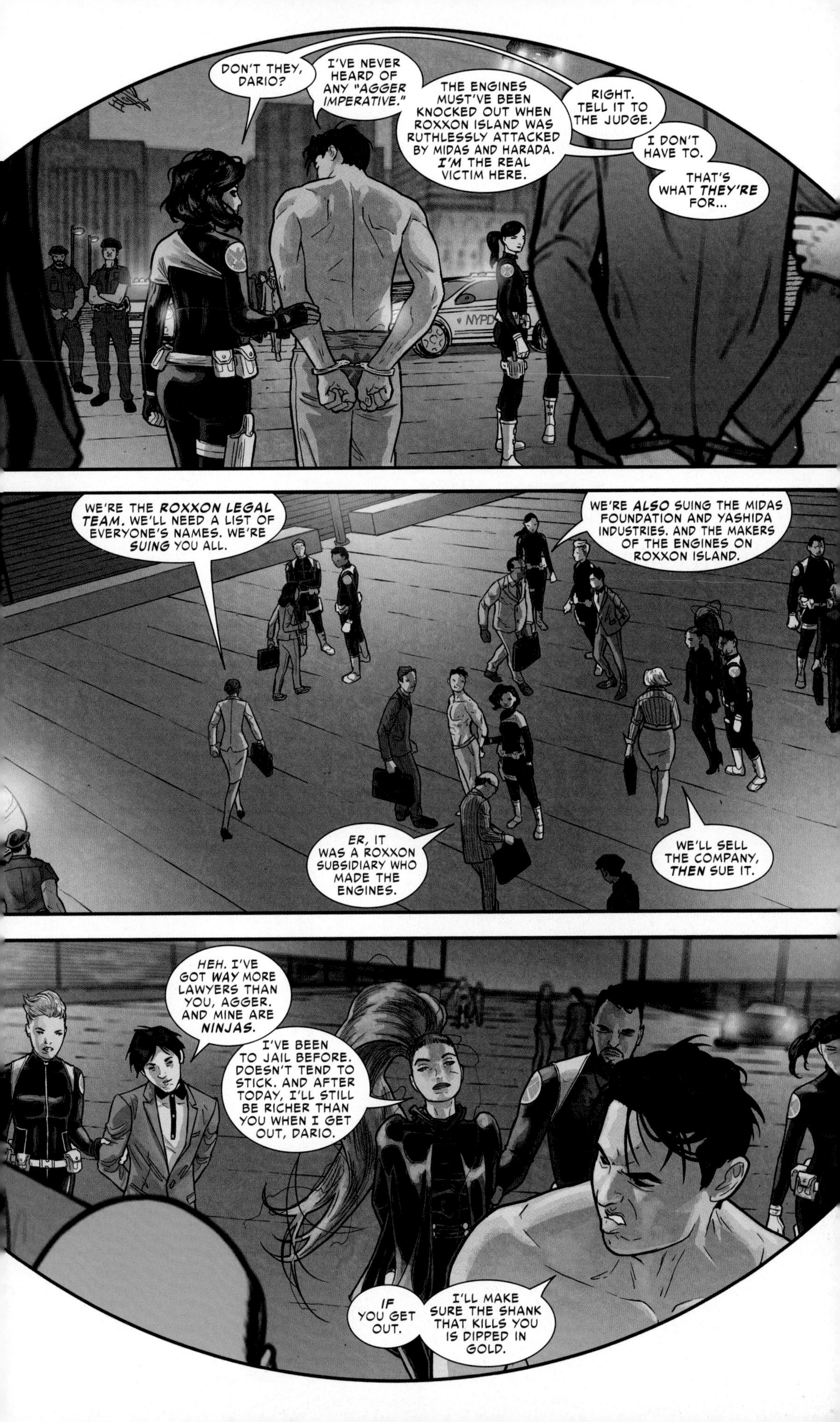
DON'T THEY, DARIO?
I'VE NEVER HEARD OF ANY "AGGER IMPERATIVE."
THE ENGINES MUST'VE BEEN KNOCKED OUT WHEN ROXXON ISLAND WAS RUTHLESSLY ATTACKED BY MIDAS AND HARADA. I'M THE REAL VICTIM HERE.
RIGHT. TELL IT TO THE JUDGE.
I DON'T HAVE TO.
THAT'S WHAT THEY'RE FOR...
NYPD
WE'RE THE ROXXON LEGAL TEAM. WE'LL NEED A LIST OF EVERYONE'S NAMES. WE'RE SUING YOU ALL.
WE'RE ALSO SUING THE MIDAS FOUNDATION AND YASHIDA INDUSTRIES. AND THE MAKERS OF THE ENGINES ON ROXXON ISLAND.
ER, IT WAS A ROXXON SUBSIDIARY WHO MADE THE ENGINES.
WE'LL SELL THE COMPANY, THEN SUE IT.
HEH. I'VE GOT WAY MORE LAWYERS THAN YOU, AGGER. AND MINE ARE NINJAS.
I'VE BEEN TO JAIL BEFORE. DOESN'T TEND TO STICK. AND AFTER TODAY, I'LL STILL BE RICHER THAN YOU WHEN I GET OUT, DARIO.
IF YOU GET OUT.
I'LL MAKE SURE THE SHANK THAT KILLS YOU IS DIPPED IN GOLD.

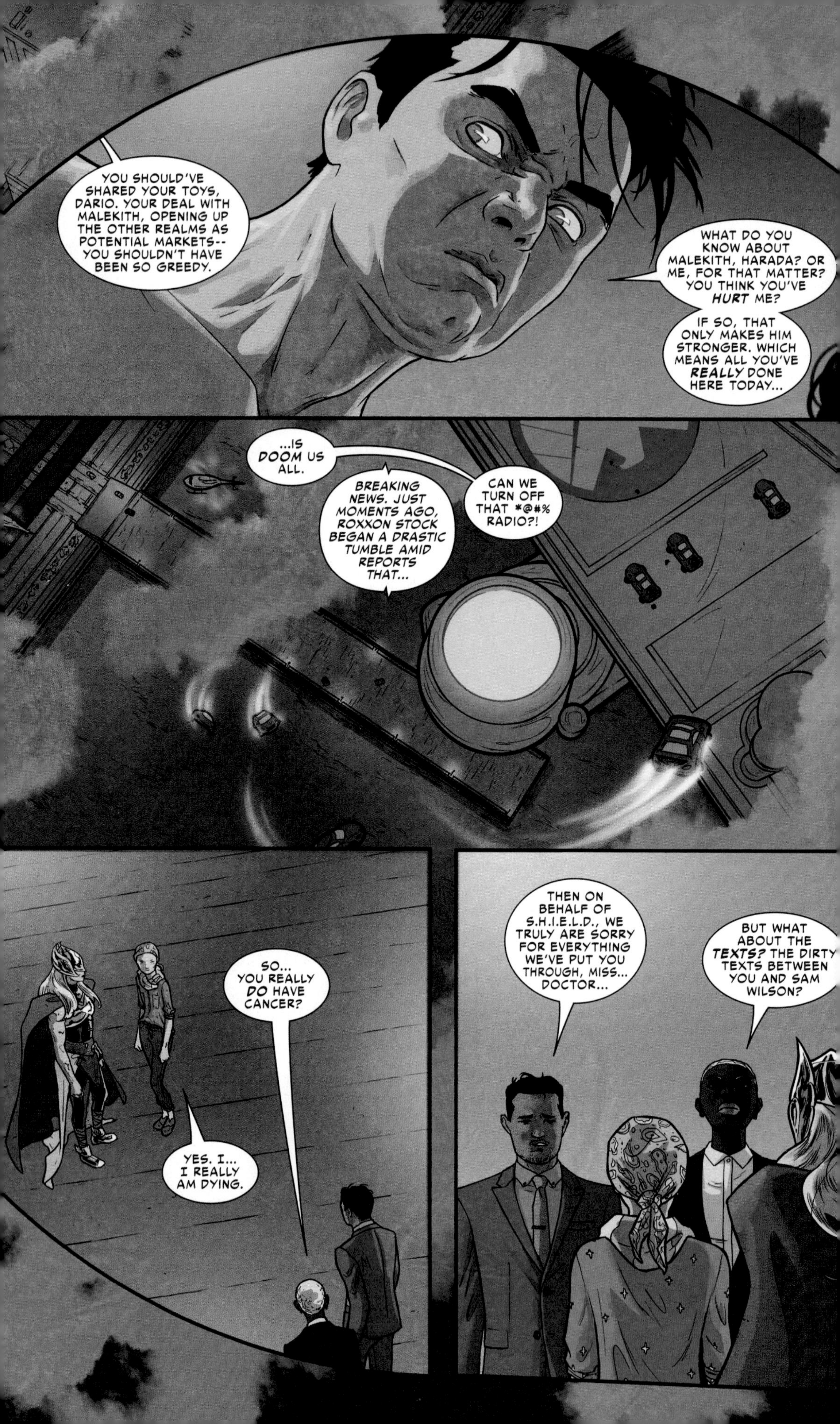
YOU SHOULD'VE SHARED YOUR TOYS, DARIO. YOUR DEAL WITH MALEKITH, OPENING UP THE OTHER REALMS AS POTENTIAL MARKETS-- YOU SHOULDN'T HAVE BEEN SO GREEDY.
WHAT DO YOU KNOW ABOUT MALEKITH, HARADA? OR ME, FOR THAT MATTER? YOU THINK YOU'VE HURT ME?
IF SO, THAT ONLY MAKES HIM STRONGER. WHICH MEANS ALL YOU'VE REALLY DONE HERE TODAY...
...IS DOOM US ALL.
BREAKING NEWS. JUST MOMENTS AGO, ROXXON STOCK BEGAN A DRASTIC TUMBLE AMID REPORTS THAT...
CAN WE TURN OFF THAT *@#% RADIO?!
SO... YOU REALLY DO HAVE CANCER?
YES. I... I REALLY AM DYING.
THEN ON BEHALF OF S.H.I.E.L.D., WE TRULY ARE SORRY FOR EVERYTHING WE'VE PUT YOU THROUGH, MISS... DOCTOR...
BUT WHAT ABOUT THE TEXTS? THE DIRTY TEXTS BETWEEN YOU AND SAM WILSON?

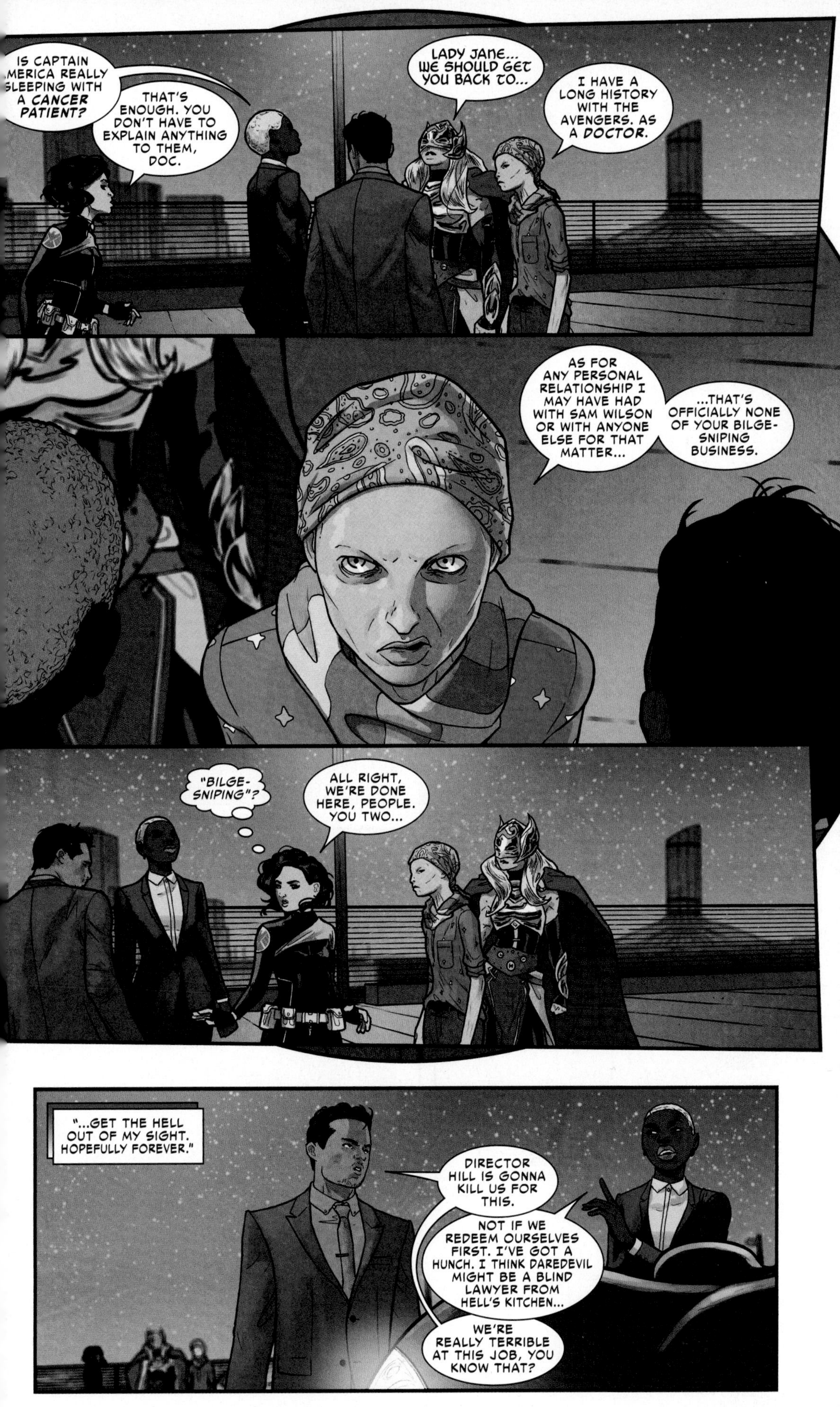
IS CAPTAIN AMERICA REALLY SLEEPING WITH A CANCER PATIENT?
THAT'S ENOUGH. YOU DON'T HAVE TO EXPLAIN ANYTHING TO THEM, DOC.
LADY JANE... WE SHOULD GET YOU BACK TO...
I HAVE A LONG HISTORY WITH THE AVENGERS. AS A DOCTOR.
AS FOR ANY PERSONAL RELATIONSHIP I MAY HAVE HAD WITH SAM WILSON OR WITH ANYONE ELSE FOR THAT MATTER...
...THAT'S OFFICIALLY NONE OF YOUR BILGE-SNIPING BUSINESS.
"BILGE-SNIPING"?
ALL RIGHT, WE'RE DONE HERE, PEOPLE. YOU TWO...
"...GET THE HELL OUT OF MY SIGHT. HOPEFULLY FOREVER."
DIRECTOR HILL IS GONNA KILL US FOR THIS.
NOT IF WE REDEEM OURSELVES FIRST. I'VE GOT A HUNCH. I THINK DAREDEVIL MIGHT BE A BLIND LAWYER FROM HELL'S KITCHEN...
WE'RE REALLY TERRIBLE AT THIS JOB, YOU KNOW THAT?

I'LL HELP YOU FILE A FORMAL COMPLAINT WHENEVER YOU'RE READY, DR. FOSTER.

JANE.

I BELIEVE SHE ONCE TOLD YOU TO CALL HER JANE.

YES, I DID. BUT...PERHAPS IT *IS* TIME FOR ME TO GET BACK TO ASGARDIA.

I CAN FEEL MY...CANCER BECOMING... *IRRITABLE.*

YEAH, OF COURSE, JANE, IN YOUR CONDITION, YOU'VE GOT TO...

NO. NOT YET.

THOR, WHAT ARE YOU...

I WANT HER TO KNOW THE TRUTH.

I WOULDN'T MIND KNOWING SOME MYSELF.

VERY WELL.

IT TOOK A TREMENDOUS AMOUNT OF POWER TO MAKE TODAY HAPPEN. I DON'T KNOW THAT WE COULD DO IT AGAIN. NOT WITHOUT A CENTURY OR SO OF REST.

IF THIS IS HOW YOU WISH THE DAY TO END, THEN SO BE IT, THOR. TRUTH BE TOLD...I WOULD EXPECT NO LESS OF YOU.

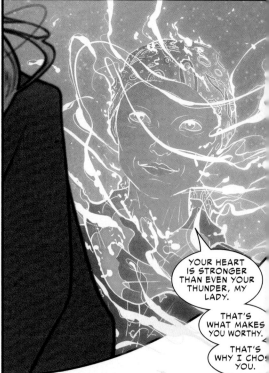

YOUR HEART IS STRONGER THAN EVEN YOUR THUNDER, MY LADY.

THAT'S WHAT MAKES YOU WORTHY.

THAT'S WHY I CHO...

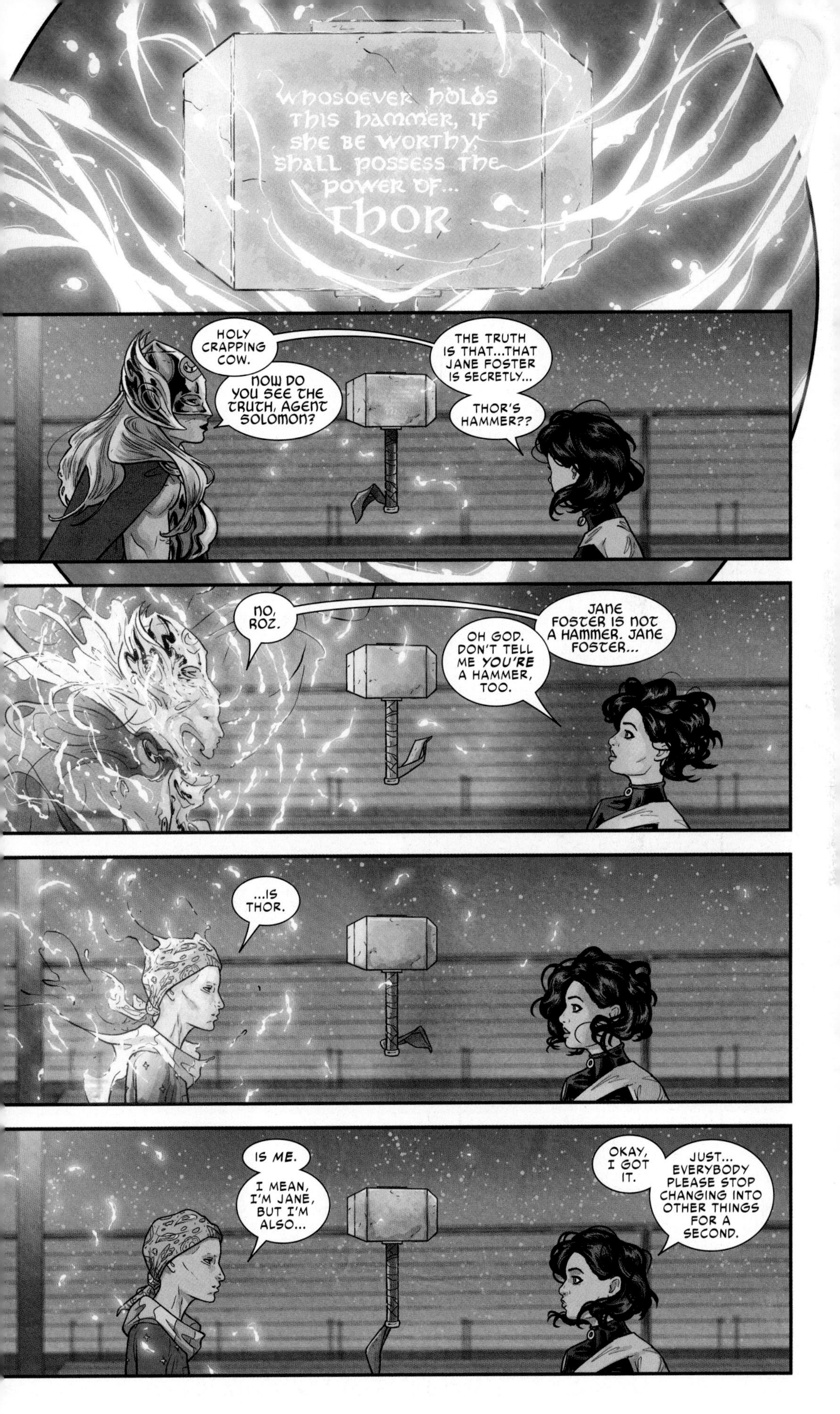
WHOSOEVER HOLDS THIS HAMMER, IF SHE BE WORTHY, SHALL POSSESS THE POWER OF... THOR
HOLY CRAPPING COW.
NOW DO YOU SEE THE TRUTH, AGENT SOLOMON?
THE TRUTH IS THAT...THAT JANE FOSTER IS SECRETLY...
THOR'S HAMMER??
NO, ROZ.
JANE FOSTER IS NOT A HAMMER. JANE FOSTER...
OH GOD. DON'T TELL ME YOU'RE A HAMMER, TOO.
...IS THOR.
IS ME.
I MEAN, I'M JANE, BUT I'M ALSO...
OKAY, I GOT IT.
JUST... EVERYBODY PLEASE STOP CHANGING INTO OTHER THINGS FOR A SECOND.

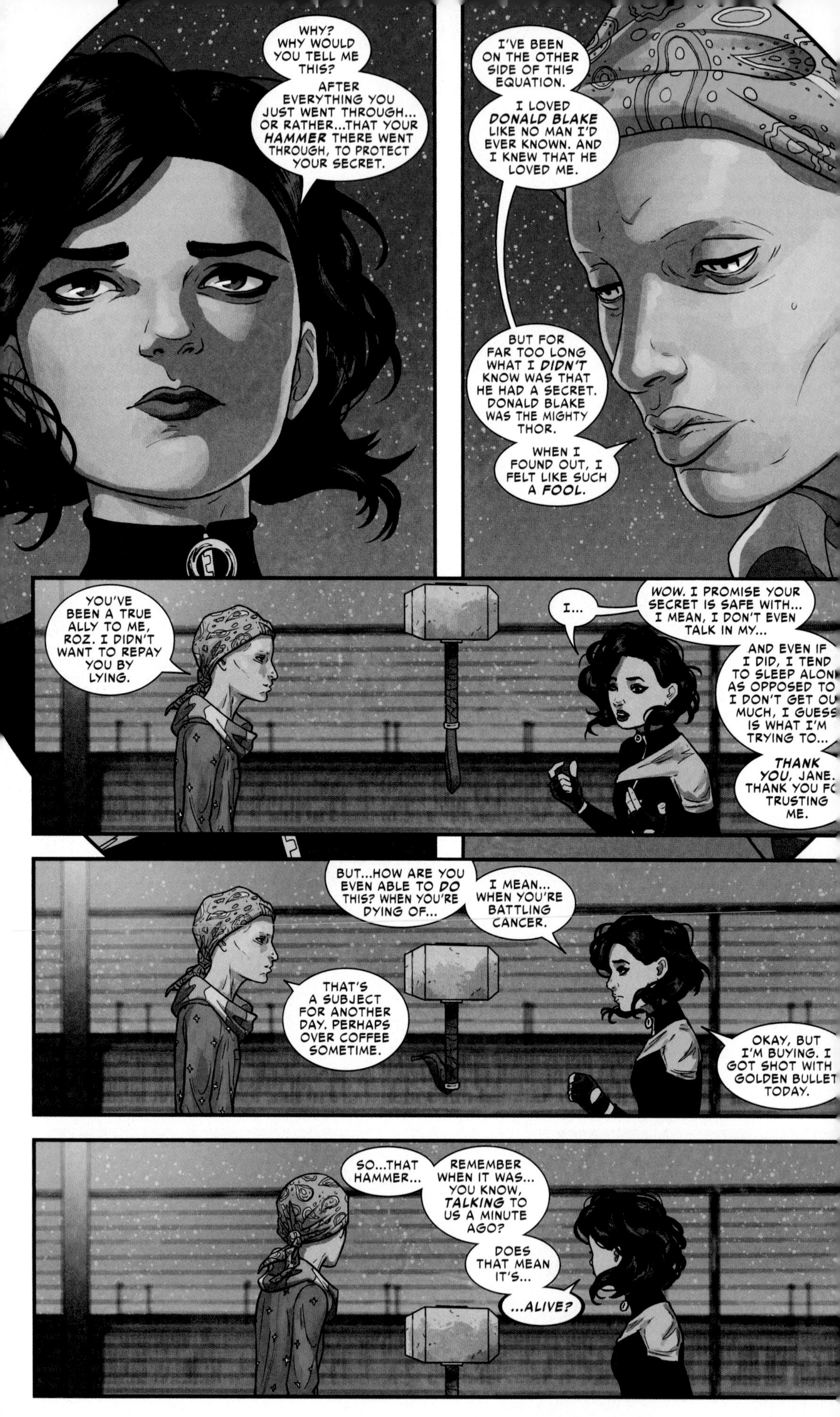
WHY? WHY WOULD YOU TELL ME THIS?
AFTER EVERYTHING YOU JUST WENT THROUGH... OR RATHER...THAT YOUR HAMMER THERE WENT THROUGH, TO PROTECT YOUR SECRET.
I'VE BEEN ON THE OTHER SIDE OF THIS EQUATION.
I LOVED DONALD BLAKE LIKE NO MAN I'D EVER KNOWN. AND I KNEW THAT HE LOVED ME.
BUT FOR FAR TOO LONG WHAT I DIDN'T KNOW WAS THAT HE HAD A SECRET. DONALD BLAKE WAS THE MIGHTY THOR.
WHEN I FOUND OUT, I FELT LIKE SUCH A FOOL.
YOU'VE BEEN A TRUE ALLY TO ME, ROZ. I DIDN'T WANT TO REPAY YOU BY LYING.
I...
WOW. I PROMISE YOUR SECRET IS SAFE WITH... I MEAN, I DON'T EVEN TALK IN MY...
THANK YOU, JANE.
TRUSTING ME.
BUT...HOW ARE YOU EVEN ABLE TO DO THIS? WHEN YOU'RE DYING OF...
I MEAN... WHEN YOU'RE BATTLING CANCER.
THAT'S A SUBJECT FOR ANOTHER DAY. PERHAPS OVER COFFEE SOMETIME.
OKAY, BUT I'M BUYING.
TODAY.
SO...THAT HAMMER...
REMEMBER WHEN IT WAS... YOU KNOW, TALKING TO US A MINUTE AGO?
DOES THAT MEAN IT'S...
...ALIVE?

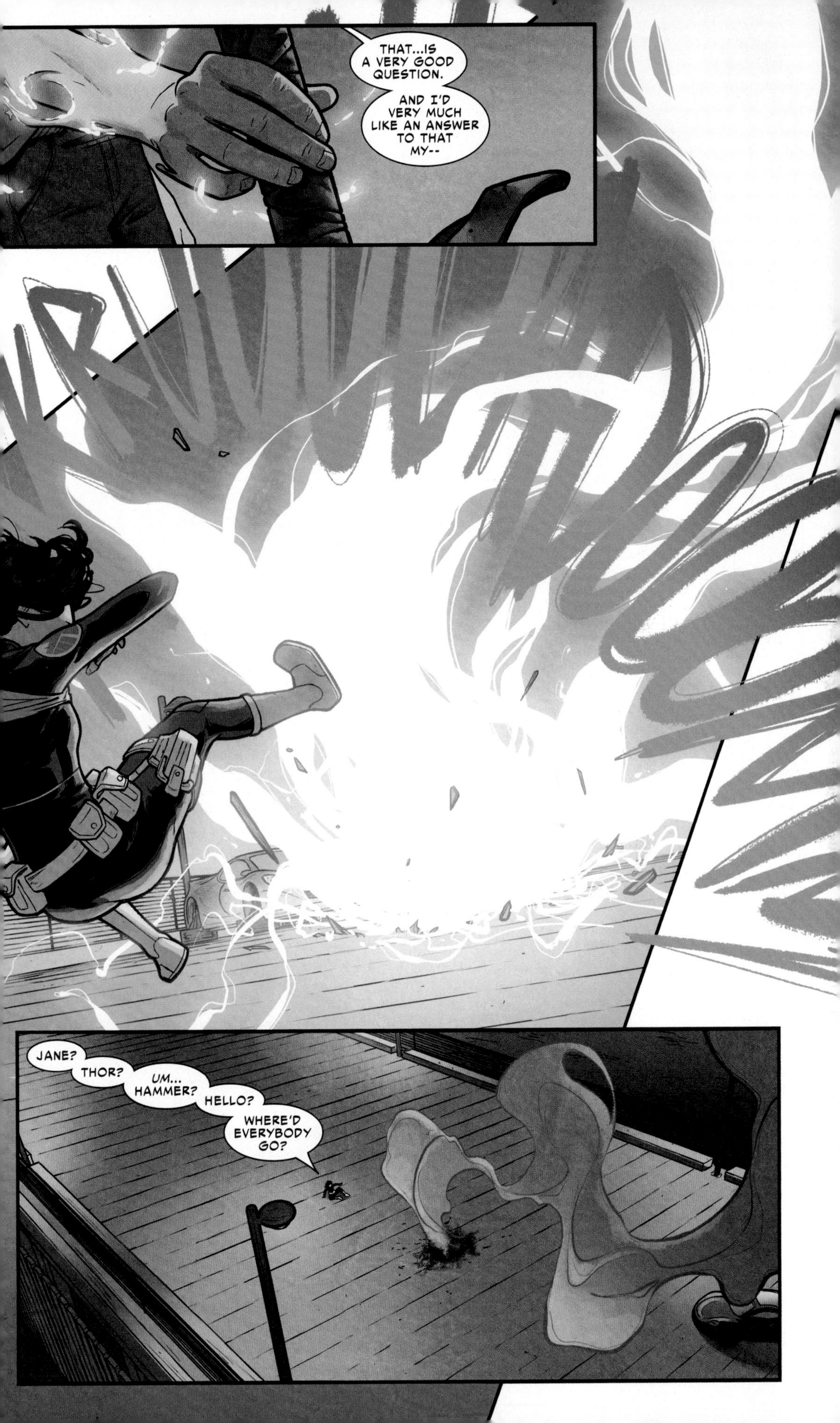
THAT...IS A VERY GOOD QUESTION.
AND I'D VERY MUCH LIKE AN ANSWER TO THAT MY--
KRUUUDDOOOOM
JANE?
THOR?
UM... HAMMER?
HELLO?
WHERE'D EVERYBODY GO?

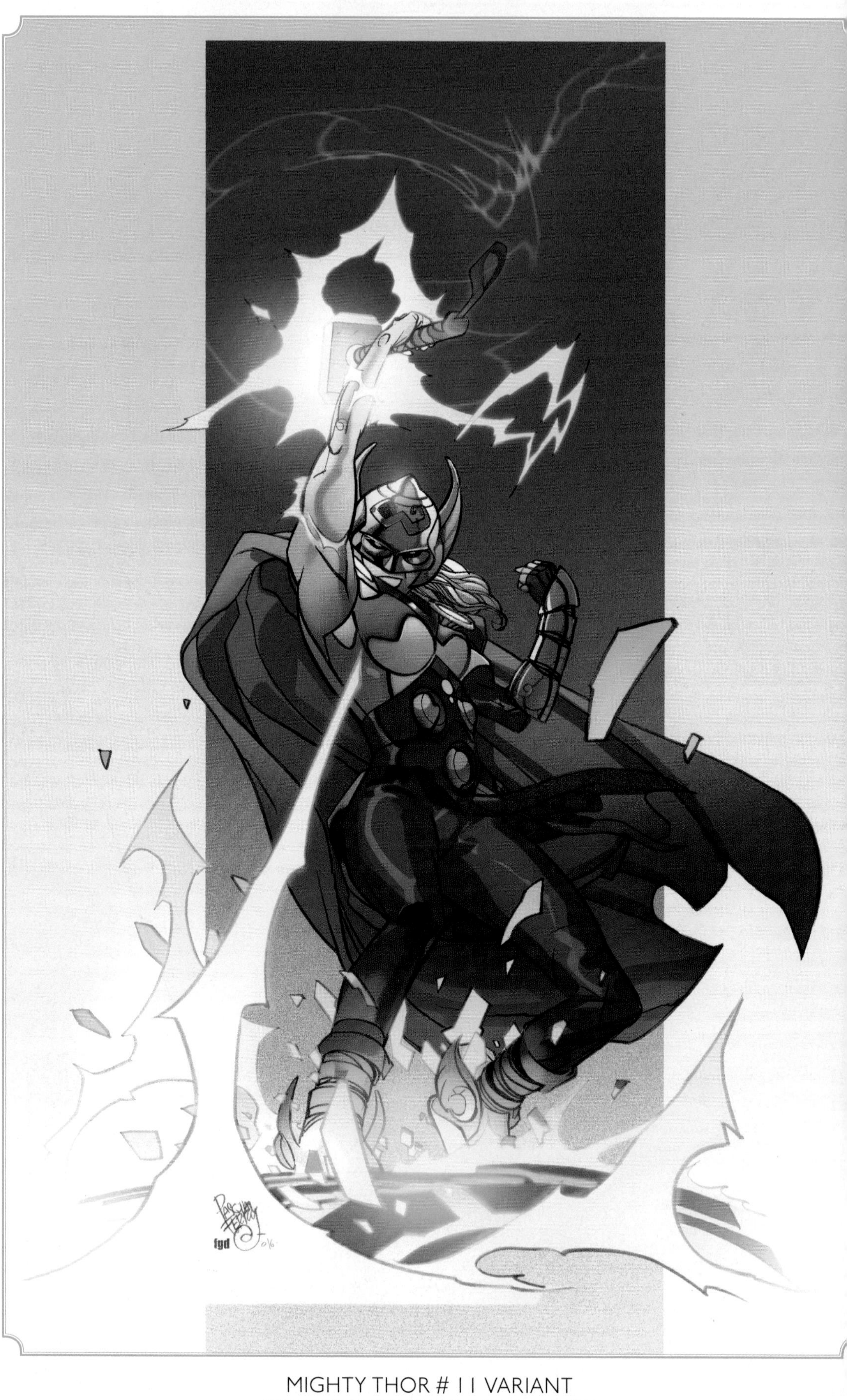

MIGHTY THOR # 11 VARIANT
BY **PASQUAL FERRY** & **FRANK D'ARMATA**

12

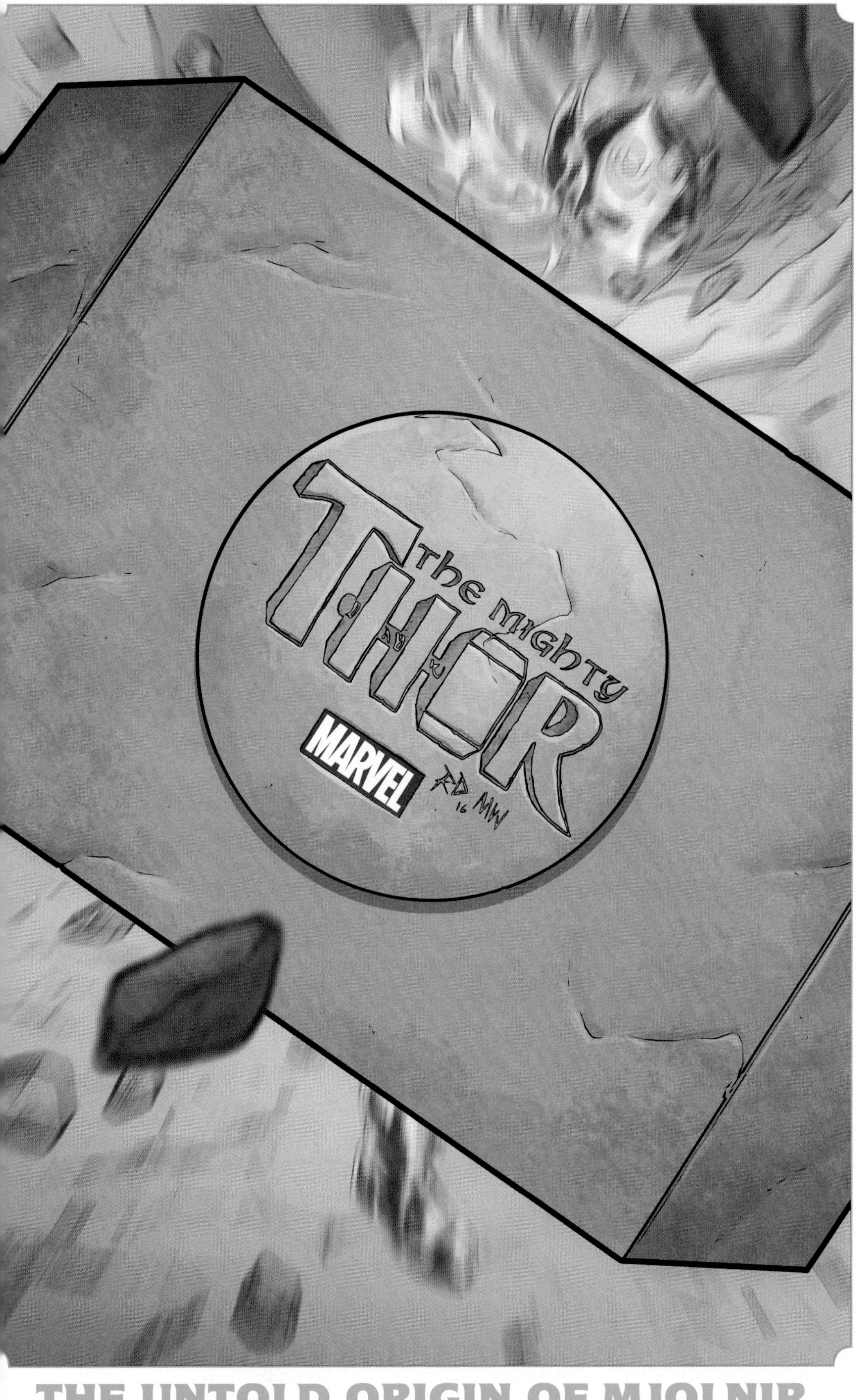
THE MIGHTY THOR
MARVEL

THE UNTOLD ORIGIN OF MJOLNIR

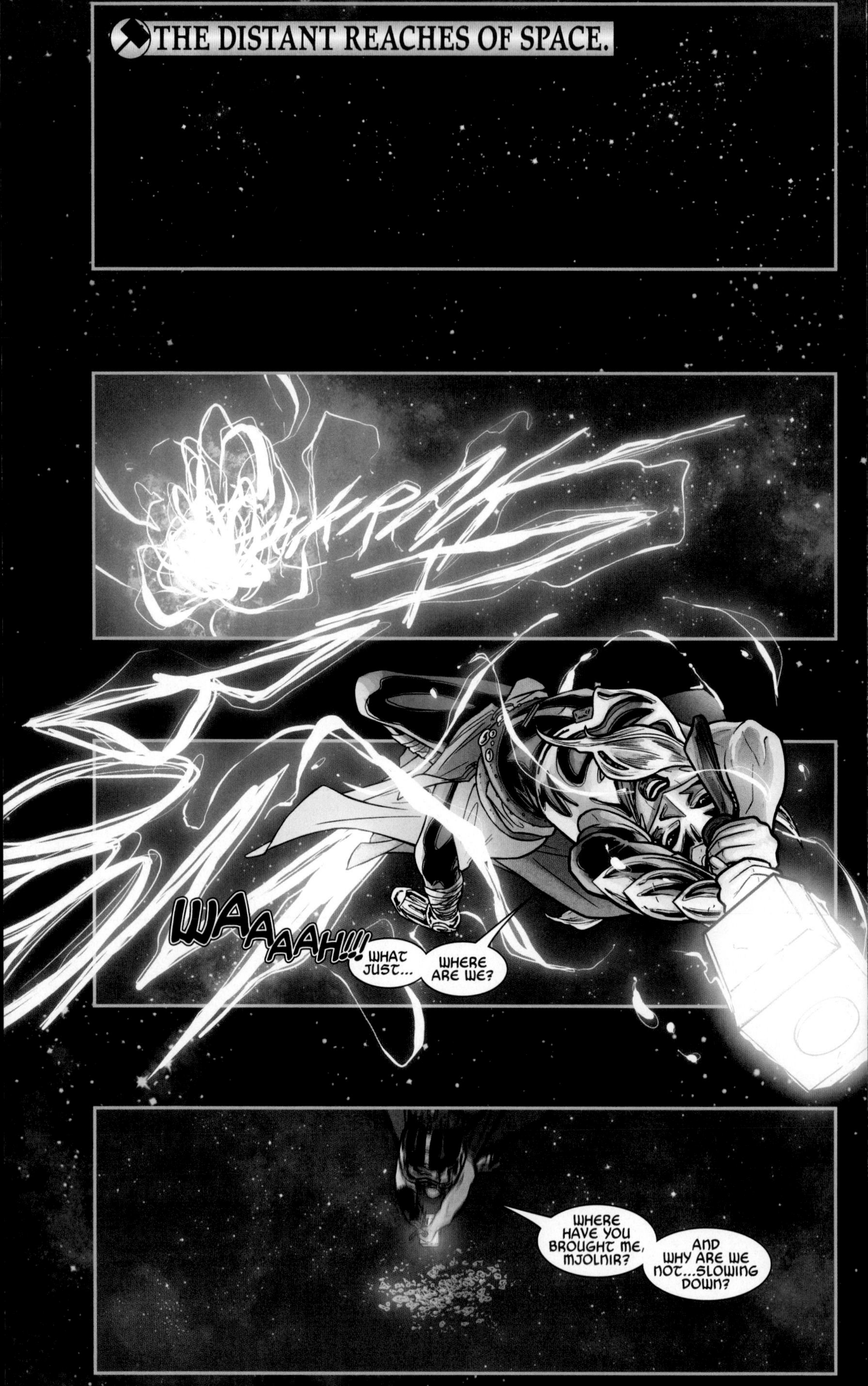
THE DISTANT REACHES OF SPACE.
SHHKRRAKK
WAAAAAH!!!
WHAT JUST...
WHERE ARE WE?
WHERE HAVE YOU BROUGHT ME, MJOLNIR?
AND WHY ARE WE NOT...SLOWING DOWN?

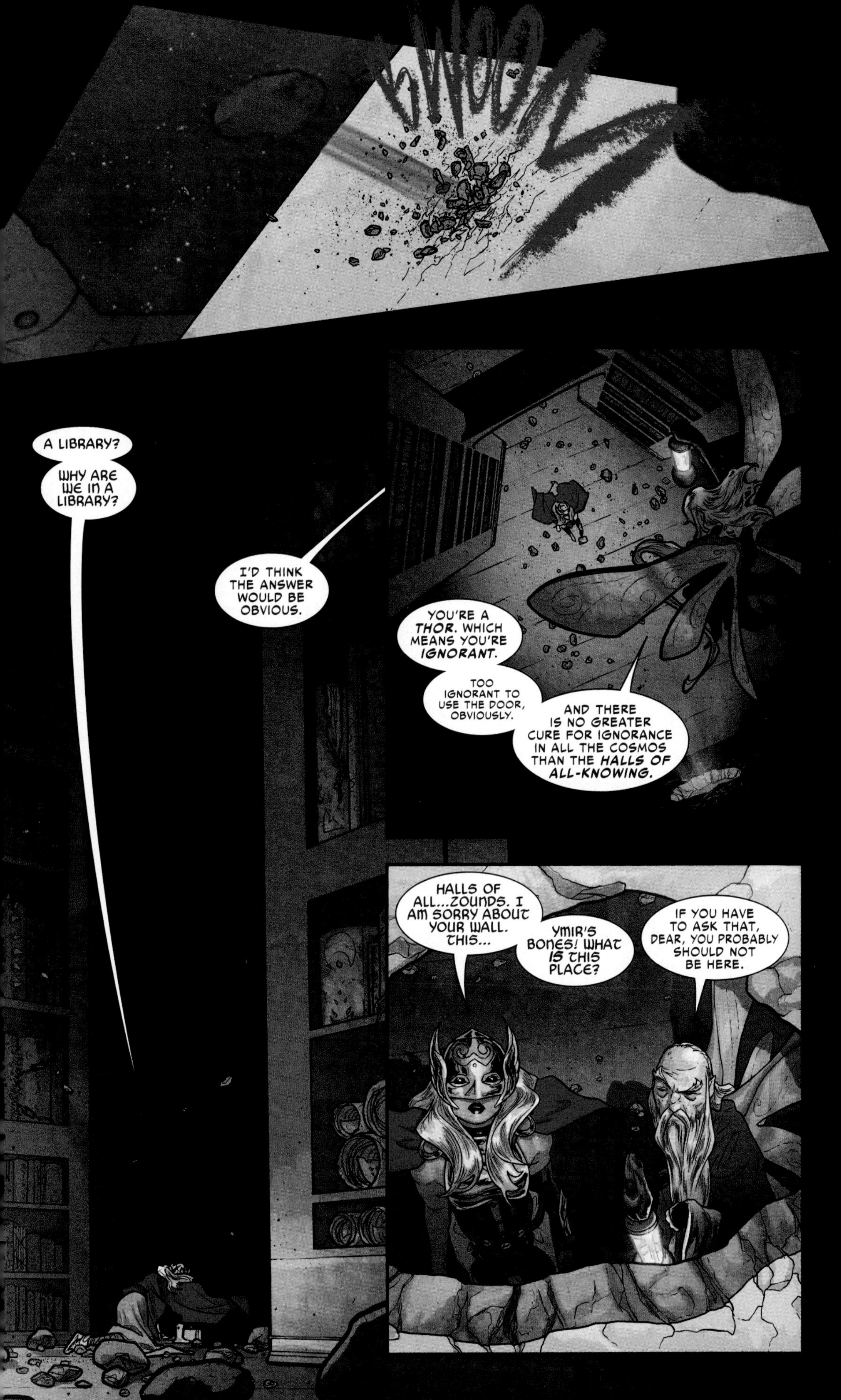

SKWOOM
A LIBRARY?
WHY ARE WE IN A LIBRARY?
I'D THINK THE ANSWER WOULD BE OBVIOUS.
YOU'RE A THOR. WHICH MEANS YOU'RE IGNORANT.
TOO IGNORANT TO USE THE DOOR, OBVIOUSLY.
AND THERE IS NO GREATER CURE FOR IGNORANCE IN ALL THE COSMOS THAN THE HALLS OF ALL-KNOWING.
HALLS OF ALL...ZOUNDS. I AM SORRY ABOUT YOUR WALL. THIS...
YMIR'S BONES! WHAT IS THIS PLACE?
IF YOU HAVE TO ASK THAT, DEAR, YOU PROBABLY SHOULD NOT BE HERE.

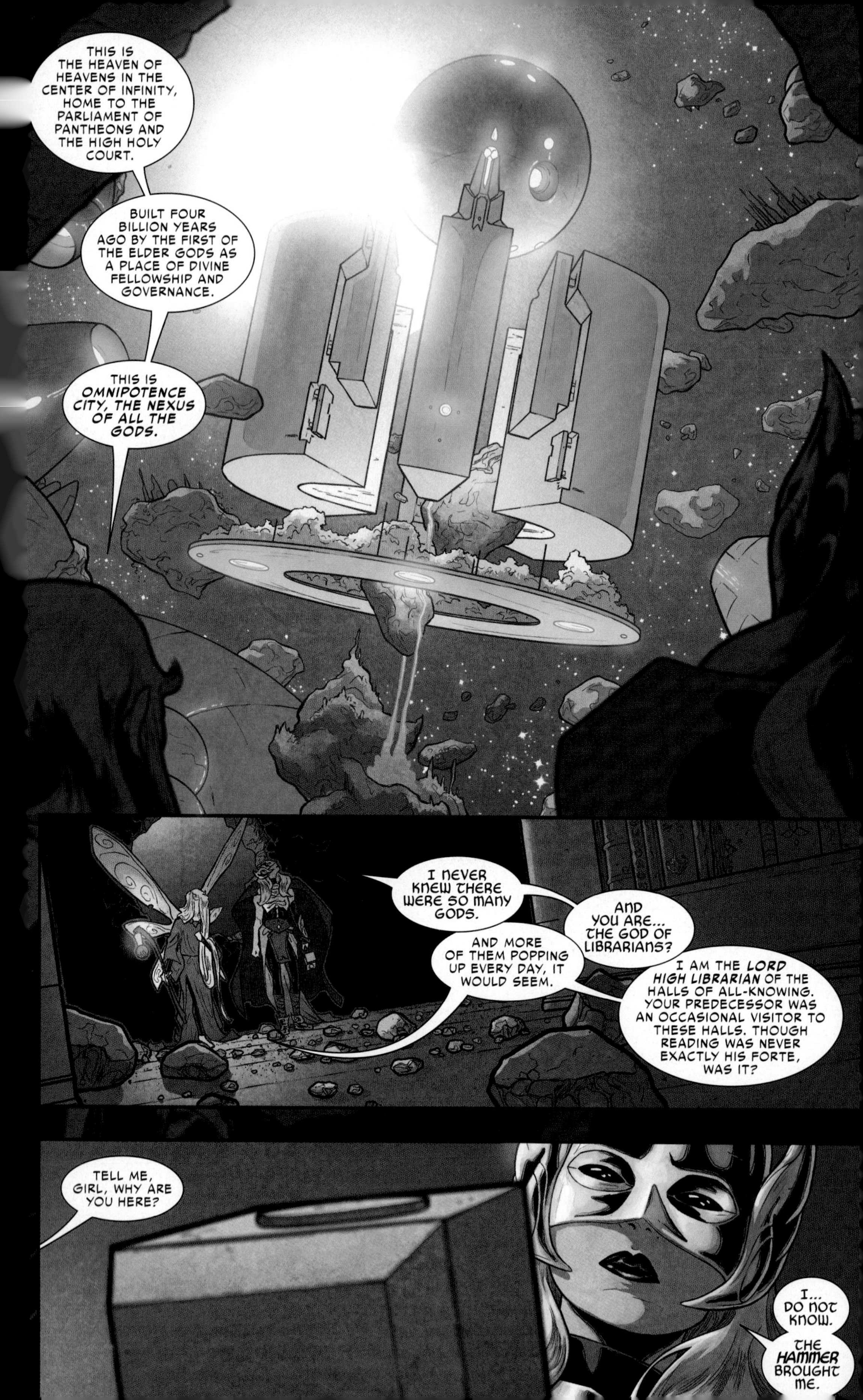
THIS IS THE HEAVEN OF HEAVENS IN THE CENTER OF INFINITY, HOME TO THE PARLIAMENT OF PANTHEONS AND THE HIGH HOLY COURT.
BUILT FOUR BILLION YEARS AGO BY THE FIRST OF THE ELDER GODS AS A PLACE OF DIVINE FELLOWSHIP AND GOVERNANCE.
THIS IS *OMNIPOTENCE CITY, THE NEXUS OF ALL THE GODS.*
I NEVER KNEW THERE WERE SO MANY GODS.
AND YOU ARE... THE GOD OF LIBRARIANS?
AND MORE OF THEM POPPING UP EVERY DAY, IT WOULD SEEM.
I AM THE *LORD HIGH LIBRARIAN* OF THE HALLS OF ALL-KNOWING. YOUR PREDECESSOR WAS AN OCCASIONAL VISITOR TO THESE HALLS. THOUGH READING WAS NEVER EXACTLY HIS FORTE, WAS IT?
TELL ME, GIRL, WHY ARE YOU HERE?
I... DO NOT KNOW.
THE *HAMMER* BROUGHT ME.

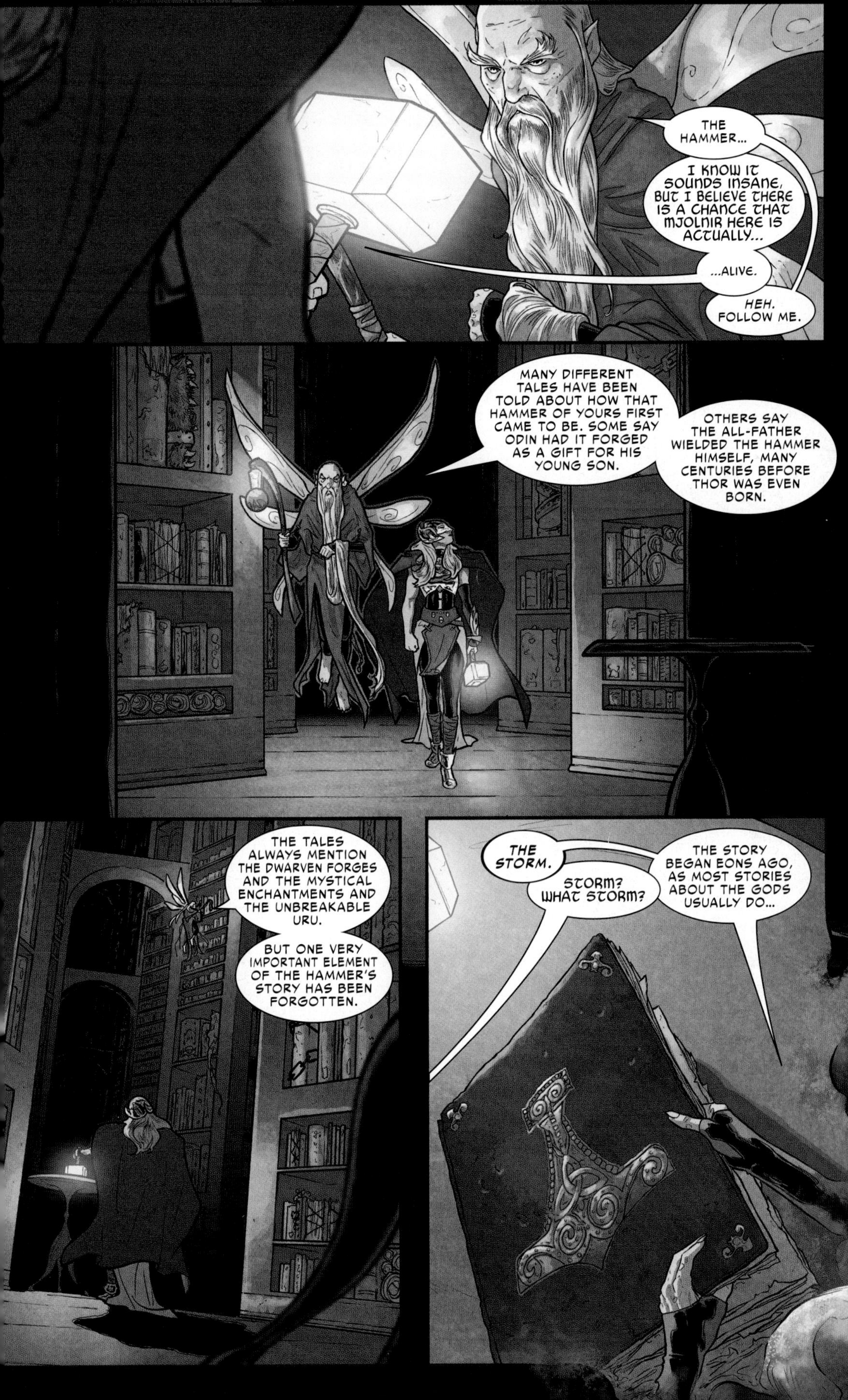
THE HAMMER...
I KNOW IT SOUNDS INSANE, BUT I BELIEVE THERE IS A CHANCE THAT MJOLNIR HERE IS ACTUALLY...
...ALIVE.
HEH. FOLLOW ME.
MANY DIFFERENT TALES HAVE BEEN TOLD ABOUT HOW THAT HAMMER OF YOURS FIRST CAME TO BE. SOME SAY ODIN HAD IT FORGED AS A GIFT FOR HIS YOUNG SON.
OTHERS SAY THE ALL-FATHER WIELDED THE HAMMER HIMSELF, MANY CENTURIES BEFORE THOR WAS EVEN BORN.
THE TALES ALWAYS MENTION THE DWARVEN FORGES AND THE MYSTICAL ENCHANTMENTS AND THE UNBREAKABLE URU.
BUT ONE VERY IMPORTANT ELEMENT OF THE HAMMER'S STORY HAS BEEN FORGOTTEN.
THE STORM.
STORM? WHAT STORM?
THE STORY BEGAN EONS AGO, AS MOST STORIES ABOUT THE GODS USUALLY DO...

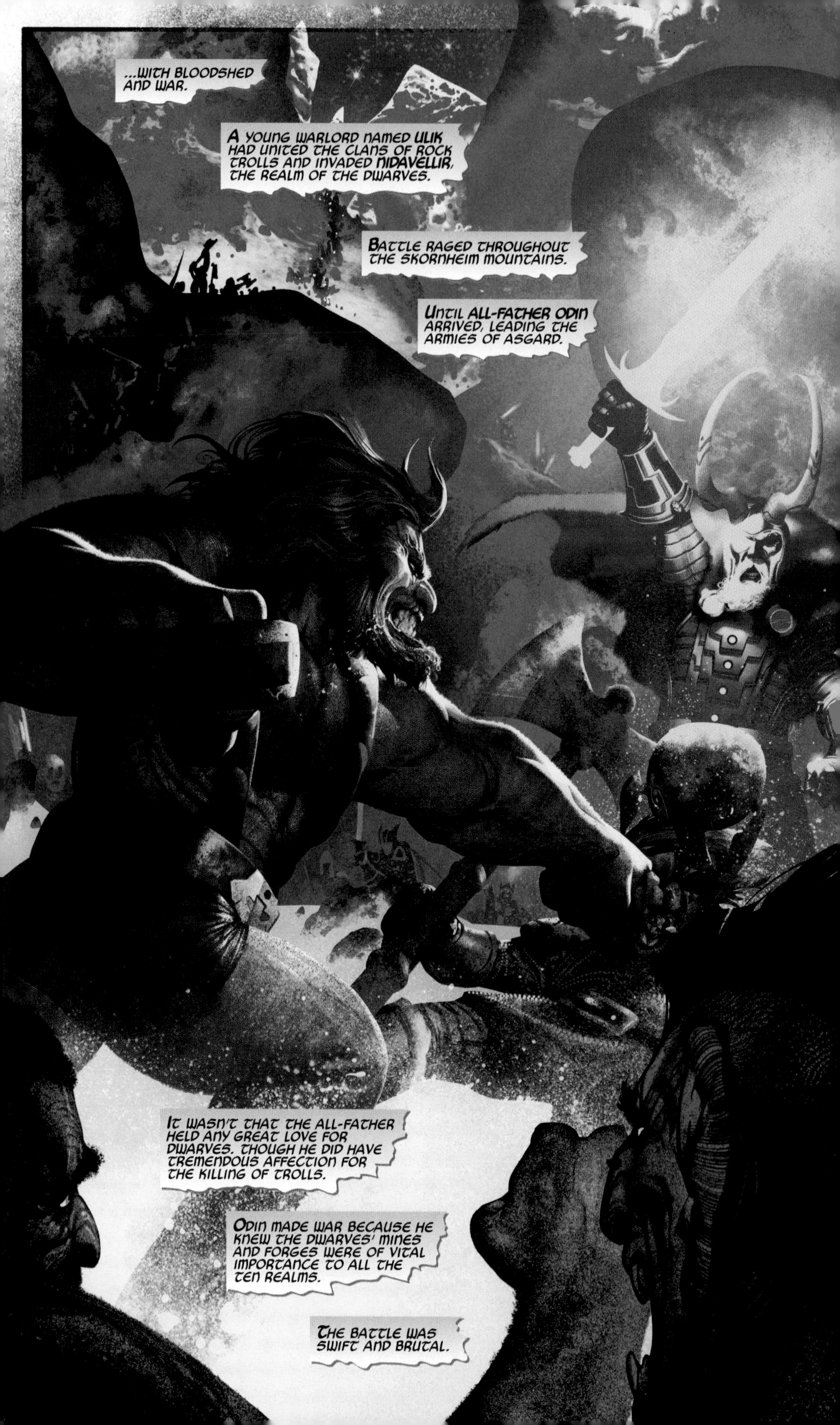
...WITH BLOODSHED AND WAR.
A YOUNG WARLORD NAMED ULIK HAD UNITED THE CLANS OF ROCK TROLLS AND INVADED NIDAVELLIR, THE REALM OF THE DWARVES.
BATTLE RAGED THROUGHOUT THE SKORNHEIM MOUNTAINS.
UNTIL ALL-FATHER ODIN ARRIVED, LEADING THE ARMIES OF ASGARD.
IT WASN'T THAT THE ALL-FATHER HELD ANY GREAT LOVE FOR DWARVES. THOUGH HE DID HAVE TREMENDOUS AFFECTION FOR THE KILLING OF TROLLS.
ODIN MADE WAR BECAUSE HE KNEW THE DWARVES' MINES AND FORGES WERE OF VITAL IMPORTANCE TO ALL THE TEN REALMS.
THE BATTLE WAS SWIFT AND BRUTAL.

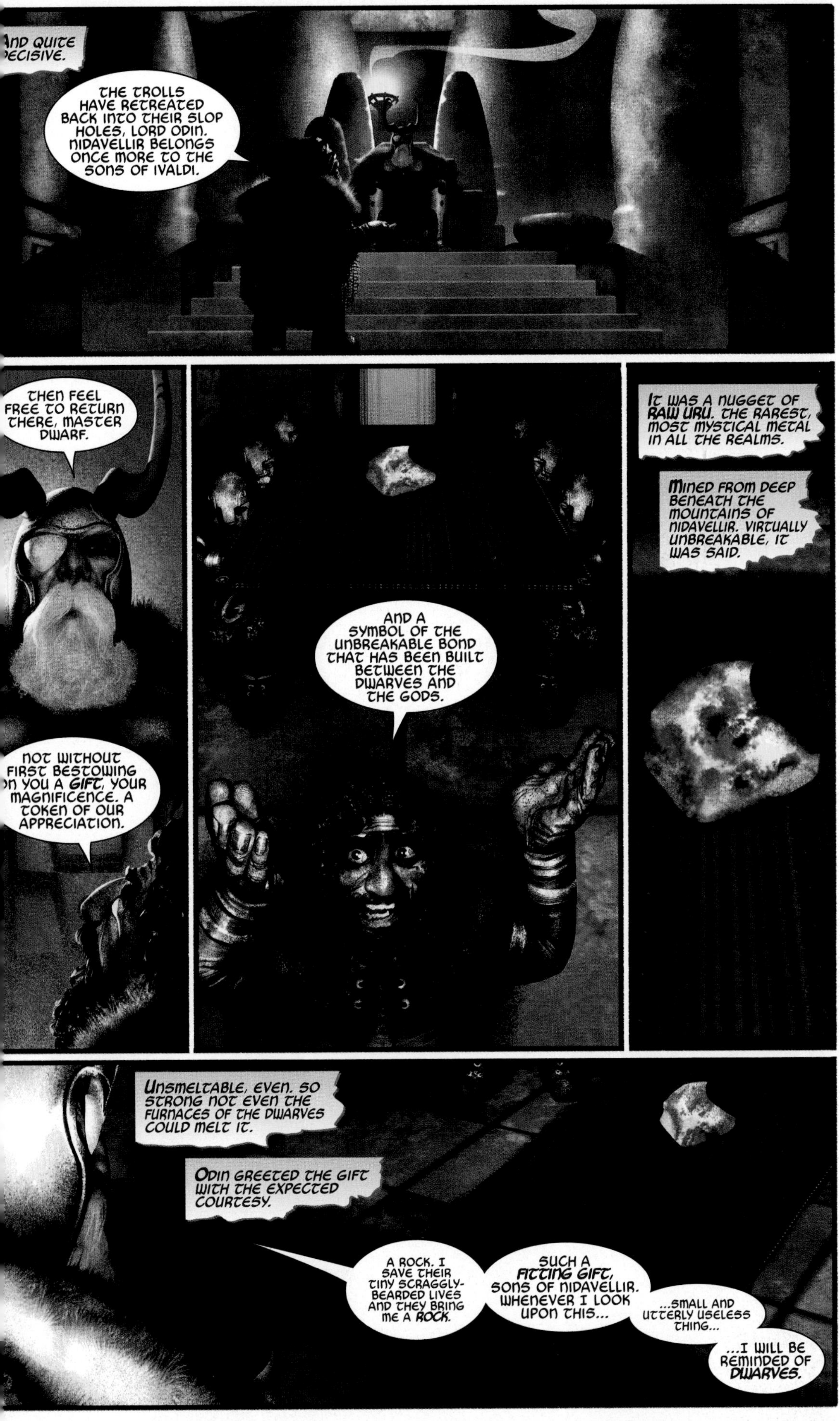

AND QUITE DECISIVE.
THE TROLLS HAVE RETREATED BACK INTO THEIR SLOP HOLES, LORD ODIN. NIDAVELLIR BELONGS ONCE MORE TO THE SONS OF IVALDI.
THEN FEEL FREE TO RETURN THERE, MASTER DWARF.
NOT WITHOUT FIRST BESTOWING ON YOU A GIFT, YOUR MAGNIFICENCE. A TOKEN OF OUR APPRECIATION.
AND A SYMBOL OF THE UNBREAKABLE BOND THAT HAS BEEN BUILT BETWEEN THE DWARVES AND THE GODS.
IT WAS A NUGGET OF RAW URU. THE RAREST, MOST MYSTICAL METAL IN ALL THE REALMS.
MINED FROM DEEP BENEATH THE MOUNTAINS OF NIDAVELLIR. VIRTUALLY UNBREAKABLE, IT WAS SAID.
UNSMELTABLE, EVEN. SO STRONG NOT EVEN THE FURNACES OF THE DWARVES COULD MELT IT.
ODIN GREETED THE GIFT WITH THE EXPECTED COURTESY.
A ROCK. I SAVE THEIR TINY SCRAGGLY-BEARDED LIVES AND THEY BRING ME A ROCK.
SUCH A FITTING GIFT, SONS OF NIDAVELLIR. WHENEVER I LOOK UPON THIS...
...SMALL AND UTTERLY USELESS THING...
...I WILL BE REMINDED OF DWARVES.

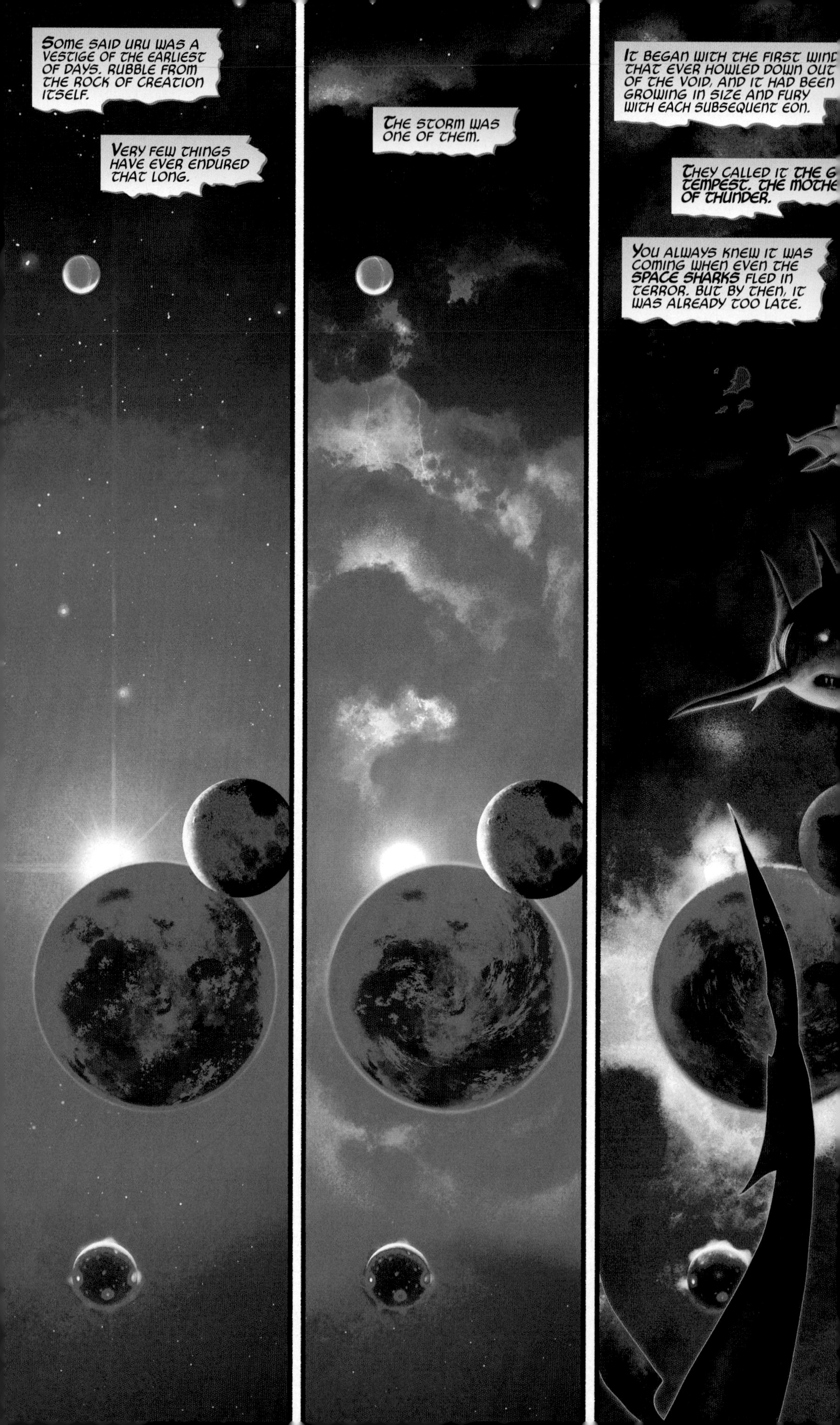

SOME SAID URU WAS A VESTIGE OF THE EARLIEST OF DAYS. RUBBLE FROM THE ROCK OF CREATION ITSELF.
VERY FEW THINGS HAVE EVER ENDURED THAT LONG.
THE STORM WAS ONE OF THEM.
IT BEGAN WITH THE FIRST WIN THAT EVER HOWLED DOWN OUT OF THE VOID, AND IT HAD BEEN GROWING IN SIZE AND FURY WITH EACH SUBSEQUENT EON.
THEY CALLED IT THE G TEMPEST. THE MOTHE OF THUNDER.
YOU ALWAYS KNEW IT WAS COMING WHEN EVEN THE SPACE SHARKS FLED IN TERROR. BUT BY THEN, IT WAS ALREADY TOO LATE.

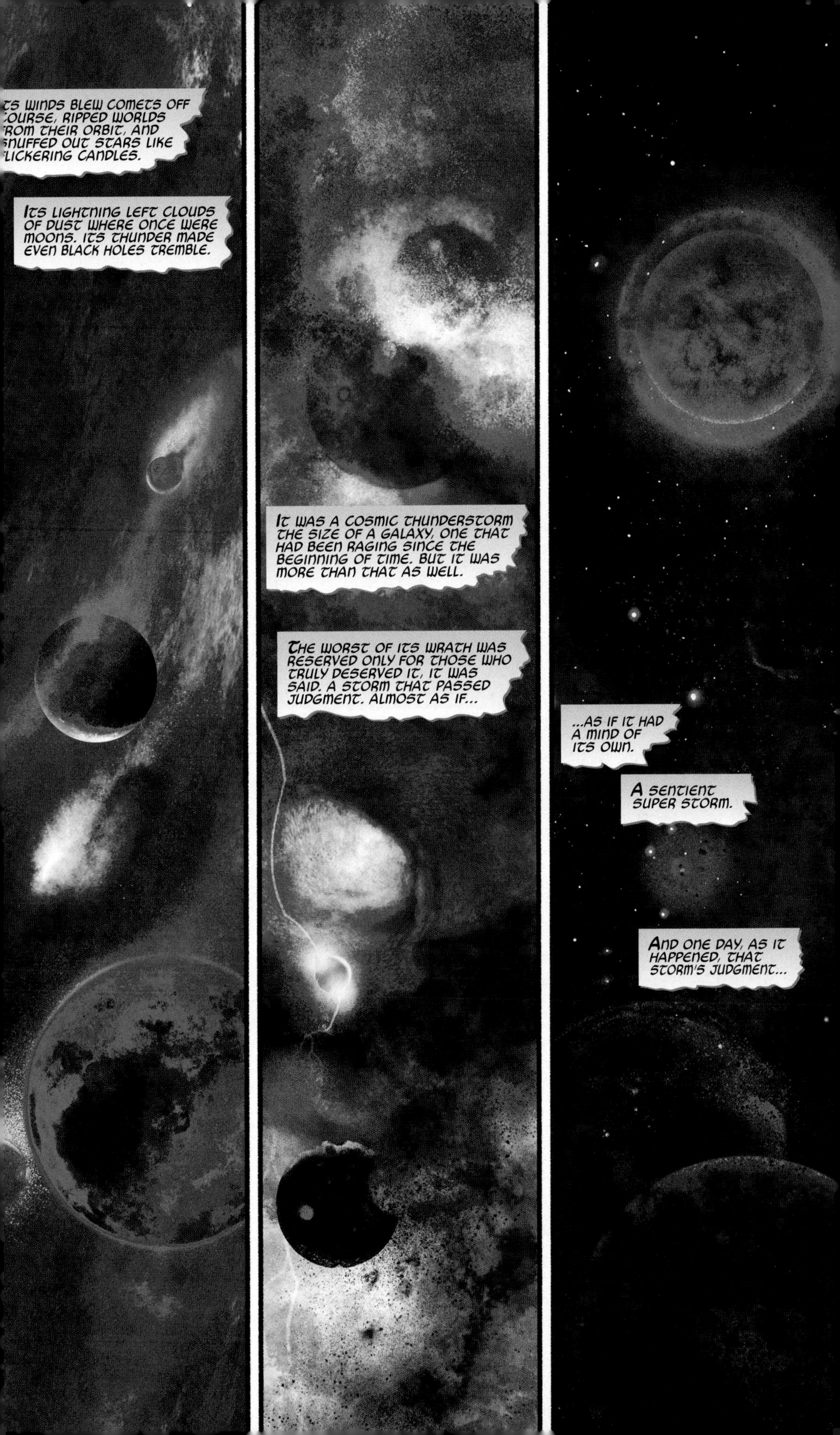

TS WINDS BLEW COMETS OFF COURSE, RIPPED WORLDS FROM THEIR ORBIT, AND SNUFFED OUT STARS LIKE FLICKERING CANDLES.
ITS LIGHTNING LEFT CLOUDS OF DUST WHERE ONCE WERE MOONS. ITS THUNDER MADE EVEN BLACK HOLES TREMBLE.
IT WAS A COSMIC THUNDERSTORM THE SIZE OF A GALAXY, ONE THAT HAD BEEN RAGING SINCE THE BEGINNING OF TIME. BUT IT WAS MORE THAN THAT AS WELL.
THE WORST OF ITS WRATH WAS RESERVED ONLY FOR THOSE WHO TRULY DESERVED IT, IT WAS SAID. A STORM THAT PASSED JUDGMENT. ALMOST AS IF...
...AS IF IT HAD A MIND OF ITS OWN.
A SENTIENT SUPER STORM.
AND ONE DAY, AS IT HAPPENED, THAT STORM'S JUDGMENT...

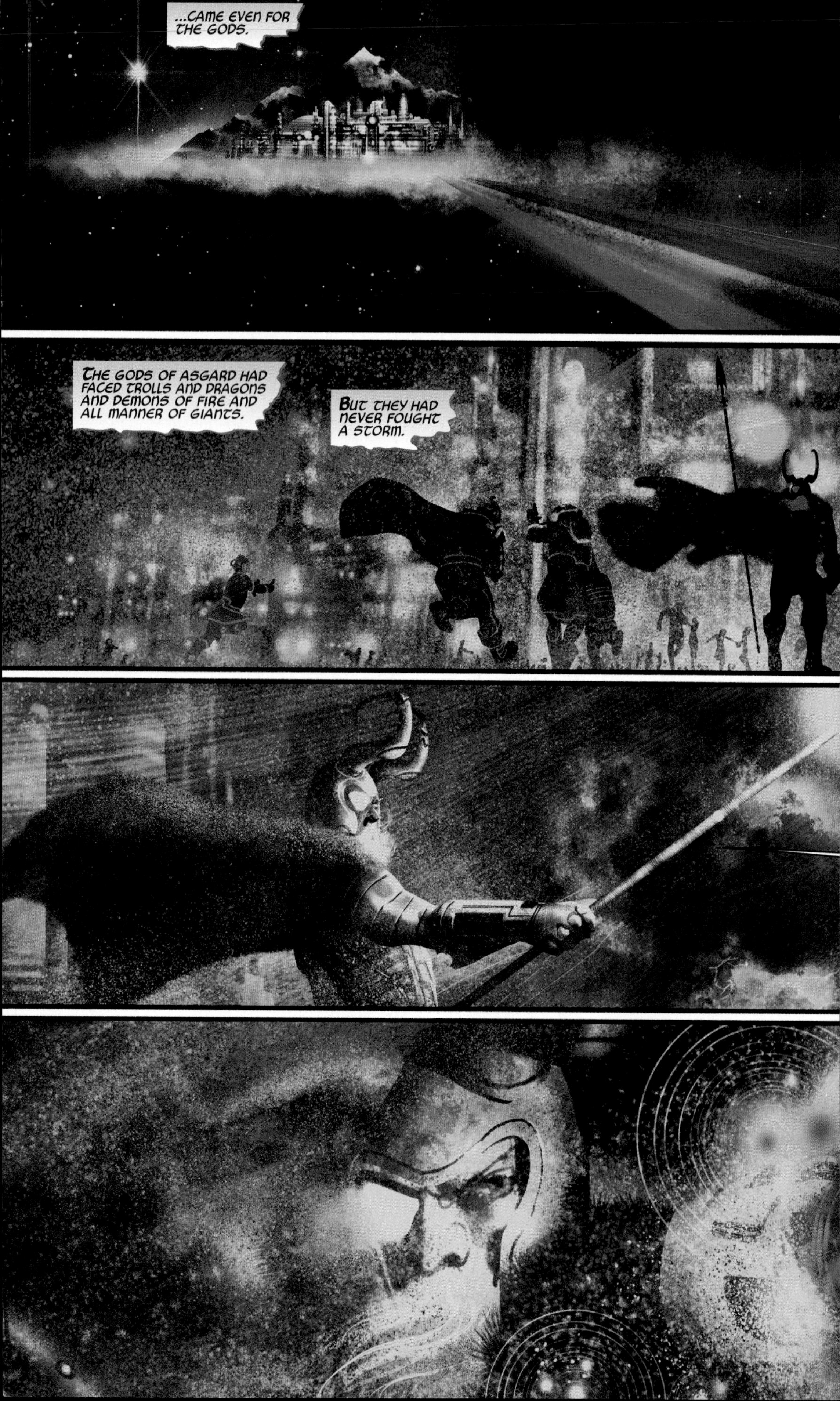
...CAME EVEN FOR THE GODS.
THE GODS OF ASGARD HAD FACED TROLLS AND DRAGONS AND DEMONS OF FIRE AND ALL MANNER OF GIANTS.
BUT THEY HAD NEVER FOUGHT A STORM.

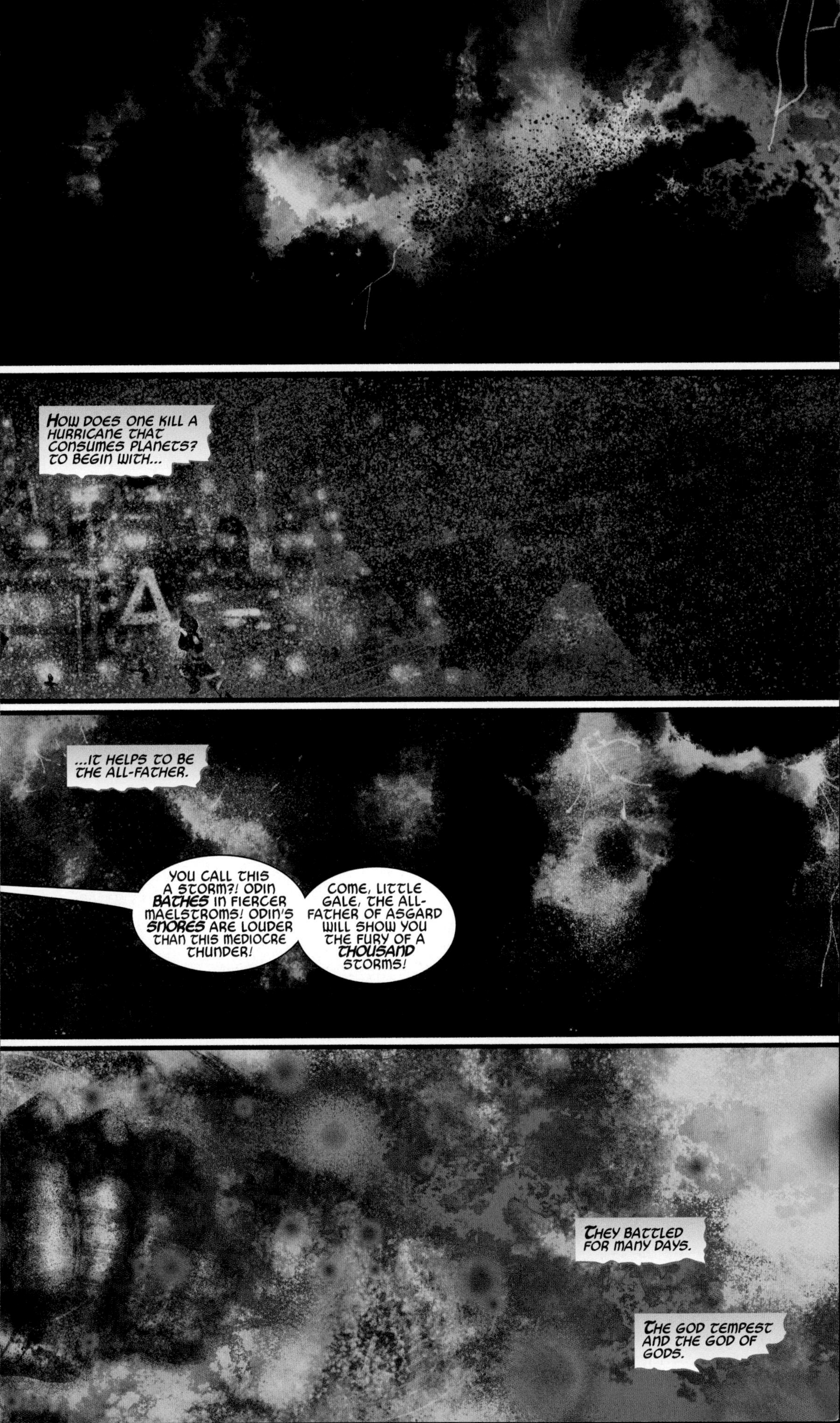
HOW DOES ONE KILL A HURRICANE THAT CONSUMES PLANETS? TO BEGIN WITH...
...IT HELPS TO BE THE ALL-FATHER.
YOU CALL THIS A STORM?! ODIN BATHES IN FIERCER MAELSTROMS! ODIN'S SNORES ARE LOUDER THAN THIS MEDIOCRE THUNDER!
COME, LITTLE GALE, THE ALL-FATHER OF ASGARD WILL SHOW YOU THE FURY OF A THOUSAND STORMS!
THEY BATTLED FOR MANY DAYS.
THE GOD TEMPEST AND THE GOD OF GODS.

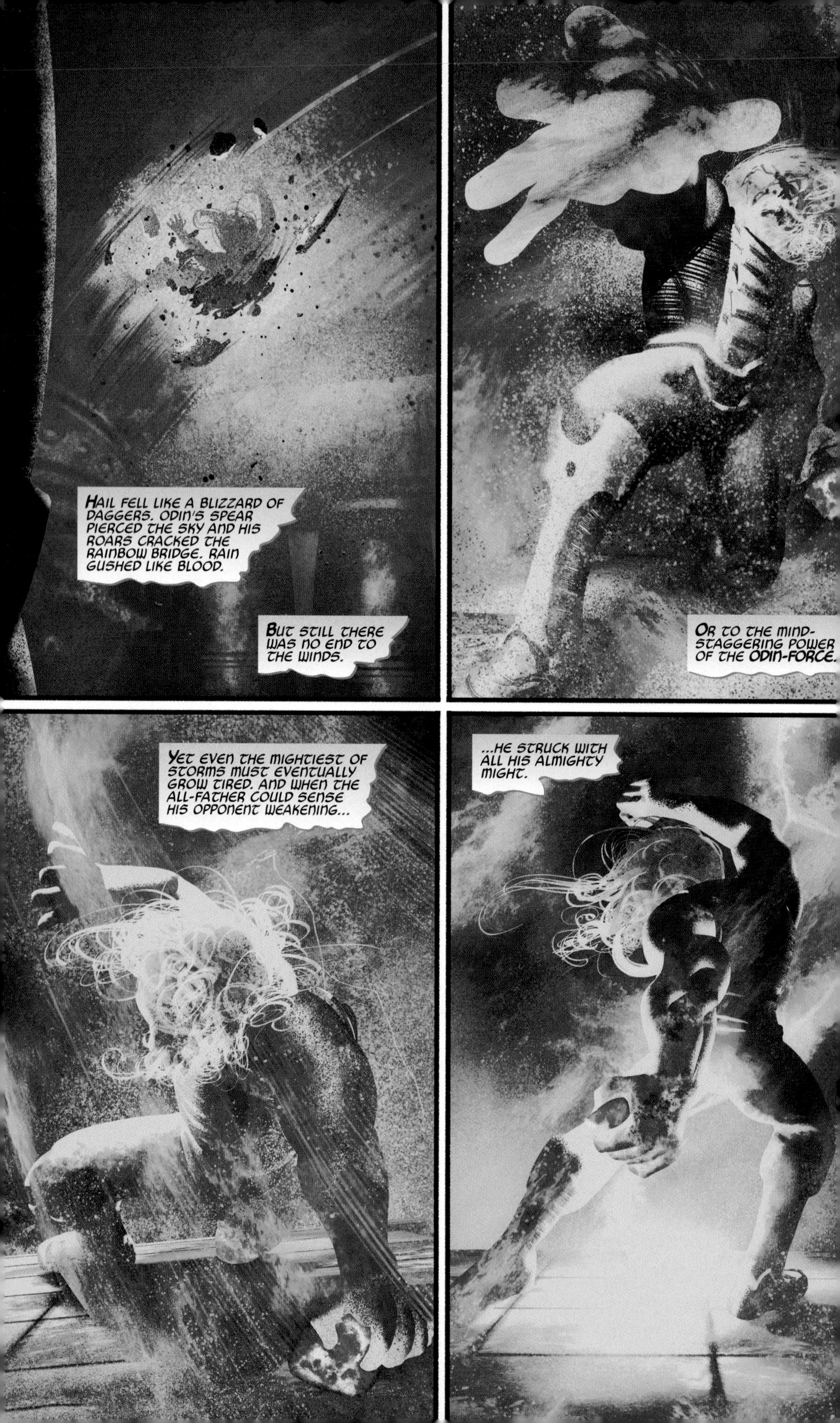
HAIL FELL LIKE A BLIZZARD OF DAGGERS. ODIN'S SPEAR PIERCED THE SKY AND HIS ROARS CRACKED THE RAINBOW BRIDGE. RAIN GUSHED LIKE BLOOD.
BUT STILL THERE WAS NO END TO THE WINDS.
OR TO THE MIND-STAGGERING POWER OF THE ODIN-FORCE.
YET EVEN THE MIGHTIEST OF STORMS MUST EVENTUALLY GROW TIRED. AND WHEN THE ALL-FATHER COULD SENSE HIS OPPONENT WEAKENING...
...HE STRUCK WITH ALL HIS ALMIGHTY MIGHT.

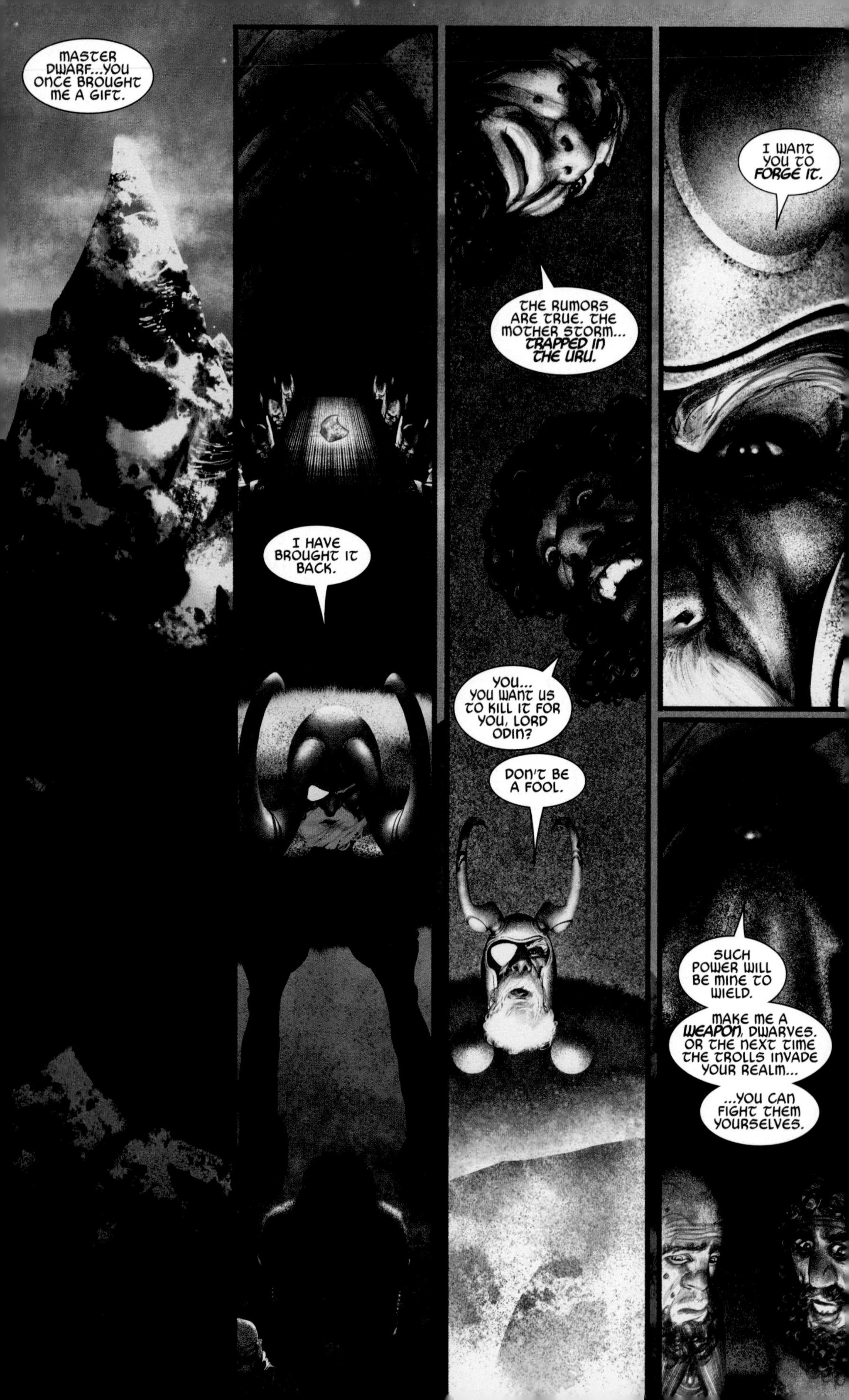
MASTER DWARF...YOU ONCE BROUGHT ME A GIFT.
I HAVE BROUGHT IT BACK.
THE RUMORS ARE TRUE. THE MOTHER STORM... TRAPPED IN THE URU.
YOU... YOU WANT US TO KILL IT FOR YOU, LORD ODIN?
DON'T BE A FOOL.
I WANT YOU TO FORGE IT.
SUCH POWER WILL BE MINE TO WIELD.
MAKE ME A WEAPON, DWARVES. OR THE NEXT TIME THE TROLLS INVADE YOUR REALM...
...YOU CAN FIGHT THEM YOURSELVES.

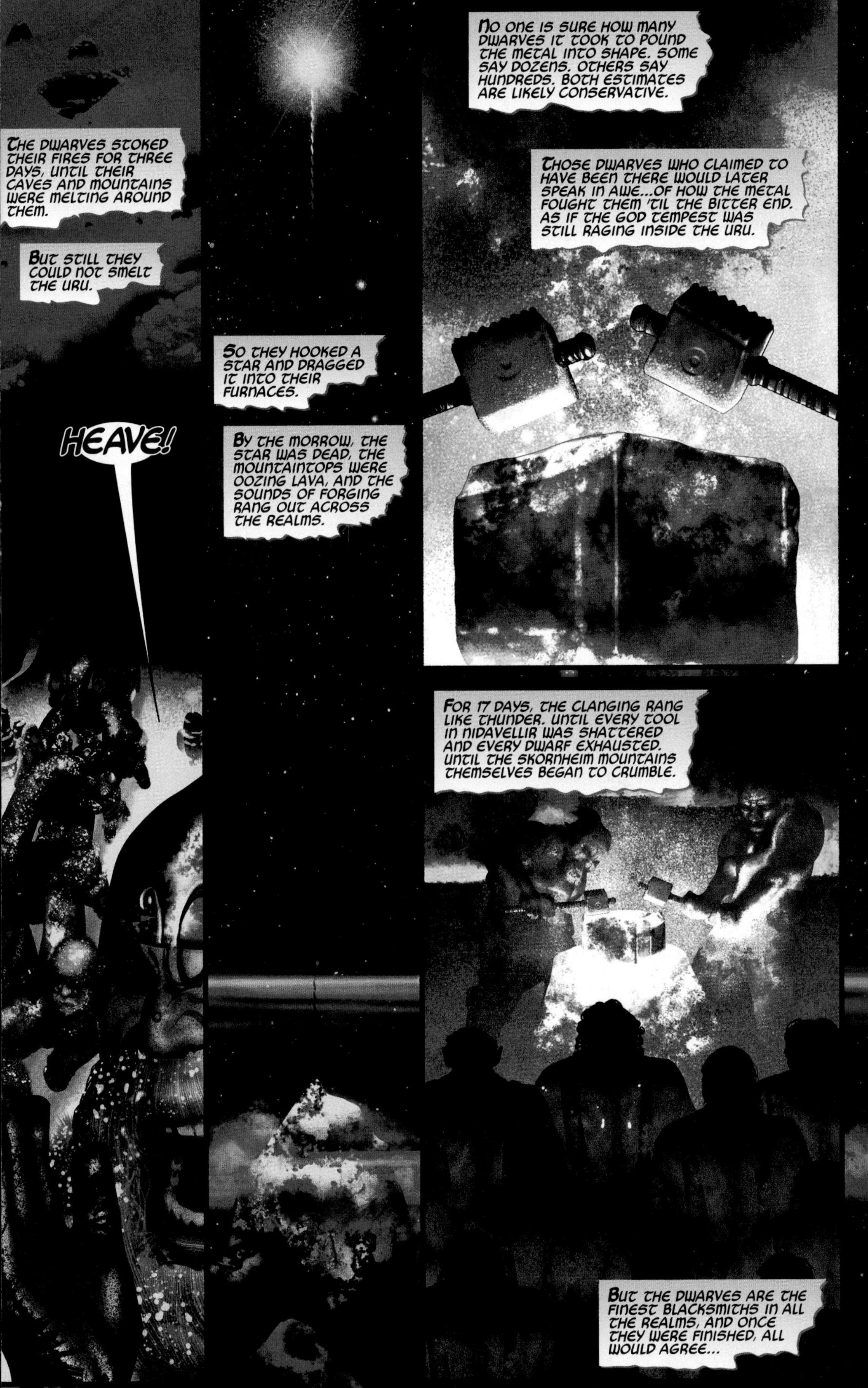
THE DWARVES STOKED THEIR FIRES FOR THREE DAYS, UNTIL THEIR CAVES AND MOUNTAINS WERE MELTING AROUND THEM.
BUT STILL THEY COULD NOT SMELT THE URU.
HEAVE!
SO THEY HOOKED A STAR AND DRAGGED IT INTO THEIR FURNACES.
BY THE MORROW, THE STAR WAS DEAD, THE MOUNTAINTOPS WERE OOZING LAVA, AND THE SOUNDS OF FORGING RANG OUT ACROSS THE REALMS.
NO ONE IS SURE HOW MANY DWARVES IT TOOK TO POUND THE METAL INTO SHAPE. SOME SAY DOZENS. OTHERS SAY HUNDREDS. BOTH ESTIMATES ARE LIKELY CONSERVATIVE.
THOSE DWARVES WHO CLAIMED TO HAVE BEEN THERE WOULD LATER SPEAK IN AWE...OF HOW THE METAL FOUGHT THEM 'TIL THE BITTER END. AS IF THE GOD TEMPEST WAS STILL RAGING INSIDE THE URU.
FOR 17 DAYS, THE CLANGING RANG LIKE THUNDER. UNTIL EVERY TOOL IN NIDAVELLIR WAS SHATTERED AND EVERY DWARF EXHAUSTED. UNTIL THE SKORNHEIM MOUNTAINS THEMSELVES BEGAN TO CRUMBLE.
BUT THE DWARVES ARE THE FINEST BLACKSMITHS IN ALL THE REALMS, AND ONCE THEY WERE FINISHED, ALL WOULD AGREE...

...THEY HAD FORGED THEIR FINEST CREATION.

THEY DELIVERED THE WEAPON TO ODIN, AS PROMISED. THOUGH WITH ONE CAVEAT...

...THAT THEY WOULD NEVER HAVE TO SEE THAT DAMNED HAMMER AGAIN.

I NAME THEE...

...MJOLNIR, THE THUNDER WEAPON.

FIRST AMONG HAMMERS. THE BREAKER OF ALL THINGS.

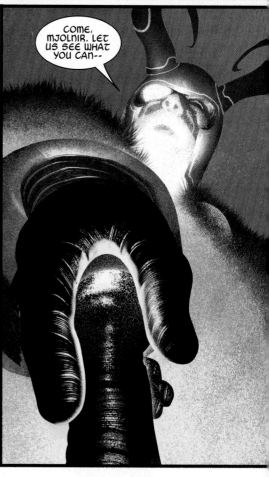

COME, MJOLNIR. LET US SEE WHAT YOU CAN--

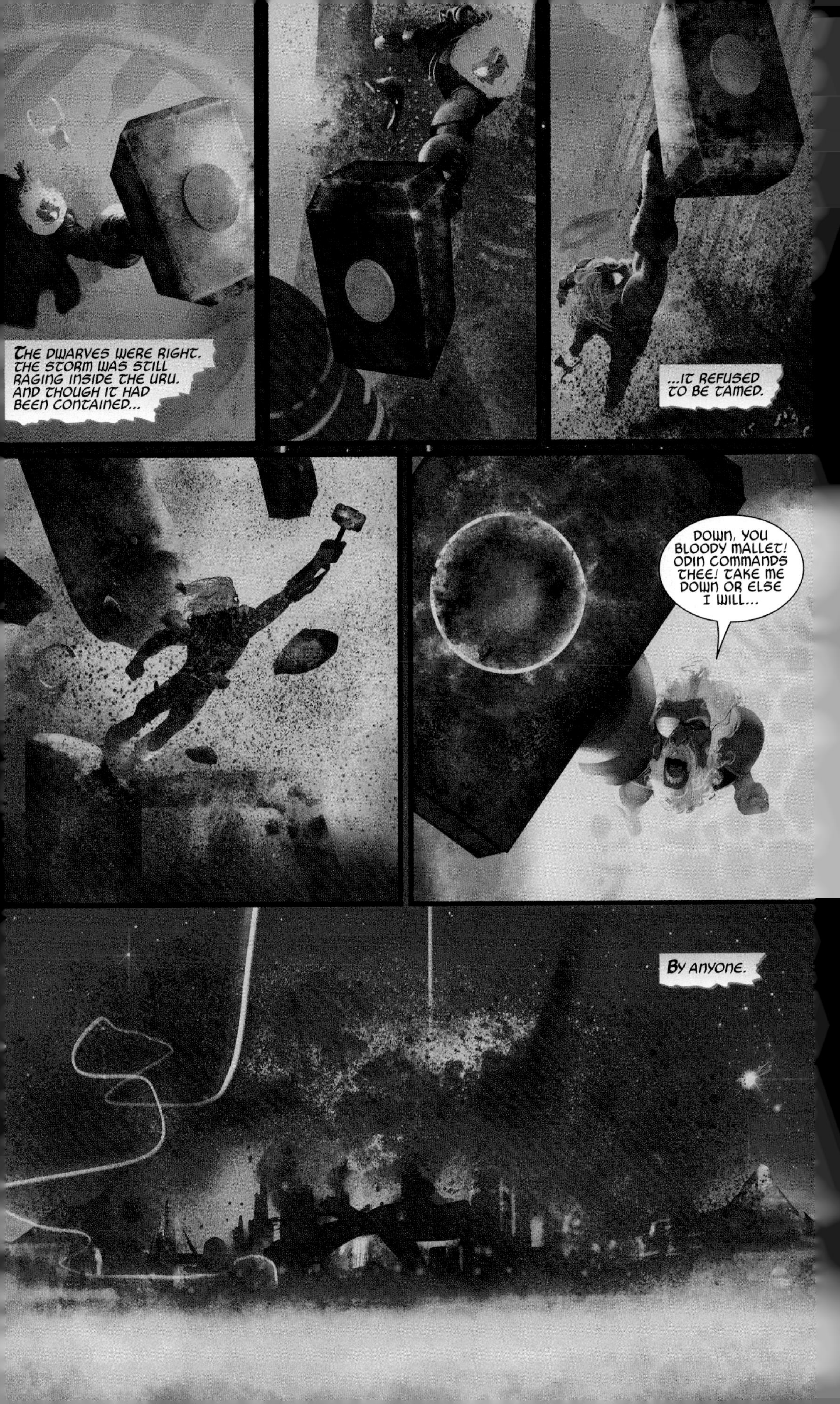
THE DWARVES WERE RIGHT. THE STORM WAS STILL RAGING INSIDE THE URU. AND THOUGH IT HAD BEEN CONTAINED...
...IT REFUSED TO BE TAMED.
DOWN, YOU BLOODY MALLET! ODIN COMMANDS THEE! TAKE ME DOWN OR ELSE I WILL...
By anyone.

ODIN'S RIDE HAD NEARLY DESTROYED ASGARD. HE FORBADE ANYONE FROM EVER SPEAKING OF IT AGAIN.

THE WEAPON WAS TOO UNBRIDLED, HE SWORE. TOO WILD AND UNTAMED FOR EVEN THE GODS. AND IF IT WOULD NOT BE WIELDED BY HIM, THEN IT COULD ROT, FOR ALL HE CARED.

SO THE ALL-FATHER PLACED ENCHANTMENTS ON THE HAMMER THAT WOULD MAKE IT ALL BUT IMPOSSIBLE FOR ANYONE ELSE TO EVER LIFT IT.

AND THEN MJOLNIR WAS LEFT TO GATHER DUST IN THE WEAPONS HALL OF ASGARD.

AND THERE IT SAT FOR MANY EONS.

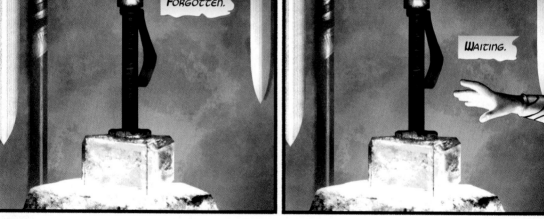

FORGOTTEN.

WAITING.

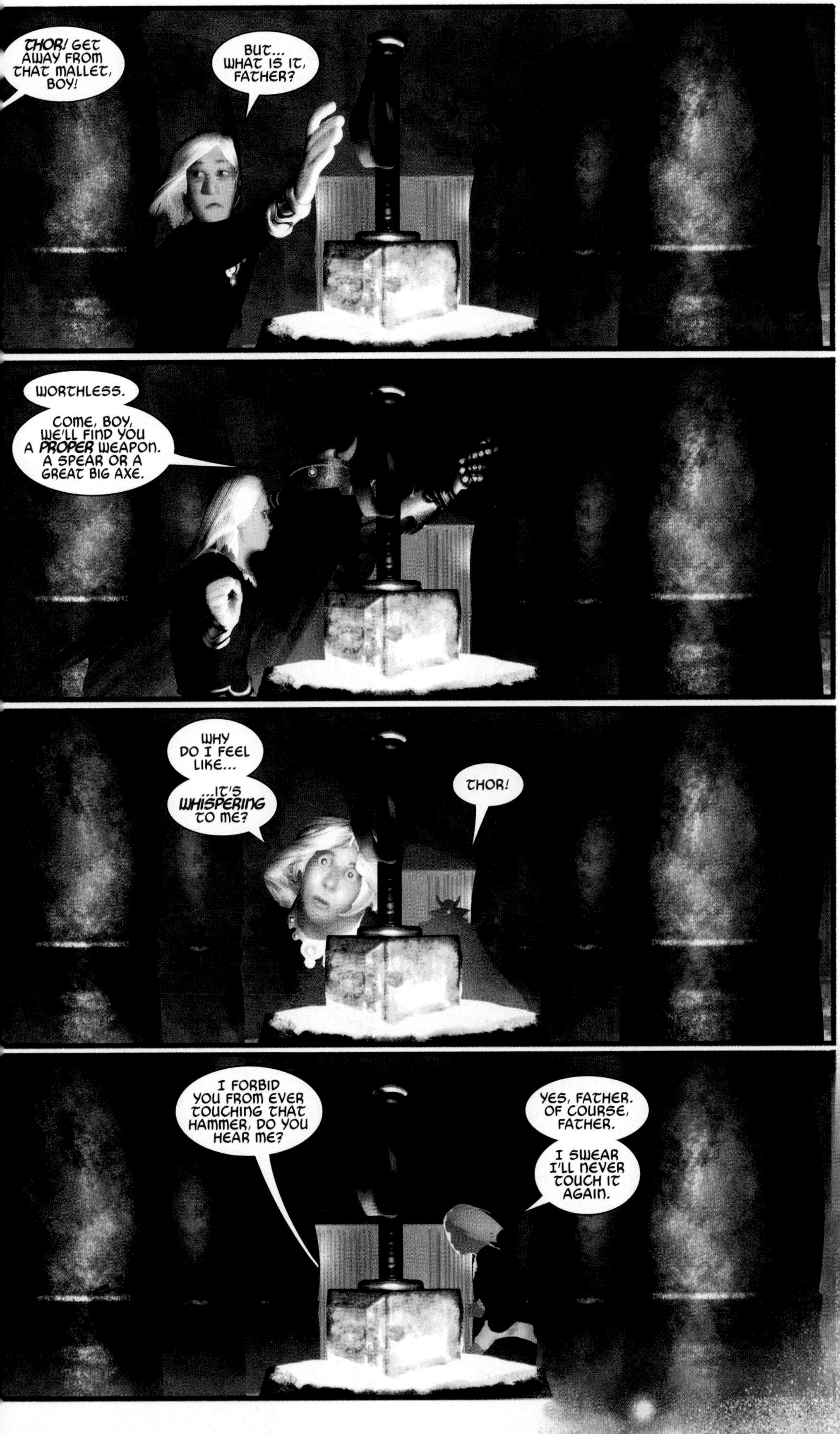
THOR! GET AWAY FROM THAT MALLET, BOY!
BUT... WHAT IS IT, FATHER?
WORTHLESS.
COME, BOY, WE'LL FIND YOU A PROPER WEAPON. A SPEAR OR A GREAT BIG AXE.
WHY DO I FEEL LIKE...
...IT'S WHISPERING TO ME?
THOR!
I FORBID YOU FROM EVER TOUCHING THAT HAMMER, DO YOU HEAR ME?
YES, FATHER. OF COURSE, FATHER.
I SWEAR I'LL NEVER TOUCH IT AGAIN.

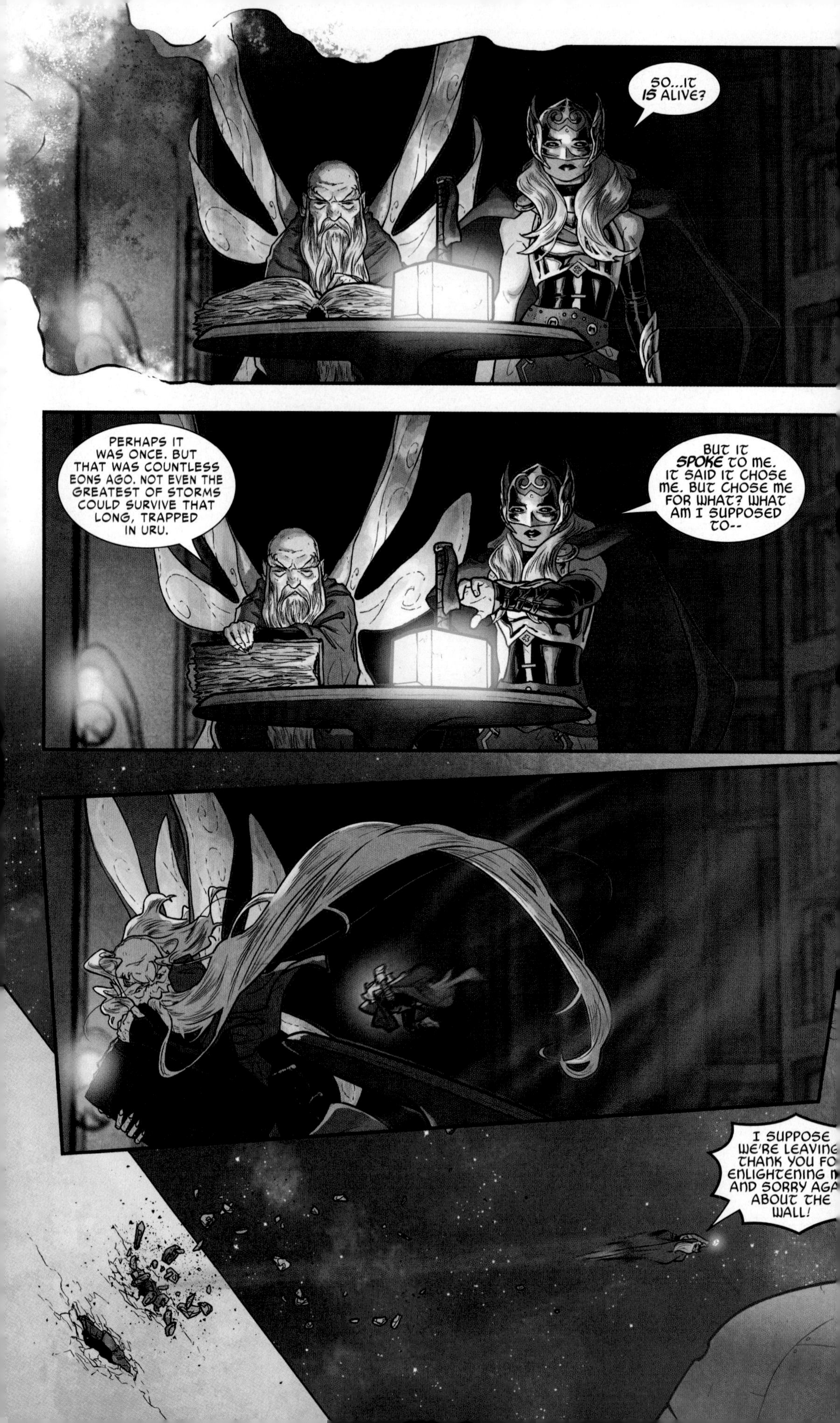
SO...IT IS ALIVE?
PERHAPS IT WAS ONCE. BUT THAT WAS COUNTLESS EONS AGO. NOT EVEN THE GREATEST OF STORMS COULD SURVIVE THAT LONG, TRAPPED IN URU.
BUT IT SPOKE TO ME. IT SAID IT CHOSE ME. BUT CHOSE ME FOR WHAT? WHAT AM I SUPPOSED TO--
I SUPPOSE WE'RE LEAVING THANK YOU FO ENLIGHTENING AND SORRY AGA ABOUT THE WALL!

POOR GIRL. STILL SO FOOLISH AND BLIND.
ALL TALES ABOUT GODS BEGIN THE SAME. AND I'M AFRAID THEY END THE SAME AS WELL.
"IN DEATH.
"DEATH AND DESTRUCTION."
AND WAR.
SO MUCH WAR...
The WAR of the REALMS
The BOOK of the MADGOG
TO BE CONTINUED.

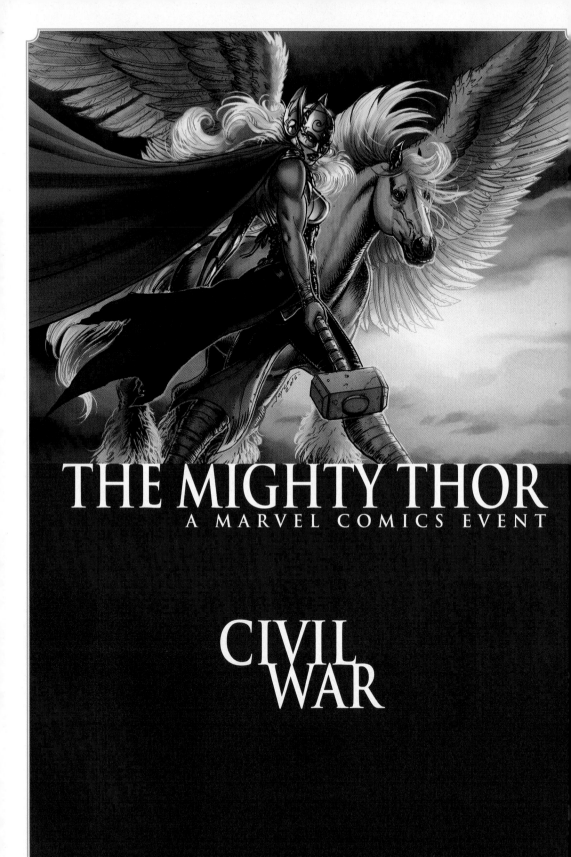

THE MIGHTY THOR
A MARVEL COMICS EVENT

CIVIL
WAR

MIGHTY THOR # 6 CIVIL WAR VARIANT
BY **JOYCE CHIN** & **LAURA MARTIN**

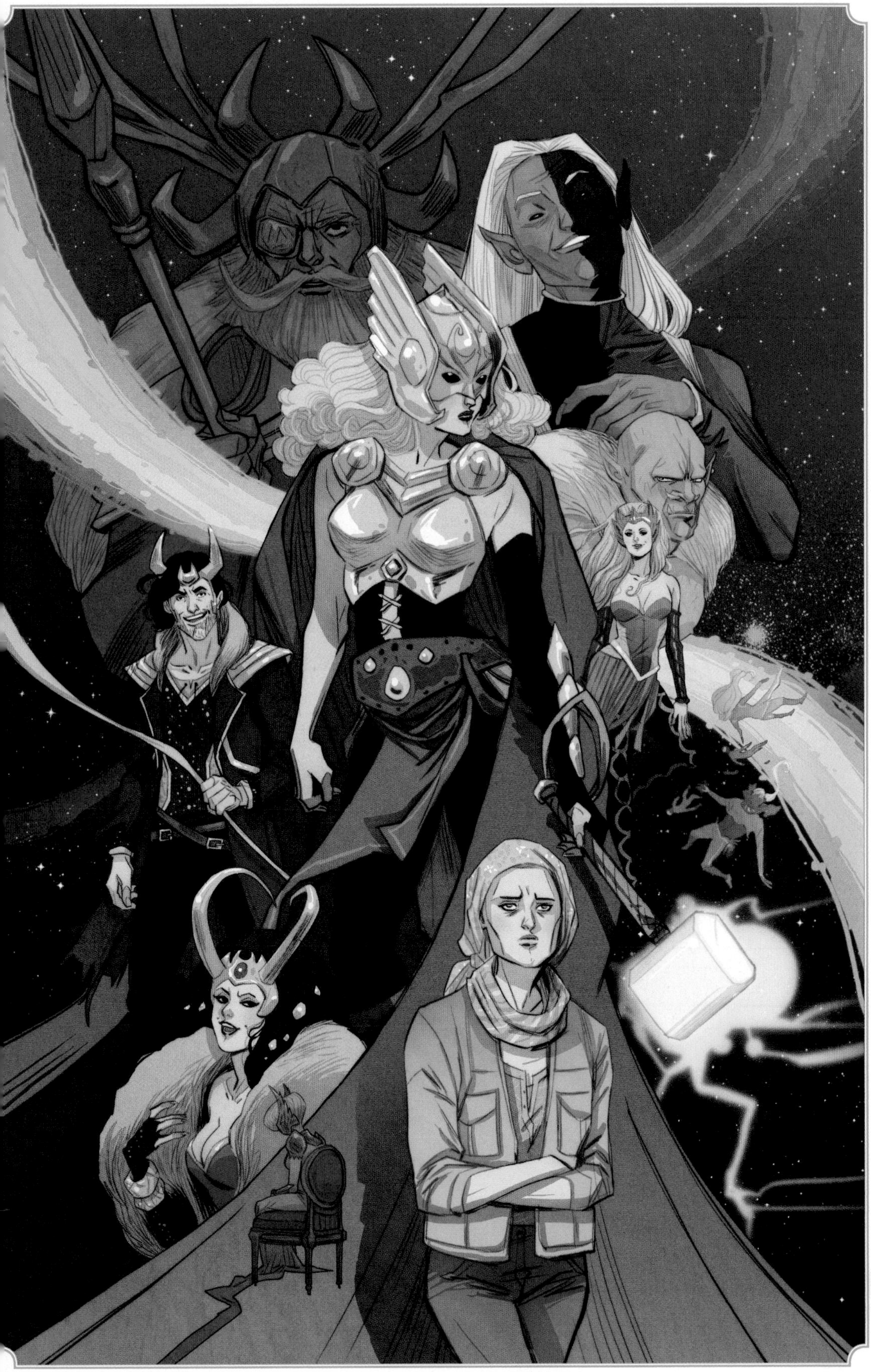

MIGHTY THOR # 8 STORY THUS FAR VARIANT
BY **MARGUERITE SAUVAGE**

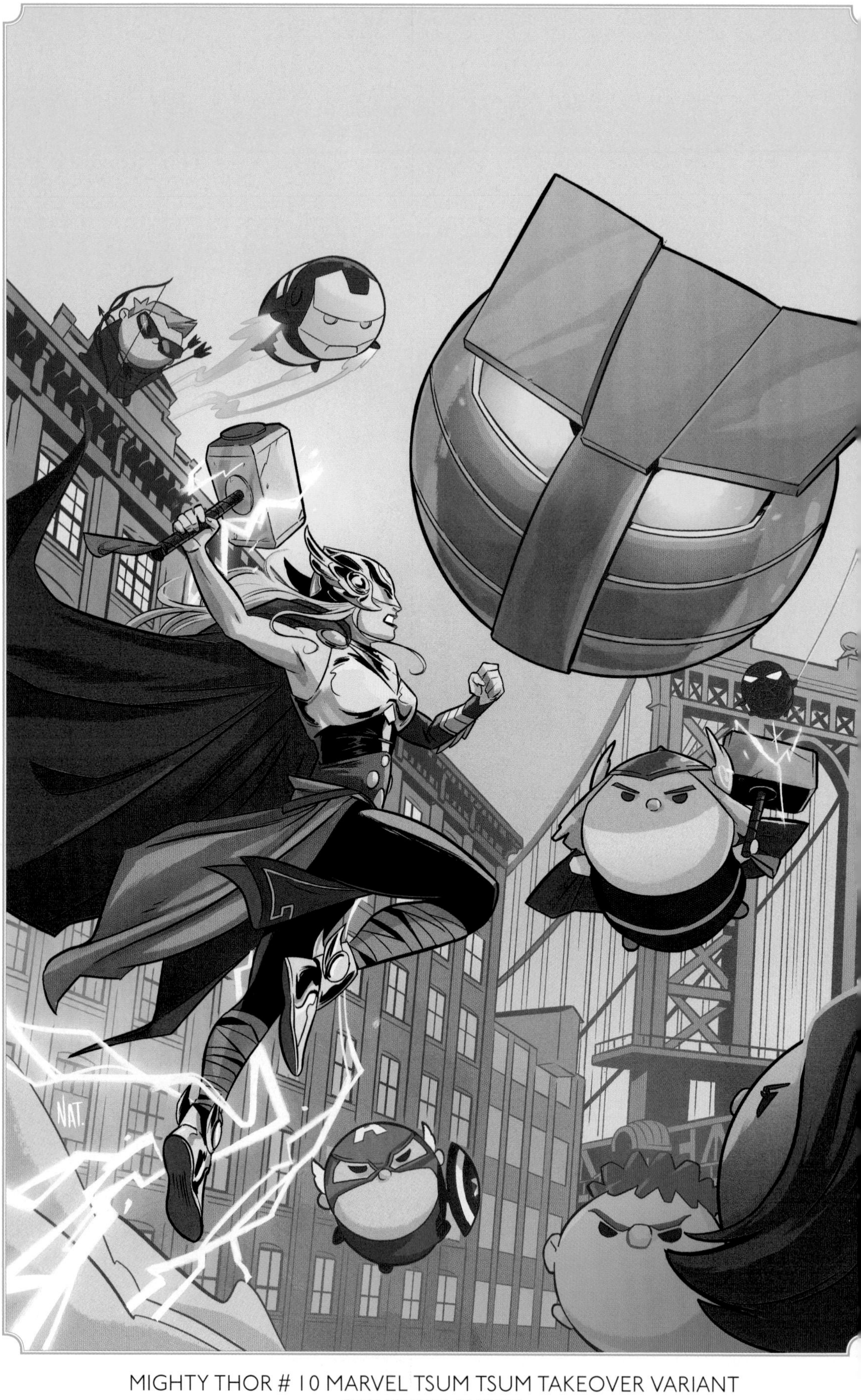
NAT.

MIGHTY THOR # 10 MARVEL TSUM TSUM TAKEOVER VARIANT
BY **NATACHA BUSTOS**

MIGHTY THOR DESIGNS
BY **RUSSELL DAUTERMAN**

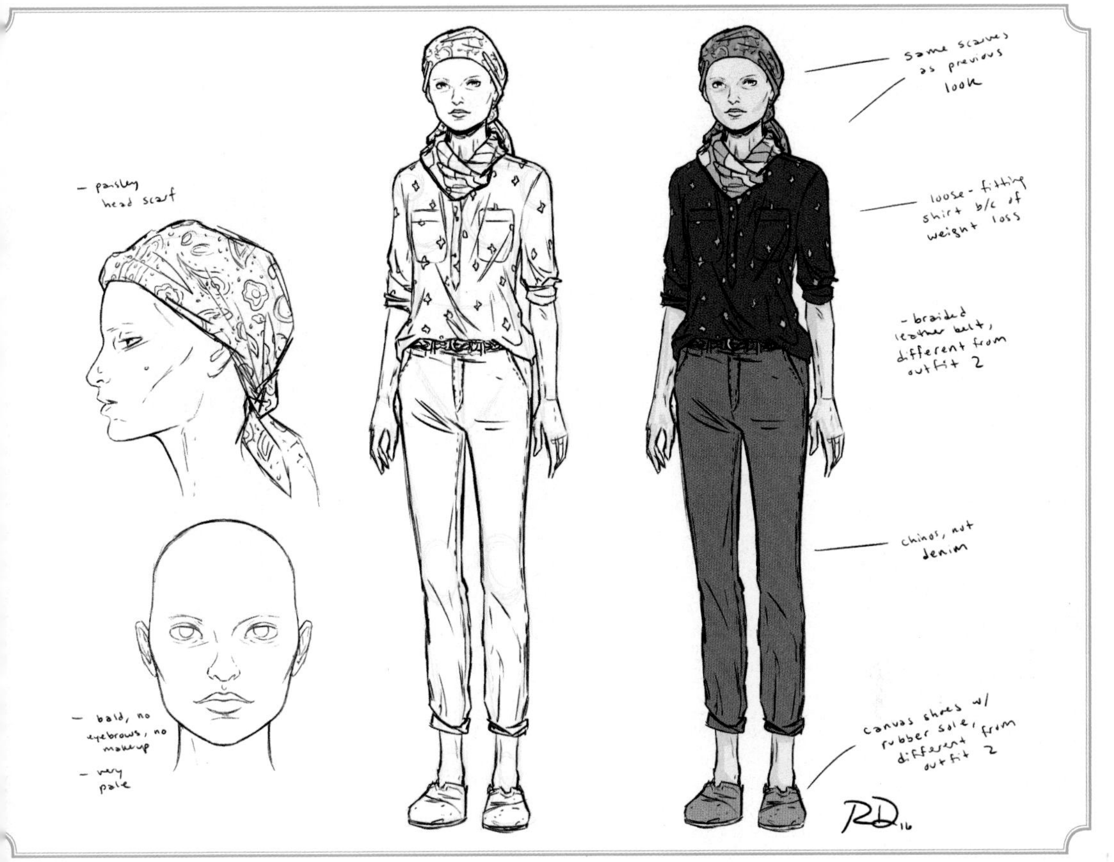
- paisley head scarf
- bald, no eyebrows, no makeup
- very pale
Same scarves as previous look
loose-fitting shirt b/c of weight loss
- braided leather belt, different from outfit 2
chinos, not denim
canvas shoes w/ rubber sole, different from outfit 2

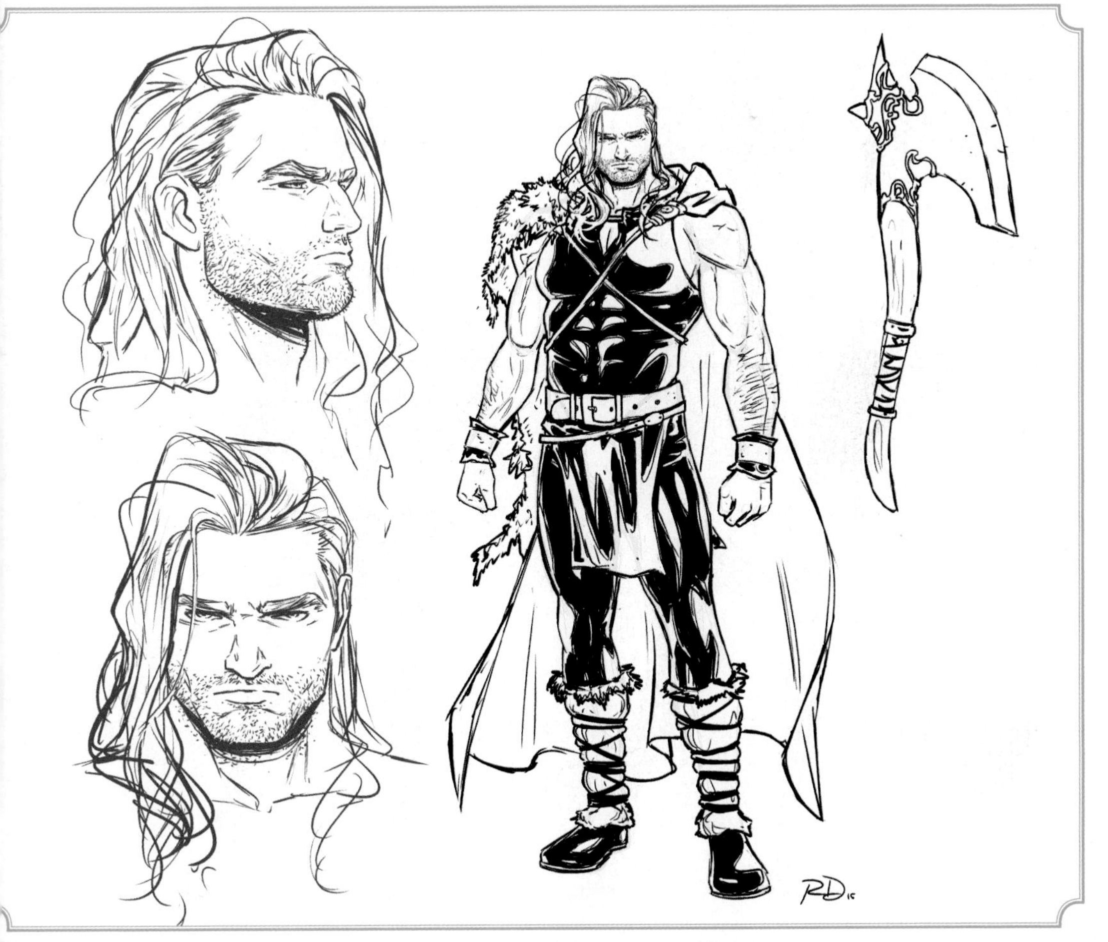

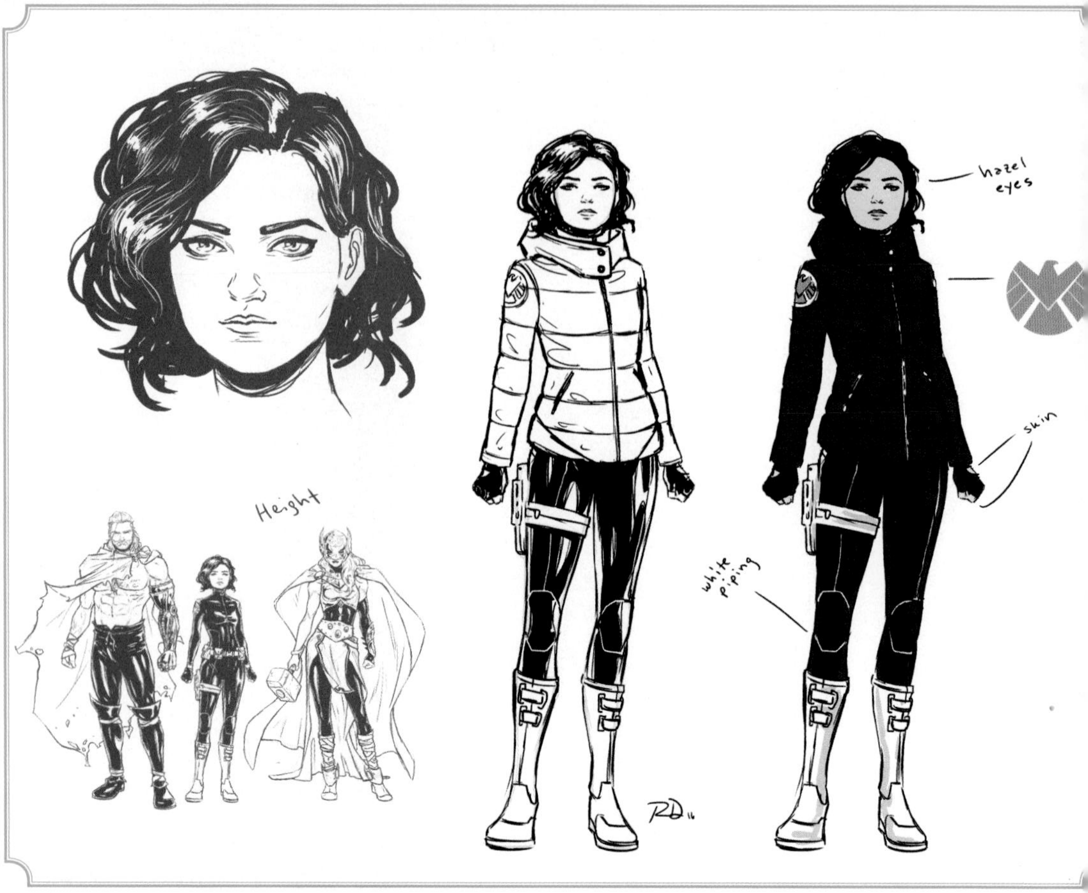
Height
hazel eyes
skin
white piping

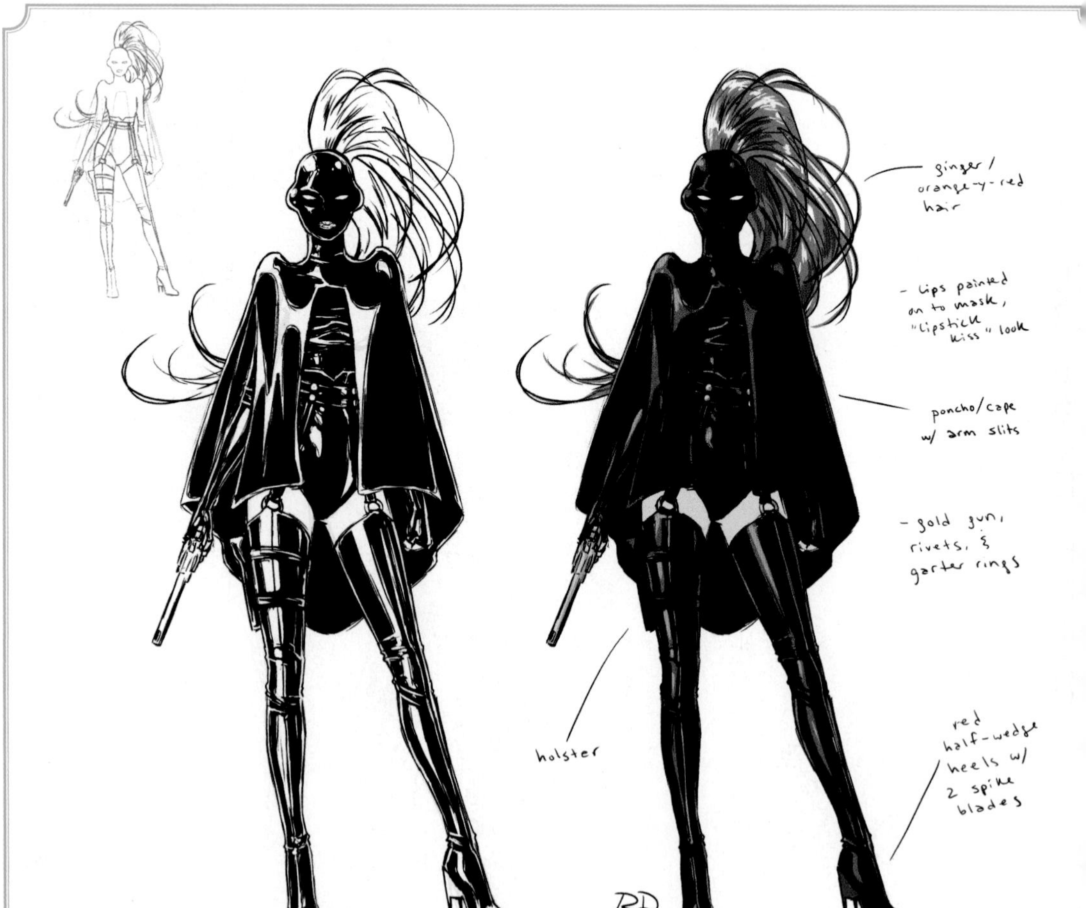
ginger / orange-y-red hair
- lips painted on to mask, "lipstick kiss" look
poncho/cape w/ arm slits
- gold gun, rivets, & garter rings
holster
red half-wedge heels w/ 2 spike blades

COVER SKETCHES BY **RUSSELL DAUTERMAN**

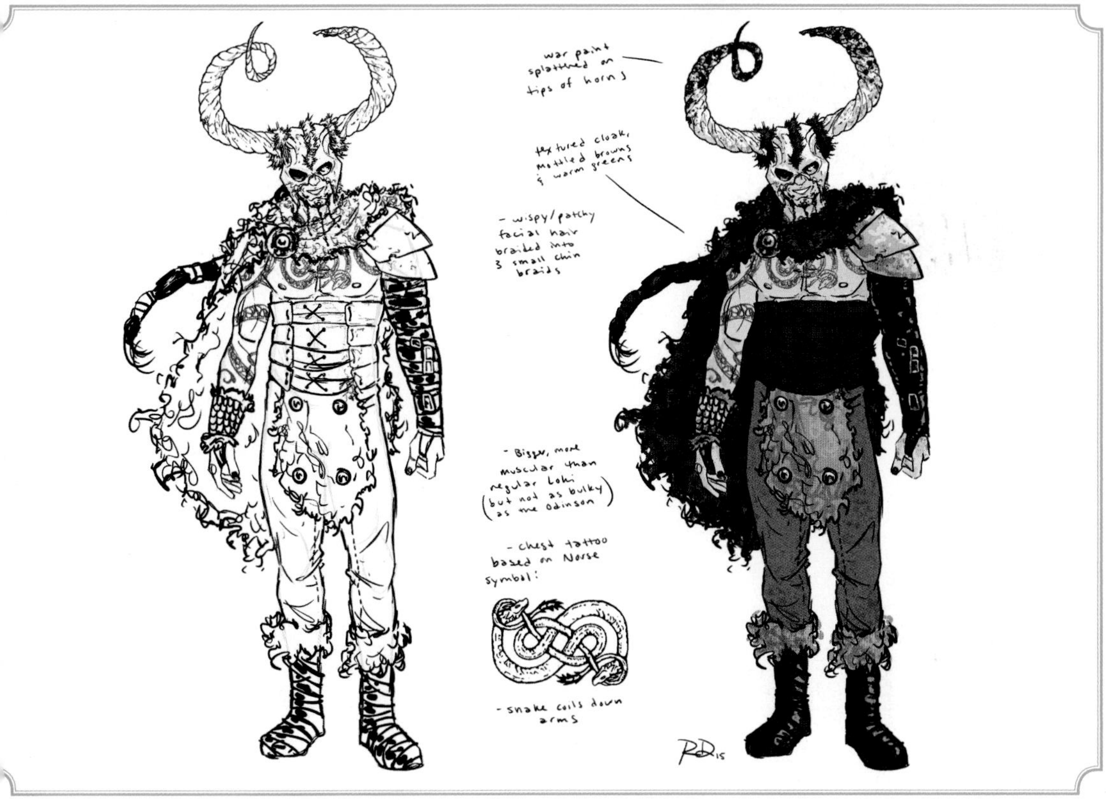

war paint splattered on tips of horns
textured cloak, mottled browns & warm greens
- wispy/patchy facial hair braided into 3 small chin braids
- Bigger, more muscular than regular Loki (but not as bulky as the Odinson)
- chest tattoo based on Norse symbol:
- snake coils down arms

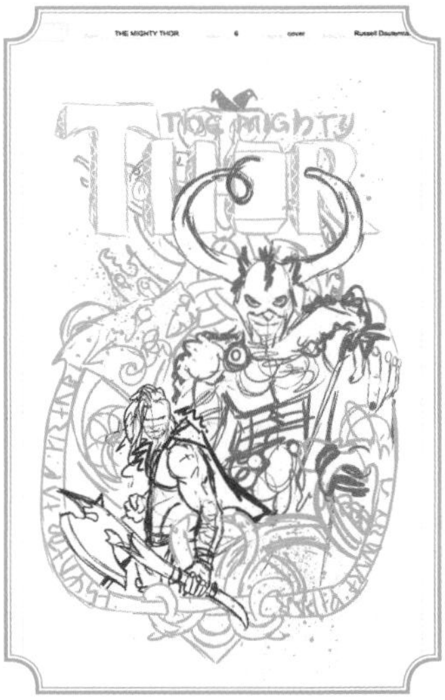

THE MIGHTY THOR 6 cover Russell Dauterman
THE MIGHTY THOR

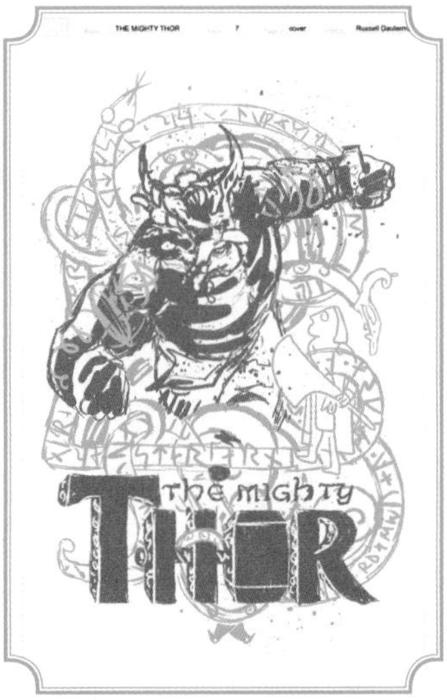

THE MIGHTY THOR 7 cover Russell Dauterman
THE MIGHTY THOR

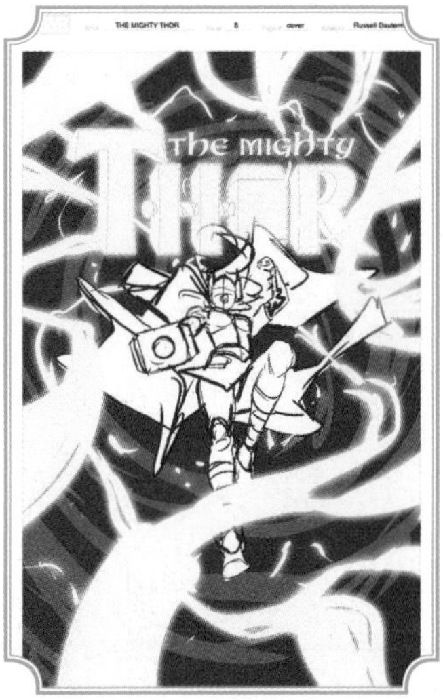

THE MIGHTY THOR 8 cover Russell Dauterman
THE MIGHTY THOR

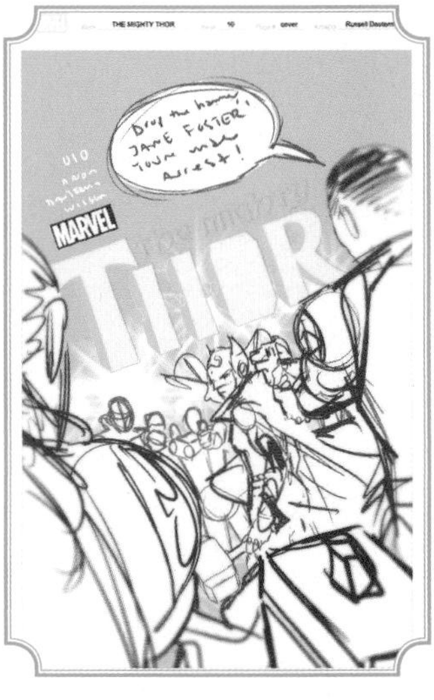

THE MIGHTY THOR 10 cover Russell Dauterman
Drop the hammer, JANE FOSTER. You're under Arrest!
MARVEL
THOR

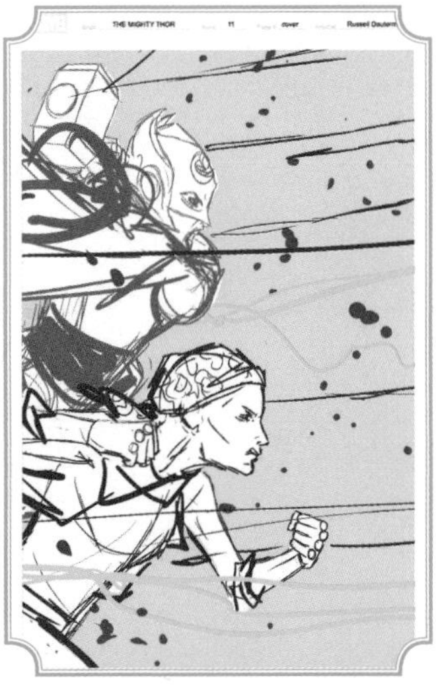

THE MIGHTY THOR 11 cover Russell Dauterman

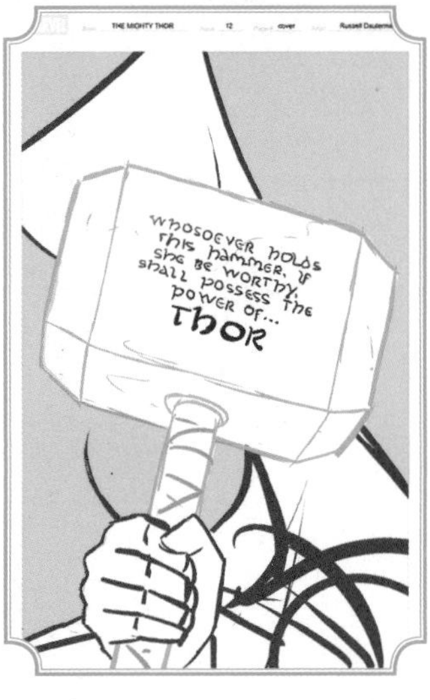

THE MIGHTY THOR 12 cover Russell Dauterman
WHOSOEVER HOLDS THIS HAMMER, IF SHE BE WORTHY, SHALL POSSESS THE POWER OF... THOR